STRATEGIC MANAGEMENT

OF PUBLIC AND THIRD
SECTOR ORGANIZATIONS

Paul C. Nutt
and
Robert W. Backoff

STRATEGIC MANAGEMENT
OF PUBLIC AND THIRD
SECTOR ORGANIZATIONS

A
Handbook
For
Leaders

Jossey-Bass Publishers · San Francisco

For sales outside the United States contact Maxwell/Macmillan International Publishing Group, 866 Third Avenue, New York, New York 10022

Printed on acid-free paper and manufactured in the United States of America

Library of Congress Cataloging-in-Publication Data
Nutt, Paul C.
    Strategic management of public and third sector organizations : a handbook for leaders / Paul C. Nutt, Robert W. Backoff.—1st ed.
       p. cm.—(A joint publication in the Jossey-Bass public administration series, the Jossey-Bass nonprofit sector series, and the Jossey-Bass management series.)
    Includes bibliographical references and series.
    ISBN 1-55542-386-8
    1. Public administration. 2. Corporations, Nonprofit—Management. 3. Corporations, Nonprofit—Planning. 4. Strategic planning. I. Backoff, Robert W. II. Title. III. Series: The Jossey-Bass public administration series. IV. Series: The Jossey-Bass nonprofit sector series. V. Series: The Jossey-Bass management series.
JF1411.N87 1992
350.007′4—dc20   91-16608
                                                  CIP

FIRST EDITION
HB printing   10 9 8 7 6 5 4 3 2 1   *Code 9189*

A Joint Publication

of

The Jossey-Bass Public Administration Series

The Jossey-Bass Nonprofit Sector Series

and The Jossey-Bass Management Series

Contents

For Nancy, Suzanne, Richard, Charles,
and Lynn-Nicole
and
Judith, Kristin, Andrew, and Julie

Preface

The strategic management of public and third sector organizations often poses "what" and "how" questions to managers who want to become strategic leaders. The "what" question concerns content. Strategic leaders want to know what a strategy looks like and how to use it to effect change in their organizations. The "how" question concerns process. Strategic leaders are equally concerned with how to create a strategy and how to get it used by their organizations. This book addresses these questions and offers a path for strategic leaders and facilitators to follow to carry out a strategic management process.

Audience

This book was developed with two types of users in mind. Strategic management is carried out by facilitators and leaders. Facilitators help the organization get started by providing guidance and direction. In some cases, this guidance takes the form of telling the organizational leader what to do. We do *not* subscribe to this position. We believe in the old Chinese proverb "It is better to teach a man to fish than to give him a fish." Facilitators who wish to help organizations develop a strategy and seek to train organizational members to continue the strategic management process will find procedures and techniques in this book that can be taught and transferred to their clients, helping them to become more proactive strategically.

Strategic Management of Public and Third Sector Organizations has special significance for the strategic leader. We encourage anyone who has the discretion and the responsibility to effect change to consider becoming a strategic leader. To become strategic leaders, managers take charge of the strategic management process by shaping the process and the techniques in this book to fit their needs. The book provides the knowledge and insights to get strategic leaders started and to keep the process moving in the desired direction. Strategic management is carried out continuously in well-run organizations. We offer several ways for a manager to act as a strategic leader by incorporating strategic concerns into the ongoing activities of their organizations.

Uses of This Book

Strategic Management of Public and Third Sector Organizations has two uses. First, it can be used in an academic setting to train future facilitators and leaders. In addition, practicing facilitators and managers can use it as a handbook to sharpen their knowledge of the what and how of strategic management.

This book can be used as the primary text or as a supplement in a course on strategic management. The focus of such a course could be a balanced treatment of strategic management, which would consider organizations with varying degrees of publicness, or such a course could concentrate on the strategic management of public and third sector organizations. The second type of course is taught in many academic programs, including business, public administration, urban affairs, political science, health care administration, nursing, pharmacy, management for the arts, architecture, and urban planning.

The cases in this book are drawn from our experiences in helping managers to strategically manage federal, state, city, and county governments as well as third sector organizations that include historical societies; voluntary organizations, such as the United Way; day-care centers; consortia like the National Kidney Foundation and the Highway Safety Program; university departments, colleges, and administrative structures; child-care services; fire and police departments; boards of regents, directors, and trustees; employment services; natural resource departments; juvenile crime prevention, youth services, and corrections programs; commerce and better business bureaus; parks and recreation services; and psychological counseling services. The book appeals to students because they can make useful career assessments by drawing on the cases and experiences that we describe.

This book has been developed for public and third sector organizations because private sector approaches have been misdirecting these organizations. Strategic management ideas developed for the profit-making organization require, at a minimum, a shift in perspective and the discarding of some ideas altogether. For instance, cost minimization has little meaning for a symphony. Profit in a hospital conflicts with goals of quality and service to the indigent. This book considers the unique needs of public and third sector organizations and folds them into the way we propose to strategically manage these types of organizations.

Innovative Features

We offer a number of new ideas in the development of strategy that extend existing theory and provide new ways to cope with the environmental turbulence most observers predict for the future. These ideas and concepts have been successfully tested in our consulting practice. First, we introduce the notion of historical context to examine the forces that have shaped the organization. This assessment establishes "directions" that may not align with the organization's "ideals." The notions of directions and ideals and their alignment are new concepts. We find that each offers fresh insights and eliminates ambiguities that often plague strategic leaders. For instance, many strategic management processes call for abstract statements of goals that attempt to capture intent. Goals are notoriously hard to identify and often are in dispute in public and third sector organizations. Ideals are easier to specify and less controversial because they deal with specifics such as clients to be served, services to be rendered, and the desired persona and regard for which the organization is striving.

Second, we form issue agendas that capture a strategic manager's attention. We use the notion of an "issue tension" to specify the opposing forces that are pulling many public and third sector organizations in two different directions at the same time. We classify these issue tensions into types to point out how equity, productivity, transition, and preservation values may be overlooked or avoided. Organizational leaders must recognize these values to "unfreeze" their organization and ready it for change. Treating issues as tensions makes these conflicts explicit and encourages win-win solutions.

Third, we have developed a way to derive a consensus view about how issue tensions and strategic actions are related. These relationships offer insight into the development and implementation of ideas.

Fourth, unlike many approaches to strategy, we offer strategic leaders a way to take strategic action. To be successful, strategic management should include the formulation and the implementation of ideas.

Fifth, we show how leaders can fashion a strategy. A leader can be successful by bringing a vision to an organization, creating a vision through the joint efforts of key people, or responding to demands for change that are alleged to have some of the ingredients to form a vision. Strategy is implemented as the strategic leader "walks the vision" with the organization's stakeholders and constituents.

Sixth, we identify how organizational transformations occur in which new services, clients, and persona are identified and can be fashioned as a strategy. Finally, we define a "mutualist" strategy, in which turbulent environments are managed by developing collaborative relationships, and show how such a strategy increases the prospects of a transformation.

Overview of the Contents

The book is made up of fifteen chapters, a conclusion, and two resources that provide worksheets for strategists. A package of material that orients people to a strategic management process can be obtained from the authors. The book is organized into five parts. Part One indicates why there is a need to engage in strategic management. Chapter One poses the challenge of strategy in terms of the dilemmas that strategic managers face and how we suggest that they should respond. Chapter Two extends these arguments by distinguishing between public, third sector, and private organizations and the unique demands placed on each type of organization to act strategically.

In Part Two, we offer a discussion of strategic management concepts and principles to ground a reader in the evolution and current thinking about strategy. Chapter Three traces the origin of strategic management ideas and provides an overview of types of strategy and how each can be used by organizations. In Chapter Four, these ideas are extended, and new ideas are developed that apply to public and third sector organizations. This chapter also summarizes some of the strategic management approaches upon which this book was built and identifies organizational types that are both susceptible to and immune from strategic action. Chapter Five provides the theoretical grounding for treating strategic issues as tensions. The chapter also provides a framework that helps to classify issues as tensions. Expressed as tensions, issues reveal the organization's core values, which identify values that are included and excluded from the strategic manager's attention. Values that are systematically excluded can become barriers to action.

Part Three lays out the strategic management process.

Chapter Six identifies key process considerations, the roles of various parties in the process, and how to form issues as tensions that guide the search for strategic action. Chapter Seven describes each process stage, including details within stage activities, and provides illustrations drawn from our consulting practice. Chapter Eight illustrates how the process can be tailored to fit one-day retreatlike sessions, how facilitators can help an organization initiate strategic management, and how the continuous strategic management of an organization can be carried out.

Part Four provides techniques that can be used to gather, organize, and prioritize the information called for in each process stage. Chapter Nine provides techniques to aid in the search for information. Chapter Ten offers techniques to tease out patterns and themes in this information. And Chapter Eleven provides techniques to set priorities among the options that emerge from each process stage. Chapter Twelve shows how to select among these techniques to fashion particular types of strategies.

Part Five illustrates strategy in practice. Chapters Thirteen, Fourteen, and Fifteen offer cases drawn from our consulting practice that describe strategic management for a mental health center, a county library, and the children's service bureau of a state government. Each case illustrates the concepts developed in the book and how the strategic management process was applied, as well as the strategy produced and its impact on the organization. The cases were selected to describe strategic management in a third sector organization, county government, and state government. The mental health case provides considerable detail on procedure, indicating the techniques and forms used, how each technique was applied, and the quantity of information obtained. The other cases also indicate what was done but go into less detail on procedure. The Conclusion discusses strategic principles that sum up what an organizational leader needs to know to create organizational transformations. We believe that organizations take shape in the "conversations" that leaders have with key stakeholders.

Our strategic principles help to frame these conversations effectively. The principles of leadership that make transformations more likely are the subject of our current research and a future book.

Using This Book

The material in this book can be tailored to fit a variety of uses and users. Strategic leaders seeking a basic understanding of how to go about strategic management can read Chapters One, Six, Seven, Eight, and the Conclusion. A brief review of these chapters provides a working knowledge of what is required to become more proactive strategically. To reinforce these ideas, it may also be helpful for this type of user to review a case in Part Five that is most like his or her organization. Facilitators should add the chapters in Part Four to those above. These chapters put more emphasis on the how of the process and provide the facilitator with a repertoire of techniques tailored to the situation he or she is confronting.

Instructors can teach several types of courses with the book. A conceptual understanding of strategic management can be presented by assigning Parts One, Two, and Three. Alternatively, a "hands-on" approach can be followed, in which a case is assigned and the techniques in Part Four are stressed along with Part Three and a brief introduction using Chapter One. Or strategic content can be stressed by using one or more of the cases to illustrate the nature of strategy and strategic change.

Many other combinations are possible. Users are encouraged to fashion the material to suit their needs. We are interested in your adaptation of the material and your results. Please contact us; we welcome a dialogue on the book and how to improve it. We also have copies of complete cases illustrating all the information that we have collected, and we would be happy to share these with users who adopt this work as a textbook.

Acknowledgments

We are indebted to many people from whom we have bor-
rowed ideas and who let us test our ideas in their organizations. We gratefully acknowledge the many contributions from
the literature dealing with strategic management. These ideas
provided a strong foundation on which we have attempted to
build. Martin Jenkins provided many insights as the ideas presented in the book took shape. We are grateful to Marty for
his many contributions. Our clients have been a major source
of inspiration and assistance by letting us try out our ideas and
offering many helpful criticisms. Susie Cinadr and Steven Meese
typed and edited the manuscript. We are grateful for their help
and their prompt and high-quality work as they maintained
their own hectic schedules. The book is dedicated to our families, the truly important people in our lives.

Columbus, Ohio   Paul C. Nutt
November 1991   Robert W. Backoff

The Authors

Paul C. Nutt is professor of management in the College of Business at The Ohio State University. His primary appointment is in the Department of Management Sciences, and he holds part-time appointments in the School of Public Policy and Management and the Department of Management and Human Resources. He also has faculty appointments in the Colleges of Medicine and Engineering at the university. Nutt has B.S. (1962) and M.S. degrees (1963) from the University of Michigan in industrial and operations engineering and a Ph.D. degree (1974) from the University of Wisconsin, Madison in industrial engineering. He is a registered professional engineer.

His research and consultation have emphasized strategic management and decision making from both a descriptive and a prescriptive viewpoint. Before his appointment to the faculty at The Ohio State University, he worked as an engineer for several companies, including Eli-Lilly, TRW, and Eastman Kodak, and was a self-employed consultant. His work experience also includes developing and operating nonprofit consortia for governmental agencies under federal contracts.

He has served as a consultant to many organizations, including the National Science Foundation, the National Center for Health Services Research, several agencies in the U.S. Department of Health and Human Services, several state governments, and many private and nonprofit organizations. He is active in several national and international professional societies and is a sought-after speaker who has written over 100 articles. He has written five books, including *Making Tough Decisions* (1989), and is completing *Managing Planned Change,* to be published in 1992. Nutt will be program chair of the Public Sector Division of the Academy of Management in 1992–1993.

Robert W. Backoff is a professor in the School of Public Policy and Management and in the Department of Political Science at The Ohio State University. He received his B.A. degree (1960) with honors from the University of Illinois in political science, his M.A. degree (1967) from Johns Hopkins University in international relations, and his Ph.D. degree (1974) from Indiana University in political science.

His chief research and consulting activities have been in the area of strategic planning and its application for public and nonprofit organizations. He has acted in the capacity of consultant to many federal, state, and local government agencies, including the U.S. Government Accounting Office and the Veterans Administration Medical Center, as well as numerous nonprofit organizations. He has contributed chapters to many books and has authored or coauthored articles on strategic planning that have appeared in the *Journal of the American Planning Association, Public Administration Review,* and other journals. In 1990, the Academy of Management awarded Backoff and Paul C. Nutt the Charles H. Levine Best Paper Award for "Organizational Publicness and Its Implications for Strategic Management."

Backoff was chair of the Public Sector Division of the Academy of Management in 1989–1990.

STRATEGIC MANAGEMENT

OF PUBLIC AND THIRD
SECTOR ORGANIZATIONS

PART ONE

■   ■

The Importance
of Strategy
in the
Public and Nonprofit
Sectors

■   ■

Part One describes the need for strategic management in public and third sector organizations. In Chapter One, we indicate the challenge that strategy poses to organizational leaders and the dilemmas that such leaders face in forming strategy. We then outline our strategic management process, which suggests how an organizational leader can respond to these challenges and dilemmas. Chapter Two extends these arguments by carefully distinguishing the private organization and its needs for strategic management from similar needs found in public and third sector organizations.

1

Chapter One

■   ■

The Need
for
Strategic
Management

■   ■

This chapter describes the concerns and difficulties that prompt the leaders of public and third sector (private nonprofit) organizations to re-energize and change their organizations. Some of the developments that signal the need for change are noted. We use our experience to illustrate the variety of concerns that prompt action and how these concerns arise. From this backdrop, we identify the variety of motivations for strategic change and how organizations can initiate strategic change through what we call *strategic management*. Strategic management is applied by leaders to align an organization's direction with the organization's aims. This alignment takes place when needed changes in clients or customers, services, procedures, policies, and the like are devised and put into practice.

3

Some Organizations Facing Difficult Times

To bring the challenge of strategic management into focus, we offer several illustrations of public and third sector organizations that are being forced to change. Each illustration is drawn from a real situation, although we must disguise the organizations and key players because we promised them anonymity. The illustrations vary in degree of failure, perceived need to act, and source of concerns. Each organization, however, was able to apply strategic management to one degree or another and cope with the turbulent conditions that were forcing change.

National Center for Assault Prevention

The National Center for Assault Prevention, or NCAP, grew out of a local group of women against rape. The alarming frequency of rape and its devastating consequences prompted a group of concerned women to form an organization and seek support for educational programs. The organization successfully obtained funding from several foundations, its city, and then the state, and initiated a number of well-received educational programs.

As the organization became better funded, its programs grew in sophistication and developed a national following. This national following led to a broadening of the organization's program development efforts and its educational offerings. The types of assault considered in its programs were expanded to include domestic violence and crimes against children.

The NCAP's national affiliation, and the outlook that such an affiliation required, brought with it many changes. An oversight board had to be formed to give the organization legitimacy. The growing public awareness of problems, such as child abuse, created new program areas that were strongly supported by several board members. New interest groups were formed by the board and gained recognition, suggesting new programs. At the same time, school systems had taken over the NCAP's rape prevention programs and educational offerings.

Tension between the NCAP's founders and some board

members began to emerge, with each group targeting a particular kind of abuse as a priority and calling for different actions to deal with the problem. The NCAP had to steer a course between feminists, who pushed the organization's rape-related issues, and women who supported child abuse programs. Both factions were vocal and not prone to compromise. Priorities and directions had become areas of contention as the two factions advocated different target groups and programs.

The NCAP could not disband its board or change its members without severely damaging the prospects for fundraising. Each of the board members had been appointed to help raise funds. The board members were to approach certain organizations and to host special events. The NCAP's executive director realized that donors respond to tangible programs that single out people at risk. To continue to cultivate corporate giving, compelling needs that stem from the plight of these people must be articulated. The fundraising that was essential to keep the organization going was being stymied by the conflict between feminists and child advocates. This conflict had to be managed. The corporate sponsors that had been cultivated were being turned off by unhappy board members grousing about organizational turmoil. The NCAP faced the difficult task of inculturating its board members into the traditions of its founders. This step was deemed essential before the power to set directions could be shifted to the board.

The NCAP was groping for a way to redefine its mission and to resolve its priorities about target groups. The executive director believed that the organization had to develop a new mandate and re-energize its old one to ensure organizational survival.

State Historical Society

A state historical society that we consulted with has a twelve-member board appointed to staggered terms by the governor of the state. The board is charged with providing oversight for the executive director and a top management team of seven professional managers. The society manages the state's historical museum, which houses documents and artifacts deemed to have historical significance. It also operates a number of smaller museums and park sites that contain historical landmarks. The society also supports historical societies in local communities and programs and events important to the state's history. The society operates a pioneer village that has preserved historically important buildings and puts on reenactments of historical events that had occurred in the state.

The society has a number of volunteer groups that assist in its programs and give input on issues thought to be important. The volunteers provide much of the labor that is required to put on special events and programs at historical sites. This free labor is essential to keep these programs and activities going.

The executive director has become frustrated with the difficulties of managing the demands from the volunteers and the board as well as finding compromises when the volunteers and the board disagree. The turnover of one-third of the positions on the board every year creates additional difficulties. Every year a massive educational effort is needed to get the new members up to speed.

During one of these annual education programs for the historical society's new board members, a new board member, who represented business, asked why the society did not plan "like a business" and volunteered to help. The society was still reeling from its last attempt to plan, which had been a complete failure. This effort had produced considerable conflict over priorities. Staff had engaged in turf battles to promote and protect their interests. Sympathetic board members were approached to gain support for the staff members' programs, areas of responsibility, and budgets. The coalitions that emerged produced a stalemate. This stalemate effectively blocked a plan in which the society had invested considerable time and money.

The executive director of the society sees planning as a good thing. However, he is reluctant to go through it again with all of the hassles and the prospect that the effort will fail. The director is planning a two-day retreat for the annual education program for board members. The new board member who advocated planning wants to initiate strategic management at this meeting and has hired a facilitator. The executive director is being forced to go along.

State Bureau of Worker's Compensation

A state bureau of worker's compensation that we consulted for operates a system that processes the claims of workers who have been injured on the job. The bureau applies guidelines drawn from legislation and makes rulings on claims by determining eligibility after reviewing medical needs statements. As in many states, this bureau had formed a partnership with employers. An employer could pay into a state fund or be self-insured. The state paid out claims from the funds collected from employers, acting like an underwriter. A few employers were self-insured. Claims from people in these organizations were handled in the same way as other claims.

The agency operated like a classic input, throughput, output system with its case management. Individuals filed claims and the bureau applied the guidelines to make recommendations. If a claim is approved, a check is written to providers to underwrite the cost of medical treatment and rehabilitation. Claimants can appeal to a commission in another agency if they are dissatisfied with the outcome of a claim. This agency schedules a formal hearing. Lawyers and state examiners assemble to hear appeals and render judgments.

The bureau had been under fire for some time. Critics contended that the long wait for a decision caused providers serious delays in obtaining payments. It took five months to process a clear-cut claim. Claimants often waited in long lines at the bureau's office without even being able to get the simplest of inquiries answered. This unresponsiveness frustrated claimants and resulted in calls to legislators, who eventually protested to the governor. Bureau procedures were in a shambles. The bureau often lost claims, in part because of its manual claim handling system and the poor management of bureau staff.

Employers were concerned about the mounting cost of

their workmen's compensation charges and called for reform.
Inefficient bureau practices were linked by critics to these increased charges. The governor was being inundated with calls
from injured workers, medical providers, and legislators, who
cited unresponsiveness of the bureau and indifference to people's needs, and from employers, who called for reduced costs
in claim processing.

        The governor, frustrated with endless complaints and the
bureau's inaction, fired its director and initiated changes that
he thought would create private sector management practices.
An oversight board was appointed. An executive director was
hired that had considerable experience in organizational turnaround. The director's annual salary of $260,000 was set in
part to signal the governor's commitment to reforming the bureau. The new executive director has to move quickly to show
that reform is under way.

County Public Library

The leaders of a public library operating in a county with a
large city and numerous wealthy suburbs had been experiencing considerable stress. Demands for services had been changing with the advent of computer systems and technological developments. The library had to continue its traditional services
and initiate new ones, which was straining its budget. There
was considerable pressure to maintain old services and to meet
the many new demands. However, the physical plants of most
library sites were too small to be technologically upgraded, and
staff members would need considerable training to operate the
new computer systems that were deemed essential.

        In the past decade, most of the population growth in the
country had taken place in the suburbs. The library had few
sites in these areas, which led to complaints about poor service.
The county board of supervisors was under pressure from
people who lived in the suburbs to provide library services and
called on the library's director to consider expanding into areas
that currently had no library facilities. In some of the more

affluent suburbs, local funding had been obtained to start a competing library. These libraries had the latest technological features, which showed what could be done with an investment of public funds. Each was making inroads into the county library's traditional service area.

The library's director felt threatened but also saw a number of opportunities. However, any plan would be stymied without new funding. The library is groping for a statement of direction that could be used to make its funding needs clear and compelling.

Triggers

The concerns and difficulties of these four organizations are typical of many we have dealt with. Many public and third sector organizations recognize the need to modify old practices and traditional ways of doing business. Each faces a number of complex and intertwined dilemmas and feels considerable pressure to act and act decisively. We have examined many such situations and believe that one or more of the developments described below triggers the need for strategic change.

New or Growing Organizations

Public and third sector organizations are constantly being created by individual initiative or legislative action. Some of these organizations quickly put together the people needed to operate, find, and secure funding, and experience some success. This success leads to legitimacy and questions about the future. Many such organizations want to grow but are not sure what to emphasize. Selecting a new or expanded role or mission is often essential before the organization can stabilize its funding and ensure continuity.

For instance, the bureau of workmen's compensation, the county library, and the historical society had to grapple with their future role before they could move ahead. New organizations face a similar dilemma. The new organization feels considerable pressure to quickly decide what it will do before the inevitable criticism about spending without taking any useful action begins.

Need to Stabilize Funding

Organizations such as the NCAP feel considerable pressure to diversify and stabilize their sources of funding. In such organizations, selling services is often limited or prohibited. For instance, the NCAP believed that fees would drive away people they hoped to reach. In other instances, the culture of the organization or mandates from one of its funding sources make fee collection difficult. For example, mental health centers faced severe funding cuts in the late 1980s. Federal funding was to be terminated, which would cut agency budgets by 30 percent. These centers were also funded by local levies, which led them to offer free care. Center boards were reluctant to authorize fees because the levy suggested that free care was expected by the voters. The leadership of these mental health centers began to see the importance of thinking strategically as they financially repositioned their organization. The advent of a financial crisis, or an impending crisis, often raises questions about the needs for change.

The perceived need to privatize often has its source in funding problems, as noted in the case of the bureau of workmen's compensation. We have been exposed to many other examples. United Way agencies are being pushed to have more services paid for by the clients of agencies and charities that they fund. Legislatures change eligibility rules to accomplish the same end. The leaders of the affected organizations see these acts as leading to cutbacks in professional staff and to clients who are unable to pay, prompting the need to rethink aims and directions.

Desire to Grow Services

Organizations often see the need to expand their services through branches or affiliates and by offering more variety in their services. Universities start branch campuses. Hospitals purchase "feeders," such as urgent care centers, hoping to increase their admissions. The county library sought funding to set up branches in the suburbs. The NCAP hoped to add services to its standard set of programs.

The organization needs a strategic plan to justify expansions to people who have oversight authority. Frequently, this requires a process in which the organization hoping to expand gradually brings along a group charged with oversight authority until its members see the need for expansion and the organization's rationale.

Expanded Roles Thrust on an Organization

An organization can be faced with a demand to enlarge its role by folding in new services. The addition of new services typically brings with it new clients that have special needs. Alcoholism programs were added to mental health agencies. Water quality was folded into the mandates of federal, state, and local offices of the EPA. Tracking abused women was forced on health service agencies. Capital expenditure review, a control function, was given to agencies with a planning function that were expected to develop shared commitments to improve health care delivery among health care providers.

Organizations that contract with a provider organization for services often have a board and executive group. The board and executives must work together toward a common aim, which now has shifted and is open to interpretation by each party. The leader of such an organization must move quickly to gain control or be swamped by special interests. To make things more complex, changes in the board are often mandated by the role shift, and the leader is apt to lose several board members who had been carefully cultivated and could be counted on for support.

Turnover in oversight groups bring in new members who must be inculturated. New working arrangements with provider organizations must be forged. The leaders of such organizations realize the need to work together toward a common goal. They seek a way to steer the new board, an executive group, and providers at the same time.

Board Education

The oversight bodies of public and third sector organizations frequently require updating. Board members periodically leave or are added, and new issues that pose threats or offer opportunities arise. Both situations call for programs to educate the board members. The state historical society had one-third of its members completely replaced every year. Oversight bodies for the bureau of workmen's compensation and the NCAP had to be educated before they could be approached to approve new initiatives.

The leaders of such organizations are often faced with the challenge of simultaneously creating awareness of traditions that must be preserved and insight into needs that call for change. Organizational leaders often struggle to find a way to meet the dual aims of getting board members to see the value in current practices and the need to change practices at the same time. The dilemma of presenting the need for preservation and transition often frustrates and stalls needed action, as noted in the examples of the NCAP, the historical society, and the county library.

Leadership Changes

The leaders of public and third sector organizations often have short tenures. University hospitals change executive directors, symphony orchestras bring in new conductors, and public school systems replace their superintendents. Some leaders bring with them a vision and try to get boards and key organization staff members to buy into their ideas. Others seek to create a vision working with these same groups. Savvy leaders realize that they must redirect momentum and establish shared aims for the vision to be adopted and change to occur. The new leader of the bureau of workmen's compensation will face this dilemma.

Leaderless organizations also need strategic development. The purpose of strategic development in these organizations is to make clear what the organization stands for, its values, and centers of excellence with distinctive competencies and to ensure that these values and competencies will be preserved. For instance, a college of business mounted a massive strategic development effort to ensure that its values were recognized by the university's top management and then looked for a new dean that shared the values.

The organization engaging in strategic development during a leadership change avoids another problem that plagues many public and third sector organizations. Public school systems, university hospitals, symphony orchestras, and similar organizations can be seen shifting between leaders who adopt "stander and shaker" and "stroker" styles. The stander and shaker wears out his or her social credit and is replaced by a stroker. The stroker gets nothing done and is replaced by a new stander and shaker. This pattern repeats over and over again, suggesting that the organization has no idea what it needs or where it is going.

For example, a symphony would not renew its conductor's contract because of the conductor's "arrogance" in making changes. The symphony's board forgot that it hired the conductor and gave him a mandate to improve the orchestra. In the same city, the public school system gave its superintendent high marks for carrying out reform by replacing administrators. Symphonies improve by getting better players and schools by getting better teachers. The conductor was condemned for getting rid of some orchestra members and the superintendent praised for keeping current teachers. Neither of these silly outcomes would have occurred if the boards of these organizations had explored what they wanted and faced up to the consequences of implementing their ideas. Being specific about needs suggests whether someone with idea skills or implementation skills is needed. The style of the leader that is selected then makes sense, in part because key people have thought through their needs and agreed on them.

Legal Mandates for Planning

Many organizations are facing new mandates that require some form of planning. Federal programs for people who are retarded or who have developmental disabilities call for states to create plans before monies are released. United Way agencies must have plans both to raise funds and to show how these funds will be used. Mental health boards must have a plan to access state support for mental health services. Hospitals must submit five-year plans before state agencies that control capital expenditure review will consider their proposal for facility expansion or modernization.

In each of these cases, plans must be skewed to fit the categories demanded by regulators and funding agents. In many instances, the organization must do ongoing agency management as it responds to these demands. Getting the most from such an effort is becoming an important part of good agency leadership.

Demands for Integration

Increasingly, states see the need to integrate services across their departments. Integration is needed to keep people from falling into an abyss created by the lines of authority that separate departments offering related services. Separate offices have been created to do coordinational planning that integrates a cluster of departments to ensure follow through. These offices have been charged with reducing duplication of effort and finding gaps in services. Departments unaware of their complementary missions are brought together to jointly fashion services and improve the efficiency of service provision.

Many states, including Ohio and Illinois, have initiated such programs. Forming cluster groups around topics such as youth services, economic development, environmental protection, utility regulation, taxation and budget, physical resources, and health services has become a widespread practice of state governments in recent years. The leaders of such groups are faced with the pressing need to develop strategic plans and to get the agencies that are affected to adopt them.

Coordination of Action

New leaders and changes in key elected officials bring new mandates and programs to the agencies of the federal, state, and local governments. The leaders of such an agency must create a shared vision of where the agency has been, its current commitments, and where it must go. These steps are needed to give everyone a common direction, creating order and continuity in the change-making process. Leaders want everyone marching to the same tune. The director of the bureau of workmen's compensation faces such a test as programs are fashioned and new aims are created. Strategic change in the library, the NCAP, and the historical society also calls for coordination.

Being Caught in a Rut

Many organizations are caught in a rut, producing the same responses over long periods of time. There is lethargy and considerable inertia. Leaders know that their organization needs renewal and are groping for a way to revitalize services and programs and challenge a bored and underused staff.

The historical society and the bureau of workmen's compensation had fallen into such a rut and were seeking ways to break out. The county library and the NCAP also recognized the need to change old ways of doing business and to create a shared commitment to support the change.

Political Threats

Some developments pose threats. Political bodies may act on a development and seriously harm an organization. The state board of regents, responding to legislators who complain about poor teaching, may allocate funds to state universities with a teaching mission and reduce funds to other universities. The county board of supervisors, hearing that suburbs are planning libraries, may cut the county's library appropriations, reducing its potential to grow. The legislature's and employers' demand that the bureau of workmen's compensation improve its practices without granting the time and resources to make the needed changes.

When political pressure becomes intense, agencies are forced to respond. Defensive strategy may be forged (as in the example of the university). Proactive strategy would be needed for the library to head off political action. A massive change is needed to keep the governor from feeling heat in the workmen's compensation situation. Although the type of response may differ, political pressure often initiates strategic change.

Visions of What Might Be

Some leaders see a way to meet previously unmet needs by clever orchestration of an agency and its oversight body. For example, the executive director for a board of regents recognized that if he could get people ready for school *and* ready for jobs he could make the regents a broker for education. He could mediate between employers and universities by recognizing and dealing with the needs of each. Universities in his state had a mandate to admit any of the state's high school graduates who apply, on a first-come basis. Universities were being burdened by compensatory education and employers by on-the-job training. Both saw their own needs but not the needs of the other. This created a new possibility. The director challenged his staff and board to creatively rethink the commitment to education in these terms and offer suggestions.

The director wanted to initiate a strategic management process that could give detail to his vision and help key people contribute to it. The link between education, economic development, technological development, and business was to be created through a collaborative process that embellished the vision. The process was to empower others by having them fill in the details. Communicating the vision (the "what") and giving it detail (the "how") is essential when strategic leaders act in this way.

Some strategic leaders see a new world and want to help in fashioning implementation plans, much like John F. Kennedy and his New Frontier. They want everyone to "walk the vision" with them. Connection with and then transfer of the plan is sought, as in the NCAP and the county library cases. Other leaders have a sense of what they want and look to others to create specific plans, much like Gorbachev's Glasnost and Perestroika. Such leaders also want key people to "walk the vision" with them but seek specific plans that will lead to connection and transfer, as in the workmen's compensation case.

What We Do

To be successful, strategic change must deal with the developments that trigger action. Each development poses questions that engage the "what" and the "how" of a strategic management process. Organizational leaders are vitally concerned with the what, or the content, of the strategy as well as the how, which indicates the steps that will be taken to develop and refine ideas as well as to implement them. Our approach to strategy management deals with the "dance of the what and the how" by moving between content and process in several waves, or stages, of activity. Each move creates content and provides a way to take the next step. In the discussion that follows, we outline our strategic management process and show how it can cope with the concerns and difficulties facing the leaders of public and third sector organizations.

Understanding History

Key staff and board members must be informed about an organization's origins and founding ideas. These educational efforts attempt to create a shared interpretation of where the organization has been. This step is essential before people can decide where the organization should go in the future.

To create a shared understanding of the organization's history, we have a key group (for example, a board or planning group) uncover directions, trends, and events. *Directions* indicate where the organization has been and where it will go without change. *Trends* and *events* capture key developments that have shaped this direction and will influence it in the future. For example, the NCAP had to immerse its new board into the trends and events that shaped its emphasis on rape prevention. At the same time, new trends and events (for example, child abuse) can be considered that suggest new directions. As these developments are discussed, the NCAP can determine what it wants to preserve and what it could change.

We use this discussion to set the stage for the development of ideals. *Ideals* represent the best situation for an organization and give strategy development a target. For instance, ideals for the NCAP could call for programs in the several areas that balance the interests of its factions. Ideals create a vision of what an organization can become stated in concrete terms, such as clients and programs, that are preferred by organizational leaders.

Exploring the Situation

Exploring history gives a planning body, such as a board, an understanding of the organization's past and from its ideals an appreciation of an idealized future. The next step is to explore factors that obstruct or enhance the prospect of reaching this desired future state. The organization's strengths, weaknesses, opportunities, and threats, or SWOTs are uncovered and explored to identify things that enable or limit strategic change. Organizations such as the workmen's compensation bureau identify competencies (strengths) and possibilities (opportunities) that will be mobilized to deal with staff and systems (weaknesses) and the political pressure to change (blunt threats).

Uncovering Issues

Historical and situational assessments help an organization develop a shared view of core concerns that must be managed.

Priority concerns arise as an *issue* agenda. Issues capture tensions in the organization that are pulling or pushing it away from its ideals. In the board of regents example, the key issue tension was between job readiness and college preparation, which called for educational change. We call this a "productivity-productivity" tension, moderated by a transition (educational change). We help organizations search for other *values* that may be in tension, such as human relationships and preservation. In the example, the learner's needs (human relations) may be in tension with educational change, and preservation (profit for firms and research productivity for universities) may be in tension with the learner's needs as well as college preparation and job readiness. Organizations that uncover values that identify issues in this way for their agenda of issue tensions are more apt to identify and deal with chronic concerns and difficulties.

Identifying Strategy

The issue agenda directs the search for actions, beginning with the most important tension to be managed. Considering the SWOTs found to be crucial, a search is mounted to find ways to manage these issue tensions by building on strengths, overcoming weaknesses, exploiting opportunities, and blunting threats. For instance, the regent's executive director could use such an approach to find ways to deal with the tension between job readiness and college preparation by asking how strengths (educational programs), weaknesses (the applicability of educational programs to the needs of firms), opportunities (co-op programs that give credit for on-the-job training), and threats (firms that boycott graduates) offer useful ideas. Following these steps helps people organize their thoughts and stimulates their creativity.

Assessing Feasibility

The resources needed to carry out a strategy and the reactions of key people who are stakeholders provide indications of feasibility. Public and third sector organizations can get resources from internal reallocations and from new financial support. For instance, the county library was able to pass a countywide levy to support its strategic plan. Mental health centers have been successful in replacing lost funds with levies. State departments of natural resources charge user fees and support up to two-thirds of their budget in this way. Strategic leaders must inventory both available funds and potential sources of support. The prospect of using these sources of support to underwrite implementation costs provides one test of a strategy's feasibility.

A second test stems from stakeholder assessments. Stakeholders must be inventoried and assessed much like resources. Stakeholders must be identified and their positions determined, and plans must be forged to capitalize on supporters and to manage antagonists. The nature and number of stakeholders in the supporter and antagonist categories suggest whether implementation is apt to be successful.

Implementing Strategic Change

During implementation, plans are devised to deal with the concerns posed by the resource and stakeholder assessments. For instance, diverting funds from employer collections to underwrite change in the bureau of workmen's compensation, although seemingly desirable and supported by key stakeholders, can be prohibited by law. Implementation in this case would identify people who must authorize such action to work for a change in agency rules. Implementation can involve lobbying, negotiation, bargaining, education, coalition building, co-optation, selling, and promotion. Stakeholders thought to be amenable to one or more of these tactics are approached by the organizational leader to win their support.

Key Points

1. Developments that capture an organizational leader's attention trigger an interest in managing the organization strategically. These triggers include: organizational growth or start-ups, the need to stabilize funding, the desire to

grow services, expanded roles being thrust on an organization, the need to educate an oversight body, leadership changes, legal mandates that call for planning, demand for integration across departments, coordination of actions, being caught in a rut, political threats, and visions of what might be possible.

2. Organizations can respond to these developments with strategic management that calls for gaining an understanding of history, exploring the situation confronting the organization, uncovering an issue agenda, identifying strategy, assessing the strategy's feasibility, and implementing strategic changes.

Chapter Two

■   ■

Why Strategic Management Is Different in Public and Third Sector Organizations

■   ■

This chapter addresses differences between what are traditionally referred to as the public and private sectors and how these
differences influence the content and process of strategic management. The notion of publicness is developed, showing that
many organizations have significant public features. These features make some of the approaches to strategic management
developed for private organizations incomplete and potentially
misleading when applied in public settings. The special needs
of public settings help to identify practices that can be useful,
providing a basis for the integration of ideas and new developments that we propose for strategic management.

   Many organizations that operate in our society have sig-

Note: This chapter received the 1990 Charles H. Levine Best Paper Award
of the Academy of Management, Public Sector Division.

nificant public features, making them more like public than private organizations. The strategic managers of these organizations should be wary of using private sector approaches that assume clear goals, profit or economic purposes, unlimited authority to act, secret development, limited responsibility for actions, and oversight through market mechanisms that signal financial results. In public organizations or, more accurately, in organizations with significant amounts of publicness, many of these assumptions are not valid. To cope with the demands posed by publicness, managers need new approaches that go beyond strategic management ideas developed for the private sector. This chapter lays out the characteristics of publicness and shows how these characteristics create demands that strategic management in such settings must address. The activities that we propose for strategic management are related to the distinctive needs of organizations with public characteristics.

There has been a long tradition of adapting management practices and ideas from the private sector to the public sector. Many if not all of the procedures for strategic management currently in use were developed in and for private sector firms. Why not just use these ideas? First, similar adaptations have been both notable successes and notable failures (Roessner, 1977). Success in the private sector does not guarantee success in organizations with significant degrees of publicness. Second, this transfer is clearly procedure specific. For instance, the success of flextime in public organizations has no bearing on the applicability to public settings of strategic management procedures derived from private settings. Flextime arrangements may get around the authority structure but the strategic manager cannot. The notion of public authority and the constraints and problems that this authority poses render the strategic management practices of firms ill-suited for public organizations.

Public-Private Distinctions and Strategic Management

According to Bozeman (1987), all organizations are public and this publicness is the key to understanding how organizations behave. The notion of publicness is useful because it draws attention to the degree to which public authority affects how organizations act. Because all organizations are influenced to one degree or another by public authority, all organizations can be seen as public.

The notion of publicness leads to considerable blurring between sectors. Public organizations are thus no longer synonymous with governmental agencies but include many for-profit service organizations as well as the third sector, which is made up of the private nonprofit organizations (Nutt, 1982a). Symphony orchestras, historical societies, charities, hospitals, nursing homes, state departments of natural resources, public libraries, welfare agencies, the Army Corps of Engineers, the academic departments of a university, children's service agencies, home health care agencies, defense contractors, utilities, employment services, rehabilitation agencies, sanitation departments, clinics, NASA, opera companies, art galleries, churches, civic organizations, Amtrak, voluntary associations, trade associations such as the American Hospital Association, and COMSAT all meet the publicness criterion to the extent that they cannot ignore publicness when dealing with the development of strategy.

Calling all organizations public is perhaps a bit extreme, but it does illustrate the need to consider the public aspects of organizational life. We believe that the constraints and empowerments that stem from public authority are crucial considerations that are often overlooked in strategic management. The purpose of this chapter is to identify these factors and show how they merit consideration by strategic managers as they fashion strategy.

If all organizations have public features, a modest extension of this argument would suggest that our strategic management process can be used for *any* organization. We do not subscribe to this view because many organizations are far removed from direct public oversight. However, for the majority of organizations, particularly those engaged in delivering services, the degree of oversight is sufficient to warrant careful consideration of publicness and its influence by the strategic manager. Now we shall turn our attention to defining the notion of publicness and how publicness influences the strategic management process.

Public and *private* are terms taken from Latin: *public* means "of the people"; *private* means "set apart." A variety of classifications have been used to distinguish between meanings as they apply to public and private organizations. Perry and Rainey (1988) identify differences in environments, constraints, incentives, and culture. Benn and Gaus (1983) distinguish between private and public organizations by whether gains and losses are communal or individual, by the openness of the organization to scrutiny, and by the degree to which the organization acts as an agent for a community and not individuals. Others distinguish between public and private organizations by using definitions of the *public interest* (Mitnick, 1982). The notion of services as *public goods* is often used to make public-private distinctions (Downs, 1967). For example, the fluoridation of drinking water has notable health benefits that would be enjoyed by all, whether they pay for fluoridation or not. Because everyone benefits if such a service is provided, tax dollars are collected to pay for the service, creating what economists call public goods. Public goods are recognized when markets fail to fairly allocate these goods or when collecting payments for use is not feasible, such as billing for clean air. Ownership and property rights also make public organizations appear distinct because these rights cannot be transferred and the risks of acting are spread among various oversight bodies.

The differences between the public and private sectors have prompted a number of studies to find a set of factors that make core distinctions between the sectors and to determine the impact of public sector distinctiveness. Perry and Rainey's review (1988) found that the unique needs of public sector organizations limit the portability of many ideas derived for the private sector, particularly approaches that deal with mission and strategic direction. Allison (1984), Neustadt (1989), and others have identified factors that capture public sector distinctiveness, but they all seem to draw on the ideas suggested by Rainey, Backoff, and Levine (1976) and updated by Rainey

(1989). This classification uses environmental, transactional, and process distinctions and provides subcategories within each category that elaborate and highlight public-private differences. We have extended this list to include factors that have particular significance for strategic management. Also, third sector organizations have been added to identify an organizational type that has an intermediate level of publicness. Table 2.1 provides an overview of the factors discussed in the next sections.

Environmental Factors

Many factors that are external to an organization contribute to its publicness. By tradition, these factors are termed *environmental*. Environmental factors identified by Rainey, Backoff, and Levine (1976) include markets, constraints, and political influence.

Markets. Most public organizations lack an economic market that provides them with resources in the form of revenues. In private organizations, the buying behavior of people is the primary source of information, suggesting organizational products that are or are not effective. Public organizations are dependent on oversight bodies for resources or on reimbursement for services based on preset formulas. Appropriations are often divorced from market mechanisms, allowing public organizations to avoid efficiency and effectiveness considerations until these questions are raised by an oversight body (Drucker, 1973). Budget allocations from these oversight bodies often follow historical precedent, creating incentives for organizations to spend at previous levels whether or not such spending has produced useful outcomes (Dahl and Lindblom, 1953; Ritti and Funkhouser, 1987).

In third sector organizations, reimbursement often stems from allowable charges that are set by oversight agencies (Nutt, 1982a). For instance, governmental agencies set rates for hospital and nursing home charges that dictate revenue possibilities and impose various kinds of limits. Third sector organiza-

Table 2.1. Factors That Capture Public-Private Differences.

Factor	Sector		
	Public	*Third Sector*	*Private*
Environmental			
Markets	Oversight bodies compose market	Market made up of both oversight bodies and buying behavior of clients	People's buying behavior defines market
	Collaboration among organizations offering a given service	Implicit or negotiated franchises to provide services in a given market area	Competition among organizations offering given service
	Financing by budget allocations (free services)	Financing by a combination of budget allocations and service charges or taxing authority	Financing by fees and charges
	Data describing market often unavailable	Market data captured by cooperatives and shared	Market data typically available
	Market signals weak	Market signals mixed, some clear, some not	Market signals clear
Constraints	Mandates and obligations limit autonomy and flexibility	Contractors limit autonomy and flexibility (for example, physicians in a hospital, users of a performing arts center)	Autonomy and flexibility limited only by law and internal consensus

Table 2.1. Factors That Capture Public-Private Differences, Cont'd.

Factor	Sector		
	Public	*Third Sector*	*Private*
Political Influence	Buffers needed to deal with influence attempts and help with negotiations	Buffers needed to deal with contractors	Political influence handled as exceptions without special arrangements
	Political influence stems from authority network and from users	Political influence stems from authority network and contractors	Political influence is indirect
Transactional Coerciveness	People must fund and consume the organization's services	Funding and use tied to contracts and arrangements that stabilize use and financing	Consumption voluntary and payment based on use
Scope of Impact	Broad sets of concerns that have considerable societal impact	Agreed-upon or negotiated mandates can limit scope of societal concerns without legislative intervention	Narrow concerns with little societal impact
Public Scrutiny	Cannot sequester the development of idea and developmental processes	Ideas and developmental activities periodically reviewed as part of accreditation	Can sequester ideas and developmental activities

Table 2.1. Factors That Capture Public-Private Differences, Cont'd.

Factor	Sector		
	Public	*Third Sector*	*Private*
Ownership	Citizens often act as owners and impose their expectations about organization's activities and the conduct of these activities	Ownership vested in users (for example, physicians in hospital), who promote their vested interests	Ownership vested in stockholders whose interests are interpreted using financial indicators
	Ubiquitous stakeholders	Many stakeholders	Few stakeholders beyond stockholders
Organizational Processes			
Goals	Goals and thus aims are shifting, complex, conflicting and difficult to specify	Goals are multiple and difficult to prioritize, making aims disputed	Goals clear and agreed upon
	Equity dominant concern	Mixed concerns about equity and efficiency	Efficiency dominant concern
Authority Limits	Implementation contingent upon stakeholders beyond the authority leaders' control	Implementation depends on securing the agreement of key contractors (for example, physicians in hospital)	Implementation vested in authority figures who have the power to act

Table 2.1. Factors That Capture Public-Private Differences, Cont'd.

Factor	Sector		
	Public	*Third Sector*	*Private*
	Agency management within a governmental umbrella	Agency management within an authority structure	Agency management largely independent of outside influences
	Limitations posed by role of public action	Limitations posed by traditional roles	No limits
Performance Expectations	Vague and in constant flux, changing with elections and political appointments, encouraging inaction	Action taking has many interpretations regarding urgency until a consensual view emerges	Clear and fixed for long time periods, creating urgency
Incentives	Job security, power, recognition, roles and tasks	Professionalization norms create expectations	Financial

tions must deal with several oversight mechanisms to alter revenue, such as hospitals negotiating rates with Blue Cross–Blue Shield and other insurers and coping with medicaid formulas. The manipulation of oversight bodies through reimbursement maximization gyrations occupy much of the time of third sector managers. Hospitals, for instance, noted that outpatient services were not price controlled in the 1980s and shifted their efforts to providing outpatient services because price controls could be avoided. This example indicates how third sector organizations can resemble private firms in some of their revenue-generating activities.

Publicness is related to a dependence on nonmarket sources for operating funds. Total reliance on budget appropriations with no opportunity to charge for service, such as in a fire department, defines the high end of the continuum. Oversight bodies make up the "market" for such an organization.

Publicness declines if charges can be made, such as in state natural resource departments that supplement their budget with license and user fees or "public" universities that raise two-thirds of their revenues from fees (tuition) and grants obtained by faculty. Budgets derived from revenues based on services with charges that cover part of the costs also suggest an intermediate level of publicness. Oversight bodies in organizations with such budgets have a role in authorizing services that avoid price controls or in approving the magnitude of fees to be charged. Thus oversight bodies make up an important element in the market. Organizations that must work through an oversight body to alter their resource base seem distinct from organizations that sell to a market. Privateness stems from direct market dealings. Publicness stems from markets that are composed of one or several oversight bodies.

The extent of competition, financing arrangements, availability of data, and strength of market signals also suggest organizations with publicness. Competition for customers can be cumbersome or even prohibited for public and third sector organizations. Public sector organizations are often expected to collaborate with other organizations offering similar services and not to compete for customers. To do so would be seen as creating a duplication of services, universally regarded as undesirable. Third sector organizations, such as hospitals, often have implicit franchises to provide services to a given catchment area. Competition arises only when negotiations among hospitals break down. New competitors are fended off using regulatory bodies to question the wisdom of adding new resources, applying a service duplication argument (Nutt and Hurley, 1981). Competitive models of strategic management have little use in organizations with significant degrees of publicness. Instead, strategy should be sought that enhances cooperation and collaboration (see Table 2.2).

Financing in private organizations depends on charging a fee. Public organizations either offer free services, obtaining their financing by budget allocations or taxation, or charge nominal fees that cover a portion of their costs in providing services. For instance, public libraries provide free service but can seek budget enhancements by asking voters to approve a property tax millage increase earmarked for libraries. Publicly assisted universities and land-grant colleges increase tuition to cover the budget shortfalls from state government. Some branches of government and regulatory agencies supplement their budgets with license and user fees. Publicness is related to the extent that a public process provides operating funds. Reliance on public subsidies creates a need to maintain this support and include its maintenance in any strategy.

Data describing service markets are often missing or unobtainable in public organizations. Many public organizations are prohibited from diverting funds from service provision to data collection on the intensity, distribution, and other features of the service delivery. Even in situations in which the collection of such information is not prohibited, professionals are often reluctant to bleed resources from the provision of services to collect such information.

Third sector organizations also tend to have primitive information about their market, although the reasons are less clear. Cooperatives, such as trade associations, provide comparative industry data in some instances, but the data are seldom

Table 2.2. Strategic Management Needs Posed by Public and Third Sector Organizations.

Factor	Consideration	Strategic Management Needs
Environmental		
Markets	Market determined by authority networks	Must identify the beliefs and demands of people in authority networks to premise strategic development and guide implementation
	Collaboration and cooperation expected	Find substitute for competitive devices
	Financing by fees limited or ruled out	Maintain financing arrangements
	Market characteristics unclear	Identify scope and nature of service use without data
Constraints	Mandates and obligations often limit autonomy and flexibility	Mandates and obligations must be understood and put in proper historical context
Political influence	Influence attempts are apt to occur	Bargaining and negotiating tactics should be incorporated at key decision points
	Political influence from users (contractors) and authority networks	Balance contractor or user concerns with those of people in authority network
Transactional		
Coerciveness	Opportunities to ensure service consumption and payment	Consider coercive opportunities as part of a formulation and implementation of strategic change
Scope of impact	Narrow conception of role can miss opportunities to act	Find ways to discover important externalities that guide aspects of strategy development
Public scrutiny	Idea development can be subject to public review	Find ways to open up process for outside participation and review

Table 2.2. Strategic Management Needs Posed by Public and Third Sector Organizations, Cont'd.

Factor	Consideration	Strategic Management Needs
Ownership	Everyone is a stakeholder or may act like one	Learn about public desires and expectations about conduct of service delivery
	Many stakeholders	Determine stakeholder views in efficient and effective manner
Organizational Processes		
Goals	Often hard to specify goals. Equity concerns as important as efficiency	Find a substitute for goals that overcomes vagueness and potential for conflict
Authority Limits	Resources needed to act beyond control of strategic manager	Offer ways to identify and manage essential resources
	Limits posed on actions of government	Learn how to deal with constrained action space
	Involve authority structure in deliberations	Ways to represent disinterested oversight bodies
Performance Expectations	Lethargy and inertia inherent in political time frames or peer assessments	Process should create urgency and need to take action
Incentives	Incentives hard to apply and based on personal achievement and recognition	Create excitement about strategic action that rewards through participation in action taking

tailored for local use. These data deficiencies are compounded by the weak or ambiguous signals in the environments of public and third sector organizations. As a result, strategy must be developed with little or no supporting data. This situation is markedly different from that of private sector organizations that have considerable market data (for example, sales by region) and strong market signals about success or failure (for example, sales changes following the introduction of new products).

Table 2.2 identifies strategic management needs that arise from publicness. Strategic management in public settings must identify the beliefs and demands of key stakeholders and deal with elaborate fictions held by these individuals to premise development and guide implementation. Strategic managers must carefully collaborate with their oversight body as they fashion a strategy.

In public organizations, norms for efficiency, effective performance, allocation, and the like are either missing or disputed. In some instances, the beliefs held by key oversight bodies can stipulate norms. For instance, a persuasive school board member in a public school can insist on graduation rates comparable to private schools. Even when the norm is stupid, these views cannot be ignored. In private organizations, expectations for efficiency and effectiveness can be tested empirically through comparisons with competitors or by marketing, which produces clearer norms. In addition, financing arrangements, competitiveness, market signals, and data depicting markets are quite different for public and third sector organizations. Each calls for special considerations not required in private sector strategy.

Constraints. Legal mandates, obligations to a charter, and traditions can pose constraints for public organizations that limit their autonomy and flexibility (Mainzer, 1973; Thompson, 1962; Woll, 1963). These organizations have less freedom to add or delete services or to carry out other actions thought to be desirable. Constraints that limit spheres of action are important considerations for strategic managers in public organizations.

Fire departments and law enforcement agencies are expected to service a particular area, precluding marketing to find new customers. In addition to fixed customers, such agencies have a stipulated set of services that they are expected to provide. Third sector organizations, such as charities, often find their missions dictated by tradition, which provides similar constraints. For instance, a Shriners children's hospital is expected to provide a designated bundle of services, such as burn care, to a particular group: children. During hard times, dropping high-cost services such as burn care is not apt to surface as an option. Dropping burn care would be strenuously resisted because of traditional commitments.

Third sector organizations also cope with constraints that limit their flexibility and autonomy. For example, physicians that make up a hospital's medical staff must be consulted about major policy changes and often push their own self-interest, even at the expense of the hospital. The salary demands of musicians in a symphony orchestra are pushed even if they create huge deficits. Any organization with a professional work force, such as a research and development laboratory like Bell Labs, faces a similar situation.

Court rulings, the demands of contractors, enabling legislation, and newly elected administrations all produce directives that public organizations must accept. As the degree of publicness increases, the force of these directives also increases, creating significant constraints on action that must be considered in strategic management. Mandates and obligations must be understood and put into a historical context that describes the organization's traditions and direction as new actions are contemplated (Table 2.2).

Political Influence. The environment of a public organization is littered with political considerations. The views of opinion leaders, outright manipulation by legislators and interest groups, and formal opposition to the agency's right to act, swamp economic issues that are crucial for private organizations (Levine and others, 1975). Disagreements and log rolling among key people can occur at any time and, within limits, are permissible ingredients in any effort to develop strategy. Bargaining and negotiation must be used to find domains of action. How things are viewed or understood by stakeholders holds more salience than the validity of claims. The meaning of a claim must be derived from opinions as well as facts. If economic reasoning such as a concern about efficiency is applied, it must be preceded by a decision to deal with efficiency, which will be politically derived. The decision to offer new services or to modify existing ones stems from the way in which implementation is handled as much as the apparent soundness of proposals. In third sector organizations, buffers are devised to deal with contractors. For example, hospitals devise special organizational arrangements to carefully manage their key clients: physicians with high admission rates.

Public opinion, interest groups, lobbying, and interventions by elected officials and contractors are attempts at influence with which public organizations must deal (Wamsley and Zald, 1973; Weiss, 1974). As publicness increases so does the need to be responsive to these interventions by using negotiation and bargaining. Private organizations can either ignore or deflect this type of intervention through legal means or rhetoric, such as damage-control advertising.

The prospect of influence attempts by key people coerces public organizations to build buffers in the form of coalitions, advisory groups, and interlocking directorates that can fend off or limit influence attempts or help with negotiations. A complex organizational structure often results, which must be considered in strategic management. Private organizations have fewer needs for such buffers and have simpler, more traceable, organizational arrangements.

Strategic managers in public organizations must anticipate and build in negotiation and bargaining opportunities as strategy is being formulated (see Table 2.2). This openness to influence helps to deflect criticism and paves the way for smoother implementation than had these arrangements been ignored.

Strategy and Environmental Factors. The influence of the beliefs of key people in authority networks and the mandates and
obligations the networks impose call for strategic managers to
carefully think through limits on action and demands for collaboration. We have strategic leaders identify and carefully appraise the *historical context* in which their organization must operate to develop an appreciation for these concerns. An
explanation of context allows strategic leaders to develop a
shared interpretation of the organization's history. Historical
events, trends, and directions provide a clear vehicle on which
to build. Action that takes into account constraints stemming
from political influence and authority networks is more apt to
be successful.

Issues arise from environmental assessments. In particular, directions that seem ill advised suggest areas of concern
for an issue agenda. We form these issues as tensions to bring
out the strong claims and counterclaims that characterize the
beliefs of people who control public and third sector organizations and the crosscurrents produced by contradictory demands from clients, politicians, professionals, and others who
are stakeholders. Forming issues as tensions brings out these
forces and shows how they are pulling and pushing the organization or agency in several ways at the same time. Managing
issues as tensions make it harder for powerful individuals in
the organization's authority network to thwart strategic management efforts.

The beliefs and demands of key people in authority networks must be identified to uncover key premises for strategy
development. These premises are also influenced by mandates
and obligations, the expectations for collaboration with others
competing for the same pot of limited funds, organizational
financing arrangements, and sources of political influence. Each
factor must be appreciated as the organization devises new ways
to act.

The rapid turnover of people and the environmental
turbulence experienced by public and third sector organizations make it essential they they periodically appraise events,
trends, directions, and issues in order to appreciate the de-

mands being posed by the environment in which these organizations must operate. This appraisal makes it easier to spot
the political factors that can render any strategy ineffective. An
appreciation of market parameters flows from these constraints, which can help organizations to target services in new
ways, change a service profile, identify services not valued by
users, and call for surrendering some services to private sector
initiative.

Transactional Factors

Public organizations develop numerous and often complex relationships with key entities in their environment to deal with
the environmental factors previously described. These relationships are mediated by coerciveness, scope of impact, extent
of public scrutiny, and public ownership factors.

Coerciveness. The mandates of public organizations often give
them coercive power (Lowi, 1969; Stahl, 1971). Individuals
cannot earmark their tax payments to avoid financing public
organizations and can be forced to use the services that these
organizations provide. For example, state license bureaus are
funded by taxpayers and force these same taxpayers to stand
in lines, adhere to obscure rules (pay in cash for self only), and
abide by deadlines. No exceptions, no excuses might be the
byword here. Parents are expected to support public schools
and send their children to these same schools unless they can
show school attendance elsewhere. In this case there is less
coerciveness because services need not be consumed, but they
must be paid for.

Organizations have less coercive power when service use
is optional and funded in part by governmental agencies. The
funding of services in hospitals and nursing homes is tied to a
contract with governmental reimbursement agencies. The contract stipulates financing for particular classes of patients, such
as the elderly or welfare recipients. Patients that offer more
lucrative payback prospects can be sought or services offered
that fall outside the purview of reimbursers.

Strategic management in public organizations can use coerciveness as a key element of strategy. Private organizations are more dependent on marketing or selling to potential customers. As publicness increases, marketing declines in importance and maintaining favorable coercive arrangements increases in importance. Strategic managers should be aware of coercive opportunities in their mandates as they fashion strategy and devise implementation plans (Table 2.2).

Scope of Impact. Public organizations have a broader scope of impact and deal with a greater variety of concerns than private organizations do (Appleby, 1945; Mainzer, 1973). For instance, the public school system is an important agent in dealing with poverty, racism, child abuse, juvenile crime, and many other social problems that go beyond its educational mandate. The local General Motors plant has no legitimate authority to deal with any of these concerns. As publicness increases, so does the need to be aware of externalities that complement the mission of the organization.

Third sector organizations have a more limited view of societal concerns than public organizations. Agreed-upon or negotiated mandates in hospitals call for reporting about possible child abuse but not an incidence of maternal mortality, unless mandated by state laws. The scope of impact is narrower but still far broader than in private organizations.

The strategy in a public organization includes opportunities to take social action (Table 2.2). The public organization, concerned with the survival of society and armed with coercive power, can and should take on tasks that the other sectors cannot (Levine and others, 1975). A key example is the creation and distribution of services, such as education and preventive medicine, that marketplace arrangements cannot manage in an equitable manner. Others deal with the residual problems in society, such as the environmental impact of hazardous waste disposal by firms and cities. As a result, the scope of plausible strategic responses in public organizations has fewer limits. Strategic managers should search for issues that embrace externalities before strategic action is taken.

Public Scrutiny. As publicness increases, so does the prospect of scrutiny (Millett, 1966; Stahl, 1971). Most public organizations do not have the luxury of keeping strategy development secret. Sunshine laws often force them to conduct business in the open, making organizations plan in front of hostile interest groups or even with the media being present. For instance, a newspaper that sensed a scandal sent a reporter to camp inside a state bureau of employment services for six months. The reporter wandered about, poking into discussions and meetings without turning up anything notable. The disruption of such scrutiny should be obvious.

Even when sunshine laws do not apply, mechanisms of accountability and oversight make all actions in public organizations, even contingency plans or hypothetical scenarios, subject to review and interpretation by outsiders. Blumenthal's (1983) term *fishbowl management* aptly describes the way in which a public organization must function to devise strategy. Floating ideas to see what happens, common in firms, can be deadly in public settings.

Third sector organizations are exposed to less scrutiny, but most cannot completely sequester their plans. Regulatory bodies and accreditation agencies can demand to see strategic plans and can leak the contents. Because accreditors and the accredited are often in the same business, such as higher education, a finely honed strategy can become available to potential competitors.

Strategy devised in the face of public scrutiny must be developed using different procedures than those used in private, sequestered settings (Table 2.2). More opportunity for participation is essential. Strategy making is both a political and a formative process. However, the political aspects of the process take on more importance in public organizations. Often, demonstrations of involvement are as important as good ideas. In private organizations, politics seldom goes beyond coping with resistance to change. In public organizations, politics involves managing many stakeholders external to the organization who control or influence needed sources of money and people whose support is essential. Third sector organizations may need defensive strategies to satisfy regulators, competitors, and others who dictate aims and directions.

Ownership. Ubiquitous ownership also distinguishes public from private organizations (Wamsley and Zald, 1973). Everyone can have an ownership stake in public organizations. The public organization is expected to show integrity, fairness, responsiveness, honesty, and accountability to citizens (Caiden, 1971). Private organizations have fewer implied obligations, and people place fewer demands on them. Publicness increases as the notion of communal ownership increases.

A form of ownership is vested in contractors for third sector organizations. Professionalism, for instance, makes a mental health clinic responsive to the whims and demands of therapists. The medical staff of a hospital acts suspiciously like absentee owners. Like owners, professionals pursue their personal interests often at the expense of the organization. Nevertheless, they represent a key group of stakeholders that must be consulted before any significant change can be made.

Strategy development in an ubiquitously owned entity is very different from that in an organization in which owners are stockholders or families. In public organizations, the strategic manager must appreciate public desires and expectations in the delivery of services. Consulting with owners this broadly construed is both essential and difficult to carry out. Cumbersome mechanisms are needed to deal with the logistics of consulting with citizens. Devices such as public meetings, task forces, and public announcements are used to determine expectations and refine understandings about what the organization should do and how the organization should act. Such arrangements are seldom necessary in private settings.

Strategy and Transactional Factors. Strategic management in public and third sector organizations creates a complex web of transactions. The complications posed by the inter and intraorganizational coordination in which agencies or work units stake out their claim for domains of action often creates considerable inertia. Agencies such as a state DNR must consult internally (for example, with the fish and wildlife divisions of the DNR) and externally (for example, with the Departments of Commerce and Labor) before taking action, which makes strategic change difficult to initiate. For example, the secretaries of U.S. governmental departments concede that their decisions often fail to produce action. This stems from their need to cross both horizontal and vertical boundaries, which makes consultation both essential and cumbersome. Third sector organizations (for example, hospitals and university facilities) face similar problems as they try to coordinate strategy formulation with professionals whose values and needs can conflict with those of the organization. Physicians in hospitals, lawyers in a city attorney's office, and the like must be consulted before action can be taken. As a result, it can be easier to ignore important issues than to grapple with ubiquitous ownership and stakeholders.

To create strategy one must emulate the Secretaries of successful U.S. government departments, who recognize that action depends on a coalition of interests that push things along. To overcome inertia, we create a coalition of interests to keep the process on track. The coalition identifies contextual features, carries out situational assessments, forms issue agendas, and identifies strategy. The discussions and interactions in the coalition are carried out to discover ideas and set the priorities needed to deal with context, situational issues, and strategy to help the coalition create a shared interpretation of interests and possibilities. Understanding these transactions brings out both the facts and the beliefs of key parties that must be understood and managed before strategic action can be taken. Vesting action in a coalition creates momentum and commitment to overcome the inertia inherent in organizations with public features.

The nature of the strategy is influenced by sector differences. Firms can undertake proactive strategies that call for divestiture, horizontal and vertical integration, and acquisition. Strategies in public and third sector organizations tend to be more reactive. Typically, a strategy must take shape as an incremental movement that balances opportunity with threat. For example, being too proactive can crystallize opposition, which may hamstring future efforts. Being too reactive can force the organization to concentrate on putting out fires. Opportunities in public organizations can also arise from the coercion to pay for and use a service found in enabling legislation (for example, legislation mandating the fluoridation of water). Also, tacit authority to deal with broad societal concerns can produce opportunity. For example, child abuse programs are feasible in public schools even though the public school's mandate may not mention such programs. Managing the tensions inherent in an issue is required to move an organization with significant publicness to a new posture that responds to opportunities in a feasible manner.

Internal Processes

The internal operations of an organization also provide clues that help to identify its publicness. Key factors that distinguish public and private organizations are goals, authority limits, performance expectations, and types of incentives.

Goals. A crucial difference between public and private organizations stems from goals (Baker, 1969; Mainzer, 1973; Weiss, 1974). Public organizations often have multiple goals that are both vague and conflicting. There is no "bottom line" that can be used as a proxy measure of success in most public organizations. Instead, the demands of interest groups, flux in missions, and manipulation by important stakeholders and third parties create a complex and confusing set of expectations that are frequently conflicting. For instance, what does the Environmental Protection Agency (EPA) do when a new administration calls for backing off the practice of fining polluters, when firms draw attention to alleged loss of jobs due to EPA action, and when environmental groups sue the EPA for inaction? More pointedly, how does the EPA infer a set of workable goals in this milieu?

Third sector organizations also have a difficult time with

goals. For instance, hospitals are judged using one set of standards by insurers and other standards by patients, medical staff, and boards of trustees (Nutt, 1980b). Insurers call for efficient operations, patients want personalized care, the medical staff demand continual improvement of resources, and trustees want prestige and tranquility. These expectations produce conflicting goals as well as vague and hard-to-interpret requirements and priorities. Charities have to deal with both fundraising and allocation, which are intrinsically intertwined. A charity's goals must involve getting money as well as seeing the need for it, using potential recipients' needs as attention grabbers to raise money. The March of Dimes Birth Defects Foundation, for example, calls attention to the needs of people it is helping or hopes to help by showcasing the programs that it funds and those that it would like to fund.

Equity in dealing with clients and providing services is more important than efficiency in public organizations. Efficiency dominates the concerns in private organizations. As publicness increases, efficiency and its comparatively clear cost-related goal proxy become less useful and equity concerns increase in importance. Measures that indicate who gets what are helpful but can be interpreted in various ways. For example, clearly specifying target groups eligible for service that were not served because of budget shortfalls is apt to create controversy. More important, equity measures may distract the organization from confronting goal ambiguity. Ambiguous goals make it difficult to identify current and future directions, a crucial aspect of strategically managing an organization.

Most strategic management procedures call for clear goals. Operating efficiently, often taken as a substitute for the bottom line, can have silly effects in public organizations. Efficiency in public libraries, for instance, would entice the library management to keep the books shelved, cut hours, and limit services. These actions sharply depart from common conceptions of what libraries are about. Thus, goals are frequently ambiguous for public organizations. The more public the organization, the greater the ambiguity. Strategy development in situations that involve ambiguous goals is difficult, if not impossible. This ambiguity provides a sharp distinction between strategic management in public as compared to private organizations (Table 2.2).

Proponents of using strategic management developed for private sector applications in the public sector decry the absence of clear goals in public organizations (Wortman, 1979). They fail to recognize that goal establishment is a crucial step in strategic management procedures needed for public organizations. However, the complex, pluralistic, and opportunistic political milieu in which strategy must be developed makes goals illusory (Levine and others, 1975). Another means must be found to establish targets to work toward public sector strategic management.

Authority Limits. Public administrators have weaker power bases and less authority to alter or reshape the system they must manage than do private sector managers (Gawthrop, 1971; Woll, 1963). Autonomy and flexibility are generally lower in public organizations, making authority limits a key ingredient in defining publicness. For instance, a welfare administrator may know how to improve the efficiency of fund disbursement but may have no way to initiate useful changes without petitioning a legislative body. Hospitals cannot promote service changes without the advice and consent of their medical staff, a group with no real commitment to the organization. Strategy development must take into account these limits to ensure that stakeholders are managed to enhance implementation prospects. Consensus building must accompany strategy formation in public organizations (Table 2.2). In private organizations, new ideas can sweep along the strategic management process or are expected to stem from it.

Strategic management for public organizations must be carried out in a jurisdictional jungle (Levine and others, 1975). Interjurisdictional cooperation is essential, but creating the needed level of cooperation is costly, frustrating, and failure prone. Resolving claims in favor of one type of claimant eliminates many of these difficulties but creates unstable strategy. The apparent selectivity or favoritism can be used by opponents to assail the strategy, leading to its modification or withdrawal. It is better to confront these forces than to allow them to periodically percolate to the surface and cause continual changes in directions. Private sector approaches to strategic management cannot cope with this pluralism and new methods are needed.

Performance Expectations. Goal ambiguity in public organizations makes performance expectations difficult to specify (Dahl and Lindblom, 1953; Schultze, 1970). Vague performance expectations have several consequences. First, success cannot be easily recognized. It is often difficult to identify and reward key contributors. Also, failure cannot be detected and corrected in a timely manner.

Second, and perhaps more significantly, there is less urgency in public organizations. Periodic elections, political appointments, and the like install new leaders who interrupt the organization's plans and projects and create inertia. The organization must delay implementation to bring these new members "up to speed" and find out their agendas. Incorporating the newcomer's ideas can be counterproductive when they lack merit and always results in a disruption of the normal flow of activity. As a result, expectations tend to be in constant flux, which makes it easy to rationalize inaction. These "scheduled interruptions" lead to cautiousness, inflexibility, and low rates of innovation (Rainey, Backoff, and Levine, 1976).

Third sector organizations are spared these scheduled interruptions but do experience difficulty in making assessments, which takes the edge off urgency. The difficulty stems from goal ambiguity; how do voluntary boards of trustees judge a symphony, an art gallery, or a hospital? Hospitals are expected to produce quality, but performance based on quality is never measured in part because the meaning of the term *quality* is both elusive and disputed. For instance, physicians claim that quality stems from using the "correct" procedure, no matter what the outcome. Elaborate systems of checking to ensure procedural fidelity are administered by physicians, raising questions about vested interests and the role of oversight bodies in quality assurance. As a result, demands for changes based on performance are difficult to initiate in a hospital. The orchestra and art gallery have similar problems when their boards attempt to judge the quality of an exhibition or a performance. Change awaits consensus that quality can and should improve, which always involves collaboration by outside experts.

Strategic management in public organizations is undertaken to prompt action and discover agendas of activities that fit within political time frames and respond to consensual demands for change based on peer review (Table 2.2). Private organizations use strategic management to slow activity to allow reflection. Dealing with premature commitments and the need to reflect on current action (for example, product viability) create a different context for strategy management in private organizations. As a result, the timing of action in public settings differs substantially from that in private settings.

Incentives. Encouraging effective performance by using incentives is much more difficult in public than private organizations (Roessner, 1974; Schultze, 1970). A key factor in defining publicness is the ease with which incentives can be devised that are likely to alter performance.

Oversight bodies seeking to improve performance often attempt to use incentives that encourage people to act in ways that produce superior performance. The more public the organization, the more difficult it is to devise workable incentives. Difficulties stem from the type of incentive that seems to be preferred in various sectors and the ease with which performance levels, individual action, and incentive payouts can be linked.

In private organizations, individual contributions to profit and related indexes can be rewarded monetarily. Reward preferences, individual contributions to performance, and the measurement of performance can create serious barriers to using incentives in organizations that have significant degrees of publicness.

Banfield (1977) found that public sector employees often prefer job security, important tasks and roles, power, and recognition over financial rewards. These rewards can be difficult to dispense. Job security and power may only be given once. Important tasks do not necessarily arrive when needed to provide a reward. Furthermore, linking people's efforts to these rewards is often difficult. Who or what, for example, was instrumental in client turnaround in a children's services agency? Various counselors, therapy programs, public school officials, and client self-motivation all play a role, and the contribution of each is often hard to sort out. The private sector can use material incentives more effectively, tying measurable performance to financial rewards. Also, there is evidence that private sector employees attach more importance to financial incentives than do public sector employees (Lawler, 1971).

Strategic management must take into account the lack of responsiveness to incentives in public organizations and use more creativity in developing incentives that match the organization's culture and touch the needs of people in the organization (Table 2.2). In general, incentives play more of an indirect role in settings with publicness. Other means are needed to encourage productive behavior, which calls for creativity during strategy formulation to devise effective mechanisms that recognize the unique features of the setting. For example, in hospitals, nurses provide most of the care a patient receives and play a key role in keeping patients alive. The nurses' need for professional identity can be a crucial factor in the installation of changes that cut costs in hospitals. "Identity-enhancing devices" that are built into cost-cutting plans can be used to entice the nursing staff to act in ways that promote hospital efficiency. However, acts that enhance identity can be hard to identify, and specific acts may be valued differently by each nurse.

Strategy and Internal Process Factors. Goal ambiguity, limits in the acquisition of resources, low expectations, and the absence of incentives pose obstacles for the strategic manager. Several steps are taken to deal with these obstacles. First, our strategic management process uses ideals in place of goals. We do not use goals because they are ambiguous in public organizations and tend to remain so after clarification attempts. Ideals provide a picture of the desired future state of the organization, giving concrete cues on which to build action. Ideals indicate best- and worst-case situations that describe clients, programs, reputation, and competence. The worst case provides a floor on which to build, and the best case provides a target to plan toward. Ideals provide intentions that can be articulated in the concrete terms preferred by organizational leaders. They provide targets and offer ways to seek compromise among competing views that dictate what the organization is (or is not) about.

Second, to build joint agreements that allow strategic action, public and third sector organizations may have to alter jurisdictions and garner resources. Both jurisdictions and resources can set precedents that require careful analysis before action is taken. Everyone is a potential stakeholder, which calls for careful assessments of a stakeholder's motives to block a strategy and his or her power to do so. Key people in the organization's authority network can be mobilized to pry resources away from other uses, to support new budget authorizations, or to authorize usage fees that can underwrite the costs needed to carry out a strategy.

People in the authority network of the public and third sector organization can draw on political influence that is seldom available to firms. Thus, organizations with public features have both opportunities to underwrite the costs of a strategy and barriers to carrying it out, no matter how financially feasible the strategy may be. Strategic managers in firms tend to ignore external negotiations and often use authoritarian postures in their internal dealings. We do stakeholder and resource assessments to form plans that cope with the needs to manage key people in authority networks and uncover the resources needed to take strategic action.

Third, participation in a strategic change offers a way out of the problems of missing incentives and low expectations. Excitement can be created in professional staff members by providing ways for these professionals to participate in the strategic management process. Participation caters to the desire of public sector employees for important tasks and roles as well as an influence over what the organization does. Private sector strategic management procedures make no allowance for such involvement.

Implications for Strategic Managers

The factors in Table 2.1 have several uses. Perhaps the most important is to identify conditions under which our strategic management procedures can be effectively used. Any organization faced with the conditions for publicness identified in Table 2.1 would be a candidate for our procedures.

The factors in Table 2.1 also point out considerations that require attention. Strategic managers in public organizations should be aware of these considerations and fold them into the bundle of concerns that must be managed in the regeneration and change of their organizations. Finally, strategic managers should seek ways to deal with the concerns posed by markets defined by oversight bodies, constraints, and so on. In Part Three, we shall turn our attention to procedural arrangements to deal with the concerns posed by markets, constraints, and the other factors in Table 2.1.

Key Points

1. Many organizations have significant degrees of publicness that pose important considerations for the strategic manager attempting to regenerate and change one of these organizations.
2. Publicness extends to many organizations that are often viewed as being more like private sector organizations, such as hospitals and utilities.
3. Publicness stems from markets that are made up of authority networks, constraints that limit autonomy and flexibility, the prospect of political interference, coercive means that can be used to fund or force the use of services, many externalities that cue action possibilities, the prospect of scrutiny by outsiders, ubiquitous accountability, vague and

argumentative goals, authority limits, shifting performance expectations, and ambiguous incentives to coax desirable behavior. The presence of just one of these factors makes an organization take on characteristics that can render private sector approaches to strategic management misleading or ineffective.

4. Strategic managers can use the factors defining publicness to identify when to use our approach, some of the key considerations and critical issues to be explored, and procedures that deal with crucial considerations.

PART TWO

■   ■

An Overview
of Strategic
Concepts and Issues

■   ■

The chapters in Part Two show why there is an increasing need for managers to act strategically and show some of the types of issues, both apparent and hidden, that prompt strategic action. We begin with a review of strategy, defining terms and briefly reviewing strategic management ideas. In today's increasingly turbulent environment, strategic management offers organizational leaders a tool to cope with the fluid and ever-changing demands placed on them, which, increasingly, call for a change in mission and a change in the historical patterns of service delivery. These pressures have spawned the notion of managing strategically. In Chapter Three, we review the origin of these ideas. In Chapter Four, we show how strategic management can be applied to public and third sector organizations. Strategy pulls an organization along a path in which internal competencies and external control are gradually increased to meet the challenges posed by new patterns of services and new service users. In Chapter Five, we discuss how signals that indicate needs can be read and formed into an issue agenda that guides the strategic management process. We treat issues as tensions that cannot be easily relaxed but can be managed through strategic action.

■   ■

Chapter Three

Types of Strategy
and Their Uses

■   ■

In this chapter, we discuss the origins of strategy and how strategy can be used by organizations. We begin with a discussion of the military lineage of strategy, showing how public and private applications of strategy have drawn on military analogies.

Strategy is used to create focus, consistency, and purpose for an organization by producing plans, ploys, patterns, positions, and perspectives that guide strategic action. The metaphors of a saga, quest, venture, and parlay illustrate how plans, ploys, positions, and perspectives can take shape as a strategy. We link these applications to strategic types called defender, prospector, analyzer, and reactor in which domains are selected, technologies marshaled, and innovations attempted or ignored. We then assess these strategic types to show how environmental conditions, defined by market volatility and competitive orientation, make the defender, prospector, and reactor undesirable strategies. Desirable strategy stems from a measured response to market signals and less extreme assumptions regarding competitor reactions, which produce the custodian, stabilizer, developer, and entrepreneur types of strategy.

The Origins of Strategy

The lineage of strategy stems from military axioms of Sun Tzu, Napoleon, and other military leaders (Evered, 1983). The term *strategic* is derived from the Greek *strategos,* meaning "a general set of maneuvers carried out to overcome an enemy during combat." The notion is one of "generalship," which Machiavelli ([1903], 1952) took to mean the planned exercise of power and influence to carry out the aims of a state.

Machiavelli thrust the metaphors of combat, adversaries, attack, and generalship into the political arena. The adversary vanquished in a political battle loses support for his or her position. The notion of securing a territory in the military context was translated to gathering support for a platform or policy. Battle is joined with adversaries using lobbying, votes, and hearings, which are analogous to campaigns, charges, and pincer movements.

Business also drew on military analogies to develop strategic concepts. The notion of market share is related to securing or pacifying territory. The term *strategy* describes the maneuvers carried out to meet the goals of a firm. Drawing on military analogies, businesses were encouraged to develop an advance plan, resources to implement the plan, and warning devices that signal when plan modification is required.

Chandler (1962) crystallized the need for strategic planning in a book that stressed practice. This practice, or applied emphasis, has endured. The term *strategic management* was introduced to include environmental assessments and implementation (Ansoff, Declerk, and Hayes, 1976). This step merged plans and intentions with assessment of the realities of the internal and external context in which the strategy must survive.

Strategic management came of age with the seminal book by Schendel and Hofer (1979) that presented conceptual underpinnings and new paradigms for the field.

Andrews (1980) offered a contemporary definition of strategy, which has been widely accepted. He contends that strategy is defined by decisions an organization makes that determine or reveal its objectives, purposes, or goals; create the principal policies and plans for achieving its aims; define the range of businesses or services the organization is to pursue; identify the kind of economic and human organization it is or intends to be; and specify the nature of the economic and non-economic contribution to be made to the organization's shareholders or trustees, employees, customers, and communities.

Contemporary Strategic Management

Strategic management continues to be rooted in the applied origins of the field. The *content,* or what is called for by a strategy, makes strategic concepts come alive for practitioners. It is much easier to talk about a merger and its features than to discuss the intellectual process that led up to the merger. Also, the situation facing the organization—its needs, novel circumstances, and traditions—must be appreciated to understand why a given strategy (such as a merger) made sense.

Strategic management has been treated in several ways in the literature. A common approach is to stress content (the merger) and leave process (how the merger was formulated and implemented) implicit (see, for example, Mintzberg and Waters, 1982). Another approach is to mix content and process, making it difficult to distinguish the "what" from the "how."

Both content and process provide insights that can be best appreciated when treated separately (Chaffee, 1985). Strategic content suggests the nature of action such as how a strategy is used, types of options, and ways to translate these ideas into action. The process of strategic management describes how strategy can be devised. It is important to note that strategy can be emergent as well as planned. Mintzberg (1978, 1987) documents how emergent strategy or unplanned ideas have a pervasive influence on the actions of an organization. In the remaining sections of this chapter and in the next chapter, the content and process of strategic action are discussed, showing how the content and process of strategy can be used by organizations.

The Nature of Strategy

Strategy has captured the attention of today's forward-looking manager because it addresses a crucial concern: positioning the organization to face an increasingly uncertain future. To position, managers try to anticipate and plan for foreseeable events, evaluate directions, and align the organization's activities with ideals that capture hopes and aspirations. Strategy provides a way to identify and make the changes called for by these ideals. It is motivated by a concern about current directions and their implications, threats that seem to loom on the horizon, and challenges to current practices and activities. In this sense, strategy identifies a new direction that makes it possible for the organization to reach its ideals. Strategy changes the organization by changing its directions so that ideals can be realized. Strategy is used to focus action, create consistency or continuity, but, most significantly, to give organizations a new or renewed sense of purpose.

Strategy as Focus

People have urges to pursue individualistic goals that can become competitive and may be at odds with the interests of the organization and its clients. Even in well-run organizations, fiefdoms often take root and grow. These fiefdoms can produce aims and traditions that differ from those the organization believes to be important. For example, staff groups resonate only to professional values and manufacturing units tenaciously cling to products in dying markets. Computer support groups become enamored with the constant updating of software, creating chaos for users. Organizational units that had special expertise in making boilers, railroad cars, and buggy whips engaged in all manner of political maneuvering to maintain their budgets, space, and other measures of status as the market for these products vanished.

Strategy helps to cope with this type of situation by focusing effort, which helps to coordinate activity toward an agreed-upon direction. Without this coordination, organizations can become little more than a collection of individuals pursuing their own ends and looking for interesting things to do. This syndrome is particularly prevalent in staff groups and public and third sector organizations without clear missions.

Focus, however, can become too rigid, which is one of the many paradoxes in strategic management. The organization with a highly focused strategy may be unable to adapt when flexible responses are required. To be successful, an organization needs both a direction and a commitment to review and modify its direction as threats and opportunities arise.

Strategy as Consistency

Strategy can reduce uncertainty by offering direction. A strategy indicates what is wanted, which concentrates effort and satisfies people's need for order and predictability in their affairs. Without a strategy, organization members must rationalize and explain their roles and activities as they deal with each new situation they confront.

Many people in public and third sector organizations experience frustration because they lack strategic guidance. Legislation can be vague both as to purpose and means, making an organization's activities subject to dispute. Consider the Highway Safety Act passed by Congress in the 1970s to provide systems for the stabilization of people injured in accidents and the safe transportation of these people to sources of emergency care. Advocates were calling for various actions, such as training and certifying ambulance drivers in handling injured people, but several organizations claimed the implied training and certification mandates. The Highway Safety staffers had to grope for a role beyond dispersing federal funds that gave their agency some reason to exist. People in some of these state-funded programs squandered much of their time searching for a mission that a strategy could have provided. Highway safety programs that were able to create an acceptable strategy to manage this ambiguity were more effective in championing legislation to license ambulance drivers, sponsor training, initiate dispatch services, develop emergency call systems, deal with treatment facilities, and set standards for people providing emergency care.

Again, consistency can be paradoxical. Control is valuable to concentrate available funds and people's energy as much as possible. People learn repertoires that can be efficiently applied for the benefit of all. To continually question a strategy leads to inaction. This situation is aptly demonstrated by one of our public agency clients who approaches us annually for help in goal setting but has never acted in accordance with these goals. Strategy allows for fast response to known or anticipated situations. Problems arise when situations are no longer recognizable, cooperative agreements to manage niches break down, and domains are foreclosed. These events call for flexibility and rapid adjustment repertoires. Strategy must be both fixed and malleable to cope with the paradox. Strategy is fixed to offer islands of stability in which to work but must be flexible enough to change as new needs and opportunities emerge.

Strategy as Purpose

Strategy not only directs effort but gives meaning to both organizational members and outsiders. Strategy provides insiders and outsiders with a way to understand what the organization is about and to differentiate it from other organizations engaged in seemingly similar activities. For instance, in one of our cases an organization moved from an image of giving grants to children with malformed feet to an image of offering services by changing its name from "crippled children's services" to "children with medical handicaps." The change in name reflects its change in strategy. This step fended off attempts to merge the bureau with another agency and gave it a renewed sense of purpose.

Strategy provides an easy way to denote the organization. As Christenson and others (1983) point out, strategy helps one to know the agency without being in the agency. For instance, organizations such as General Electric (GE) create excitement by merely articulating a strategy. The announcement that GE would focus on three segments—core businesses, high technology, and services—was used to make inferences about the company's leadership and potential (Mintzberg, 1987a). The use of strategy as a proxy for understanding GE's future financial prospects can be questioned, but the symbolic power of the strategy should be clear. The challenge is to articulate a strategy and an organizational name that create a desirable image: one that resonates to organizational ideals. Strategy making and name changes often go hand in hand because there is a need to draw attention to a new set of purposes.

Paradox again poses a dilemma. For organizations seeking a new sense of purpose, periods of groping may be desirable and may not always indicate a moribund agency vegetating with public money. Blandness can be useful when it allows groping for a new strategy to take place at a pace that permits appreciation of what can be done, what can be desirable, and the intersection of the desirable and doable. What seems a period of lethargy can be one of deep probing for new direction and purpose to form a new strategy. If this process is disturbed or disrupted, the labeling of strategy, as in the GE illustration, may temporarily deflect criticism and even garner accolades. However, this temporary relief may keep the organization from attempting to cope with emerging issues, that, unattended, could have serious consequences.

How Strategy Is Used

Strategies have multiple uses in organizations (Mintzberg, 1987b). The use of a strategy as a plan is widely understood, but a strategy can also be used as a ploy, pattern, position, and perspective. The interrelationships of these uses add further insight into how strategy can be applied and its value.

Plan

Strategy as a plan provides a way to take action, such as attempting to capture a market with changes in product pricing. Plans are intentionally drawn before taking action. Purposeful action calls for conscious development of an idea in the advance of action to advocates of plans and planning. In strategic management, planning is carried out to ensure that the objectives of an organization are met.

Ploy

Strategy can also be used as a ploy. As a ploy, strategy can be used to outwit an opponent. The assumption of competition is inherent in this notion of strategy. Corporations that threaten to enter a market can discourage a competitor by altering their thinking about the desirability of the market. Such a strategy has no intention of being realized. Porter (1980) discusses how announcing moves and making threats, such as antitrust suits, can be used to ward off competitors and keep them off balance as the firm formulates its own preemptive response. Defensive strategy (Porter, 1985) uses several ploys to reduce the prospect of retaliation by a competitor. Ploys are also used in bargaining situations by companies seeking to outwit rivals.

Johnson Controls used a ploy to hide its $20 million next-generation building automation system that integrated computers and digital technology to control heating, security, and other building functions from Honeywell, Johnson's primary competitor. Both Johnson and Honeywell had about 30 percent of the building control market, valued at $2 billion a year. Even though elaborate secrecy was attempted, Johnson believed Honeywell had found out that a major development was in the works. To hide its efforts, Johnson Controls created a smoke-screen. Johnson Controls promoted a slight modification to their existing control system, calling it LOBO (logical option for building systems). They used a flashy advertising campaign, complete with helium balloons, thereby buying time for the company to complete its new product. The diversion was covered in trade publications and distracted Honeywell, illustrating how ploys are used to protect new ideas. Ploys often take shape as cloak-and-dagger activities, such as phony publicity for nonexistent products with catchy names. Many companies will not reveal their security methods, making the Johnson Controls anecdote particularly notable.

Pattern

Used as a pattern, strategy becomes a stream of actions. Seen in this way, strategy is made up of both emergent and intended ideas. Successful moves gradually take shape and combine into a grand strategy. According to Mintzberg (1978, 1987b), this stream of action has a pattern that connects emergent opportunity with intended planned action, discarding some aspects of what was planned as new insights about opportunity arise. The pattern tends to be strategist-situation specific, creating what might be termed a continually evolving notion of a grand design in the strategist's mind. This view of strategy discounts the value of planned action and relies on the cleverness of managers to see opportunity and graft it onto the organization's current conception of its markets, products and services, customers, clients, and the like.

Position

Strategy can also be used as a position. To position, a strategist explores the environment to find services or products that seem needed (Hofer and Schendel, 1978). The internal and external context, which make up an environment, create a niche for which a strategy is fashioned. Finding a niche, or "niche prospecting," is often treated as a key responsibility of top management. If products and services are well matched to this niche,

the strategy that results will provide sustainable economic returns on investments or benefits to citizens. These product or
service niches create "domains" to which resources are directed.

An organization can compete for a niche using ploys or
can seek a niche to exploit, hoping to avoid competition. Service organizations often seek out such domains and present
arguments, such as duplication of effort that wastes tax dollars,
to fend off other organizations. Cooperation among organizations can be carried out by dividing up niches to produce max-
imal benefit or efficiency. For example, home health agencies
that service a single area could divide up groups of patients by
using specialization or some other criterion.

Self-protection can also motivate cooperation. Collective
strategies can be carried out for mutual self-protection, allowing service organizations to protect their budgets. Firms use
franchising to limit competition for similar reasons, hoping to
reduce the expected force of competition. Strategy as a position can call for consortia, shared boards, venture subsidiaries,
or even mergers.

Perspective

Strategy can also be seen as a perspective. Organizational traditions are captured in the products or services thought to be
of high priority and how they are regarded (or believed to be
regarded) by members of important constituencies. These traditions make up the organization's culture, ideology, or world-
view. For instance, American Electric Power (AEP), a well-known
utility, has considerable pride in its transmission capability and
has concentrated its strategy on protecting this core value.
Measures of performance, such as maintaining low power
transmission costs, are used by AEP to emphasize this core value.
In this sense, strategy becomes a concept that is widely shared
and the touchstone of all future action. This preoccupation is
useful as long as the strategy provides sustainable benefits. In
this sense, organizations use strategy to create a persona that
captures their desires and aspirations.

Combining the Uses

As a plan, strategy sets direction, establishing what the organization hopes to become. These intentions are subject to change as new opportunities are recognized, which produces a pattern in which both intended and emergent ideas combine to form a strategy. Perspective shapes a plan in which opportunities are embraced and incorporated. As a position, strategy identifies several niches that can be exploited by the organization by applying its distinctive competencies, such as AEP exploiting its transmission capability. And ploys are used by organizations to maneuver, in the hope of producing an advantage by sealing off desirable domains or by sharing them in ways that are acceptable to organizational players.

   These views of strategy have many interesting interrelationships. Perspective can form the pattern from which a plan emerges. For example, utilities caught up in their transmission capability are apt to make decisions in which this technological capability is enhanced, protected, and nurtured. This stream of decisions produces a pattern of technology enhancements that becomes the grand strategy, misguided or not. As a result, marketing or new ventures are unlikely strategies. Management views the result as a plan that, in reality, has self-imposed constraints combined with new directions. The strategic manager maneuvers within the constraints, selecting positions and even ploys to maintain this view. Examples include: Volkswagen's nearly self-destructive devotion to its "bug," the "people's" car (Mintzberg, 1978); a former Big 8 accounting partner as a university business school dean who identified the accounting department as a center of excellence and saw all educational needs in terms of benefiting the accounting faculty; and Wendy's move into the breakfast market with products that had the same package, production, and advertising approach as their upscale burgers. Volkswagen nearly choked on its commitment, the dean saw his college slip in national stature, and Wendy's stock fell by two-thirds before corrective action was taken. The enduring influence of perspective can be self-destructive.

Strategists should consider various ways that the organization can be positioned that depart, to one degree or another, from traditions. Such an approach would create several competing views that challenge conventional thinking (Mason and Mitroff, 1981; Quinn, 1988). Scenarios can be built that take pacesetter and reactive positions for comparison purposes. Also, interesting perspectives can be created by comparing new versus current technologies, new versus current markets, turbulent versus predictable use or demand, and relying on political influence versus cost cutting. Juxtaposing across categories, such as positioning with a marketing versus an engineering orientation, opens up even more possibilities. The organization open to testing its strategy in this way will be more innovative and better able to cope with unexpected shifts in the environment that can make its products or services obsolete.

Taking Strategic Action

Past, present, and future temporal orientations are required in a strategy (Ackoff, 1981). The future orientation provides a target that shapes action to achieve long-run aims. By designing a desirable future, a range of moves can be tested to determine which seem best. A present orientation stresses immediate action, concentrating on what can be dealt with today. Piecemeal shifts or moves are made as opportunities arise and needs are recognized. The past can be used to explore historical commitments that represent real values the organization wishes to retain in future efforts and create an understanding of what has made the organization successful.

Rubin (1988) dramatizes these temporal postures in terms of risks, adversaries, challenges, wins or losses, and the like to characterize the types of strategic action that can be taken. The metaphors of the saga, quest, venture, and parlay indicate both the temporal orientation and assumptions about the environment embodied in various kinds of strategic action.

Saga

The saga depicts a historical orientation toward time in which the past offers cues for action. A recounting of a heroic exploit is used to create something with which people can identify, providing glue that binds together the image of the organization. An appreciation of the past is built by depicting the exploits of people as they overcame seemingly unsurmountable obstacles and saved the organization when it appeared headed for oblivion. As these exploits are recounted, the core values of the organization are revealed. The revelation dramatizes a situation or event in which these core values are in danger of being lost because of changes outside or inside the organization. These changes can stem from declining organizational capacities, conflicts, or shifts in the support needed from key benefactors, such as a legislature.

The saga is configured to reinstitute or to protect a strategic position thought to be threatened by events and trends. For example, the Citadel, a tax-supported military institute located in Lexington, Virginia, used a saga to rally support for its fight to block the admission of women fifteen years after the Big Three military academies went co-ed. The tale of a Union army general's march through Lexington, the burning and sacking of the school, and the faculty's rebuilding of the campus stone by stone was recounted to rally support for tradition, which just incidentally excluded women. The civil rights movement used this approach by pointing out that the core values in the Constitution and Bill of Rights were never put into practice for minority groups and, as a result, were in danger of being lost for everyone (Rubin, 1988).

The saga may change with each retelling, even to the degree that all but the core elements are abandoned. Some heroes, victories, and encounters may enter or exit to make the saga cogent to a current situation. This approach to strategy formation allows key players to see and appreciate the core values to be maintained and how new conditions may alter these commitments in undesirable ways. In this way, the mission that lies behind the saga reproduces the original aims of the organization, often drawing from the core values of now departed leaders. For example, only after their deaths do U.S. presidents become charismatic leaders. This allows a certain revisionism to occur in which the leader's views are reinterpreted to champion contemporary causes. To call for reform follow-

ing the congressional money grubbing and influence peddling
scandals of the late 1980s, people cited anecdotes such as the
one about Harry Truman using his own stamps to mail letters
during his administration.

Sagas capture long-term commitments to change that
must be included in responses to trends and events believed to
be serious and real. Sagas can be undesirable, as illustrated by
Volkswagen's "bug" design. Volkswagen saw the bug as the
symbol of its commitment to a "people's" car, on which the
company was founded. This commitment was applied as a saga
to hold back new car designs that were necessary because of
changes in consumer taste and the growing demand for Japanese automobiles in U.S. markets. Massive leadership changes,
as in a merger, or deep-seated conflict among key members of
the organization also provide opportunities to use sagas. Stories are told by the merger partners or antagonists to support
their position during the sorting-out period that follows the
merger.

Sagas represented about one quarter of the cases studied
by Rubin (1988) and were found to use restorative, reformative, and conservatory strategies. A *restorative strategy* seeks to
capture a lost prior state by new policies and mandates. For
example, port organizations in the early 80s engaged in dredg-
ing and facility construction to bolster the use of these facilities
in spite of clear declines in the patterns of use for ports that
were being refurbished. A *reformative strategy* modifies existing
policy and mandates that seem inappropriate. Public indigna-
tion caused the Internal Revenue Service (IRS) to revise its policy
on confiscating the bank accounts of children when their parents had delinquent tax bills. A *conservatory strategy* is carried
out to protect values embodied by people and organizational
arrangements that seem to be threatened. For example, historical societies take action to hold up zoning that would lead to
razing structures that have historical significance.

Quest

Strategic managers who focus their efforts and resources with
a vision of what is desirable or compelling use the metaphor of

a quest. The quest is intended to capture the sense of adventure and tests of courage in a search for something of value. A quest is a saga that draws on the future and not the past. (Although, at some future date, today's quest may become tomorrow's saga.) Strong and inspired leadership is needed to infuse key players in the search with a sense of destiny. The leader often provides a new vision that calls for bold initiatives to replace current strategy. Mikhail Gorbachev used the images called forth by Glasnost and Perestroika as a quest that brought reforms to Soviet society. A quest can also arise when new leaders feel compelled to show that they are setting new directions during a honeymoon period or when the organization's future is threatened.

Like the saga, a quest responds to long time periods but unlike the saga, future environments are anticipated and believed to be understood. A quest has an answer or remedy for the issues believed to be salient. The leader mobilizes people by describing what will be done. Politicians often coax people to follow a quest. Success depends on the politician's ability to describe his or her vision with compelling imagery that inspires people to commit their energy and resources to the "cause." For example, John F. Kennedy's New Frontier offered a new vision of public service that is credited with inspiring young people to work in federal programs. Lyndon Johnson's Vietnam policy could be termed a failed quest.

Quests also arise when key people are locked in conflict. Offering long-run goals creates a vehicle to promote agreement among conflicting parties. Setting aside the short-term aims that produced the conflict and replacing them with a future target creates a new set of ideals to work toward that the competing interests may be able to embrace.

Rubin (1988) found that quests depicted strategic action in one quarter of the organizations studied. Quests were carried out by new agenda, grand vision, and alternative course strategies. The *new agenda strategy* can be used to balance tensions between parties favoring and opposing change. The structure of an agenda allows the leader to protect new initiatives by packaging them with other projects that bring in people who can be sold on the new directions. The agenda can be

organized around the new directions and other topics known
to be of interest to certain people. A group made up of these
individuals is asked to provide an assessment of ways to act, in
the hopes of creating a coalition that can be mobilized to prevent opposition.

The *grand vision strategy* captures an image of future possibilities and paints a proactive picture of what the organization
can become. Such an approach has been used to mobilize support for economic development in cities like Baltimore. A
physical plan that provides a vision of what Baltimore can become has guided its urban renewal decisions for decades. An
alternative course strategy is used to deal with an issue that suggests a crisis. The organization's resources are mobilized to resolve the issue. The quest is directed toward resolving this one
burning issue and precludes working on anything else. For instance, if a crucial service program is failing, it captures attention until the crisis is averted.

Venture

A venture is an action that deals with perceived opportunities
or needs. A present or near-future orientation is used. Ventures are based on speculations about the prospect of occur-
rence and impact of emerging issues that would demand
immediate attention. The orientation is similar to a "predict-
and-prepare" posture in that it recognizes the limitations in
predicting the salience of emergent issues and the risks involved in making contingency plans. Complex and poorly
understood situations on the horizon often provoke the venture approach. Short-term experiments are conducted for situations in which outcomes are going to be ambiguous because
it is not clear how to deal with the emerging issues. Examples
include premerger discussions among potential merger parties. Cooperative arrangements, such as the National Kidney
Foundation, go through a venture stage before the consortium
is formed (Nutt, 1984a).

Ventures were used in more than a third of the organizations studied by Rubin (1988). They were carried out by

strategies called targets, trials, and compacts. The *target strategy* in the private sector concentrates financial resources to deal with the emergent issue. In the public sector, targeting frequently must improve the organization's capacity before an emergent issue can be addressed. The *trial strategy* deals with emergent issues by using experiments or temporary arrangements, such as temporary assignments. Organizations apply stopgap measures that can be modified as needed later on, such as coping with sharp jumps in demand for services by reassigning personnel and at the same time checking on state regulations to determine the acceptability of acting in this way. A *compact* as a strategy calls for short-term agreements among parties to cope with an emergent issue that involves organizations with overlapping responsibilities or ambiguous roles. The first year of a new project can be managed in this way, with a renegotiation to follow.

Parlay

The parlay is used when the organization's attempt to read signals fails to produce a coherent pattern of trends and events that will become issues. In this situation, a parlay is used to make a move that creates an opportunity to make a subsequent move. To illustrate, in playing poker you bet a high-risk hand with small stakes early in the game to convince opponents that your strategy is to bluff. Later in the game, the other players are more apt to stay in the game and match raises when you have a superior hand, thereby increasing the size of the pot. In organizations, a parlay is used to exploit an opportunity to position for a better opportunity. This approach is based on incrementalism (Quinn, 1980). The environment is seen as too complex to read and understand. Taking small moves creates feedback and the possibility for adjustment without "betting the barn" in turbulent situations. The incremental movement is thought to seek out and explore opportunities as they come to be recognized.

Parlays can arise in budget hearings, media reports, and crises. For example, during periods of retrenchment, an organization competing for funds plays its cards "close to the chest." Ideals and new directions are revealed in small doses to read how key parties react. Changes can then be made to influence legislators and others that make budget decisions.

Parlays were used in 13 percent of the organizations studied by Rubin (1988). Strategies of hedging, leveraging, and advancing were identified. The primary motivation for a *hedging strategy* is to cope with the uncertainty of several equally likely future conditions looming on the horizon. In periods of budget scarcity, public organizations put forward a variety of programs and avoid prioritizing them so rebudgeting is possible should budget shortfalls develop.

A *leveraging strategy* draws on the strategist's store of "social credit." The strategist's contacts in social and work networks are exploited to increase his or her influence over events. Some department chairs in universities agree to serve on every imaginable committee and project to build social credit that can be used to promote self-interests, such as pay and promotion, and the interests of their academic programs, such as budget support during periods of retrenchment.

An *advancing strategy* is a parlay designed to lower risk by seizing an unexpected windfall opportunity. The strategist uses this parlay to advance toward a goal in situations that lack control (that preclude leveraging) and have a single, well-defined aim (that preclude hedging). For example, a hospital administrator knew that his institution had the lowest cost in the region because the cost of constructing the facilities had been paid off years ago, eliminating depreciation expenses. He also knew that the facility had to be refurbished in the next few years or face a loss of accreditation, which would decertify a large number of the institution's beds. The discovery of the lowest operating cost in the region was used to argue that fiscal prudence had been exercised in the past, justifying to regulators the spending of huge sums of money to modernize and expand. The hospital now has the highest cost in the region, but the administrator has parlayed his reputed "success" in both building and running a tight ship into a new and more prestigious position.

Types of Strategy

Table 3.1 shows attempts to classify strategy by type. The typical framework shows how environmental conditions are responded to using classes of actions that can be grouped according to a dominant theme. These themes capture some of the content of strategies carried out by organizations. As such, they provide examples about the nature of strategic action under a variety of conditions and how an organization puts its sagas, quests, ventures, and parlays into practice.

The Miles and Snow (1978) typology offers an interesting classification that has been widely adopted. Drawing on the environmental definitions of Emery and Trist (1965), environmental types were defined in terms of market volatility and the orientation of competitors, as shown in the top half of Figure 3.1. Disturbed environments have volatile markets that frequently change and in which competitors adopt a defensive posture. The placid environment is also defended but the market is stable. A clustered placid environment has stable features but competitors take steps to grab clusters and become offensive. The turbulent environment has aggressive competitors that are attempting to cope with a volatile and rapidly changing market.

Miles and Snow (1978) fit strategies to these environmental types, suggesting how to select domains, marshal technology, and promote innovation under these four conditions, giving the framework a contingency perspective. These strategies describe how domains can be determined and technologies garnered, and when innovation is needed in the private sector. Public and third sector applications will be offered in the next chapter.

Classifying Strategy by Environmental Adaptation

Miles and others, (1978), Miles and Snow (1978), and Miles (1982) classify strategy types in terms of actions prompted by shifts in the environment. Effective organizations identify and maintain viable market-product (or service) alignments. Effec-

Table 3.1. Classifications of Strategic Content.

	Content Classifications
Miles and Snow (1978)	Defender, reactor, prospector, analyzer *Dimensions:* risk orientation
Miles and Cameron (1982)	Domain offense, domain defense, domain creation *Dimensions:* market orientation and innovation
Galbraith and Schendel (1983)	Harvest, build, continue, climb, niche, cashout *Dimensions:* level of investment and specialization
Meyer (1982)	Weather the storm, ignore the storm, experiment *Dimension:* leader attitude
Mintzberg (1978)	Entrepreneurial, adaptive, planning *Dimensions:* source of idea
Paine and Anderson (1977)	Adaptive, planning, entrepreneurial *Dimensions:* amount and control over change
Porter (1980)	Cost leadership, differentiation, focus on control *Dimensions:* strategic and advantage target
Harrigan (1980)	Early exit, milk the investment, shrink selectively, hold position, increase investment *Dimensions:* amount and timing of investment

Figure 3.1. Strategies Matched to Private Sector Environments.

Types of Environment

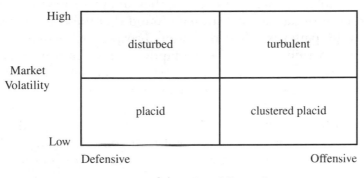

Orientation of Competitors

Types of Strategy

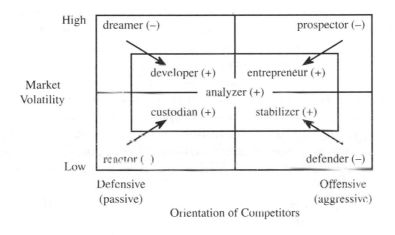

Orientation of Competitors

tiveness stems from continually adjusting to significant environmental shifts by selecting products or services that match the new market realities and the actions of competitors. Strategic managers make strategy as they adapt to new realities. Studies of organizational strategy found that these adaptations had four patterns called defender, prospector, analyzer, and reactor. Within each of these adaptive types, entrepreneurial, engineering, and administrative tasks are carried out. The entrepreneurial task identifies domain: the product or service line and its market niche. The engineering task creates the means to manufacture and market products or the means to deliver services. Administrative tasks deal with control, ensuring that needed activities are carried out efficiently according to present procedure.

Defender. Strategic managers become defenders when they try to protect their domains to maintain current products or services and markets. Steps are taken to close off a portion of the market from competitors or to protect turf. Entrepreneurial tasks include lobbying, selling or seeking franchises, seeking import barriers and taxes, using advertising and promotion, and forming trade associations that defenders can use to protect a domain. For example, Miles (1982) shows how tobacco companies used these tactics to defend tobacco products in the face of governmental action that linked smoking and health problems. Lobbying was used to turn aside attempts to limit smoking, such as smoke-free workplaces. The Tobacco Institute was founded by and continues to be funded by firms with an interest in promoting tobacco use. The Tobacco Institute attempts to counter all publicity that draws attention to the health hazards of smoking.

    Engineering tasks in a defender strategy stress efficiency in the production and distribution of goods and services. This often leads to huge investments in production capacity. The tobacco industry, for example, is well known for its highly efficient manufacturing and sophisticated distribution systems. Control tasks are carried out to ensure that efficiency continues to be realized in manufacturing and distribution systems.

The defender strategy is useful for organizations with stable, well-defined markets and technology. Because efficient operations are valued, cost is often used to measure organizational performance. Serving a market or market segment with products and services that can be efficiently produced and delivered is believed to provide long-term benefits and organizational survival. However, when technology or customer needs become volatile, this strategy can lead to poor results or even organizational failure, which is indicated by bankruptcy, mergers and buyouts, or the termination of tax support.

Prospector. Strategic managers following a prospector strategy seek out new products or services and market opportunities. Being an innovator becomes an important aspect of the organization's culture. The Limited, 3M Company, and Hewlett-Packard Company are innovative firms. The entrepreneurial task is to create new products that fill needs in particular market segments. Organizations using this approach to strategy invest heavily in people to scan for opportunities and provide the creative energy needed to come up with new ideas. Strategists continually match innovations with market niches. Strategy tends to be quite fluid in order to seize each opportunity as it emerges.

The engineering task in this strategy is to maintain flexibility that permits rapid responses to new opportunities. Efficiency is seldom a priority because several redundant technologies must be available for possible use. Administration is loose and designed to facilitate and coordinate many projects in various stages of completion. Facilitation, not control, is emphasized.

Revenues tend to be stressed as a measure of organizational performance in firms following a prospector strategy. Such a strategy requires flexibility but results in a loss in efficiency and an increase in risk. Rapid response can lead to windfall payoffs, but through miscalculations an organization may fail to capture the windfall, leaving only high cost. Being the first to see opportunity in a turbulent market has high initial payoffs that decline as others attempt to reap the benefits of exploiting this market. This decline commits the organization to a prospector mentality, in which it continually searches for innovative ideas to replace its products in maturer markets.

Analyzer. Some organizations combine prospector and defender approaches, creating what is called an analyzer strategy. The strategic manager who has an analyzer perspective attempts to lower risk and increase opportunity. The analyzer combines the strengths of a defender (domain defense) and the prospector (domain offense). The entrepreneurial task is to look for new product-market opportunities *and* maintain current customers. New products or services are introduced after others have tested their viability. Analyzer strategy is based on imitation: adopting products and services that prospectors have initiated with good results. These new initiatives are slowly added to the traditional products and services and their associated customers and clients.

Key engineering and administrative tasks deal with creating a balance between the demands for control and flexibility. New products or services are partitioned off from old ones, and different tactics are adopted for each type of product or service. For old products or services, standardization and mechanization are stressed, and for new ones fluid arrangements, such as venture management teams, are used. Administrative tasks call for distinguishing between these two engineering tasks. Each is dealt with separately using appropriate tactics, such as matrix organizational structure and liaison between research and development and manufacturing or delivery units for new products and standardization for the old products.

Analyzers produce two organizational cultures, the prospector and the defender, that can have considerable friction. This friction can be illustrated by the Lego block division's conflicts with its parent company, Samsonite luggage. The Lego block division stressed innovation and new ideas and the luggage division placed less emphasis on new ideas and more on cost control. People working for the Lego division believed that cost-control mentality was holding them back and people in the luggage division were aghast at the "wild-eyed," undisciplined behavior of the Lego people.

The coexistence of two cultures makes it difficult for a company to be an industry leader. As a result, costs are higher than in defender organizations and revenues are lower than in prospector organizations. The profit picture can be better than in either of these types of organization with effective management. Current profit becomes the key indicator of organizational success.

Reactor. The pattern of adjustment to environmental shifts can be inappropriate and in a constant state of flux. Reactor strategy represents an ineffective form of strategy in which initiatives either miss markets or select products or services that the organization is ill equipped to provide. Failure leads to alternating between a passive posture when aggressiveness is needed and overly bold initiatives that lead to unwarranted risk taking. The reactor strategy stems from failing to act effectively as a defender, prospector, or analyzer.

Reactor strategy can arise in organizations dominated by a single strategic manager who is no longer creative or who departs, due to death or raiding by another organization. Departure leaves a vacuum that produces groping to replace or maintain the organization's historical strengths. Reactor strategy may also stem from a new leader whose style differs sharply from his or her predecessor. For example, organizations may be unable to absorb a strategy that shifts their culture from prospector to defender. Apple Computers had difficulty switching to cost standards because it was accustomed to the constant change called for by innovation. Shifts from a defender to a prospector strategy would produce similar dilemmas for an organization. Culture can also make it difficult to alter strategic commitments when markets cease to be viable. These commitments have tradition and many vocal defenders who create roadblocks that stand in the way of a change in strategy.

Extending Adaptive Strategy

In the framework of Miles just two of the strategic postures are viable (prospectors and defenders). Analyzers are a combination of viable types but match no particular environment, and reactors are ineffective, leaving the disturbed and the placid environments without a viable strategy. Also, the defender and the prospector types represent extreme responses to environmental conditions.

In response to these criticisms, a framework was proposed by Acar (1987) in which more and less effective strategies have been suggested for each environmental condition, as shown in the bottom half of Figure 3.1. Ineffectiveness stems from being overly committed to assumptions about markets and competition. Overreactions to volatility in markets and the prospect of competition are believed to produce ineffective strategy types, denoted with a minus sign in Figure 3.1. A restrained response seems more apt to produce successful strategy. The more effective types of strategy are called custodian, stabilizer, entrepreneur, and developer and are denoted by a plus sign in Figure 3.1.

Custodian. Strategic managers who take a defensive posture in a stable market assume that environments are not apt to change. Either a reactor or a custodian orientation toward strategy can be adopted. Maintenance is the preferred strategy because it makes less extreme commitments to future market stability and the prospects of competition, creating a custodian strategy. Custodians maintain distinctive competencies and nurture markets in which the organization's capacities can be used to exploit historically viable market niches. A reactor strategy tends to read information into trends and events that are more apparent than real and more urgent than important (Kolb, 1983).

The custodian takes a position that defends historical commitments (such as those expressed in sagas) without being reactionary. Subsidies in the form of protectionism, such as limits or taxes on imports, are often sought. The bureaucracy is devoted to using devices such as patents to seal off its key product ideas from exploitation by others. Competitive threats are ignored and standardized operating procedures (SOPs) are used to produce goods or provide services. Organizations following a custodian strategy accept slow growth and react to competitors cautiously, limiting risk and tightly controlling capital investments. According to Acar (1987), the steel industry in the United States has successfully used a custodian strategy for decades.

Stabilizer. When markets are seen as stable with many aggressive competitors, a clustered-placid environment is assumed to exist. Within each cluster, there is little change, but the clusters can have different features. Either a defender or a stabilizer strategy can be adopted. Defenders overreact by assuming that demand is fixed and aggressively defending each product or service in each cluster that is threatened. The stabilizer takes steps to respond to each important cluster, recognizing that demand as well as market share can shift. The U.S. automobile companies adjusted to slow growth in traditional lines of business with renewed emphasis on efficiency in all product lines with a stabilizer strategy. Product lines were treated as heterogeneous autonomous units in which separate tactics (for example, parlays) were used to deal with engineering and control problems. Stabilizers tend to react to changes in the environment with cost cutting and related efficiency-seeking tactics. Only strong signals that indicate shifts in demand and market share would be recognized by stabilizers.

Developer. A defensive posture toward changing markets assumes that a disturbed environment exists in which some change is inevitable. Either a dreamer or a developer strategy can be used. Being overly defensive leads to a dreamer strategy, in which unrealistic assumptions are made. Competition is ignored, and the market's volatility is thought to be temporary. Dreamers cling to tradition long after products or services have lost their vitality because these products and services are powerful symbols of a company's commitment to its distinctive competence. For example, making railroad cars had become a fine art in a few U.S. companies that maintained this product long after its market had been played out.

The developer sees the environment as disturbed and believes signals must be carefully read (as in the venture). Competitive moves that jeopardize market position or erode profits are carefully noted. Benchmarks of competition, such as market share, are used to signal when innovation seems needed. According to Acar (1987), the response of International Business Machines (IBM) to competitors illustrates this posture. Much like Japanese firms, IBM emulates innovations by others as a way to refine and update its products and marketing approaches.

Entrepreneur. Turbulent environments result from changing markets that a strategist seeks to capture by aggressive action. Either a prospector or an entrepreneurial strategy can be used. Prospectors can overreact to weak signals and see competitors as more of a threat than they actually pose. The United States's posture toward the "Soviet menace" during the cold war is an illustration. In contrast, entrepreneurs take a more restrained posture toward signal reading and innovative developmental activities. This type of strategy has been pursued by Intel, Disney, and Apple Computer and has led to rapid growth and excellent profitability for each organization. The entrepreneurial strategy is employed when firms carefully read weak signals and develop novel products with risky or unknown market potential. Products with promise are pursued. Efficient operations tend to be unimportant. Few firms maintain this posture (that is, many continuous quests) over long periods of time. Switching from an entrepreneurial to a custodial strategy allows the aggressive firm to consolidate gains before engaging in a new round of innovation.

Key Points

1. Strategic management provides a way to realize organizational ideals. Trends and events that pose issues, actions to take in response to issues, and political and social forces

that facilitate or constrain action are considered as an organization reaches for its ideals. Strategic management is initiated by an organization to make needed changes in its strategic direction in order to move toward its ideals.

2. Strategy is used by an organization to focus effort and create consistency in reaching for its ideals (purposes). Strategy is used as a plan, ploy, pattern, position, and/or perspective to guide action.

3. Strategic action takes shape as sagas, quests, ventures, and parlays. Sagas reaffirm values and ideologies that the organization wants to preserve. Quests launch new initiatives that take shape as grand visions. Ventures and parlays provide ways to steer a course through the immediate tension field of issues that are pulling or pushing the organization in various directions at the same time.

4. Four types of strategy can be identified that respond to environmental conditions produced by market volatility and the competitiveness of others in the same market. These strategic types show how domains are selected and technologies marshaled and indicate the need for innovation. Strategists are cautioned to avoid overreacting to environmental conditions and to maintain flexibility in their strategic orientation. Custodian, stabilizer, developer, and entrepreneurial types of strategy were recommended because they produce flexible commitments that can be modified as new environmental conditions arise. Custodians seek to maintain distinctive competencies and to nurture markets in placid environments. Stabilizers develop a variety of responses for important clusters, based on consideration of each cluster. Developers make careful moves that are forced by the actions of competitors that can jeopardize market position or erode profit. Entrepreneurs respond to market opportunities with innovative products or services.

Chapter Four

■   ■

Applying Strategic Approaches to Public and Third Sector Organizations

■   ■

This chapter identifies types of strategy that fit environmental conditions relevant for public and third sector organizations. The authority network of public and most third sector organizations defines their market. This market is made up of the needs calling for action as seen by voluntary boards, legislative bodies, and mandates that make up the authority network to which the organization must respond. Like markets, these needs can be stable or shifting. The notion of reacting to competitors is replaced by responsiveness to emerging needs for organizations with public features. Using these definitions, strategies for public and third sector organizations are identified that have positive features (director, bureaucrat, accommodator, compriser, and mutualist) and negative features (dominator, drifter, and posturer). These strategies show how organizations with public features can move toward high responsiveness coupled with appropriate action taking. In this chapter, we also discuss strategic management processes that can be applied to produce a strategy and public and private portfolios of activities, showing how they are alike and how they differ. Finally, we discuss the strategic aims of public and third sector organizations to increase their external control and internal capacity. Control and capacity are used to identify types of organizations in which strategic change can occur and organizational types insulated from change.

Public and Third Sector Strategy

For organizations with public features, concerns about market volatility and competitors are replaced by need volatility that creates pressure for action and the responsiveness required to meet needs. Perceptions of the responsiveness expected and the pressure for action identify the environments recognized by public and third sector organizations, as shown in Figure 4.1 (top). In this figure, the plus signs indicate potentially effective strategy and the minus signs strategy that is apt to be ineffective. The arrow indicates a path to take to increase the effectiveness of a strategy.

Instead of merely responding to the competitive position of others, organizations with public features can alter their relationships with organizations and stakeholders that make up their environment, as shown by the arrow in Figure 4.1. The level of responsiveness is modified by the organization as it makes commitments to act. The organization can move to accommodation, compromise, or collaboration and can attempt to sustain this kind of relationship with its environment. These positions define environments that can be fashioned in part by the actions of an organization with public features, as shown in Figure 4.1. Depending on the response to needs that are stipulated by the organization's authority network, one of the strategies shown in Figure 4.1 (bottom) is created by the organization. Organizations that respond to needs as they have in the past limit their choices by continuing to use their old strategy. Organizations that match their responsiveness to emer-

Figure 4.1. Strategies Matched to Public Sector Environments.

Types of Environment

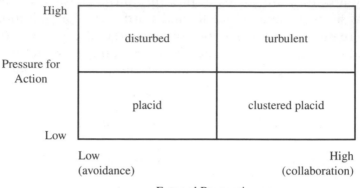

External Responsiveness

Types of Strategy

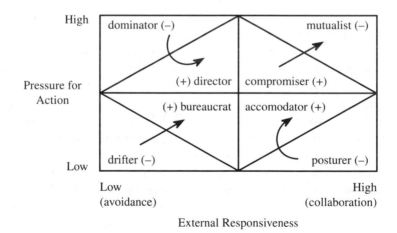

External Responsiveness

gent needs recognized by legitimate authorities have a broader repertoire of strategic responses and better prospects of using a strategy best suited to their situation.

The most successful strategy moves toward and up the diagonal indicated by the arrows in Figure 4.1. This calls for changes in the pressure for action to be matched by organizational responsiveness. Strategy located off the diagonal is less effective because responsiveness is out of phase with the pressure for action.

High Action Types of Strategy

Dominator. Dominators produce strategy that takes action to deal with rapidly emerging needs with little responsiveness to legitimate authority, as shown in the upper left quadrant of Figure 4.1. The motivation is to produce discretion in the choice of action and divorce it from accountability. For example, the IRS promulgates rules that create such a strategy. The Motion Picture Association of America (MPAA), which gives motion pictures ratings that control viewing by certain age groups, has a similar impact on film producers. Both organizations use coercive power to define needs for action with little accountability. The IRS changes and implements tax rules as it sees fit and can be challenged only through lengthy and costly litigation. The MPAA uses the threat of an "R" rating that would keep a film from being seen by the 13- to 17-year old age group, the largest market segment for most motion pictures, to force film producers to remove what the MPAA perceives as objectionable scenes. To reach their primary market, film producers must let the MPAA censure their products.

The EPA tried to create a dominator strategy and failed because the organization was forced to maintain close ties to various parties who insisted on a role in rule making. The Reagan administration and trade associations that were hired to protect the interests of violators made it difficult for the EPA to enforce its rules and legislative mandates.

Director. In a disturbed environment, attempts should be made
to move a dominator strategy to a director strategy. This change
brings an increase in the responsiveness to needs thought to
be significant, as shown in Figure 4.1. A director strategy has
a moderate to high action orientation and assumes modest accountability. For example, the Great Society programs of the
Johnson administration created thousands of nonprofit organizations with a social change agenda, which called for roles
and missions outside the normal channels of governmental accountability. Organizations with a director strategy include
mental health centers, agencies regulating the expansion of
health facilities and utilities, and area health education centers. These and related organizations have been called "paragovernments" because their authority to act seldom had clear
legal grounds and their accountability was limited to self-
appointed boards and rules in the disbursement of federal
funds.

　　　　Organizations can survive for long periods of time with
a director strategy if their environments continue to allow action without full accountability. A shift in which accountability
increases would force movement toward a mutualist strategy,
moving toward and up the diagonal in Figure 4.1. The need
for such a movement is often signaled by new mandates, such
as new legislation, which create new missions for the organization. The paragovernments of the 60s and 70s often failed
because they were unable to adopt a compromiser or mutualist
strategy when their environments became turbulent. The Regional Medical Programs, for instance, were unable to shift their
commitments away from medical schools and high-tech medical centers to the needs of people and to grapple with the hard
choices inherent in improving the quality of medical care. When
choosing between closing radiation treatment centers offering
low KV cobalt or offering educational programs to upgrade
radiotherapy practice, the latter course was typically selected,
although it would have little impact. Educational programs assume that behavior change is possible. This was unlikely because radiotherapists that were motivated by their fees disputed the danger of using low KV cobalt.

Low Action Types of Strategy

Posturer. A strategy of inaction is called a posture. Strategists following this approach read every signal to see if a call for action seems warranted and make statements about planned responses. These responses never materialize, often because the agenda is so full of low-priority issues that action is crowded out by a preoccupation with reading issues. Such strategy lacks closure and any sense of priorities, making it less effective than one that couples needs with some degree of action.

Many third sector organizations have adopted a posturer strategy. Illustrations include Common Cause, the Grey Panthers, and the NAACP. In each case, the strategy is to continually make lists of issues that are brought to the attention of others to deal with. This lack of closure can make such an organization seem inconsistent and even irresponsible. The inconsistency stems from ignoring the gap between what is intended and what can be realized. Issues that pose questions that are irresolvable or resolvable only at prohibitive cost create frustration and friction. This frustration is magnified by the organization's unwillingness to seek solutions, which creates an image of irresponsibility.

Organizations faced with the termination of federal funds often adopt a posturer strategy. The list of unresolved issues that the termination of funding would leave unattended is used to call for a restoration of funds and continuation of the program. Head Start programs and the Office of Economic Opportunity successfully used a posturer strategy to prevent program termination. The Regional Medical Programs and the Partnership for Health Acts of the 60s and 70s also used this strategy, but were unsuccessful. Success depends on having a large and vocal constituency that trumpets the list of issues. The Office of Economic Opportunity and Head Start had such a constituency, and the health programs did not. In congressional testimony, spokespersons for the partnership for health came across as arrogant physicians who advocated only self-interests and resisted any change that would influence their personal prerogatives and incomes. Cutting off funds for agencies with this kind of image is the dream of politicians and is good politics.

Accommodator. Strategy as accommodation has some of the same ingredients of a posture, but incorporates more commitment to action in the agenda of issues. This makes the accommodator strategy more effective than the posturer strategy, as shown by the movement toward the diagonal in Figure 4.1. Trade associations, like the American Hospital Association (AHA), use such a strategy. Such organizations serve a particular constituency. The AHA serves the interests of America's nonprofit voluntary hospitals. The concerns of this constituency make up the issues that the trade association must pursue. When changes are proposed, such as reimbursement plans that cut margins in nonprofit hospitals, the AHA is expected to take the lead in testifying in front of Congress and promulgating the point of view of hospitals.

During periods of low need for public relations, trade associations must have something to do. Many adopt service programs that benefit their constituencies, placing them in the low level of action initiation in Figure 4.1. The AHA, for example, provides data services to its members that compare costs and margins by service area among hospitals grouped by type, such as size, service intensity, or geographic region. Data describing individual hospitals is provided by the subscribing hospitals and combined, for a fee, into these reports. The data also allow the industry access to information that can be selectively used to defend its position on various issues. The fees for these services supplement membership charges to keep the trade association well budgeted.

Organizations with an accommodator strategy can be effective if they exhibit moderate responsiveness and their environment remains predictable, which results in a series of activities to manage known clusters. A shift toward a compromiser strategy would be needed if the environment shifts to more turbulent conditions. Organizations adopting a compromiser strategy and moving toward a mutualist strategy are more apt to survive. For example, the Hospital Research and Education

Trust (HRET), a research arm of the American Hospital Association, moved from a passive data collection agency to an aggressive grant seeker after budget support was reduced by the AHA. HRET sought out partnerships with university faculty. HRET used the faculty members' names to promote their staff team's capability when responding to grant and contract request for proposals (RFPs), and retained all of the overhead payments (compromiser strategy). In the future, HRET may be called on to deal with significant societal problems that will require true partnerships, creating a mutualist strategy.

Coupling Action and Responsiveness

The diagonal in Figure 4.1 captures the movement needed to become successful in public and third sector organizations. At the lower left corner in Figure 4.1, an organization is functioning without much of an agenda. The aim is to move this organization to an appropriate point along the diagonal. Movement up the diagonal is prescribed, gradually making the organization more proactive in recognizing needs and forming cooperative arrangements.

Drifter. Some organizations see themselves in placid environments that call for little action. Drifter strategy can be followed in an environment that makes few demands on people, which allows the equivalent of goldbricking. Many organizations founded with vague missions that stem from legislation with unclear goals, such as the "coordination" of education programs in an area health education center, develop such a strategic posture. The doldrums set in and people can become comfortable in roles that call for little effort. Make-work programs and routines are followed to create the aura of action. New leadership or fear that make-work will be discovered periodically coaxes such an agency to search for a strategy that gives the agency a sense of purpose.

Drifter strategy also represents a state that some organizations pass through during periods of recovery after intense campaigns in which considerable energy was expended. Low

periods of activity can be used to reward people who were expected to work at overload levels during budget shortfalls.
However, the "easy life" game (Bardach, 1977) can be an insid-
ious trap for the organization when it tries to return to normal
operations. The lower level of activity becomes a norm that is
used to justify a slower pace and less effort.

Bureaucrat. Organizations operating with modest action taking
for clear-cut needs employ a bureaucratic strategy. This approach is the minimal acceptable posture in a placid environment (Figure 4.1). The strategy calls for an organization to
demonstrate moderate responsiveness by using programmed
routines with standardized responses. For example, a state bureau of employment services can treat its role as making decisions about who qualifies for unemployment compensation and
processing checks for successful claimants. The task of finding
jobs for the hard-core or temporarily unemployed is avoided
because finding jobs would require a more proactive posture
in which environmental turbulence must be recognized and dealt
with. Only token efforts at employment would be mounted in
a bureaucratic strategy. Periodic contacts would be made with
employers following long-established routines, such as running
through available people without attempting to match skills with
employer needs.

Bureaucratic strategy depends on routinized programs
and standardized procedures, much the way the custodian
strategy does for firms. A defensive posture is taken to protect
these routines through maximizing budgets and hiding unused
funds for the recurring periods of decline in public funding.
The routines and procedures are treated as distinctive competencies that are defended in budget hearings and the like, in
which the need to maintain things such as computer capability
or work-force skills is stressed. The equivalent of protectionism
in a firm is sought; rules are promulgated that treat the funding of these routines and procedures as sacrosanct. This approach attempts to seal off the organization from budget cuts
that others face during retrenchments.

Compromiser. Organizations that are experiencing several distinct calls for action must become more proactive than they can be in operating a rule-bound bureaucracy. The compromiser strategy attempts to prioritize these needs and the actions each implies by playing one constituency off against another. One tactic is to meet the needs of important constituents, another is to deal with needy constituents. For example, a mental health agency can choose to treat the severely retarded, offering life-maintenance skills that are poorly reimbursed by third-party payers, or it can deal with court-assigned substance abusers that go through programs with very high recidivism rates and receive payment for all services rendered. This type of choice would pose a serious dilemma for the mental health agency. A compromise is often struck to serve clients following certain rules that balance people's needs with revenue generation to keep the agency solvent.

Compromiser strategy deals with several clusters in a turbulent environment. Within each cluster, stakeholders with significant needs can be identified, but not all clusters can be managed with available funds. The compromiser strategy allocates funds among the clusters using criteria that attempt to capture the agency's role. These criteria often become quite complex and make up a large part of what is assumed to be key strategic considerations. The compromiser strategy calls for steps to defend decisions that deal with some clusters and not others by involving oversight bodies in the decisions. Each cluster may call for special programs and services, which makes the compromiser strategy much more complex than the bureaucrat strategy. This match of clusters of needs and programmed responses, such as services, makes up the strategic content. Only strong signals to change clusters would be recognized, making strategic change long term.

Organizations that are pulled into turbulent environments often treat emergent needs as just another cluster to be managed. If sufficiently compelling, these needs must be met through the allocation of resources and development of programs. When new needs emerge at an ever-increasing rate, the clamor for action becomes strident and the understandings that set priorities among clusters are upset. At first, attempts are made to meet these demands by reallocations and use of slack resources. Another approach, the mutualist strategy, is required when new needs emerge at a rate that makes reallocation infeasible.

Mutualist. The most proactive strategy in the typology is called a mutualist strategy. This strategy is needed for turbulent environments in which needs are rapidly changing and collaboration is required to respond, as shown in Figure 4.1. Mutualist strategy responds to a diverse and ever-changing set of needs through action designed to meet these needs. Collaboration is substituted for the competitive orientation of firms. Competition has little relevance to public organizations that have mandates to meet the needs of people. Instead, cooperation to meet these needs is emphasized. For example, fire departments do not compete in markets for customers. Service areas that do not overlap are negotiated with taxing authorities to cover service obligations.

Agencies with overlapping service areas or mandates, such as home health agencies supported by United Way and city health departments, can develop a collaborative approach to strategy to avoid duplication of effort. This collaboration can be difficult to achieve, pushing strategy to a compromise position in which each agency serves its own perception of important clusters. This approach can leave some important needs unmet or underserved. The mutualist strategy calls for cooperation to promote collaboration to serve these needs by devising consortia or other kinds of umbrella organizations and cooperative arrangements that merge the interests of organizations with overlapping mandates or missions. Examples include the National Kidney Foundation and the Highway Safety Program.

The National Kidney Foundation created a consortium to manage the activities required to treat end-stage kidney disease that were under the control of various medical delivery organizations, such as tissue-typing centers and hospitals offering transplantation and dialysis services. The foundation promoted organ donation laws and data bases for kidney patients undergoing dialysis who were candidates for transplantation. As kidneys become available, the foundation ensured that the interests of patients, especially the most needy and best matched for transplants, were considered over the desires of providers for treatment revenues and large patient volumes to justify a "center designation." The Highway Safety Program also merged the interests of many disparate agencies, such as technical centers offering training for people operating emergency vehicles and hospitals providing emergency care. The consortium enacted laws to ensure that all ambulance attendants were trained and vehicles were properly designed, promulgated standards for hospitals offering emergency care that categorized them by level of care, and organized communication networks to dispatch emergency vehicles.

In both of these illustrations, a collaborative approach ensured that needs in a changing environment would be met. In each case, the environment had become turbulent because long-standing needs were suddenly recognized. For kidney disease, the opportunity to improve the survival of people with end-stage renal disease called for action. In Highway Safety the awareness that more injuries were caused by untrained ambulance drivers than the accident itself, provoked a public outcry for action. The mutualist strategy ensured that this kind of turbulence, stemming from changing attitudes about needs in these areas, would be managed with resources and programs drawn from appropriate agencies. The self-interests of these agencies were subordinated to the greater interest of people's needs that were now visible and compelling.

The mutualist strategy marshals the support of internal and external stakeholders. The initiative can begin either internally, with key people in leadership positions calling for action, or externally, as legislatures and others identify needs that should be met. The mutualist strategy calls for a dialogue in which insiders respond to outsiders or reach out to outsiders with their ideas. Once this dialogue begins, it is nurtured as collaborating parties move toward a shared vision of appropriate action. For instance, the U.S. Public Health Service recognized the outcry for better emergency services by raising funds from Congress. Organizations were created to administer the funds and to use them to forge change. A shared vision emerged in which insiders and outsiders collaborated toward resolving the emergency transportation crisis.

Mutualist strategy calls for organizational relationships that jump across traditional lines of authority, creating complex structures. Once collaboration is seen as essential, cluster groups or consortia are usually formed. These can be followed by a divestiture in which some organizations give up functions and others take them on. Privatization via contracting out services may also follow, leaving only a coordinating role for the initiating agency. The mutualist strategy calls for organizations to change their structural relationships to deal with emergent needs. The U.S. Public Health Service contracted and delegated to others to carry out essential activities that initiated and sustained needed functions for regional EMS programs.

A mutualist strategy is analogous to a prospector strategy in a firm. The mutualist responds to volatile needs that emerge with the same amount of urgency and force as rapid changes in customer preferences, which creates a volatile market for a firm. An organizational structure and a policy are fashioned to deal with urgent needs. Signals are read and interpreted, such as changing attitudes that permitted organ donation laws to be enacted in emergency medical service legislation. Developmental activities that produce strategy based on these needs are initiated by seeking novel arrangements.

Transformational Strategy

Organizations with public features can go through a number of phases in which they switch strategic postures, such as going from accommodator to compromiser or from director to compromiser. The movement to a mutualist strategy is more difficult to justify and to sustain. To initiate this movement, the demands for action must be seen as clear and compelling by key people in the authority network in which the organization operates. Outsiders are mobilized and dialogues between insiders and outsiders begin that develop a call for action. When this call becomes unequivocal and strident, the organization has the option to initiate consortia and other mechanisms that provide the means for collaboration. These collaborative arrangements must be sustained until the issue is managed. At this point, the organization may shift to a compromiser strategy. Mutualist strategies are sustainable only when the environment remains turbulent and key people in the organization's authority network recognize the turbulence. Effective organizations shift from using compromiser to mutualist strategies as this turbulence is recognized.

The mutualist strategy may periodically give way to a compromiser strategy as the organization attempts to consolidate gains or reconnect with its traditions. Organizational leaders can feel pressure to serve their traditional clients by allocating more of the organization's resources to this group. The organization may also have the actions called for by a mutualist strategy, which take it beyond its charter, questioned by an oversight body. Either development will pull the organization away from a mutualist strategy toward a compromiser strategy. Like the prospector and entrepreneurial strategies for a firm, both compromiser and mutualist strategies can be useful. However, mutualist and prospector strategies are more apt to produce breakthroughs.

Mutualist strategies are needed to create organizational transformations in which an organization makes significant changes in its services, clients, roles, obligations, and persona. These transformations occur in periods when needs are extremely volatile and demand collaborative responses. Using collaboration can bring dramatic change in which new visions of what the organization can become are born. Transformations are possible when organizations recognize that needs are volatile and choose to respond in a collaborative fashion.

Some public organizations may never have to cope with volatile needs. In such a situation, a less proactive strategy can be maintained over long periods of time. These organizations can be effective but are seldom innovative. In other situations, organizations ignore the pressure for action as needs become volatile. These organizations are neither effective nor innovative. Finally, emergent needs may be dealt with using accommodation or compromise. Organizations using these strategies are not as effective as they could be.

Ways to Create Strategy

There are several ways to create strategy that can be grouped by focus and dominant activities. Table 4.1 presents an overview of these approaches. Approaches that stress analysis have a problemlike focus. The emphasis is to evaluate by sorting key activities (such as products or services) into categories to identify the activities that need modification or elimination. A search for problems to be rectified is mounted. Conceptual approaches tend to have either an actor or an agency focus. Approaches that focus on an actor are concerned with understanding claims for action directed toward the organization by insiders or outsiders. A focus on an agency examines the capacities of the organization and sorts them out to identify attractions and repulsions, things to emphasize and avoid. Organizational capacity then becomes the focus of attention. The emphasis in actor and agency approaches is on discovery, not assessment, which is stressed in approaches with a problem focus. Each of these approaches, in each of these categories, has provided many useful ways for leaders to think strategically. This section sets out these ideas and how they are used to go about strategic management.

Analytical Approaches

Analytical approaches typically call for some form of portfolio analysis. Analysis is carried out to determine how well various product lines fit into a firm's strategy and to make resource allocation decisions. The most widely used framework was developed by the Boston Consulting Group (BCG).

Table 4.1. Comparison of Strategic Management Approaches.

Type	Focus	Approach	Procedure	Key Uses	Limitations
Analytical	Problem	Portfolio Approaches (Henderson, 1979)	Classify products or services or activities by market share and growth potential to determine value.	1. Balancing portfolio to evaluate activities against criteria. 2. Applying noneconomic criteria.	1. Analysis assumes a strategy to assess. 2. Dimensions are sector specific. 3. Rules for use (such as divestiture of wildcats) are in dispute.
		Issue Portfolios (Ring, 1988)	Classify issues by stakeholder and tractability to determine priorities.	1. Balancing issues so success is possible. 2. Building credibility to attack more difficult issues.	1. Issues must have been identified. 2. No way to do issue discovery.
Conceptual	Actor	Industry Analysis (Porter, 1980, 1985)	Analyze forces that shape industry to find entry and exit barriers and threat from rivals.	1. Assessing competitive behavior of organizations and strategy options that are given. 2. Predicting success of strategy.	1. Identifying an appropriate referent industry often ambiguous or not relevant. 2. Noneconomic factors swamp the economic. 3. Collaboration may dominate competition.

Table 4.1. Comparison of Strategic Management Approaches, Cont'd.

Type	Focus	Approach	Procedure	Key Uses	Limitations
		Stakeholder Analysis (Freeman, 1984; Mason and Mitroff, 1981)	Find priority stakeholders and what they expect. Develop ways to deal with each in strategy.	1. Alerting an organization about key claims and claimants. 2. Fitting in with most other approaches.	1. No way to prioritize stakeholders via importance and impact. 2. Stakeholders not limited to strategy formation and implementation.
		Interpretive Strategy (Pettigrew, 1977)	Capture culture and symbols to motivate stakeholders.	1. Finding social contracts and treaties. 2. Constructing legitimacy.	1. Interpretation is a difficult skill. 2. Creating useful symbols is difficult.
Conceptual	Agency	Harvard Policy Model (Andrews, 1980; Child, 1982)	Analyze SWOTs to capture management values and obligations to find strategy with best fit to the environment and the competencies of the organization.	1. Analyzing SWOTs. 2. Defining a strategic planning unit. 3. Identifying strategic planning team.	1. Means to devise strategy from SWOTs is unclear.
		Issue Management (Ansoff, 1980, 1984)	Recognize and resolve issues that must be managed for organization to meet goals.	1. Linking issues to SWOTs. 2. Using issues to identify strategic responses.	1. No way to identify or articulate issues beyond SWOTs.

Table 4.1. Comparison of Strategic Management Approaches, Cont'd.

Type	Focus	Approach	Procedure	Key Uses	Limitations
		Adaptive Strategy (Miles and Snow, 1978)	Match opportunities with distinctive competencies.	1. Choosing domain. 2. Selecting technology. 3. Managing systems.	1. Environmentally driven. 2. Implementation steps not clear.
		Planning Systems (Lorange, 1980)	Apply systems ideas of integration across organizational levels and coordination of functions.	1. Integrating and coordinating. 2. Giving stages and steps to follow.	1. Politics and implementation needs not considered.

Portfolio Approaches. Developers of the BCG matrix found that business cost follows a "one-third rule," in which unit cost falls by one-third as volume doubles (Henderson, 1979). This "experience curve," as it has come to be known, suggests that increasing market share will pay significant dividends. Profit will increase because unit cost will fall. Therefore, *gaining market share* was proposed by Henderson as a generic strategy. The BCG matrix can be used to assess businesses, product lines, and products and can be used for still other levels of analysis. Although not proposed for this purpose, it can be used to analyze services as well. First, the selected level of analysis, such as products, is identified. Then an assessment is carried out determining each product's growth and its market share, as shown in the upper half of Figure 4.2.

Four categories emerge:

1. *Stars*—The star category has products or services with high growth and high market share. They produce substantial cash and require continuing investment to maintain this position.
2. *Cash Cows*—The cash cow product or service has low growth but high market share, which produces large cash flows with little investment. Cash cows often produce profit (or margin) that is siphoned off to be used elsewhere in the organization.
3. *Dogs*—The dog category has products or services with low growth and low market share. There is little cash flow and little prospect for increasing market share.
4. *Wildcats*—High-growth and low-share products or services are risky ventures that require considerable investment to grow into either a cash cow or a star. The likelihood of this growth gives a measure of risk.

To apply these ideas, the strategist looks at the growth of a product or service relative to the market share of an industry leader. If a product or service is the market share leader, it will be located on the far left of the horizontal axis. High growth puts the product or service toward the top of the ver-

Figure 4.2. Public and Private Sector Portfolios.

Product/Service Portfolio

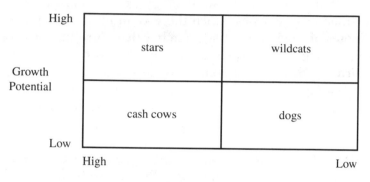

Issue Portfolio

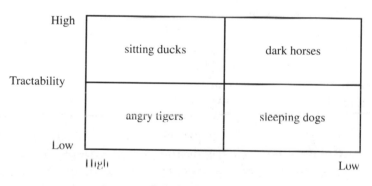

tical axis, making it a star. The usual prescription calls for taking profits from cash cows to fund growth for stars and a few select wildcats, selling off the dogs and the remaining wildcats.

This approach treats strategy as the management of a portfolio of businesses, much the way an investor acquires and disposes of stocks and bonds. Each activity (product or product line, service or service line) is managed to bring in the best return to the organization. This approach can be related to custodian and stabilizer strategies, but not the more proactive developmental and entrepreneurial strategies that require new ideas.

Portfolio Approaches in Public and Third Sector Organizations.
The ideas in the portfolio approach can also be used for issue management in a public or third sector organization (Ring, 1988). In this adaption, relative stakeholder support and tractability are substituted for market share and industry growth, respectively. Issues are then analyzed instead of products or services.

The term *tractability* indicates the prospect that an issue can be successfully attacked by the organization. Tractability depends on technical problems, target group mix, the proportion of the population included in the target group, and the extent a target group is expected to change. Issues with low tractability, such as AIDS, have poor prospects for successful treatment, a diverse mix of people in the target group, a large potential target group, and call for life-style changes that people will not accept to prevent recurrence or spread. High tractability issues, such as kidney problems, have good prospects for successful treatment, clearly defined target groups, and call for life-style changes to prevent recurrence that people will accept.

Relative stakeholder support indicates the attitude of people who will be affected by the agency's actions to serve people with needs. Dealing with end-stage kidney disease patients is apt to create public support, whereas coping with AIDs carriers is not.

Tractability and stakeholder support produce the categories shown in the lower half of Figure 4.2. The public sector manager can use these categories to classify issues facing the organizations and derive recommendations for issue management.

1. *Angry Tigers*—These issues have low tractability and considerable public support. Such an issue calls for action when no action is currently possible. Deflection of these concerns by dealing with issues in the other cells is recommended. Concerns about the hard-core unemployed, the educational achievement of minority children, and "stagflation" (high inflation with no growth) are angry tigers.

2. *Sitting Ducks*—These issues are high in tractability and high in support, making them easy to manage. Acting to deal with important tractable issues creates credibility for an agency and buys time to cope with angry tigers, much the way that the national kidney program and Highway Safety Program brought new vitality to the U.S. Public Health Service.

3. *Dark Horses*—This category of issue is tractable, but action is not apt to create public support. The ability to meet needs suggests that the agency should deal with these issues and publicize the benefits achieved. Providing life-management skills for the severely mentally handicapped would be one example.

4. *Sleeping Dogs*—These issues are neither on the public agenda nor tractable. Such an issue is best left off the issue agenda of an agency, unless it can be put into a bag of more manageable problems. AIDS treatment is an example.

Conceptual Approaches with an Actor Focus

Approaches with an actor focus stress gaining an understanding of the pressures put on the organization. These pressures stem from stakeholders and competitors. Actor-based approaches to strategic management tend to emphasize one or the other.

Industry Analytic Approach. Porter (1980, 1985) developed a competitive analysis model using industry norms. The forces that shape an industry are used to predict the success of strategy. Porter and others (Harrigan, 1981) identify six key forces that shape an industry. Success is influenced by the relative power of customers and suppliers, the threat of competitors and new entrants, the competitiveness or rivalry among key players in the market, and exit barriers that keep organizations from leaving a market. Porter claims that strong forces lower financial returns for both the industry as a whole and the organizations that make up the industry.

Stakeholder Approach. Approaches that focus on stakeholders (such as those of Freeman, 1984; Mason and Mitroff, 1981) treat strategy as a way to build the means to serve an organization's interests. Stakeholders are defined as individuals in a position to influence the organization or place demands on it. Customers, employees, suppliers, shareholders, financial institutions, and partners or partner organizations are often stakeholders in private organizations. Clients or service users, professional staff, oversight bodies, legislatures, political appointees, elected officials, reimbursement agencies, and contractors (for example, the medical staff of a hospital) are frequently stakeholders in public and third sector organizations. Organizations in both sectors must deal with regulators, the courts, environmentalists, trade associations, local zoning boards, and land-use agencies. According to Freeman (1984) political and social actors are as important as economic actors (such as banks). Strategy is sought that can satisfy the interests of key stakeholders.

 Stakeholder approaches attempt to integrate social, political, and economic considerations. The strategic manager is challenged to figure out what aims are relevant to each stakeholder or differentiate responses to provide a way of satisfying key stakeholders (Bryson, Freeman, and Roering, 1986).

Interpretative Approach. The interpretative approach attempts to fold in considerations such as culture and management of symbols and thus provides more emphasis on implementation.

The notion of a "social contract" (Keeley, 1980) is used. An organization is treated as a collective of individuals who have made implicit treaties that regulate the organization's affairs. Change depends upon marshaling the support of these key individuals. Thus, strategy is the product of environmental opportunities and the dilemmas faced by key constituents. These dilemmas go beyond "who gets what" to commitments that recognize tradition. Symbols become a central part of a strategy, and the construction of legitimacy becomes a crucial goal (Pettigrew, 1977). Interpretative approaches focus on desired relationships, such as promoting consensus and treating customers as valued informants, not complaining nuisances. Symbolic acts and communications are used to deal with the environment. Strategic managers convey meanings to motivate stakeholders, such as using poetry to promote tourism in the Grand Canyon (Chaffee, 1985). Although useful, such an approach is clearly a skill that may be as demanding as leadership, if not more so.

Conceptual Approaches with an Agency Focus

An agency focus occurs when the organization's capacities and its place in the environment become key considerations. Approaches to strategic management with an agency focus make assessments of the organization's distinctive competencies and look for ways to apply them.

Policy Model Approach. The policy model has its roots in courses taught as far back as the 1920s in the Harvard Business School. The notion of finding actions that fit the environment is stressed (Andrews, 1980; Child, 1972). Strategy is defined by the pattern of goals and activities that make up the organization and define what it is about. Strategy is determined by analyzing internal strengths and weaknesses and external threats and opportunities posed by the environment. The organization's management searches for SWOTs (short for strengths, weaknesses, opportunities, and threats) that characterize its position and seeks an appropriate response.

This approach is often applied to a "strategic business unit," or SBU. An SBU is any activity that has competitors and discretion in its activities, such as an agency of city or state government. The SBU is constrained in some ways but has sufficient latitude to act and enough narrowness of purpose to focus actions. Any division or department of an organization with latitude to act can be viewed as an SBU. For example, a university department can act as an SBU but so can colleges and even larger organizational entities in the university.

Issue Management Approach. The issue management approach makes issues the focal point for analysis (Ansoff, 1980, 1984). Issues are treated as emergent developments that are apt to influence the organization's ability to meet its goals. Issues can arise internally or externally and may have beneficial or negative effects. Issues are used to fill the gap between a SWOT analysis and strategic development. This approach allows for the continuous revision of SWOTs, suggesting a process that periodically updates strategy with the insights drawn from recent developments. Annual strategy sessions are planned to resolve a few pivotal issues, with SWOT review and revision done every five years. Using issues as the focus of inquiry allowed strategic managers to become more flexible and responsive to emergent developments.

Adaptive Approach. The adaptive approach attempts to find a match between opportunities in the environment and the organization's capacity to exploit these opportunities (for example, Ansoff, 1984; Hofer and Schendel, 1979; Steiner, 1979). Strategic development takes shape as recurring cycles of activity in which domain (business or market) choices, selection of technology, and implementation take place. Adaptive strategy also includes subtle nuances, such as style, and involves several layers of the organization. Whether action is proactive or reactive, the environment is the focus of attention as the organization strives to read signals that contain salient information about opportunity. The organization is called on to change with the environment, but may not be able to deal with all significant trends and events that are recognized.

Planning Systems Approach. Strategic planning has also been treated in systems terms (for example, Chandler, 1962; Andrews, 1980; Drucker, 1974; Lorange, 1980; Nadler, 1970, 1981). The key notion is to link mission, strategy, resources, and direction so their interrelationship can be identified and carefully managed. These approaches tend to be formalistic and highly prescriptive, which give them the appearance of rigidity (Bryson, 1988).

Planning systems often use a variety of checklists that structure and guide activity. Chaffee (1985) calls these approaches linear strategy to denote the tendency to require sequential action and a step-by-step procedure. The aim is to produce new markets or products through formal planning that recognizes competitors and marshals resources to attain preset goals. Strategy is developed to anticipate environmental shifts and events. Emergent strategy tends to be ignored. These approaches assume that organizations are responsive to directions from strategic managers, that desirable futures can be imagined, and that environments (such as the purchasers of products) can be influenced by clever leaders. The weakness of planning systems stems from the attention to procedure and detail that can distract the strategic manager from dealing with political and implementation questions.

An Integrated Approach

Each of the approaches summarized in Table 4.1 has useful applications and limitations when applied to public and third sector organizations. Industry analysis shows how forces shape what organizations can and cannot do. In public and third sector organizations, important forces are frequently concentrated in clients or users and agency rivalries. Suppliers are less important. Exit and entry are rarely concerns for most third sector and public organizations. Collaboration, not competition, is the dominant theme in providing services.

However, industry (agency) analysis may shed light on collaborative potential and barriers, which can help to predict programs destined to face funding difficulty. At another level, these organizations compete vigorously for public funding and reimbursement during periods of fiscal restraint. If a strategic manager can identify competing parties, he or she can benefit from understanding the forces at work influencing the organization's behavior. Knowing these forces poses questions and suggests possibilities.

Applied to city government or state departments, the industry model has much less value. In other cases, industry types can be misleading. For instance, hospitals fall into three categories: the voluntary nonprofit segment, the for-profit segment, and the governmental segment. The forces in each segment are more different than alike. However, examining homogeneous segments may be useful using the Porter (1980) model.

The stakeholder, interpretative, and adaptive approaches offer several useful ideas. The notion of performing well in the eyes of key stakeholders and developing ideas are useful ways to think about strategic needs and implementation. These approaches can be improved by offering ways to prioritize and classify stakeholders in terms of their importance and impact through linking the notion of stakeholder interests to strategy development and implementation and by dealing with the pressures to preserve a culture.

The policy model provides insightful ways to capture stakeholder values. These values are crucial in public and third sector organizations because strategy can seldom be evaluated solely on economic grounds. The notion of finding a strategy that fits with the environment, with environments defined in collaborative not competitive terms, seems essential. The means to devise a strategy, however, is not provided in the policy model.

Issue management calls for the recognition and resolution of issues as an intermediate step between a SWOT analysis and action. The relationship of issue to strategy is similar to the relationship of problem to solution. The notions of periodically updating an issue agenda and how issues are embedded in a SWOT analysis offer useful clues in devising strategy. However, ways to identify and articulate issues are essential. Some clarification is provided by the issue portfolio in which issues can be classified by risk and opportunity. More clarification seems necessary. Planning systems provide stages and steps to follow that help to routinize practice by guiding the strategic manager who is applying these ideas for the first time.

Analytical approaches have much less value for public and third sector organizations than conceptual approaches do. The assumption of economic returns is seldom the only or even the most important aim of these organizations. Henderson's (1979) aim of increasing market share in the portfolio approach has little meaning for organizations such as a city police department.

Together, the approaches in Table 4.1 offer many useful ideas. In Part Three we have selected the best features of strategic management approaches, such as those in Table 4.1, added some of our own, and tailored the approaches for application in public and third sector organizations.

The Prospects for Strategic Change

We often find public and third sector organizations in situations of limited capacity and low responsiveness. Their capacity to initiate action is often eroded through years of budget cutting, limitations on prerogatives from court rulings, rule making by legislatures, assignment of duties to other agencies during reorganization, and chronic staff turnover. When capacity reaches a low ebb, the organization can become complacent about its obligations. All but the most dependent clients have gone elsewhere for help.

External control in public and third sector organizations is low when the organization is buffeted by events it is unable to manage. Such an organization experiences demands at a rate that exceeds its ability to respond or even its ability to fully understand the nature of the proposed action or request. The organization may react by adopting the equivalent of the psychological concept of "learned helplessness," in which elaborate rationales for avoiding action supplant building capacities. Strategic management attempts to move such an organization toward increased capacity and increased control over its environment. In this section, we discuss how organizations get in undesirable situations and when it is possible to move such organizations along the diagonal, running from lower left to upper right as indicated by the arrow in Figure 4.3, toward a more proactive posture by applying strategic management.

Organizational Types That Resist Change

In Figure 4.3, organizations are classified by competence and the extent to which perogratives are dictated by outsiders (for example, legislatures). The organizations located in cells off the diagonal in Figure 4.3 represent stable types with little motivation for change. These types exist when internal competence and external control have become seriously imbalanced. Because either competence or control dominates, attention is focused on the maintenance of the competence or control and not on using competence to exercise useful control.

Professional Organization. Organizations or agencies with high internal capacity and little external control over their actions are called *professional.* Activity is directed internally by professional values. Control is low when the political, legal, and economic strictures that ordinarily direct and channel the energies and ensure accountability are not in place. Typically, such an

Figure 4.3. Types of Organizations.

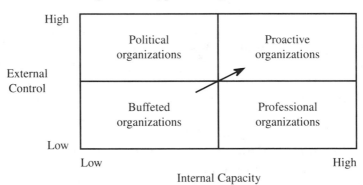

agency has protected its budget or resource base and has considerable prerogative to act in a prescribed arena. The Federal Bureau of Investigation (FBI) under J. Edgar Hoover, the Department of Defense under the Reagan administration, and the IRS are examples. Organizations that rely on highly skilled and self-regulated staff members to provide key services can also become professional-type organizations. Examples include most hospitals, medical centers and clinics, university facilities, social work agencies, public defender offices, and other organizations dominated by a professional elite who control the terms of services that are provided. Strategic management with professionals who seek to maintain this kind of control is not apt to be successful.

The professional organization can ignore client or stakeholder preferences, the political agenda of reformers, and public support and may even be insulated from budget cutting. In some instances, the professional organization can even turn aside legal mandates and judicial orders. Such organizations have little motivation to change and often adopt the drifter strategy shown in Figure 4.1.

Strategy in a professional organization rests on maintaining its internal capacity. If internal capacity erodes, a drifter strategy becomes untenable. For example, the FBI's reputation after Hoover's death went into eclipse, forcing the FBI to become more concerned about public relations and to reexamine its role. A decline in competence (real or perceived) is a necessary precurser for change to occur in professional organizations. Strategic management is then focused on maintaining the image of competence as new practices are slowly being forged and adopted. The bureaucratic strategy (Figure 4.1) often emerges to signal that a change in strategic posture has occurred. As real or perceived competence declines, such an organization requires new positioning. A mixed strategy of defending past practices coupled with small adaptations is carried out. For example, the IRS, stung by reports that they confiscated the bank accounts of children and gave inaccurate tax advice, mounted strategy to do damage control and to reform a few of its procedures.

Strategic management with a professional organization is often difficult unless forces calling for more control over the organization's actions are clear and compelling or if the organization's capacity is thought to be declining. The organization is moved toward the diagonal in Figure 4.3 as perceived competence falls or as external control increases, making strategic change seem both possible and desirable.

Political Organization. Organizations or agencies with high control over their actions that lack internal capacity are termed *political.* Such an organization exploits this dependency by carving out a domain in which it has an exclusive right to act. Legislation can be written to give exclusive rights or responsibilities. For example, the Iowa legislature gave the University of Iowa Medical School exclusive rights to provide all tertiary care in the state. In a political organization, old-boy networks are carefully maintained to deflect criticism and routine accountability and to harness the forces that would normally be used to monitor actions. Control of turf in this way by organizations or agencies creates little incentive to improve capacity and makes the organizations quite political.

Organizations that take a political orientation and ignore building capacity end up in the upper left corner of Figure 4.3. The strategy in such an organization is to maintain the old-boy network and other arrangements that protect turf. Real change is not apt to occur unless these arrangements erode. Erosion of turf or prerogatives can occur when organizational patrons lose elections or leave office or when an old-boy network ceases to function. Periodically, the political organization is tossed into the mainstream by these events. The political agenda of newcomers or a shift in power among stakeholders signals the need for action. The clear and compelling call for better services and the like can no longer be ignored. The organization must give up control and increase its internal capacity, shifting it toward the diagonal in Figure 4.3.

A state department of public welfare experienced such a shift, moving from a protected position to one of increased expectation after a new governor took office. The status quo was no longer acceptable and a posture of incremental change was adopted (Wechsler and Backoff, 1988). The welfare department had to abandon its dominator strategy, in which clients were expected to respond as directed, and move toward a posture that emphasized helping clients, which provided the impetus for strategic change.

Increased awareness of low internal capacity often accompanies shifts in environmental control. Exposing this low capacity invariably forces rapid action to improve matters, increasing the need for and desirability of strategic management. Changes in leadership and increased consensus to adopt a planned change perspective often results.

Organizational Types Amenable to Change

Organizations on the diagonal fall into less stable states in which change is more acceptable. This occurs when internal capacity and external control are balanced. The match of capacity and control calls into question whether the organization's directions are going to produce hoped-for outcomes. This questioning can arise externally through the preferences of stakeholders, shifts in political agendas, erosion of public support, budget shortfalls or windfalls, and legal rulings. It can also arise internally as the result of shifts in consensus or changes in leadership. Internal and external pressures to change make strategic management seem pragmatic and lower barriers erected by political or professional strategic behavior.

Buffeted Organization. Organizations and agencies low in internal capacity and low in control over their affairs are called *buffeted*. Such an organization or agency is constantly being pulled about by fickle public support, changing legal mandates, shifting political agendas, and shifting preferences of clients or key benefactors. As mandates shift, budget support may shrink and constraints on the use of resources may be imposed. As a result, priorities provide moving targets that can lead to frustrated staff and frequent turnover of key personnel. Turnover forces large investments in training that further bleed away resources.

Consider the EPA. This agency has been faced with mandates that continually shift. Periodically, a preference for activism and use of the courts shifts to a more passive posture of dealing with environmental threats by negotiating with polluters. And then the mandate shifts back. Policies can literally change from one day to the next, as noted in the case of the Exxon oil spill of 1990. As the EPA shifts from one posture to another, charges of irresponsible activism are made by one faction and dereliction of duty by another, enticing the EPA to engage in an action one day and abandon it the next. Regulations are promulgated and then rescinded with no apparent logic or pattern.

Strategy in a buffeted organization adapts to changes by posturing, which shows that each new issue has been recognized. To accommodate shifts in competence, the organization is encouraged to move toward the mutualist strategy in Figure 4.1, assuming that a measure of environmental control is possible.

Strategic management can help the buffeted organization come to grips with the forces at work in its environment. Capacity to act is built by finding ways to increase control over the environment. This control can lead to happier and more challenged staff and reduce turnover. As capacity is built and environmental control established, the organization develops an increased interest in strategic change.

Proactive Organization. High internal capacity with external control and the obligations this control brings lead to an ideal type: what is called the *proactive* organization. Such an organization adopts either a compromiser or a mutualist strategy in which parties to strategic action develop a shared understanding of needs and potentials to act.

Consider a state department of natural resources (DNR). In one of our cases, the DNR moved toward a proactive organization with high environmental responsiveness by strategic management. Key stakeholders that expressed criticism were folded into task forces to deal with important issues such as wildlife protection, natural areas, hunting and fishing rights, waterways, and recreation. Programs were identified and funds sought to operate them through licensing the use of wild areas, through park programs, and through fishing and hunting licenses. The fees charged in these programs were turned back to fund program development, which produced more fee-generating activities until two-thirds of the DNR's funding was outside the state's budget process. By responding to stakeholders in this way, the DNR became a self-sustaining proactive organization pursuing a mutualist strategy that is highly responsive to stakeholders and high in action.

Key Points

1. The need for action and responsiveness to these needs identify placid, clustered placid, disturbed, and turbulent environments for public and third sector organizations.
    a. In placid environments, a custodial approach can be used to realize sagas that reaffirm values and protect important competencies, using a bureaucratic strategy.
    b. Environments that have placid clusters call for stabilization, in which parlays can be useful to allocate the resources among the clusters through an accommodator strategy.
    c. Disturbed environments require a developmental approach in which new ways to meet needs are tried as new ventures, using a director strategy.
    d. Turbulent environments call for an entrepreneurial spirit in which quests are mounted to deal with emergent needs and new circumstances, following a mutualist strategy.
    e. The preferred strategic orientation is to match environmental responsiveness with an appropriate level of action, striving to produce a mutualist strategy.
2. The mutualist strategy recognizes the need for novel ar-

rangements to meet emergent needs. The tactics called for include:

a.   key people who set the tone by subordinating personal and organizational interests
b.   issue-centered focus of effort
c.   a consortium that draws key stakeholders into a body seeking to address emergent needs
d.   using the consortium to create a vision and/or shape a vision to meet needs
e.   seeking win-win arrangements for all affected parties
f.   promoting trust so that stakeholders will cooperate toward meeting needs
g.   shepherding the consortium members away from competition toward cooperation

3.   Stakeholder support and tractability of issues identify the portfolio of issues facing public and third sector organizations. Sitting Ducks are issues that are resolvable and have stakeholder support. Angry Tigers have stakeholder support but pose issues that are difficult to successfully resolve. Dark Horses can be resolved but stakeholder support is lacking. Sleeping Dogs are issues that lack both stakeholder support and tractability. The balance of issue types in the organization's issue portfolio gives a picture of environmental conditions that may or may not be recognized in the selection of strategy.

4.   An organization with an imbalance between external control over its actions and internal capacity seldom engages in strategic change. A balance in control and responsiveness will make strategic management seem both desirable and pragmatic.

Chapter Five

■   ■

Understanding
Strategic
Issues

■   ■

This chapter discusses the role and importance of strategic issues and provides a way to form and articulate an issue agenda.
An *issue* is defined as a trend or event, arising inside or outside
an organization, that can have an important influence on the
organization's ability to reach its desired future (Ansoff, 1984;
Nutt and Backoff, 1987). In strategic management, issues are
used to direct the search for strategic responses. Issues that fail
to capture significant trends and events can misdirect this search.

  In practice, strategic managers often add issues to their
issue agenda quickly, with little reflection. Issue agendas that
take shape in this way can miss weaker signals that identify
significant opportunities or threats. Signals that are recognized
can be more urgent than important or can be symptomatic of
deeper concerns. The apparent urgency directs attention away
from the more important but hidden issues that lie at the heart

of making significant change (Kolb, 1983). For example, the clamor for service from a vocal group of users can keep organizations from examining the viability of service arrangements such as service intensity and impact on users. Finding crucial issues in the bewildering blizzard of signals that often confronts the strategic manager is a difficult task.

Most strategic managers are not fully conscious of issues that pose barriers to achieving a desired future. They need a way to uncover issues that tend to be overlooked. Also, strategic managers need to reveal what is "at issue" in an issue. To do so, a deeper understanding of the relationships at work is needed. We believe that these relationships give rise to tensions in which opposing forces push or pull the organization in several ways at the same time. Strategic managers who deal with one of the poles in this tension while ignoring the other are apt to miss opportunities and fail to deal with threats.

A tension format is used to describe issues. Issues are formed by noting that one pole in a tension that calls forth its antithesis. We use a competing values format to reveal the dialectical elements that shape issues as tensions (Quinn, 1988; Nutt and Backoff, 1992). The trigger for the issue, called a *development,* is classified using the framework and then paired with other generic developments to produce tensions. These tensions and the tensions not involving the triggering development are used to uncover a set of issues for the strategic manager to ponder. What emerges becomes the issue agenda.

This chapter describes the role of issues in strategic management, how issues are often recognized in practice, the potential for bias in these practices, the nature of issues, and ways to recognize and articulate issues as tensions to form an issue agenda.

Role of Issues in Strategic Management

Issues in strategic management have a role analogous to problems in problem solving. Issues set out an arena in which a search for a strategic response is conducted that tends to preclude other arenas and associated responses. Beginning with Dewey (1910, 1938), many researchers have recognized the relationship between statements of intention and subsequent action (for example, Drucker, 1945; Maier, 1970; Posner, 1973; Mintzberg, Raisingham, and Theoret, 1976; Nutt, 1984b). Statements of intention emerge from the recognition and diagnostic acts of strategic managers, which, for good or ill, channel the search for ways to respond. Lyles (1981) reviewed case histories and found that people repeatedly reverted to the original perceptions of how a situation was construed during strategy formation. Initial perceptions and understandings have an enduring quality.

In practice, issue agendas can form rapidly, often without careful study or reflection (Dutton and Jackson, 1987). When strategic managers deal with misleading issues or issues that lack salience there is considerable risk that ill-advised strategies will result.

Tactics for Reading Issues

Several strategic management approaches call for issues to guide the search for strategy (for example, the approaches of Dutton and Jackson, 1987; Backoff and Nutt, 1988; Ring, 1988; King, 1982; Ansoff, 1980). Less attention has been directed toward ways to articulate an issue and determine what makes an issue worthy of attention. Freeman's (1984) "stakeholder approach," for example, examines how actors are apt to react to strategies but not how issues were identified to form the strategy to which a stakeholder responds. Mason and Mitroff (1981) start with competing policies and prioritize assumptions about them but do not search for the issues that provoked the policies. Cobb and Elder (1972) seek out important players and determine their views to form issue agendas.

In these approaches, issues are either implicit or emerge from an impressionistic prioritization scheme. Few strategic management approaches offer ways to uncover and articulate an issue or ways to test issues for comprehensiveness and substantive content. This oversight seems quite important because issues that fail to deal with core concerns will direct strategic responses away from important threats and key opportunities. The tools for the discovery and articulation of strategic issues need considerable sharpening if these problems are to be avoided.

Misleading Issues

Without procedures that help to uncover and frame issues, strategic managers must rely on their powers of judgment and intuition to identify and describe issues that merit attention (Mintzberg and Waters, 1982). Dutton and Jackson (1987) point out the limitations of intuition when it is applied by top managers to make judgments about issues. There is a tendency to use very limited information in determining the saliency of issues (Nisbett and Ross, 1980). Initial positions become even more extreme if an issue is viewed as a threat (Tversky and Kahneman, 1974). Perceived threats were found to provoke more certain and larger responses than perceived opportunities (Jackson and Dutton, 1988). New information is then selectively chosen or distorted to fit this view, magnifying the bias and making it harder to back away from initial commitments. Positions harden and revision becomes difficult (Hogarth, 1980). Strategic managers who follow this pattern apply incomplete information to select issues, search for confirmative cues, and resist modifying the resulting issue agenda.

Cobb and Elder (1972) offer additional insights. Concrete issues are favored as are issues thought to be both important and enduring. This view is supported by the vividness and representativeness biases identified by Tversky and Kahneman (1974). Bias arises because vivid information (a person's plight) is more apt to be acted on than pallid information (statistics) and because one's experiences, no matter how provincial, are often seen as representative. The claims of stakeholders become salient when supported by information that is more vivid than important (Downs, 1972). Issues often gain good currency from the clamor for action instead of from an appreciation for the causes of the clamor. As the clamor for attention grows louder, strategists feel pressure to take decisive action to show that they are in control. Superficial concerns in the novel, tangled, and open-ended considerations that make up issues (Ackoff, 1981) are responded to in predictable ways that stress tradition and ignore innovation (Smart and Vertinsky, 1977; Nutt, 1984b).

Beliefs and political interests can produce misleading cues that may further bias the recognition of issues. Axelrod (1976) demonstrates how beliefs about causality produce a lens through which the world is viewed. This lens can be wide angle or telephoto and produces a window with distinct fields of view that can illuminate issues, fog them, or miss them entirely. Political concerns can produce a different kind of bias (Narayanan and Fahey, 1982). Issues can awaken parochial interests in stakeholders. These stakeholders may distort, shape, or interpret signals to pose an issue that caters to their self-interests. Conflict among protagonists pushing self-indulgent interpretations can force the strategic manager to choose among the equally undesirable implied issues.

The content of an issue often focuses on something tangible, like services, and ignores social forces (Arcelus and Schaefer, 1982). Social forces, such as workplace safety and minority employment, have life cycles much like service programs (Ackerman and Bauer, 1976). Social forces often go undetected, in part because the scanning tools used by strategic managers are not equipped to recognize that social demands are in tension with operating efficiency and other values held by the organization.

Language and labels used to describe an issue can also have biasing effects (Staw, Sandelands, and Dutton, 1981; Dutton, Fahey, and Narayanan, 1983). Pfeffner (1981) shows how labeling can rally support or opposition by the manipulation of linguistic elements, such as calling a new profits tax *excess* or *windfall*. Even simple changes in semantics used to express these perceptions and understandings have an influence on what is sought as a response (Volkema, 1986). Furthermore, the direction of the strategic manager's attention influences the type of issue that is recognized. Issues with an internal focus are apt to provoke strategic responses such as tinkering with the organization's structure. An external focus, in contrast, is more apt to produce liaison and building support networks as strategy.

Treating issues as problems produces another kind of labeling bias. A focus on problems creates convergent thinking around the parameters of the problem (King and Cleland, 1978). The problem specifies dysfunctions, such as rising costs, and implies the need to take action to deal with the dysfunctions. Identifying cost problems requires a cost response, thus illustrating one form of convergent thinking. Problems also lead to finding guilty parties and norms to judge departures from expectations, such as determining who is responsible for a cost increase and what level of cost can be justified. Issues emerge from many forces for which blame is obscure and precise measurement elusive and unnecessary. Viewing issues as problems is apt to provoke blaming, which creates unproductive actions to avoid being tarnished instead of productive actions to find remedies.

Dilemmas in Recognizing Issues

One of the more curious metaphors in strategic management involves the frog that, depending on who tells the story, underreacts or overreacts to pressures to act. A frog that fails to act will get boiled when sitting in a pan of water that is heated very slowly. The frog seems to have the option of jumping but does not act because change is gradual, and the frog ends up cooked. Managers who refuse to see things "heating up" can also fail to act until it is too late (Tichy, 1983). Janis (1989) calls this behavior "defensive avoidance."

Frogs are also used to describe managers who constantly overreact to signals that capture their attention. Frogs have their brain coupled to their eyes to trigger rapid flight at the slightest threat. Unlike frogs, managers can think before they act but may do so less often than is desirable. A "hypervigilant" manager superficially scans for the most obvious responses and picks one that lets him or her react to escape an immediate danger (Janis, 1989).

Strategic managers, like frogs, run both kinds of risk, depending on how they respond to emerging concerns that face the organization. The top management of an organization is continually barraged by both unconfirmed reports and the realities of budget cuts, reduction of prerogatives or responsibilities, changes in those eligible for services, service intensity increases or decreases, price controls, workplace safety claims, unionization votes, strikes, erosion of image, shifts in the views of oversight bodies, judicial renderings, technological advances, pollution and environmental awareness, minority hiring, demand for equal opportunity, lawsuits, user-need shifts, changes in those eligible for service, leadership changes, and claims of declining workforce competence. These all create a background of tangled concerns.

When trends persist or events occur that seem salient, one concern emerges to capture the attention of the manager, creating a development. Trends take shape as changes in important indicators, such as the erosion of budget support. Some trends become apparent to the strategic manager only after long periods of scanning. Events occur periodically that suggest threats or opportunities to the strategic manager. One example is legislative action that changes the eligibility requirements for services or creates new program initiatives. Trends and events draw attention to developments that appear to have a significant influence on the organization's prospect of reaching a desired future (Ansoff, 1980; Dutton, Fahey, and Narayanan, 1983; Daft and Weick, 1984; Nutt and Backoff, 1987).

Developments are embedded in the inner and outer environments in which an organization must function. Signals that call attention to a development can be strong or weak, and the development may or may not have sufficient importance to become an issue. Developments such as grievances over work schedules may be symptomatic of deeper concerns caused by resentment over the organization's unresponsiveness to employees' aspirations or feelings about working conditions. The clamor to deal with work schedules can distract the strategic manager from dealing with aspirations or working conditions.

Organizations face environments that are increasingly turbulent. Ansoff (1984) attributes this turbulence to internal and external developments that are becoming more numerous and more frequent, harder to decipher, and more novel. When developments are unfamiliar, appear to change as they are being monitored, and have murky implications, they are less amenable to "lessons" drawn from historical ways of doing business. Strategies for regeneration and change are needed if an organization facing such an environment is to maintain its viability.

Consider a public organization whose budget has been eroded by inflation, that clashes over turf with other organizations, and that serves a clientele that is changing faster than new user categories are being recognized. This organization is facing a turbulent environment in which the recognition of trends and events that signal budget erosion, the emergence of conflict, and shifting clientele is essential. The failure to identify and articulate developments is a prime cause of organizational decline (Ansoff, 1984). Decline is averted or reversed by strategic action that correctly interprets important signals.

The implications of a given development in such a milieu are seldom clear and often difficult to determine. To impose order and infuse a development with meaning, labels such as threat or opportunity are imposed (Dutton and Jackson, 1987). The label classifies the development and suggests how to respond. If a declining number of customers for a utility that generates electric power is viewed as a threat, promotional strategies designed to increase the use of electric power would be a likely response. It can be just as logical to see declining market share as an opportunity that suggests the need to explore new markets, which calls for a totally different response (Nutt, 1989a). Also, developments from inside or outside of the organization can be interpreted as either a strength or as a weakness (Ansoff, 1980; Nutt and Backoff, 1987). A development may be viewed as fortuitous, such as using a strength to capitalize on an opportunity, or troublesome, such as blunting threats that could lead to an internal weakness. Developments that get defined by loaded words, such as *weakness* or *threat*, can bias the selection of a strategic response.

Strategic managers often find uncertainty intolerable and take decisive action to explain away ambiguity in developments by labeling them as issues (Mintzberg, Raisingham, and Theoret, 1976; Nutt, 1984b). Responding in this way can be disastrous. Opportunities for significant improvements can be missed, and the organization's capacity can be diminished. Threats that go undetected can result in an erosion of organizational performance, leading to decline or failure.

The range of issues that organizations should consider before acting by selecting a strategic response needs to be broadened. This broadening seems essential for two reasons. First, some types of issues can be overlooked by organizations with particular values (Quinn, 1988). A way to comprehensively explore a variety of concerns is needed if crucial issues are to be recognized. Second, issues require a means of expression that captures what is "at issue" in an issue. We use the notion of tension to highlight the conflict inherent in most issues and provide a means to describe and articulate issues. The rationale for treating issues as tensions is discussed in the next section of this chapter. Following this discussion, we turn our attention to a framework that identifies a set of generic issues, which are framed as tensions that help to uncover, test, and then articulate issues to form an issue agenda.

Issues as Tensions

We define an issue as a tension between two developments that represent polar opposites or contradictions within the organization or between the organization and its environment. For instance, a hospital may be experiencing sharp reductions in revenue due to low occupancy, which suggests the need to cut back its workforce. Cutting back on the workforce is in tension with a union contract that controls the rate of layoffs. Many such tensions are at work in most organizations, creating a field of tensions. The resolution of forces in the tension field creates a direction which may lead to undesirable outcomes. Recognizing the issue tensions at work on the organization prompts the organization to search for responses that deflect an undesirable direction toward the organization's ideals. (We describe the

concepts of directions and ideals and their role in strategic
management in Chapter Seven.)

Why Tensions Must Be Faced

Framing issues as tensions attempts to capture the tangled web
of political and market forces that confront an organization
and tug it in many different ways at the same time. Strategic
managers who deal with one of these forces and neglect the
others are less apt to be successful (Cameron, 1986). For example, public organizations must confront the need to control
spending and at the same time expand to meet their service
commitments to disadvantaged groups as stipulated by judicial
renderings and legislative edicts. Responding either by curtailing spending or expanding services without dealing with the
other issue can create a potentially dangerous situation.

In a mental health center, dealing with court-specified
clients creates conflicts with funding agents who call for budget
reductions. If these issues are not managed as tensions, the
mental health agency can be whipsawed by powerful people in
its authority network. Also, tensions can be produced by advocacy on both sides of an issue raised by media, professional
interest groups, and branches of government. A utility, for example, can be pulled in various ways as it considers how to deal
with a forecasted power capacity shortfall. Environmental groups
are apt to block the damming of wild rivers that could provide
cheap power. Regulatory agencies may refuse to allow the
opening of a nuclear power plant. State legislatures may call
for the use of local soft coal when federal pollution control
strictures make the use of soft coal prohibitively expensive. In
contrast, tensions in firms stem from the actions of competitors
and the limits on rapidly entering or exiting markets that competitors have successfully exploited (Porter, 1985).

Rationale for Treating Issues as Tensions

The rationale for treating issues as tensions stems from several
sources. The notion of a tension is related to the notion of

paradox (Van de Ven and Poole, 1987). The contradiction between two defensible interpretations of something creates a paradox. The arguments that can be posed for each interpretation are cogent, but when put together they become contradictory. The opposing interpretations are mutually exclusive, but together offer insights that are missing when viewed separately (Cameron, 1986). A paradox does not imply a choice to be made or the need to reconcile the opposing interpretations. The tension posed by the paradox identifies the interpretations as opposing forces that exist simultaneously in an organization. Viewing issues as tensions produced by paradoxes suggests the contradictory forces impinging on an organization. Seen in this way, an issue can be expressed in terms of opposing forces that are pulling or pushing an organization toward or away from its ideals (Nutt and Backoff, 1987).

Treating issues as tensions is consistent with several schools of thought pertinent to strategy formation. For example, Jantsch (1975) contends that strategic management should balance opposing forces, such as budget cuts and the treatment of the disadvantaged needing care in a mental health center. Tensions are similar to the dialectical ideas used by Mitroff and Emshoff (1979) and Mason and Mitroff (1981) to frame needs in policy making as opposites. The opposing ideas produce strong claims and counterclaims that create tensions for which a response is devised. Cobb and Elder (1972) identify issues as conflicts between interest groups. Each approach implies that issues should be seen as opposing forces that capture the dilemmas in contradictory needs. Both Mason (1969) and Sussman and Herden (1985) found that exploring these opposing forces led to superior results in policy making. Strategic managers that deal with one of the two opposing forces and ignore the other create potentially dangerous situations in which the barriers to action or opportunities posed by the unrecognized force may be overlooked.

Organizations that classify developments with little thought and label them in predictable ways, using knee-jerk orientations such as productivity, are not apt to find an innovative strategy. Opening up issue identification to new possibilities follows widely accepted maxims derived from studies of problem solving, expert practitioners, and master managers. The problem-solving literature implies that strategy formation should be issue centered (for example, Maier, 1970). Delaying action until the nature of needs and opportunities becomes clear is an essential step in successful action taking (Mason and Mitroff, 1981; Nutt, 1984b). Studies of expert practitioners find that the best results occur when both means and ends are kept fluid (Schon, 1983). Master managers have an appreciation of competing values and examine issues from the perspective of each of the values before acting (Quinn, 1988). Treating issues as tensions keeps strategic managers "issue centered," forcing them to linger in formulative activities until an understanding of needs and opportunities has emerged.

Types of Developments That Organizations Recognize

The direction of attention and nature of attention indicates how strategic managers scan the environment for developments that are confronting the organization. Figure 5.1 identifies the type of development that will be identified when a strategic manager directs attention internally or externally with flexible or control aims. Direction of attention and scan approach were selected as discriminating factors because similar dichotomies occur frequently in the strategic management literature.

Strategic managers can direct their attention either inside or outside the organization to scan for developments (Ansoff, 1979). There is considerable agreement that an internal as opposed to an external focus of attention provides an important dichotomy (see, for example, King, 1982; Ring, 1988; Nutt and Backoff, 1987; Dutton and Jackson, 1987; Bryson, 1988). An internal focus of attention picks up developments in terms of organizational functioning, such as performance measured by information systems or the insights of key confidants. The observations of confidants describe how opinion leaders and power centers typify classes or groups of people in terms of needs, satisfaction, or complaints. Performance-centered ob-

Figure 5.1. Types of Developments Facing Organizations.

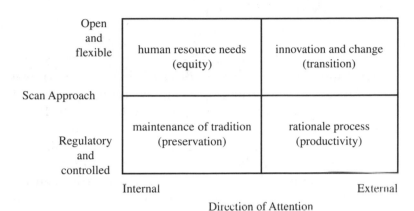

servations detect problems with operations such as measuring cost, quality, and user satisfaction. An external orientation directs scanning for developments outwardly and allows managers to view people and performance in terms of norms based on expectations derived from similar agencies and other reference groups.

Either an *open and flexible* approach or a *regulated and controlled* approach can be adopted by strategic managers to scan for developments (Morgan, 1980; Quinn and Rohrbaugh, 1983). Morgan (1984, 1986) finds that perceptions of needed actions fall into broad categories of regulation and change. These distinctions indicate what strategic managers are apt to see and the aspect of reality they will recognize. An open and flexible response leads to interpreting events and trends in terms of developments that identify potentials for change. Developments often take the form of innovations that the organization should consider adopting. The regulated and controlled response sees developments in terms of ensuring predictability and stability. These types of attention can lead to imperatives for change or the restoration of tradition.

Strategic managers that select one of these ways to direct and focus their attention are prone to see developments in terms of needs for equity, preservation, transition, or productivity (Nutt and Backoff, 1992).

Equity

An open and flexible response directed inwardly is drawn toward human resource developments by using indicators of cohesion, morale, and motivation (Quinn and Cameron, 1983). This type of scanning focuses on the network of relationships that run an organization to identify needs. To deal with individuals in this network, the strategic manager must confront equity, determining if people are treated fairly. A human resource development is often recognized in terms of intended and unintended incentives that alter peoples' behavior and encourage certain kinds of actions. Consensual views about events and trends that create incentives are interpreted in terms of norms that are applied to how, for example, appointments are kept by service users. The sanctions that are available to the service providers to encourage people to keep appointments are also considered. A human resources development often takes shape as the need for training or the revision of a reward system.

Preservation

An inwardly directed focus on control and regulation emphasizes developments in terms of the need to maintain tradition. A control model is imposed on events or trends, which calls for a return to a previous status quo or maintenance of a current one. The need to maintain traditions underlies these developments. The value of tradition is often interpreted in terms of the preservation of cultures, practices, or treaties forged and validated over the life of the organization. For instance, attempts to introduce management skills into the U.S. Department of State have been unsuccessful. First, attempts were made to retrain ambassadors. When this failed, attempts were made to shift power from the ambassadors and the Diplomatic Corps to the people who man desks for each country in Washington

(Warwick, 1975). The tradition of ambassadors as spokespeople for the United States abroad and their old-boy way of doing things was forcefully maintained, even as power shifted away from the State Department to the National Security Council.

Transition

The need for change (transition) emerges from externally directed attention using an open and flexible lens. Reading environmental signals, the strategic manager looks for needs that must be met or opportunities that give the organization leverage. The organization would be called on to adapt in the ways required to exploit the opportunity or meet the need, creating a transition. The transition captures how the organization must shift to accommodate the changes that are implied. Developments are often articulated as new services the organization may offer that have the potential to meet emergent needs or mandates, expand influence, or increase budgets.

Productivity

Viewing the outer environment from a regulatory perspective stresses rationality in how things are done and calls for changes to enhance productivity. Developments are recognized that can produce the best possible output level. Developments posed in terms of productivity often call for changes in practices and processes that can improve performance prospects, such as efficiency.

Forming Issues as Tensions

Developments that signal the need for action can be located in one of the four cells of the framework shown in Figure 5.1. To use the framework, the triggering development is paired with the three other types of developments. An issue is defined as a tension between generic developments in the four quadrants of Figure 5.1. For example, a development triggered by new services and paired with productivity enhancement creates an issue called the *transition-productivity tension.* Six types of tensions can be identified in this way, as shown in Figure 5.2. Moderators are found in the adjacent cells. Moderators are directly linked to the tension and will tend to relax it or stress it still further. The triggers, tensions, and moderators provide a way to define an agenda of issues that will always merit consideration before action is taken.

Examples that describe a single tension are difficult to provide. This stems from our basic premise: an issue is connected or implicated in all six tensions. Each example that we use to illustrate the tensions can be reframed to make it fit any of the other tensions, either as one pole of the tension or as a moderator. We believe that all issues have this characteristic. A complete representation of an issue must involve all four cells in Figure 5.1.

Transition-Productivity Tension

Meeting demands during a change often leads to a transition-productivity tension. This tension can occur in several ways including "cut-back management" (Levine, 1978), dealing with new mandates, replacing an old with a new order, and domain foreclosure such as coping with fixed markets, like those of a fire department. Organizations face such a tension when they experience difficulties stemming from budget cutbacks or shortfalls in cash flow as new programs are mounted. A transition-productivity tension occurs when there is a clear need to maintain customers (or clients) while the change takes place to produce revenues needed to meet expenses that occur during the transition. For example, during an expansion, hospitals must maintain their occupancy in order to produce the cash flow needed to meet the payroll and the bond obligations floated to fund the expansion.

This tension also arises as organizations attempt to get services efficiently delivered while they attempt to maintain the political legitimacy and support required to ensure continuing program support. Policy makers in government who attempt to get new programs in place often clash with agency managers

Figure 5.2. The Six Issue Tensions.

1. Meeting Demands During Change

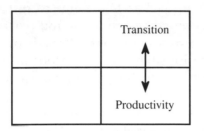

2. Determining Who Gets What During Change

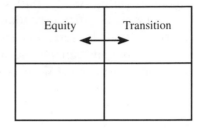

3. Fairness Clashing with Tradition

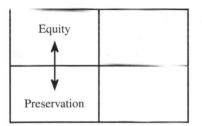

4. Squeezing a Stressed Tradition-Ridden System

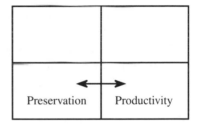

5. Reconciling Cost Cutting with Human Commitments

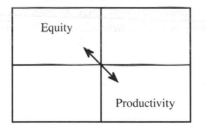

6. Dealing with Inertia During Change

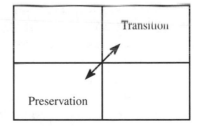

concerned about maintaining sensitive political ties to legislators and powerful constituents. Weinberg (1986) describes such
a tension in a state department of transportation. The engineers in public works had set up elaborate systems to install
new highways efficiently that ignored citizen input and participation. Road location decisions and the choice of roads over
other modes of transportation ultimately created serious problems for the department because the transition-productivity
tension had been ignored.

The transition-productivity tension can be moderated by
equity or preservation. Concerns about equity can surface when
a decline in economic activity dramatically cuts revenues for a
state government and prompts service managers to anticipate
cuts in programs and in service intensity. Equity draws attention to the needs of people who can no longer be served, calling for well-conceived cutbacks. Equity can relax the tension
when the needs of key clients are recognized and stress it when
people's needs are ignored or treated in a cavalier manner.

Concerns about preservation can stress the tension when
traditionalists who want to keep things the way they are mount
campaigns that challenge the wisdom of a change. Change brings
new practices that must be learned, causing temporary confu-
sion and inefficiency. These problems can be exploited by
preservationists who contend that the change is a failure and
call for a return to past practices. Preservation can act to relax
the tension when traditions that have important implications,
such as culture, are used to support a change. Attempts are
made to forge agreements that graft traditions onto the change,
much the way legislatures offer grandfather clauses to exempt
constituents adversely affected by legislation.

In cut-back management (Levine, 1978) developments
take shape in terms of the magnitude and timing of a cut. The
proposed cut and the need to maintain or even increase output, produce a strong tension. (Note the "and" relationship.)
One cannot be managed without attending to the other. The
tension is moderated by the rules of the game (preservation),
such as dealing with the culture of the organization to make
cuts. The cutbacks must adhere to organizational traditions

spelling out how cutbacks are to be carried out through devices such as hearings, consultation, commitments, and priorities. Valued aspects of the culture, such as leaving the centers of excellence in a functional state, must also be considered. Equity provides another strong moderator, ensuring that cuts adhere to standards of fairness that are understood by affected parties.

Equity-Transition Tension

The equity-transition tension is often signaled by disputes over anticipated spoils. A new service or internal operation that offers potential to enhance prestige creates a vehicle for advancement and will be claimed by upwardly mobile executives. If the change is accompanied by generous budgets or funding, the competition can become fierce. The reverse is also true: new ideas that lack budgetary slack and prestige become "someone else's problem" (Bardach, 1977). Transition without equity considerations can create a potentially explosive situation.

The equity-transition tension is moderated by preservation and productivity. Preservation claims can take shape as protests about adhering to accepted procedures during change, stressing the tension. When precedent is followed, the tension is relaxed. If precedent is not followed, tradition will combine with equity and provide powerful arguments to set aside planned changes. Preservation may call for the use of implicit treaties that have been negotiated in the organization to decide who inherits the new service or operation (Lippitt and Mackenzie, 1976) and how the change will be instituted. Violating such traditions will stress the equity-transition tension, adhering to them will relax the tension.

Productivity can stress the equity-transition tension when productivity norms are imposed that lack fairness or make the change especially painful. For instance, hospital departments experiencing price controls for the first time saw no way to maintain productivity because the main source of their cost, physicians, was outside of the department's influence. Productivity as a moderator can slow change by showing how cost will rise and performance fall during a transition and can thus ease the tension. Claims for rapid change are often slowed using such tactics.

Equity-Preservation Tension

The equity-preservation tension emerges when the notions of fairness cannot be reconciled with tradition. When Congress attempted to institute performance-based compensation (transition) for key federal civil service people, it was confronted with rules that based rewards on seniority codified by the equivalent of a union contract (equity). Similarly, rewards for managers, such as vacation time, are typically based on length of service. Linking vacation time to a reward structure would be strenuously resisted.

Equity-preservation clashes are moderated by transition and productivity. For example, the need to show external watchdog agencies an increase in the average compensation level for women can entice organizations to compensate women, with comparable experience and performance, better than men. This change raises the average compensation for women but creates fairness concerns. The tension is stressed because males can claim that reverse discrimination and quotas violate the organization's traditions regarding compensation. A transition that puts such a compensation system in place can also act as a moderator. Reactions during the transition may call for a graduated change in compensation for women, perhaps ensuring that equity within job classifications be maintained for people with comparable jobs and performance levels. This may relax the tension.

Authority limits can also surface as equity-preservation tensions with powerful transition and productivity moderators. During budget cutting, public agencies often find their resource base depleted and their positions frozen. This creates a tension between equity concerns about who gets served by whom and concerns about what part of the service delivery system will be preserved. Productivity questions arise as a moderator when ways are considered to meet these demands with inadequate staffing. Meeting traditional commitments can be impossible for a period of time, causing limits in service productivity and attempts to go outside the system to supplement the lost funds (transition), such as the license or user fees initiated or increased by state departments of natural resources.

Preservation-Productivity Tension

A preservation-productivity tension is often produced when an organization that is deeply committed to tradition experiences hard times. The need to increase output is compelling and can no longer be ignored, but tradition arises as an argument to resist the new production norms. Resistance is justified in terms of the cost and time that are essential to adhere to the new expectations. Traditionalists mount campaigns that enumerate the litany of their woes produced by the new norm. For example, university faculty members confronted with the need to increase their research productivity often cite a long list of obligations, such as student services and university committees. A university department chairperson can respond to budget cuts in the same manner. The chair may retain funds for his or her junkets but eliminate typing and copying support for research papers in the hopes of forcing faculty members to write grants that underwrite the costs of their research. The preservation-productivity issue emerges when funds to support research are eliminated while the chairperson preserves personally valued activities.

Equity and transition are moderators to the preservation-productivity tension. The department chair in the previous example may be confronted by senior faculty members who see the lack of equity in his or her allocation of funds. As a moderator, equity can place limits on the use of funds, relaxing the tension. Transition moderators can stem from the budget shortfalls that prompted cutbacks. Ongoing transitions moderate the budget reductions that are carried out.

Equity-Productivity Tension

The equity-productivity tension often occurs when organizations attempt to square budget cuts with their commitments to people. This tension can create havoc when organizations are forced to cut costs but must do so in accordance with union contracts or long-standing commitments for continuing employment to managers and staff specialists. For example, replacing union janitors in a hospital with an outside cleaning company can be cost effective but may violate the terms of a union contract. The need to close down a service because of lost federal funding can violate long-standing commitments to service users and commitments made to professional staff members when they were hired.

Clashes between productivity and equity can build until they set off waves of protest, which can be moderated by preservation and transition. A welfare department in one of our cases experienced continuous problems in handling its daily caseload, which created employee burnout. There seemed no time to invest in human resources. Employees gradually lost their motivation because there was no way to sustain the required level of activity. After burnout, employees resorted to goldbricking to deal with the stress that was inherent in the unrelenting push to meet the day's needs.

Job specifications were used to moderate this tension, keeping things from changing. Employees were reminded of their job description, and the real problems the jobs created were ignored. Here the moderator damped the tension and blocked its emergence. We introduced transition as a moderator to amplify the tension. The idea of using a team approach in handling claims forced equity needs to surface. The transition also introduced the notion of automation to replace the manual claim-handling process. Dealing with equity concerns by using employee flextime in the claim-handling teams (team members developed their own work schedules, including hours to be worked) made it possible to automate when automation had been blocked for years.

Veto power inherent in the authority system to which public organizations must respond can also create an equity-productivity tension. For example, a utility can find its summer shutoff plans to deal with nonpayers vetoed by a regulatory body or the courts. The utility cannot be efficient if nonpayers get service, but the courts find that human commitments call for utilities to serve people whether they pay or not.

Transition-Preservation Tension

Many organizations find inertia to be a major roadblock inhibiting change, which creates a preservation-transition tension. Inertia can be rooted in a tension between the need for transition and the bureaucratic momentum inherent in organizations that tend to reproduce the same activities. Inertia causes organizations to get stuck in a cycle that becomes degrading. Entropy sets in, and things get steadily worse, with no apparent way to break out.

Political patronage (preservation) can slow the need for transition and can prevent strong rationales for change from emerging. Similarly, forces such as learned incapacity that stem from restrictive work rules in unions can require strict adherence to work rules that reinforce the status quo.

The transition preservation tension is moderated by equity and productivity. Equity concerns often occur, such as the need to retain nonpaying clients (for example, the severely mentally retarded in a mental health center). Performance can also act as a moderator, producing two types of forces. First, legalisms in accounting for performance, such as legislatively mandated measures to count job placements in a state employment commission, can distort performance positively or negatively, enhancing or dampening the need for change. Placements can be next to impossible in regions that traditionally have high unemployment, which makes superior placement performance impossible. Second, performance can call for documentation mechanisms, such as accreditation and audits, or categories, such as the PIMS model (now widely used by hospitals), that can be interpreted to ratify the status quo or challenge it. These tensions and their moderators can be termed the *bureaucratic-pathology issue,* which produces inertia rooted in a transition-preservation tension.

Another kind of transition-preservation tension occurs when organizations attempt to blend old and new services. The old service represents tradition and the new service, transition. Concerns often arise that the new service will bleed off resources from the old services, which symbolize the organization and what it stands for. Budget limits can create a transition-preservation tension. Tradition stipulates how an allocation is to be made, but approved budgets may create a shortfall in appropriations. The shortfall can be allocated by across-the-board cuts or earmarking that specifies how some of the funds will be used. For example, colleges of medicine had to create family medicine departments when legislatures provided funds specifically for this purpose and cut their budget at the same time. The administrations of the colleges had to deal with productivity and equity concerns as cutbacks were made.

Using the Framework

To form an issue agenda, trends and events that identify developments are treated as signals that guide a search for underlying concerns. Two steps are taken. First, the triggering development is paired with each of the three other developments in Figure 5.1 to produce tensions. For instance, to ascribe meaning to a dispute about perks among key executives, the conflict about perks (equity) is paired with other developments that may be in tension with it. The equity-preservation, equity-productivity, and equity-transition tensions pose three additional considerations: dealing with the clash between fairness and tradition, reconciling cutbacks with human commitments, and determining who gets what during change, respectively.

Second, the three generic developments not involved with the triggering development (equity) are explored as tensions. The transition-productivity, preservation-productivity, and preservation-transition tensions pose issues such as meeting demands during change, squeezing a stressed tradition-ridden system, and dealing with inertia during change, respectively. These tensions treat the triggering development as a moderator. They go beyond the initially recognized development to explore the other tensions to see which, if any, may merit further attention.

Issue agendas created in this way helps the strategic manager to take a balanced perspective and to search for underlying possibilities before acting. The equivalent of framing takes place, which broadens the arena of action and goes beyond the arena implied by the trend or event that initially captured the strategic manager's attention. This step is crucial to improve the conduct of strategic management. Also, by moving through the six generic tensions, the parties and interest groups influenced by each can be recognized.

Treating issues as tensions makes win-win strategies more likely. First, by moving through the six types of tensions, the parties and interest groups affected by each tension become easier to spot. Second, the "and" relationship between the developments that make up a tension points out the need to search for a strategy that deals with both developments. By considering the tension between opposing developments, such as looking for equity concerns in transitions and transition opportunities in equity concerns, the need to deal with both components of the tension becomes explicit. This coaxes the organization to consider a strategy that may otherwise be ignored, increasing the chance of finding a win-win result.

Examining issues as mutually exclusive and contradictory developments produces divergent thinking, which is essential for complex tasks such as fashioning strategy (Cameron, 1986). Contending with the mutually exclusive opposites in a tension is more apt to produce breakthroughs than dealing with a single development. Rothenburg (1979) found that breakthroughs in the work of fifty-four creative scientists and artists stemmed from their accepting that opposing forces are equally valid or accurate. The tension that resulted from these seeming incompatibilities produced a springboard from which creative insights emerged that reconciled the opposing forces. Examples include musicians who thought of dissonance and harmony in constructing a musical chord and artists who painted dissonance and harmony in the same scene. Thus, an issue posed as a tension does not identify a problem to be solved but a paradox to be transcended. Transcending the opposites in a tension produces a win-win strategy. Peters and Waterman (1982) show how excellent organizations have learned how to recognize and manage tensions.

Even when breakthroughs are not realized, the tension and its contradictory elements hold the organization's attention and spark creativity (Schumaker, 1977). The tension may capture a currently insolvable situation that can be translated into a solvable one with new insights and opportunities that may emerge in the future.

Considering issues as tensions does not guarantee that win-win strategies will emerge. This approach does make it more difficult to ignore hidden concerns by raising consciousness about them. This heightened awareness promotes a commitment to search for ways to deal with issues that are often shunted aside. Quinn and Cameron (1983) point out that organizations often respond to strategic concerns in highly predictable ways. These knee-jerk responses lead organizations to, for example, see issues exclusively in human resource terms and never as a transition. The persistent interpretation of human resource concerns as issues will make strategy become unbalanced, and the action implied by the other three quadrants in Figure 5.1 will be ignored. Exploring issues in terms of the six types of tensions opens up inquiry and makes it harder to ignore the forces at work on an organization.

Key Points

1. Issues are crucial to the conduct of strategic management because they direct the search for strategic responses, much like problems in problem solving.
2. Trends or events produce developments that capture the strategic manager's attention, becoming issues. Tests are applied to ensure that these developments are not just symptoms of deeper concerns that merit attention.
3. Developments are treated as strong signals that guide the search for underlying concerns which identify the needs

for equity, preservation, transition, or productivity. The triggering development is paired with another development to create an issue formed as a tension. Forming issues as tensions has two benefits. First, the pairing uncovers underlying concerns that always merit attention, helping to reveal weak signals that can be overlooked. Second, tensions show how organizations are pulled in several ways at the same time by important issues.

4. The framework of issue tensions helps an organization test its issue agenda for comprehensiveness and identify issue tensions that tend to be overlooked. Issue tensions missing from an issue agenda can provide insight into issues that pose weaknesses and threats that may have been overlooked.

5. Strategy is sought that attempts to balance the opposing forces in a high-priority issue tension so that strategic action is taken to deal with one development in the tension while being cognizant of the other. Managing tensions in this way gives managers a better chance of fashioning win-win responses than does selecting among competing developments that make up poles of a tension.

PART THREE

■   ■

The Strategic
Management
Process

■   ■

In Part Three, we describe the process that we propose in order to carry out strategic management. In Chapter Six, foundation ideas are presented. Chapter Seven provides a detailed description of the required process stages and steps. In Chapter Eight, ways to carry out various types of strategic management efforts are assembled from combinations of the six process stages.

Chapter Six

■   ■

Organizing
the Process

■   ■

Public and third sector organizations must articulate, evaluate, and manage the evolution of their strategies to ensure the efficient and effective provision of services that have become a part of our life-style expectations. A strategy identifies, among other things, service profiles and aims, such as growth or stability. For example, a strategy in a state department of natural resources could modify fees for various kinds of licenses and target these revenues to support wildlife programs, environmental protection plans, hunting and fishing regulations, and the development of state parks.

The unique problems public and third sector organizations have in fashioning strategy are often overlooked. As we discussed in Chapter Two, these organizations face considerable ambiguity, real and potential conflict, and severe limits on choices and domains, as compared to firms. In these organizations, premature closure and a misplaced focus on analytical precision can have devastating consequences. Analysis creates a false sense of security that can displace political issues, which, if left unattended, can lead to failure and recrimination.

We provide a process designed to cope with the problems of doing strategic management in public and third sector organizations. The approach is novel in several ways but also builds on several of the key ideas discussed in Part Two, modifying them to deal with the unique needs of strategic management in public and third sector settings. Its novelty stems from the addition of several stages, several new activities, and the sequencing of these stages and within stage activity, which will be discussed in the next chapter. To set the scene for this discussion, this chapter presents crucial foundational ideas.

Foundational Ideas

Strategic management calls for a process that blends the old with the new and considers both formulation—creating new ideas—and implementation—putting these new ideas into practice. As the process unfolds, there is a shift in emphasis from the old to the new, as shown in Figure 6.1. The organi-

Figure 6.1. The Old and the New in Strategic Management.

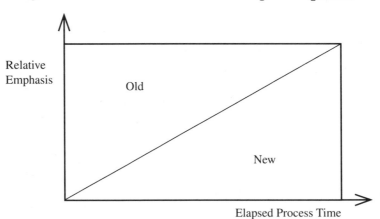

Figure 6.2. Thinking and Acting in Strategic Management.

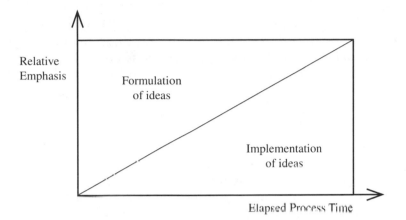

zation's current practices, culture, beliefs, and traditions form a foundation on which change must be built. The first step in strategic management is to review and uncover and then explore these historical commitments to reacquaint decision makers with the basis on which the organization was built. Changes flow from an appreciation of what must be preserved in these practices. A dialectic between the old and the new is created to produce a new synthesis on which to build the future.

The process begins by emphasizing formulation and gradually shifts in emphasis to implementation. As shown in Figure 6.2, formative and implementational concerns arise in every process stage, only the relative emphasis changes. Early in the process, discovery is emphasized. To formulate strategy, views about what is and what might be are uncovered and explored. This exploration moves through a series of activities designed to promote disclosure of what is and creativity in considering what might be. Both are essential in managing any change process. Historical commitments identify core values around which new ideas can attach and grow.

The notion of joint action during formulation of strategy is used to encourage acceptance of the strategy by key strategic decision makers, which promotes implementation. To implement strategy, social and political forces become paramount. These forces are managed by making preservation commitments early in the process and encouraging stakeholder acceptance through consensus building around these commitments. To take action, steps that manage these social and political forces take priority. Formulation, however, still plays a role by identifying who and what need to be managed and steps to deal with stakeholders that control the resources needed to implement changes. This shuttling between formulation and implementation, gradually moving from ideas to commitments that allow action, is an important hallmark of the process.

For these reasons, implementation as well as formulation (or acting and thinking) are included in the strategic management process (Ansoff, 1984; Nutt and Backoff, 1987). The process merges short- and long-term considerations by seeking immediate actions that simultaneously address short- and long-range issues. Strategic planning is integrated with the ongoing management of an organization, making the process one of strategic management. These steps remove barriers that have made the creation of ideas a staff function insulated from the action taking of responsible agents.

The Strategic Management Group

Strategic management is an ongoing process carried out to inform and build a consensus among key stakeholders. By developing ideas together, stakeholders can appreciate the needs and viewpoint of others, which creates a consensus to act. The process builds an understanding of these needs and then develops ideas to address needs.

A key vehicle in strategic management is the strategic management group, or SMG. The SMG is made up of people who represent interests and power centers internal and external to the organization. The SMG becomes the key source of ideas about change and how to make the change within the organization. The strategic management process draws out these ideas and how to make the needed changes from the SMG.

The SMG need not be comprised solely of the dominant

coalition or top managers. Over time, as the issue agenda brings in new concerns and changes, the membership of the SMG may also change to bring in the expertise called for to address these emergent issues.

Purposes

The strategic management group is involved in both innovation and consensus building. First, the process draws on techniques that can tap the creative potentials of people who are intimately familiar with the organization and its unique needs. Second, participation in an SMG addresses the problem of incentives in public and third sector organizations discussed in Chapter Two. Serving on an SMG can be used to reward key employees, allowing them a significant role in fashioning the future directions of the organizations. Third, participation leads to "buy-in" of both the process and its product through co-optation (Selznick, 1949). The social world of the SMG arises out of these interactions, in which members explore and interpret one another's views (Berger and Luckman, 1966). What counts are the constructions that people make to characterize a situation or event (Boulding, 1956). If shared meanings can be created, these constructions will be sustained. If not, no basis for action will emerge. The process is designed to allow the SMG to become a management team with the knowledge, insight, and authority to take action. Participation allows members to appreciate what can be done and their role in carrying out desired changes.

SMG Formation

An SMG is made up of people who appreciate the wants and needs of clients, can speak to professional values, and understand the authority system in which the organization must function. Research shows that nearly three-fourths of the information needed in strategy building is organization specific, which means that informed insiders should be involved in the process (Tichy, 1983). Typically, the chief executive officer, the senior staff members, and up to three levels of management are involved. It is not unusual for representatives of oversight boards or key stakeholder groups to participate. Outside stakeholders are involved in legitimizing the process at the beginning and become involved again during the formulation and implementation of strategies.

SMG Size

The ideal size for a group varies according to the kind of action that is expected. Small groups are best for evaluation and judging, and five members is the ideal size (Nutt, 1989a). A small group encourages equal participation, which is important in making judgments and assessments. Influence attempts are eased in small groups because those being influenced can be gradually coaxed to go along, a process that cannot be rushed. Larger groups are preferred for developmental tasks because innovation is an individual matter that benefits from exchanges of ideas that stem from many different viewpoints. Information exchange is limited by communication opportunities, so group process (discussed in Chapter Nine) rather than size inhibits information flow.

Four-person groups solve more problems than two-person groups, and groups of thirteen are superior to a group of six to eight members in problem solving (Faust, 1959). The quality of solutions increases with group size (Cummings, Huber, and Arndt, 1974). Both the amount and quality of discussion among group members are important determinants of whether a group will provide a quality solution (Holloman and Hendrich, 1972). Group process techniques (Chapter Nine) are used to ensure both the amount and quality of discussion.

Judgment, in contrast with problem solving, takes longer in large groups because of the additional time needed for compromises (Hinton and Reitz, 1971). Large groups require more time to make judgments than small groups. Small-group productivity is better when dealing with concrete problems, and large groups are better with abstract problems (Thibaut and Kelley, 1959). For instance, studies of subcommittees of the

U.S. Senate find that the mean size of action-taking committees was five, compared to an average size of fourteen for committees that did not take action.

Member participation and reaction are also related to size. As group size increases, so does tension, but the number of suggestions per member and the prospect of agreement decrease (Hare, Bogatala, and Bales, 1955). The least active member's participation declines rapidly as the group's size goes from three to ten members (Bales, 1951).

Without group processes as an aid, elaborate patterns of interpersonal relationships develop in large groups. Information is lost because some group members are unable to assimilate it. Lost information causes errors and judgments that seem ill advised to the better-informed members. Sensitivity to other points of view decreases as group size increases (Collins and Guetzkow, 1964). Delbecq (1968) finds that large groups require attention to many viewpoints, considerable computational ability, great psychological concentration, and empathy that are beyond the capacities of most group members. As groups increase in size, a few high-status members will tend to have more influence over group activities (Stogdill, 1969). With these considerations in mind, the ideal size of a strategic management group is between five to fifteen key members of the organization.

SMG Leadership

Leadership for the SMG stems from one of two sources. Either a facilitator, the titular leader of the organization (or work group), or a trusted staff member can be used to guide the activities of the SMG. The choice between these types of leaders depends on several factors. Facilitators are used when the titular leader wants to participate as a group member. The facilitator's role is to ensure that the process is followed, freeing the leader to become immersed in the content of strategy. Process management is delegated. Facilitators can be used to teach the leader or others in the organization how to manage a strategic management process. The facilitator has two roles: to guide the process effectively and to show others how to carry out the required procedures. Several SMG members may be selected to participate in part to learn these procedures. Some leaders want the process to unfold without their views influencing the outcome. To keep this type of influence at a minimum, such leaders may choose not to participate as either a group member or a group leader.

Other circumstances may call for the chief executive officer of the organization or manager of the work unit to assume the role of SMG leader. Strategy development can be a sensitive matter that could disclose practices and plans to outsiders who could benefit from them or use them to whipsaw the agency. Organizations that can sequester strategic discussions prefer to do so, often to permit the exploration of hypothetical situations and possible responses that could be inflammatory. Also, participants may not be candid when outside facilitators are present. Disclosure of important weaknesses and threats and even opportunities can be used by outside interests to the disadvantage of the organization engaged in strategy development. For instance, a medical school department kept its slush fund, collected from practice fees, secret because it feared the dean would cut its budget in proportion to the outside earnings and thus keep it from using the slush fund to underwrite new initiatives. Some organizations would prefer to exhaust ways of coping with weaknesses and threats before seeking outside help.

The most compelling reason for a leader to assume SMG leadership stems from the need to manage an organization strategically on a continuing basis. The role of strategic managers is to position their organization for the future. Strategic development is no longer done via the annual weekend retreat but has become a crucial part of the progressive manager's work life.

The best organizations anticipate and adjust to issues as they emerge. Strategic management is the best way to deal with the steps needed for anticipation and adjustment. The well-trained manager of the future should have strategic management skills and should apply them continuously. Thus, facilitators are useful to initiate strategic planning but should be phased out as the notion of managing strategically takes root in an organization.

Primary Concerns of an SMG

Managing an organization requires the continual balancing of opposing tensions such as differentiation and integration, morphogenesis and morphostasis, change and stability, and collectivism and individuality (Jantsch, 1975). Steering a viable course through these tensions is the primary concern of strategic management.

The SMG explores the past and projects a future for the organization using a "tension field" metaphor (Figure 6.3). Organizations exist in a tension field made up of capacities, which can be visualized as strengths and weaknesses, and potentials, which can be visualized as threats and opportunities. These SWOTs (short for strengths, weaknesses, opportunities, and threats) identify a tension field that pushes or pulls the organization. The tension field acts as a lens that brings together opposing developments to focus their effects, creating a direction for the organization. The resolution of these forces creates a direction of movement toward or away from the organization's ideals.

The SMG must come to a collective understanding of the organization's current situation by identifying its clientele, programs and services, and reputation and competence in order to picture a current "persona." The organization's future situation is extrapolated by using the SWOTs tension field to imagine how clients, programs, reputation, and competence are likely to change, given the directions inherent in the tension field. This projection is used to identify who will be served, what programs will likely be adopted, and the reputation or regard these programs and clients would likely produce to create the organization's future persona.

This projected persona is assessed in two ways by the SMG. First, attempts are made to imagine how authority systems that control the organization's resources, such as a city

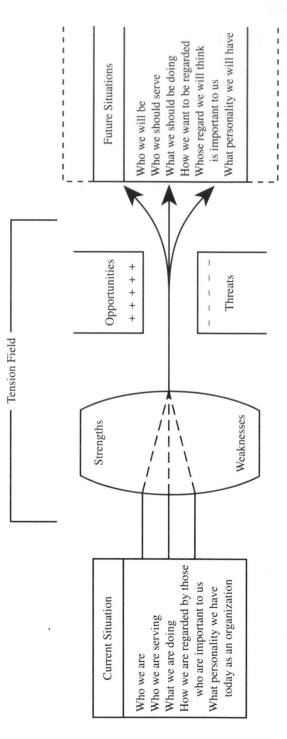

Figure 6.3. The Tension Field Lens.

Tension Field

Current Situation

Who we are
Who we are serving
What we are doing
How we are regarded by those
  who are important to us
What personality we have
  today as an organization

Strengths

Weaknesses

Opportunities

+ +
+ + +
+

Threats

– – – –

Future Situations

Who we will be
Who we should serve
What we should be doing
How we want to be regarded
Whose regard we will think
  is important to us
What personality we will have

158

council, are apt to view the evolved persona. Second, the SMG compares the projected persona to its ideals. The first assessment determines the prospects of a push toward a desired future, the second, the chance of a pull toward a desired future. To alter a future situation, the tension-field elements (SWOTs) must be managed by taking actions that build on strengths, capitalize on opportunities, blunt threats, and overcome weaknesses. Coherent themes in these SWOTs take shape as issues, which guide the search for strategy.

The SMG's explorations of the tension field serve as a vehicle to uncover actions that alter a future situation so it is more closely aligned to the organization's ideals. The SMG identifies and critiques the organization's strategic direction as a vehicle for change. Stages in the process are carried out to (1) depict the organization's historical context in terms of trends in its environment, its overall direction, and its normative ideals; (2) assess the immediate situation in terms of current strengths and weaknesses and future opportunities and threats; (3) develop an agenda of current strategic issues to be managed; (4) design strategic options to manage priority issues; (5) assess the strategic options in terms of stakeholders affected and resources required; and (6) implement priority strategies by mobilizing resources and managing stakeholders. Once the process is under way for at least one issue and one strategy to manage the issue, the stages of the process may be repeated in whole or in part. Ways to carry out the process from short one-time applications, such as one-day retreats, to the management of continual strategic change are described in Chapter Eight.

Within each of the stages, the SMG engages in three steps. The first step is to *search* for information and ideas. The second, or *synthesis,* step is used to find generalizations, patterns, or themes in the pool of information and ideas. The final step of *selection* applies criteria to set priorities for action as the process moves from one stage to the next. In Part Four of the book, planning techniques that can be used for each of these steps are discussed, using examples. The process stages and steps that we propose are discussed in the next chapter.

Formation of Issue Agendas

In strategic management, issues are used to direct the search for strategic actions. Issues identify an arena of action in which a search for a strategic response is conducted. Because issues that are symptomatic or misleading can misdirect the search for a strategy, creating an agenda of issues to be managed is one of the most important activities in strategic management.

Trends or events often capture the attention of strategic managers but fail to reveal the underlying issue tensions at work in the organization. For instance, in one of our cases, the leader of a family medicine department in a medical school recognized the demand to increase the department's research activity but did not see the demand as in tension with the department's needs to service its large and growing patient population, which provided most of the funds to underwrite departmental expenses. Expressed as a tension, the pushing and pulling of scholarship demands and patient care clarified the contradictions in these demands, both within the department and between the department and key outsiders. The department searched for ways to manage the tension between research productivity and funding with patient fees by recognizing that both factors are important and that both must be considered in any strategy that is implemented.

Issues are formed as tensions by identifying developments that depict observed or anticipated trends or events, inside or outside the organization, that can have a significant effect on the organization's ability to achieve a desired future. For example, the demand for increased research productivity by the family medicine faculty suggested how the department had to change to keep its reputation from declining. To pose this development as an issue tension, one looks for the most significant factor that is pulling in the opposite direction. The time demands for increased research and the time demands for patient care, which created the funds that subsidized the salaries of the department's residents and the operating costs of the department, posed a clear tension to the SMG. Note that tensions are organization specific. Other departments of family medicine may have demands to increase research productivity but tensions may not involve subsidies.

To form an issue agenda, developments as trends or events are elicited from the SMG, using techniques described in the following chapter. This agenda is tested to ensure comprehensiveness by classifying tensions with the framework in Chapter Five. Six types of tensions will emerge:

- transition-productivity
- equity-transition
- equity-preservation
- preservation-productivity
- equity-productivity
- transition-preservation.

The "research-patient care" issue can be classified as a tension between transition (new research emphasis) and productivity (funding the department). This tension was pulling the family medicine department away from its ideals of national recognition and thus demanded attention. In this case, the triggering development, the need for more research, created the strongest tensions. In other situations, the trigger can become a moderator to more important tensions that lie lurking beneath the surface of SMG considerations.

Organizations often develop blind spots in which certain tensions emerge and others remain hidden. By classifying the issue tensions identified by the SMG according to the six types noted above, these blind spots can be identified For example, the need for improved teaching of residents in a family medicine department is also in tension with doing research. Because of an impending retirement, a new chairperson was to be appointed, which created concerns in the faculty members that old commitments would not be kept. Concerns about growth and the funds to support it were also noted. These tensions could be classified as follows:

- Transition-equity (more research and doing right by students)
- Transition-preservation (new chairperson and maintaining historical commitments)
- Transition-productivity (need for growth and lack of funds to support growth)

This assessment indicated that the SMG in this case was preoccupied with transitions. The group was able to see the tensions in several impending transitions but did not see the tensions among equity, preservation, and productivity that were influencing people's behavior and blocking needed change. By introducing equity-preservation, equity-productivity, and preservation-productivity tensions into the discussion of issues, we brought out several new concerns. This allowed the SMG to grapple with fairness in assignments, the fear of failing to get tenure, and maintaining the commitments to teaching upon which the department was founded. Steps were taken to deal with the assignments—tenure, assignments-teaching, and tenure-teaching tensions—before the SMG (composed of the department's faculty) could deal with research questions. This tactic is often useful in helping an SMG broaden its issue agenda and bringing out tensions that must be addressed so change can occur.

Issue agendas formed as tensions that deal with each of the four kinds of developments (productivity, equity, transition, and preservation) and consider all of the six possible issue tensions are more likely to uncover useful strategy. By testing the initial list of issue tensions in this way and broadening it to encompass concerns that are initially missing, an SMG is more apt to have a balanced perspective before acting. The parties and interest groups potentially in conflict over taking various types of actions are more apt to become clear when issues are represented in this way. This way of thinking about issues also promotes the search for win-win strategies that cope with both poles in the tensions that most organizations must deal with. For example, by considering the need to deal with equity concerns during a transition, the SMG can make explicit the concerns about transitions that can be sidetracked by equity considerations. This coaxes the SMG to look for ways to manage the tension by addressing the conflicts that must be managed to be successful. The cases in Part Five of the book provide additional illustrations of the value of issue tensions in creating successful strategic change in a variety of organizations.

Types of Public and Third Sector Organizations

Three types of organizations can be found in public and third sector settings: traditional organizational types, consortia, and mixed types, which have features of both consortia and traditional organizations. The *traditional organization* has permanency (which leads to the creation of a history) and employees with various standings and longevity (which creates a culture). Organizations that fall into this category include: federal and state departments, academic departments of a university, fire and police organizations at the local governmental level, and state historical societies.

The *consortium* is a loose confederation of organizations that band together to accomplish some aim (Nutt, 1979, 1984a). Cooperation among many interests is needed because dealing with strategic management for kidney disease, highway safety, and the like cuts across the mandates of several organizations. A consortium is made up of people drawn from organizations that have the resources, leadership, and mandates that are required to act. The consortium marshals these resources, leaders, and mandates through membership of organizational representatives in the decision-making body that controls what the consortium will do and become. Some consortia become relatively permanent, such as the National Kidney Foundation. Others are disbanded and their functions are given over to another agency after certain activities have been carried out. The Highway Safety Program, for example, has delegated training to vocational centers and emergency-system maintenance to local municipalities now that it has accomplished one-time projects, such as organ donation legislation. Consortia can also be found in loose confederations that represent several interests such as colleges (for example, medicine or education) in a university, the Veterans Administration's district offices (see Chapter Eight), the 648 boards for a state mental health plan (see Chapter Thirteen), and booster organizations.

The mixed type organization has an oversight board that resembles a consortium, although the agency the board directs is similar to the traditional organization. Examples include: mental health agencies (see Chapter Thirteen), libraries, crippled children's service bureaus, nonprofit nursing homes, children's hospitals, symphonies, cultural centers, and alumni associations.

Conducting strategic management in these three different settings calls for careful formation and management of an SMG. Chapters Thirteen, Fourteen, and Fifteen provide some illustrations.

Roles Played by the Strategic Manager

Strategic managers are called on to combine thinking about action with acting thoughtfully as they support a process to formulate and implement strategy. It is also important for strategic managers to see themselves in roles that are required to support acting as well as thinking if they are to become involved in strategic management (Howe and Kaufman, 1979). The strategic management process calls for a manager to be a facilitator, teacher, and politician as well as a technician, with the aid of support staff. Strategic managers are facilitators when they help to carry out the process, teachers when they demonstrate the need for each stage, and politicians when they aid in stakeholder management.

In the role of a facilitator, the strategic manager not only guides the SMG through the process stages and steps but also recommends and helps to apply appropriate techniques, discussed in Part Four. For new strategic management teams, the strategic manager also takes on the role of teacher. To be a strategic manager, an individual must communicate the rationale behind stages and steps, handle informal questions, and provide guidance. Strategic managers also help to link the process to political considerations within the SMG and to stakeholders who affect or are affected by the deliberations and actions. Strategic managers provide a means to solicit points of view as a strategy emerges from the process. Strategic managers must be prepared to adopt the roles of analyst, facilitator, teacher, and politician in each process stage if they are to deal with the ambiguous and politically sensitive business of fashioning a strategy and promoting its use.

Key Points

1. A strategic management group (SMG), composed of key people inside and outside the organization, is the primary vehicle used for strategic management. The SMG develops ideas and builds a consensus for action, translating ideas into plans that can be implemented. The SMG creates shared meanings about needs and prospects for action, which build momentum for feasible change.

2. Strategic management is done in a tension field that defines the past and suggests a future. The strategic management group explores the past and uses it to forecast the future and then examines this prediction to see if it aligns with the collective desires of important stakeholders. A misalignment creates the impetus for change and poses questions about how clients and services can be modified to alter the regard and persona that are implied by current directions.

3. Issues are expressed as tensions that show how most organizations are being pulled in several ways at the same time. The six types of tensions provide a way to test an issue agenda for comprehensiveness and provide insight into weaknesses and threats that can be overlooked.

4. The strategic manager should lead the SMG. Facilitators provide a period of transition in which leaders learn how to shape the strategic management process to fit their needs. The strategic manager of the future must be prepared to adopt various roles, including facilitator, teacher, and politician, to deal with ambiguous and politically sensitive activities needed to shape strategy and create an environment in which the strategy can flourish.

■   ■

Chapter Seven

Formulating and Implementing Strategy: A Step-by-Step Approach

■   ■

This chapter describes the process proposed to strategically manage organizations. Activity is broken into stages and stages are broken into steps to make explicit how to carry out the strategic management process. In this discussion, we describe the rationale for each activity, the relevance of the activity to public and third sector organizations (drawing on Chapter Two), and what to do to carry out the process. This discussion attempts to make the why, the what, as well as the how clear and compelling.

Our approach to strategic management has two types of processes, as shown in Table 7.1. One calls for a movement through six stages that are essential for strategic management. In the other, the strategic management group, or SMG, moves through three steps that are repeated for each of the six stages.

Table 7.1. Stages of the Strategic Management Process.

	STEPS		
	Search for:	Synthesis of:	Selection of:
Stage One: Historical Context 1. Trends and events 2. Directions 3. Ideals			
Stage Two: Situational Assessment 1. Strengths 2. Weaknesses 3. Opportunities 4. Threats			
Stage Three: Strategic Issue Tension Agenda			
Stage Four: Strategic Options 1. Action sets 2. Strategic themes			
Stage Five: Feasibility Assessment 1. Stakeholder analysis (internal/external) 2. Resource analysis			
Stage Six: Implementation 1. Resource management 2. Stakeholder management			

Search, synthesis, and selection steps are carried out for the stages to describe the historical context, conduct situational assessment, form an issue agenda, generate strategy, assess feasibility, and implement the strategy. Techniques for search, synthesis, and selection are presented in Part Four. Stages are discussed in this chapter.

The stages offer sets of activities that have distinct purposes and provide a way to break up complex activities into

Figure 7.1. Simplified Systems Model.

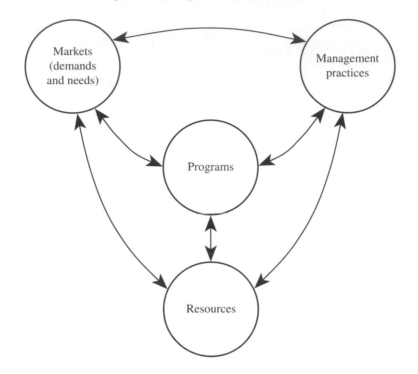

digestible parts. These activities are guided by the SMG leader, who draws on staff support to carry out the collection and summarization of information required by each stage of the process. The process stages begin with an emphasis on exploring old ideas and move toward developing new ideas. The early stages of the process emphasize formulation. In the latter stages, emphasis gradually shifts to implementation.

Stage One: Historical Context

In the first stage, the SMG identifies trends, events, and directions that characterize the pressures being directed toward the organization. Steps are then taken to identify the organization's ideals.

The SMG is asked to reconstruct aspects of the history of the organization that have special significance. Trends, events, and directions are examined, noting how they have changed in the past and may change in the future. For example, a trend in a mental health center could be decreasing federal funding, an event could be the cost containment initiative of a state legislature, and a direction could be increasing demands from the center's board of trustees to increase productivity.

Changes in direction are classified using the four components of a system—markets, programs, resources, and general management practices—as shown in Figure 7.1. *Markets* in public and third sector organizations are made up of the demands placed on the organization by oversight bodies and the perceived needs of people the organization is to serve. Demands identify things that the organization should respond to, and needs stem from the wants and desires of clients or publics recognized as important by the organization. *Programs* are the services offered and the clientele targeted by each service. *Resources* are the means at the organization's disposal to carry out its programs, including human and physical means as well as fiscal. *Management practices* identify the competencies and strategies around which the organization's administrative mechanisms are organized. Some examples of possible shifts in the system include markets shifting from service on demand to rationing, resources shifting from governmental budgeting to periodic voter approval, programs shifting from nonspecialized services for low-income clients to specialized services for local businesses, and management practices shifting from a reactive to an anticipatory posture.

Collecting Information Depicting Trends, Events, and Directions

Information depicting historical context is collected by the facilitator or staff prior to or at the first SMG meeting, using a survey. Several approaches can be used to get this information (see Chapter Nine). Forms that can be used to gather the required information can be found in Resource A. Form A.2 provides a format that can be used to collect information describing directions. Form A.2 provides definitions of each component that makes up a direction and allows space for SMG members to indicate their views by listing things the organization or agency is moving away from and toward. Some illustrations of directions obtained for a radiology department in a college of medicine and a county-financed public library are summarized below.

Moving Away From   *Moving Toward*
                        Radiology Department

General radiology	Subspecialization
Manual systems	Computer technology
Diagnosis only	Increased treatment role
One person	Team (to cope with technology)

Public Library

Patron self-help	User assistance
Day only service	Service expansion
More is better	More selectivity
Slow growth	Rapid expansion
Modest reference service	Quality reference service
Shotgun acquisitions	Central control
Overstaffing	Understaffing

Directions for a bureau of crippled children's services, sorted by the system components in Figure 7.1, shown below.

Moving Away From   *Moving Toward*
                        Demands and Needs

Disregard of politics and special interests	Responses to politics and special interests
Fragmented treatment plans	Standard plans
Few centers and intensive service	Local centers and local support

Resources

Well funded   Cost containment
State dependent   Other support
Isolation   Part of health care system

Programs

Hospital stays   Outpatient
All handicapping conditions   Limited number of condi-
                                 tions
Prevention   More emphasis on complex
                                 handicaps

Management Practices

Short term   Planning
Manual operations   Computerized
Crisis management, reaction-   System-based responses
  ary

These illustrations demonstrate the added explanatory power derived from segregating directions by system components.

The format to collect information for external events and trends is provided by Form A.3 (see Resource A). Examples of events and trends collected in this way are listed below for a radiology department and a bureau of crippled children's services.

Radiology Department

1. Computer systems in all phases of work
2. New technologies and treatment modalities
3. Imaging technology
4. Expensive support required
5. Governmental regulation
6. Licensing staff

Bureau of Crippled Children's Services

1. Authorizations via computer
2. Office automation

3. Governmental cost-containment programs
4. Block-grant funding phaseout
5. State budget cuts and increasing demands for services
6. Pressure by parents to expand services
7. Better treatment modalities that increase cost

This information is collected by surveying the SMG members or by using a group process, with the SMG members as participants (see Chapter Nine). Copious information is typically produced. Several techniques can be used to combine and then rank events, trends, and directions to create salient information that can describe historical context. These techniques are described in Chapter Eleven.

Identifying Ideals

The final activity in Stage One calls for the SMG members to create idealized images of the organization several years into the future with the trend and event and shifting direction analysis still fresh in their mind. Ideals are derived from the best- and worst-case future conditions that could face the organization. The best case identifies a target to be moving toward, and the worst case identifies a floor to be moving from. The SMG is asked to describe attributes that make up these two visions for their organization. For example, the SMG in a bureau of crippled children's services identified the best case as the authority to see all children at a comprehensive care center, with sliding-scale fees based on ability to pay. The worst case was seen as a decline in number of services offered, delays in treatment, and failure to deal with children who could be helped.

Many service organizations see their ideals as creating balance between tensions. Examples of these tensions include: meeting particular client needs and maintaining high standards of services for all, dealing with income sources (third party, self-pay, levy, state funds, and industry contracts), and allocating resources among programs. The idealized vision of the organization captures the tensions in these opposing forces that will take shape as issues. Ideals also provide a target, which offers a way to assess a strategy in terms of its ability to produce movement toward an ideal. Ideals are used in place of goals to overcome the difficulty in specifying outcome states in some future situation (Ackoff, 1981). Ideals give direction and bearing without demanding outcomes.

A useful format for a facilitator or leader to collect information about ideals is provided by Form A.4 (see Resource A). This information is obtained by a survey of the SMG or by using a group process with SMG members as participants (see Chapter Nine for details). The information collected from the SMG is aggregated by the facilitator to capture what the SMG sees as the best- and worst-case future situations facing the organization or agency. The SMG leader combines like elements and has these elements ranked to identify components that make up a statement depicting ideals (see Chapter Eleven). For example, a bureau of crippled children's services produced the following ideals.

Best Case Scenario
Bureau has the authority to see all children in the program at a comprehensive care center, with sufficient funding to increase conditions covered and drop income eligibility.

Worst-Case Scenario
Bureau must reduce services although need is increasing. Bureau is slow in providing services, delaying treatment, and does not provide services needed to totally rehabilitate clients.

Why the Historical Context Is Important

The first process stage gets members of an SMG to examine their initial mindsets by using directions and trends to reconstruct the organization's history. Ideals provide a picture of the organization's desired future that pushes the planning horizon forward. Discussion allows the SMG to develop a shared interpretation of the organization's history and its idealized future.

The rationale for Stage One is based on the value of reconstructing history. Studies of time horizons show that going

back into history is an essential step in making useful conceptual forecasts (El Sawy, 1985). The further back in time a stream
of events can be recalled, the longer into the future a potential
action or stream of events can be projected. For example, Weick
(1979) shows how envisioning an auto accident that happened
in the past resulted in more precise and vivid descriptions of
conditions that could surround such an event in the future.
Boland (1980) found that data describing actual situations helped
managers of a film library articulate a desired future. These
studies suggest that past events provide a vehicle with clear and
compelling imagery on which to build.

Events serve as temporal markers, depicting a happen-
ing that punctuates a trend or direction. They allow the SMG
participants to recall situations in which they got burned, to
reflect on what they want to avoid, and to identify what had
been useful. Each area suggests many possible actions. Trends,
such as regulatory growth, are more easily interpreted through
the lens of a salient event, such as the controversy that precip-
itated regulation. Directions provide "reference projections"
(Ackoff, 1981) that suggest likely trends that may be desirable
or undesirable. Directions and events are used to "unfreeze"
the SMG (Lewin, 1958), enticing the SMG members to walk
into the turbulent environment that they must confront.

By recalling history, SMG members can set ideals that
are both realistic and clear. Ideals provide specifics about the
desired future state of an organization (Ackoff, 1981), giving
the mind cues on which to build. Ideals provide a target that
proximates what is desired and desirable in concrete terms
preferred by strategic managers (Mintzberg, 1975, 1978).

Public-Private Distinctions

The operating environments of public and third sector organizations differ from those of a business firm. The firm sets
strategy for its lines of business by selecting markets or market
segments in the industry in which it is located. Strategic managers can test the appropriateness of specific strategies by obtaining feedback on profitability from sales to customers in the

marketplace. Public and third sector organizations, however, must be responsive to oversight by external political authorities as well as to their clients in the provision of services. Their strategic emphasis, therefore, shifts from simple marketplace dependence to a more complex set of political, economic, and legal considerations. Typically, the oversight function in governmental and third sector organizations is vested in elected officials and appointed boards.

Strategic management in such organizations includes the building of joint commitments to carry out new strategies. Strategists must take into account all parties who either affect or who are affected by the organization's strategies (stakeholders) by including them directly in the process, consulting them, or considering their views. The authority systems in which such organizations operate suggest that many individuals and groups can have stakes in the organizations' strategy. These stakes will be communicated not only by client demands (similar to market-based exchanges) but also by political mandates, voting, bargaining, budgeting, and judicial renderings. A business firm's stackholders are its stockholders, which leads firms to maximize short-term profit as demanded by the managers of retirement and mutual funds that hold most of their stock.

Reconstructive history is particularly useful in public and third sector organizations to help deal with ill-defined markets, constraints, political influence, authority limits, and broad ownership, as discussed in Chapter Two. Authority networks make up the market in organizations with significant degrees of publicness. The strategic manager must identify the beliefs and demands of key people in these authority networks to premise strategy development. These premises are also influenced by mandates and obligations, the expectations for collaboration with others competing for the same pot of limited funds, organizational financing arrangements, and sources of political influence. Each factor makes up a part of the historical context, which must be appreciated as the organization devises new ways to act.

The rapid turnover of people and the environmental turbulence experienced by public and third sector organizations make it essential to periodically appraise events, trends, and directions to appreciate the demands being posed by the environment in which these organizations must operate. This appraisal makes it easier to spot the political factors that can render any strategy ineffective. Noting these factors alerts the SMG to key constraints. An appreciation of market parameters flows from these constraints, which can help the SMG to target services in new ways, change a service profile, identify services not valued by users, and call for surrendering some services to private sector initiative. Market signals that call attention to needs in firms are meaningful only when interpreted in the context of authority networks for public and third sector organizations.

In private organizations, historical context has less importance because data depicting signals are available and can be interpreted more directly. Organizations that lack significant publicness are not influenced as pervasively by trends and events and have directions given by market segmentation. Making forecasts about current and prospective market segments captures directions typically expressed in terms of market share or growth. In public organizations, key factors that make up directions as well as the influence of these factors on the organization's desired future are vague and must be uncovered from a mass of conflicting information. Objective measurement of these factors is seldom possible and may not be desirable. An appreciation of market forces specifies an arena of action which indicates what is to be included and excluded as strategy is fashioned. Services can be stipulated for inclusion or exclusion by legislation, user preferences, tradition, the demands of key people, the emergent needs of users, opportunity, and a host of other factors. Measuring these factors is both difficult and not apt to clarify the arena of action.

Our strategic management process uses ideals in place of goals. Goals are not used because they are typically ambiguous in public organizations and tend to remain so after clarification attempts. Private organizations, such as business firms, can assume a goal of profit. Most strategic management approaches developed for firms use some form of profit measurement to select among courses of action (Henderson, 1979; Porter, 1985). There is no equivalent for profit that applies to organizations with significant publicness. In such organizations, goals tend to be both vague and in dispute. Attempts to sweep away this ambiguity encounter two related situations. The first is "goal mania," which can lead to continuing the current implicit strategy. Goal mania results when the difficulty of goal setting supersedes the development of strategic options. Goal-setting processes that become ends in themselves stymie action. However, leaving goals implicit makes it difficult to modify or even evaluate current practices. Without some concept of the organization's aims, all change becomes contentious and the organization's strategy tends to stay rooted in past practices and conventional wisdom. To provide targets that identify intentions, we use the notion of ideals. Ideals suggest aims that can be articulated in concrete terms to capture goallike targets and offer ways to seek compromise among competing views that dictate what the organization is (or is not) about. Our strategic management approach is designed to aid the managers of public and third sector organizations as they steer their organizations toward ambiguous ends in the context of political authority systems and the claims of multiple stakeholders.

Stage Two: Situational Assessment

Specifying historical context brings the SMG to an understanding of its past and, through it, an idealized future. In the next stage, the immediate situation facing the organization is considered. To carry out this stage, the SMG identifies and ranks the organization's current strengths and weaknesses as well as its future opportunities and threats, or SWOTs (Ansoff, 1980). This stage makes an SMG candidly confront crosscurrents in the pressures that the organization faces. Reviewing history in Stage One and conducting a situational assessment in Stage Two make it possible for an SMG to face the organization's weaknesses and threats without attributing blame to others (Ansoff, 1984). Clarifying strengths allows the SMG to see capabilities that the organization possesses and reinforces a sense of competence in managing its weaknesses and threats. The idealization process stimulates a more active search for opportunities in the direction of the organization's ideals.

Collecting SWOTs Information

SWOTs information is initially collected using a survey, filled out at the same time as information is collected describing historical context. This information can also be collected prior to the first meeting or as a part of the first meeting of the SMG. A format to collect SWOTs information is provided by Form A.5 in Resource A. (Group process approaches that can be used to manage this collection of information are found in Chapter Nine, and techniques to integrate and prioritize the information are in Chapter Eleven.)

SWOTs information is often quite revealing, offering significant insight into windows for subsequent action. Table 7.2 summarizes priority SWOTs for a state mental health department, a bureau of crippled children's services, and a radiology department.

Why Situational Assessment Is Important

The Harvard policy model (Christenson and others, 1983) provides the inspiration for this stage, as it has for many others. The notion of situational assessment has been strongly influenced by the Harvard perspective as it was originally devised. Many people have used the SWOTs perspective to pose questions for strategic management (for example, Ansoff, 1980). Steiner's (1979) "WOTS" approach and Rowe, Mason, and Dickel's (1982) "WOTS-UP" approach are two of many derivations. Each provides examples of how a SWOTs-like framing can help to uncover insightful as well as candid assessments of the current organizational situation.

Our approach, however, is more faithful to the Harvard model, in which attention is directed toward the values of key stakeholders, not just senior managers, in determining strengths and weaknesses. We also adopt the Harvard view that mandates

Table 7.2. SWOTs for Three Organizations.

	Mental Health Department	Bureau of Crippled Children's Services	Radiology Department
(S) Strengths	1. Community Regional forums 2. Top staff with new insights 3. Clear objectives and mission	1. Exceptions and appeals mechanisms 2. Internal review 3. Staff expertise 4. Commitment to clients by general public	1. Diagnostic (new imaging) capability 2. Clinical expertise 3. Rapport among faculty 4. Good case material (huge referral pool)
(W) Weaknesses	1. Poor relationships with media and legislature 2. 50 percent of budget used for hospitals with few patients 3. Displaced workers 4. Civil service disincentives to employees	1. Budget cuts leading to service cutbacks 2. Influence of outside agencies over bureau 3. Increasing health care costs 4. Political vulnerability 5. No way to evaluate program impact	1. Poor collaboration 2. Poor work environment 3. Lack of research effort 4. Poor staff support
(O) Opportunities	1. Close hospitals and use funds for community centers 2. Train displaced staff 3. Train former patients 4. Patient tracking	1. Legislation 2. Grass-roots support 3. Climate calling for innovation and change 4. Effective lobbies 5. Public support	1. Become more consultant oriented 2. Hire research oriented junior faculty 3. Divert resources to support scholarship (reward scholarship) 4. New leadership
(T) Threats	1. Unstable budget 2. Community fear of released patients 3. Special-interest groups 4. Prisons holding former patients	1. Budget cuts and funding cuts 2. Poor understanding of bureau's role by legislature and state administrators 3. Vague legislation and rules 4. Close identification with welfare	1. Apathy (no interest in changing) 2. Poor administrative support 3. Governmental regulation 4. Turf wars

and social obligations influence the threats and opportunities that impinge on an organization. Many contemporary adaptations tend to ignore values, mandates, and social obligations.

Public-Private Distinctions

The emphasis in the content of SWOTs varies markedly across sectors. First, firms have tight markets and weak political linkages. The reverse is true for public and third sector organizations; markets are loosely defined and authority systems impose constraints such as sunshine laws that force strategy to be created in a "fishbowl" (Blumenthal and Michael, 1979). Second, firms are pulled toward opportunities and public and third sector organizations tend to be driven by threats. Strategy making can be difficult in an environment in which governmental and, often, third sector organizations are expected to do as little as possible, spend as little as possible, make wise use of tax dollars, and avoid acts that deprive firms of the chance to make a profit. In firms, the challenge for strategic management is to recognize threats in an ocean of opportunities. In public and third sector organizations, the process provides a way to identify opportunities in a turbulent sea of threats.

The internal-external distinctions that are made in the Harvard model do not apply to public and third sector organizations. In the Harvard model, strengths and weaknesses arise internally. In public organizations, strengths and weaknesses can arise internally and externally and are not limited to organizational capacities. For private organizations, strengths and weaknesses tend to be more internal and to deal with the organization's distinctive competencies. The Harvard model treats threats and opportunities as external. Organizations with significant degrees of publicness have threats and opportunities that can arise both internally and externally. In firms, opportunities are seen in market terms as propitious niches that can be exploited and threats are seen as vanishing markets. Publicness brings with it the notion of internal threats, such as professional values, that can conflict with organizational aims. Internal opportunities (for example, the realization that collaboration among similar agencies is desirable) as well as external market-based threats and opportunities can also arise.

Stage Three: The Issue Agenda

The first two stages build pressure to get at the core issues that must be managed and usher in Stage Three: establishing the issue agenda. An issue is defined as a difficulty that has a significant influence on the way the organization functions or on its ability to achieve a desired future for which there is no agreed-upon response (Ansoff, 1980). Issues can be internal or external to an organization or both. Public and third sector strategic management groups typically uncover several issues that are priorities for active management, thus creating an issue agenda. The dynamic nature of both the organization and its environmental relations ensures that, over a year or two, the strategic issue agenda will shift, with new items entering and old items disappearing. As a result, the strategic manager must periodically review and update the issue agenda.

As described in Chapter Five, issues are framed in terms of opposing forces pulling or pushing the organization in various directions and away from idealized images of its future. These forces identify the underlying tensions at work on the organization. This format for expressing issues points out contradictions within the organization or between it and other external actors. For example, a mental health center faced with a 50 percent cut in its revenue base due to the phaseout of all federal funds identified "humanitarian values of service for all, without regard to a client's ability to pay, and the need for businesslike approach in the collection of fees for service" as a key issue. The tension in the issue arose from the clash between being "businesslike" and "humanitarian." By forming issues as tensions and confronting the historical context and situational assessment, the SMG begins to appreciate the need to reconcile contradictory pressures, like those faced by the mental health agency. The strategic management group uncovers, discusses, and then ranks developments. The priority developments are then paired with their opposites. A format that

can be used to construct issues as tensions is shown in Form
A.6 (Resource A). The top-priority issue tension is selected for
management.

The issue agenda marks a turning point in the process
for two reasons. First, the remaining activity focuses less on the
context and more on identifying substantive actions to manage
key issues. Second, the issue tensions are reviewed using the
framework in Chapter Five to ensure that each of the considerations posed by the six types of issue tensions have been
weighed. This step expands the horizons of the SMG. It can
be carried out by testing the issue tensions for comprehensiveness at two points. First, the six types of issue tensions can be
used to expand the issue agenda before the first attempt to
fashion strategy. Second, this review can be carried out as a
prelude to revising the issue agenda for another round of fashioning strategy. Ways to carry out process recycles are discussed in the next chapter.

Note that goals are not needed to orient strategic thinking. Instead, participants use reconstructed history and idealized future targets to create an anticipatory mindset. By shifting to an emphasis on currently relevant tensions, the SMG is
able to uncover an agenda of issue tensions to be managed now
instead of goals to be achieved at some distant future. A network of relations is the underlying focus of action, not a linear
movement toward preestablished goals. Our concern with goal
mania is resolved by this shift.

How to Elicit Issues

Issues are identified, organized, and prioritized in a group session with the SMG, using group process and other techniques
described in Part Four of this book. A worksheet useful for
this task is provided by Form A.6 in Resource A.

Issue tensions have important relationships that must be
explored to clarify the order in which the issue tensions should
be attacked. A key relationship is precedence, which captures
the order in which issues should be addressed. Another is producer-product, which captures the causal elements in issue ten-

sions. The primary causal issue merits considering as well. To make these assessments, the SMG compares the issue tensions using procedures described in Chapter Ten. Figure 7.2 shows how the precedence among issues (shown by the direction of the arrows) can be captured to guide SMG activities. Note that precedence is organization specific. Another mental health agency may have similar issue tension but a very different ordering of the issue tensions.

The SMG interprets the network by noting the dangers in dealing with a particular issue tension. For example, the billing issue tension could be selected because it precedes most of the others in Figure 7.2, indicating it has priority. The three issue tensions in the center of the figure show issues with feedback or interaction because the arrows flow both to and from these issue tensions, indicating reciprocal influence. Each of the issue tensions in the center of the figure must be managed along with the billing issue tension to avoid nasty feedbacks. The SMG must keep financial stability, allocation, and staff quality in mind as they consider strategy to deal with the billing issue tension.

Why Issues Are Critical

Issue management is supported by several streams of research. First, issues are emerging as the preferred conceptual focus from which to develop strategy. The notion of an issue agenda is consistent with the way effective managers frame strategic concerns (Kingdom, 1984) and prefer to operate (Buchholz, 1982). Second, framing issues as tensions follows from the arguments we laid out in Chapter Five. In summary, using tensions is consistent with Janusian thinking (Rothenberg, 1979) and the steps Argyris and Schon (1978) find to be essential in cognitive learning. Tensions are similar to the dialectic used by Mason and Mitroff (1981) to fashion policy (strategy). The dialectic produces strong claims and counterclaims that create tensions from which synthesis can emerge. Both Mason (1969) and Sussman and Herden (1985) found that issues expressed as tensions lead to superior planning results.

Figure 7.2. Issue Precedence for a Mental Health Agency.

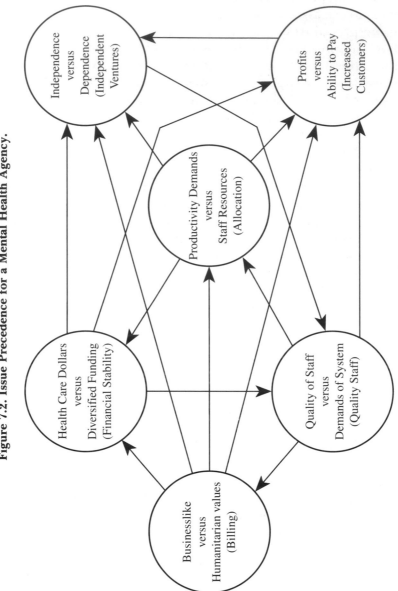

Public-Private Distinctions

Forming issues as tensions seems particularly appropriate for public and third sector organizations. The web of political and market forces facing these organizations often pulls them in several directions at the same time (see Chapter Two), as in the dictum of separation of powers, which causes conflict between judicial renderings and legislative edicts. Responding to one tension without dealing with the other creates serious dilemmas. For instance, dealing with latent demand creates conflict with funding agents calling for budget cutbacks. If this tension is not managed, the organization can be whipsawed by powerful individuals in its authority network. Also, actions by public and third sector organizations often provoke advocacy on both sides of an issue and from many sources, including: the media, treatment professionals, interest groups, and formal branches of government. In firms, these tensions are less complex, typically stemming from the actions of competitors and responses to these actions (Porter, 1985).

Stage Four: Strategic Options

In Stage Four, the strategic management group identifies possible strategic actions to deal with each issue tension on the agenda, beginning with the most important issue tension to be managed. We find that different issue tensions bring out different configurations of strengths, weaknesses, opportunities and threats and different rankings of the items in each. The shifting SWOT priorities allow an SMG to see the complex dynamics at work in the organization. Using the SWOTs as guidelines to generate ideas for action helps the organization come to grips with its complex dynamics.

How to Elicit Strategies

To identify strategic actions, SMG members are given a sheet of paper listing the priority issue tension and priority strengths, weaknesses, opportunities, and threats of the organization. Form A.7 (see Resource A) provides a format. The SMG considers the organization's ideals, suggesting concrete actions to manage the issue tension to *build* on strengths, *overcome* weaknesses, *exploit* opportunities, and *block* or *blunt* threats using an appropriate group process (see Chapter Nine). Actions that address a strength, a weakness, an opportunity, *and* a threat are of particular interest because they can be synergistic (Ansoff, 1980). The issue tension of expanding the role of a bureau of crippled children's services vis-à-vis handicapped children (equity) during a period of fiscal restraint (productivity) coupled with the SWOTs for the agency (shown in Table 7.2), produced the following suggestions.

Building upon Strengths

- Make the public aware of the costs of care and the costs of not receiving care.
- Draw upon outside expertise to sell the program to the counties, the staff, the medical advisory committee, and so on.
- Lobby the legislature using outside support groups and professional organizations to show how the bureau contains costs.

Overcoming Weaknesses

- Work on IHC rules and state law.
- Use staff and consumer groups to influence the state health department director, legislature, and governor.
- Redefine program as preventive and expand prevention activities.
- Coordinate preventive aspects with genetics, family planning, and child health departments.

Exploiting Opportunities

- Collaborate with other state department of health programs, other agencies, and the medical advisory committee to expand on health prevention activities for children.

• Project the program's image as innovative, preventive, and cost saving.

Blocking Threats

• Market, sell, and lobby the bureau to the legislature and get other departments to help.
• Emphasize quality of care, uniqueness, and differentness from welfare (for example, middle-class families are helped).
• Do planning using diagnostically related groups (DRGs) or prospective payment, long-term, and contingency plans if not enough funds.

Strategic Themes

A strategy is made up of action ideas that have a common theme. The SMG is asked to identify a label for related ideas to suggest themes, using techniques discussed in Chapter Ten. Themes can emerge from ways to initiate action that launch a new program, identify resultant consequences and outcomes of actions, or describe a process made up of a series of actions. The themes that emerged from SMG consideration in the bureau of crippled children's services are shown in Figure 7.3 (a full discussion of these themes appears in Chapter 15).

The relationships present in strategies are determined using procedures like those applied to issue tensions. The SMG compares each strategy to all other strategies to identify the degree to which the strategies influence one another and the magnitude of these effects. (This ranking procedure is described in Chapter Ten.) The resulting relationships are captured by a network like that shown in Figure 7.3. Note how feedback influences the relationship among these themes and causes important linkages between every one of the strategic themes. This figure illustrates how a strategic action becomes dependent on a multitude of other strategic possibilities that can never be fully divorced from the focal strategy that is receiving attention by the strategic manager.

Figure 7.3. Producer-Product Causal Relationships Among Strategies for Bureau of Crippled Children's Services.

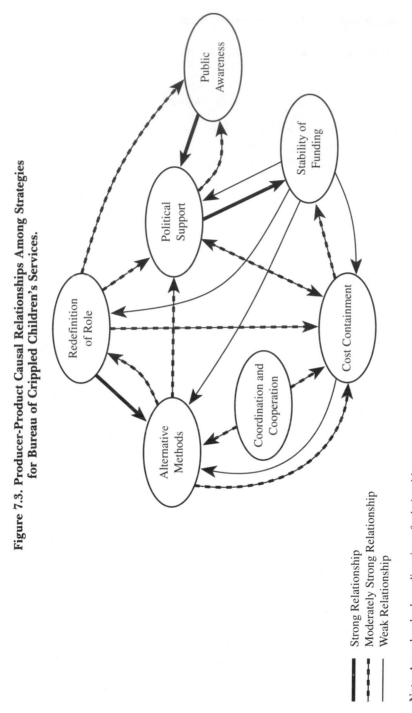

Strong Relationship
Moderately Strong Relationship
Weak Relationship

Note: Arrowheads show direction of relationship.

Why Using Situational Assessment and Ideals to Develop Strategy Is Important

The guarantors for Stage Four stem from the strategic principles inherent in building on strengths, overcoming weaknesses, exploiting opportunities, and blunting threats. The inference that springs from joining the SWOTs with an issue, framed as a tension, leads to more innovative strategic actions than other approaches we have tried.

Public-Private Distinctions

Firms can undertake strategies that call for divestiture, horizontal and vertical integration, acquisition, and other proactive moves that change their domains. Strategies in public and third sector organizations tend to be more reactive, in part because these organizatons typically have jurisdictional or domain limits. For instance, Porter's (1985) "low-cost leadership strategy," which merely segments a market, has no meaning for a fire department or a mental health center. Pure opportunities occasionally arise for service organizations (stemming from new social concerns) and produce honeymoon periods, but these periods tend to be short lived.

Typically, a strategy must take shape as an incremental movement that balances opportunity with threat. For example, in the EPA, being too proactive can crystallize opposition that may hamstring future efforts, but being too reactive forces the EPA to concentrate on putting out fires using threat-management tactics. Opportunities in public organizations can also arise from the coercion to pay for and use a service found in enabling legislation, such as the fluoridation of water. Also, tacit authority to deal with broad societal concerns can produce opportunity. For example, child abuse programs are feasible in public schools even though the public school's mandate may not mention such programs. Carefully managing the tensions inherent in an issue and the SWOTs moves organizations with significant publicness to a new posture that responds to opportunities in a feasible manner.

Stage Five: Feasibility Assessment

The operating environments of public and third sector organizations tend to be complex, as pointed out in Chapter Two. The attempt to introduce new strategies in such organizations ushers in considerations that go far beyond forecasting what services consumers will purchase. In addition to the standard concerns about customer and employee views of changes, political, financial, and legal implications of new strategic actions must be considered.

To deal with this broader set of considerations, a different kind of feasibility assessment is needed—one that differs from traditional feasibility assessments in several ways. First, we call for extended discussions of who will be affected by the new strategy and how other parties could affect successful implementation. This activity is called *stakeholder analysis* because it identifies specific parties who can affect or are affected by the strategy to be introduced (Freeman, 1984). The approach is similar to Mason and Mitroff's (1981) "assumptional analysis" but is modified to deal with stakeholders instead of assumptions (Nutt, 1984a). We focus on the people and organizations with political, financial, managerial, and professional interests or stakes in the strategy and try to anticipate how they might respond as the strategy is communicated and implemented.

Second, our approach determines resources that are required to implement the strategy. Here we also extend our assessment to go beyond finances to consider political, legal, managerial, and professional resources and who can allocate them. Stakeholder and resource analyses clarify the range of joint commitments that must exist or be built between the organization and its stakeholders and resource suppliers to successfully implement the strategy. Top management is largely responsible for building these commitments. The installation of operational and technical designs is delegated to subordinates. The assessments in Stage Five identify key people and power centers that must be managed and resources that must be obtained during implementation.

Identifying Stakeholders

The limitations of time and resources call for the targeting of the high-priority stakeholders. First, the SMG identifies stakeholders for the strategy under consideration. This list often includes users of services, key providers of support, cooperating units, and providers of services. Form A.8 (Resource A) provides a format to collect the needed information.

After the list has been compiled, each stakeholder is ranked in terms of importance and position on the issue. Forms A.9 and A.10 (Resource A) provide a format to collect the SMG's rankings of importance and position. Tallies are made averaging the ratings of the SMG. (The logic behind these rating procedures is discussed in Chapter Eleven.) The ratings are plotted on a grid shown in Figure 7.4. Stakeholders can be interpreted by referring to the grid classifications. Ranking clarifies how much and what kind of power each stakeholder has, suggesting the extent to which each stakeholder can influ-

Figure 7.4. Stakeholder Assessments.

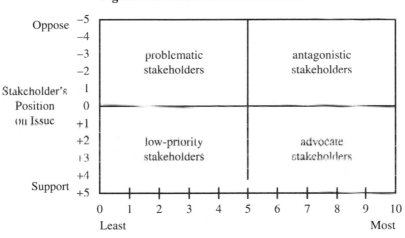

ence the actions required by the strategy. This analysis is used in the next stage for stakeholder management.

Identifying Resources

Resource analysis follows a similar procedure. First, the types of resources required to carry out the priority strategy and who might supply them are listed. Figure 7.5 is presented to the SMG to suggest cues about resources that are crucial and may, at the moment, be excluded.

Both internal and external resources and resource suppliers are often relevant. The forms of assistance can be fiscal and nonfiscal resources, such as labor, power and legitimacy, status, acceptance, knowledge or expertise, time, and existing programs. A resources worksheet is provided by Form A.11 (Resource A). Strategic themes are listed on the left. For each potential strategy, the SMG members list resources thought to be needed for this strategy, specifying type and who or what supplies the resource. This listing is followed by an assessment of actions aimed at getting needed resources.

A ranking procedure similar to that used for stakeholders is used. Resources required by the strategy are assessed in terms of their criticality (importance) and potential availability (ease of finding or mobilizing) by the SMG. Form A.12 is used to obtain ratings of each resource's criticality and Form A.13 is used to get ratings of each resource's potential availability and can also be used to tally the ratings of a group (Resource A).

Average ratings, which reflect group consensus, are plotted on the grid shown in Figure 7.6. The grid allows resources to be interpreted as one of four types. These four types are called *essential scarcity* (critical with low availability), *core support* (critical with high availability), *auxiliary support* (noncritical with high availability), and *irrelevant* (noncritical with low availability). This ranking identifies the resources that must be obtained to ensure that a strategy can be implemented. Using this test before moving to the implementation stage ensures that a strategy has some chance of success.

Figure 7.5. Dimensions of a Strategy Calling for Exploration.

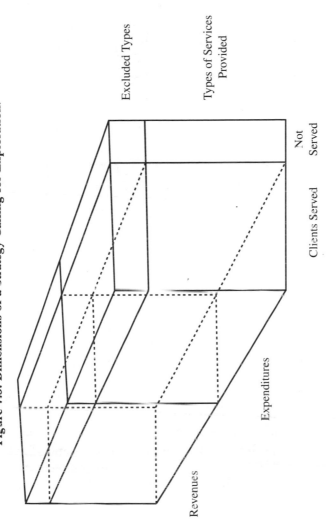

Excluded Types

Types of Services
Provided

Not
Served

Clients Served

Expenditures

Revenues

Boxes identify rules, norms, and criteria for drawing boundaries regarding clients served, types of service, and so on.

Figure 7.6. Resource Assessments.

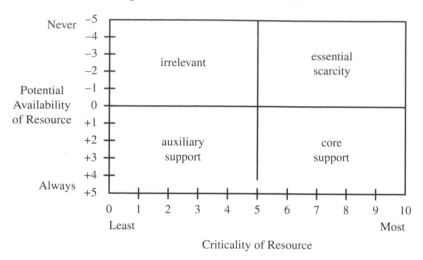

Why Identifying Stakeholders and Resources Is Important

The identification of stakeholders and resources is needed because a cooperative ecology must be in place before public and
third sector organizations can offer new initiatives, such as a
new service. In building these joint commitments, public and
third sector organizations must consider whether this service
could have harmful effects on both users and firms and whether
it can be supported by fees, levies, or tax authorizations (Mokwa
and Permet, 1981; Archebal and Backoff, 1981). The firm, in
contrast, has only to ensure that its products or services are
safe for consumer use and can be sold to consumers. This suggests that the actions of public and third sector organizations
come under close scrutiny from a variety of sources, including
firms. Each action must be managed if implementation is to be
successful.

Public-Private Distinctions

To build joint agreements, public organizations may have to negotiate with oversight bodies to alter jurisdictions. For example, a new Tennessee Valley Authority (TVA) program would have to deal with a host of agencies, such as existing water authorities and bureaus responsible for land reclamation and development. The needed agreements often set precedents that require extensive internal and external negotiations (Allison, 1984).

Everyone is a potential stakeholder in a public organization, which calls for careful assessments of a stakeholder's motives to block the strategy and his or her power to do so. Key people in the organization's authority network can be mobilized to pry resources away from other uses, to support new budget authorizations, or to authorize usage fees that can underwrite the costs needed to carry out a strategy. Either an actual or a potential strategy can be described to call for financial support. Both users and people in the authority network of the organization can draw on political influence that is seldom available to firms. Thus, organizations with public features have both opportunities to underwrite the costs of a strategy and barriers to carrying it out, no matter how financially feasible the strategy may be. Strategic managers in firms tend to ignore external negotiations and often use authoritarian postures in their internal dealings (Nutt, 1986).

Stage Six: Implementation

Our approach to implementation deals with the broad-scale concerns raised by a change in strategy, not with steps to install new procedures. Implementation at this level is described elsewhere (Nutt, 1984a, 1986). In strategic management, programs are devised to monitor and evaluate stakeholders' predicted actions and to manage resource suppliers. Tactics for the management of resource suppliers follow the same line of reasoning as that used for stakeholders.

The SMG examines each of the stakeholder categories in Figure 7.4—the antagonistic , advocate, problematic, and low-priority stakeholders. First, the numbers and proportions of stakeholders in each category are determined. Additional analyses are carried out to suggest the extent of each stakeholder's support or opposition, determine the homogeneity of the stakeholders in each category, determine the prospects for a coalition, and identify neutral stakeholders who could be targeted for lobbying. Finally, the SMG selects tactics for dealing with each of the stakeholder categories (Freeman, 1984).

Tactics to consider for potentially antagonistic stakeholders include the following:

1. Identifying potential coalitions by determining which neutral actors in the problematic and low-priority categories are closely aligned or related to the antagonistic stakeholders
2. Taking steps to block coalitions of antagonistic stakeholders with those in the problematic category
3. Preventing antagonistic stakeholders from undermining supporters
4. Determining which antagonistic stakeholders must be surprised (kept in the dark) to prevent them from mobilizing their opposition
5. Anticipating the nature of objections and developing counterarguments for selected antagonistic stakeholders
6. Engaging selected antagonistic stakeholders in bargaining and determining strategic changes that will ensure their neutrality, if not their support

Potential advocates are managed differently. The following tactics are suggested:

1. Providing information to reinforce advocates' beliefs
2. Co-opting key supporters into some of the SMG's deliberations or as members of the group
3. Asking supportive stakeholders to sell the strategy to those who are indifferent

4. When a balanced perspective is needed, asking stakeholders who are thought to be nearly neutral to react to the strategy after supporters and critics have taken their positions

Problematic stakeholders pose fewer management problems. Some precautions are desirable, however, such as the following:

1. Preparing defensive tactics to be used if a coalition of problematic stakeholders emerges and takes a public position opposing the strategy
2. Targeting moderates for education attempts
3. Redefining the strategy so strongly negative stakeholders opt out

Finally, low-priority stakeholders need to be managed only under special conditions, such as when they are homogeneous and numerous. Tactics include the following:

1. Providing low-cost education for those near the boundary of important and unimportant stakeholders
2. Promoting involvement with supporters to demonstrate depth of support for a strategy

Scenarios are often used to simulate how key stakeholders will respond and to develop tactics that deflect their claims. For instance, Bardach (1977) offers archetype situations that can be explored to anticipate how key stakeholders may react (Nutt, 1983, 1984a).

Stakeholder Management

Figure 7.7 identifies stakeholders for the mental health center and its "scholarship" strategy. (The scholarship provides a grant of a specific sum to a patient to defray treatment costs, with the proviso that the agency can pursue fee collection with appropriate parties when the grant runs out and will charge one

Figure 7.7. Classification of Stakeholders for a Mental Health Center.

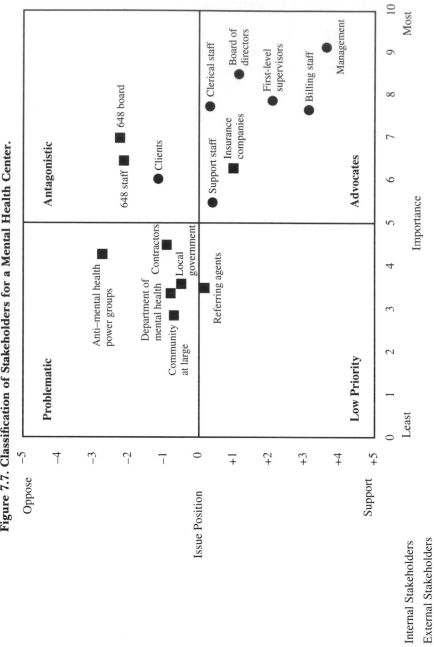

● Internal Stakeholders
■ External Stakeholders

198

fee for each type of service. See Chapter Thirteen for details.) The importance of the stakeholders in the antagonistic category suggested a need for considerable caution. Stakeholders who were closest to a neutral position (clients) were approached initially. The SMG attempted to win these individuals over. The center held public meetings to involve clients in careful discussions of the issues, asking for their suggestions of ways to replace lost sources of revenue.

Many of the external stakeholders were problematic because they were very important. For the problematic stakeholder, initial implementation avoided prematurely drawing attention to the scholarship strategy. The SMG also assessed those stakeholders to determine whether coalitions among them were possible and the probable implications of such coalitions for the scholarship strategy. For example, a coalition was possible between the state department of mental health and local governments. So the SMG took steps to allay local government officials' fears, assuring them that the mental health center did not anticipate asking for funding from local governments.

Next, the community at large was targeted for education attempts, using the mass media. From that point, the implementation moved to industry contractors. The center made presentations attempting to convert these stakeholders to at least a neutral, if not a supportive, position. Then, the center was ready to deal with the members of the contracting agency's board and its staff. This agency was empowered to contract for mental health services using state funds. These potentially antagonistic stakeholders presented a crucial barrier to implementation. The SMG anticipated objections to dropping the sliding-fee scale and developed counterarguments.

The center also developed a "downside" scenario: it described various actions, such as cutbacks in services and the like, that the center would have to take if a larger proportion of its service costs could not be reimbursed. The analysis included the proportion of its costs that it currently captured and showed different targets, associating various downside possibilities with each target. For example, after federal cutbacks, revenues would be at 50 percent of costs; therefore, the center articulated scenarios at the level, at 65 percent, and at 95 percent, representing the current untenable situation, a problematic situation, and a good situation, respectively. The mental health center's scholarship strategy was presented as a way to preserve the humanitarian nature of its mental health services while assuring the center's survival. (This use of the scenario technique is discussed in Chapter Nine.)

Resource Management

The SMG examines the resources found in each resource category in Figure 7.6 to determine the number and proportions of resources in each category. The first assessment contrasts the number of resources in the "essential scarcity" category with those in the "core support" category. A strategy that relies on scarce resources, not deferred in the last stage, may be feasible if one of two approaches are followed. First, some resources can be shifted from auxilliary support to core support by changing their targeted audience or intended use. This step may require outside approval by the organization's authority network. Second, internal reallocations, dropping some activities, and rebudgeting, may be desirable for very important strategies. This step also may require outside approval. Third, appeals to key stakeholders known to be advocates can be made to promote more funding, user charges, and reallocations among programs that would make the strategy feasible.

Stakeholder management can be carried out for proactive promotional activities as well as defensive ones. Calling for support from key users and important people in the organization's authority network is often feasible and useful.

If sufficient resources can be found in the core support category (or shifted there, using the tactics cited previously), the SMG is polled to verify the actions needed to tie these resources to the strategy. Information gleaned from Form A.10 is summarized and reviewed to ensure that all appropriate bases have been identified. With an appreciation of this information, the strategic manager is prepared to act to install the strategy.

Why Resource and Stakeholder Management Are Important

Resource and stakeholder management are often overlooked in strategic management procedures. A careful consideration of what is needed to make strategy implementation possible and steps that must be taken to secure the needed support are essential components of strategic implementation. These steps are important because barriers to action can be pervasive in public organizations. In dealing with stakeholders and resource suppliers, strategic managers must use political instead of power tactics. Tactics such as edicts and intervention (Nutt, 1986, 1989b) assume a level of power that does not exist in most public and third sector organizations. Indirect tactics, such as co-optation, must be used in forums that include legislatures, courts, open hearings, public and press briefings, and interest group negotiations (Bryson, 1984).

Public-Private Distinctions

Publicness brings with it constraints, political influence, authority limits, scrutiny, and ubiquitous ownership, as discussed in Chapter Two. These factors make implementation more complex in public organizations, calling for more elaborate procedures that differ from those used in private organizations, such as the local steel mill.

The beliefs and demands of key people in an authority network and of users can be fickle, shifting without notice, but still play a major role in determining what types of change will be accepted in welfare reform, whether or not to drop a popular concert series, and the like. Constraints and authority limits make it essential to carefully manage external as well as internal stakeholders. Authority limits often pose significant problems in finding the resources needed to underwrite strategic action, no matter how meritorious. Private organizations have fewer needs to manage external stakeholders and face fewer constraints in finding needed resources. As a result, private organizations have less difficulty with implementation.

Key Points

1. The strategic manager is called on to work with the SMG to discover or rediscover historical context, carry out a situational assessment, develop an agenda of issue tensions, identify strategic options for priority issue tensions, assess feasibility by exploring the resource and stakeholder support needed to carry out priority strategy, and engage in stakeholder and resource management to implement the strategy.
2. The strategic manager works with an SMG to carry out process stages by dealing with a series of activities that gradually build a shared understanding of needs and various ways to act. This process of "coming to know" is an essential ingredient in both strategy formation and implementation.
3. The proposed process is built on key ideas in strategic management, augmented by steps and stages designed to deal with the unique needs of organizations that have significant degrees of publicness.

Chapter Eight

■   ■

Tailoring
the Process
for Specific
Needs

■   ■

A strategic management process is assembled from the six stages discussed in Chapter Seven. This chapter provides facilitators and strategic leaders with three approaches to strategic management called *focused action, regeneration,* and *continuous change.* Strategic management for focused action can be applied in a one-day retreatlike setting, where the organization seeks to establish an arena in which to act or to introduce strategic concepts. Regenerative strategic management provides the organization with an in-depth exposure to strategic possibilities as a prelude to making a critical change or becoming more proactive strategically. The continuous change approach calls for ongoing strategic management in which a strategic leader moves through process stages to update and revise an action program that continually identifies and appraises change possibilities.

Strategic Management for Focused Action

A one-day retreat to do strategic management can be organized in several ways, depending on organizational needs and the success of previous attempts at taking strategic action. A common request is to reorient the thinking of a key group, such as a board of trustees or a group of senior managers, to get them to begin to think strategically. Third sector organizations such as chambers of commerce, state nursing associations, and university departments increasingly face watershed situations in which the organization's leadership must find new ways to do business. Public organizations tired of periodic upheaval and lack of progress are also becoming restive and are looking for new ways to rethink their aims and programs. Such organizations want to explore different ways of doing business.

Another frequent reason for holding a retreat is to work on a crucial issue that has nasty implications and calls for rapid action. For example, the Veterans Administration (VA) hospital system was faced with severe budget cuts that would curtail development of new programs and force the termination of some existing programs in VA hospitals. Key VA managers had to develop an awareness of this issue and see its ramifications before they could work out "who gets what." Both fairness as well as current and future programs that were thought to be excellent had to be considered to make choices for the next budget cycle. The leaders of organizations confronting the need for strategic change often test what they can do in a one-day retreat that involves senior managers and other key stakeholders.

To fit the process into a one-day time frame, several abbreviations can be made. The stages related to historical context and implementation (Stages One, Five, and Six) are deleted. Situational assessment, agenda building, and fashioning strategy are then carried out in a truncated fashion. Although these abbreviations prohibit the kind of reflection we believe to be important, this approach does give an appreciation of the nature of strategic development and can help key people come to grips with short-term needs that call for strategic action. By participating in the development of strategy, these actors acquire an appreciation of the nature of strategy and its importance. Ideas for focused action provide a useful by-product for awareness sessions. Organizational leaders interested in making a highly focused strategic change can put the change in context and begin to see crucial interconnections that pose barriers to action by using a one-day retreat.

Format for a One-Day Retreat

The one-day session is typically carried out to collect some of the information required by process Stages Two, Three, and Four, although many variations are possible. In the discussion that follows, an overview of the steps for a one-day session is provided, along with an example and notes about the insights that can be realized from a single day devoted to strategic management.

Steps. Activity begins with an introduction that orients the participant's thinking. Each of the activities to be undertaken is reviewed and its purpose and the expected results are pointed out. (The orientation discussed in the next section of this chapter can be used.)

A group made up of key participants lists SWOTs using a silent reflective group process (see Chapter Nine). Form A.5 can be used to gather and record the results (see Resource A). Each group member silently makes a list of the strengths, weaknesses, opportunities, and threats believed to be important. The listing of the SWOTs is done simultaneously by a facilitator, who takes one strength, weakness, opportunity, and threat from each group member with each pass. Ranking (see Chapter Eleven) is used to prioritize the SWOTs. Usually only the two or three top-ranked SWOTs are considered to avoid becoming overloaded with information. The orientation and SWOTs listing usually takes about one-half day.

In the afternoon session, the group uncovers issues, again using a silent reflective group process. Form A.6 can be used (see Resource A). The issues are prioritized using one of the faster rating techniques described in Chapter Eleven. The priority SWOTs and issues are listed together using Form A.7. Each group member reflects to find strategic actions that build on strengths, overcome weaknesses, exploit opportunities, and blunt threats. Again, a silent reflective group process is used along with one of the rating techniques that can be carried out quickly.

An Example. A VA district with thirteen member hospitals used this approach to confront anticipated budget cuts. The district's budget was to be reduced, perhaps severely, and a contingency plan for cuts was needed. VA district leaders were asked to oversee the development of contingency plans without any real authority to enforce changes such plans would bring. Each hospital had distinctive competencies, and each had proposals to increase its current range of services, many of which would duplicate services elsewhere in the district's hospitals. The need for cutbacks had to be jointly appreciated and agreements concerning the need to give up some current activities had to be secured.

A planning group made up of each of the thirteen hospitals' chief executive officers was formed for a one-day session. After orientation, the SWOT procedure was carried out with the following results, listed in priority order.

Strengths

1.   Program diversity.
2.   Medical school affiliations and professional staff.
3.   Political support of veterans.

Weaknesses

1.   No bases to allocate resources among hospitals.
2.   Nearby hospitals offer the same services.
3.   Declining budgets and no way to reduce manpower because of union contracts.

Opportunities

1.   Shared service program in Department of Defense hospitals offers a prototype.

2. Political support for VA hospitals is strong.
3. Sharing among hospitals currently being done on a limited basis could be expanded.

Threats

1. Veterans are moving to the Sun Belt, which signals future declines in occupancy.
2. Loss of budget and weak VA image as source of care.
3. Competition among hospitals for esoteric services.

The afternoon session produced two key issues: mission changes for each VA hospital and ways to deal with the declining VA population. The following tensions were identified for these issues:

1. Mission changes (transition) versus fairness (equity)
2. Mission changes (transition) versus excellence (productivity)
3 Declining population (productivity) versus mission change (transition)

The tension of mission change versus excellence was used to identify strategic actions. Themes in these actions suggested the need to redefine each hospital's mission to ensure excellence and led to the following actions:

1. Each hospital would inventory its services and identify at least two services that could be dropped without damaging the hospital's distinctive competence.
2. Each hospital agreed to modify its mission to account for the downsizing.
3. Demographics would be studied to determine the ideal location of new services, given expected shifts in population. (For example, needs of older veterans would be declining and the Vietnam and Gulf War veteran's needs would be stable or increasing.)
4. Each hospital agreed to make at least two proposals for downsizing of operations in which costs would be cut.

The movement of this group in one day was quite re-markable. Most of the group members expressed surprise at the extent of cooperation and compromise that was achieved.

Uses of the Insights Produced. The one-day session can seldom fully penetrate the complex set of concerns that confront most organizations and offer remedies. The absence of ideals makes targets implicit. As a result, different images of a desired future may be used by each group member to make suggestions, and these images may not be shared. Disagreements often stem from these unspoken assumptions about aims. Also, a historical context must be assumed. Again the assumptions made by each group member can be off target or not agreed to by others.

So what can be learned? The one-day retreat suggests what can be done with more effort and a more realistic time commitment. The notion of strategic action can be conveyed, helping key groups get up to speed about strategic management and pointing out whys and hows. Coming to know an issue and its importance allows key participants to see the need for compromise in order to take action, as in the VA case. The VA hospitals were able to produce a workable agreement in which each hospital agreed to give up something of value to preserve crucial capabilities.

Strategic Management for Regeneration

Organizations faced with the need to alter their programs and practices but struggling to find an approach that can be used to make the needed changes often carry out one cycle of a strategic management process with a facilitator in the role of group leader. The facilitator is both the teacher, showing how to carry out strategic management, and the focus of action taking for the initial cycle of the process. The organizational leader usually participates in the SMG or, in rare instances, merely observes the process. This approach to strategic management offers process learning coupled with idea development. The facilitator shows how the process can work and in doing so trains people by demonstration. Drawing on this book as a reference, facilitators can select process stages and techniques that can be used to carry out each process activity, thereby shaping the process to user needs. After this initial cycle, strategic management becomes the obligation of the organization leader. The need for and virtue of strategic change would be periodically considered as dictated by trends and events. One cycle of the process can uncover an agenda of issues, provide strategies to deal with the priority issue, and provide an implementation plan for this strategy.

Figure 8.1 depicts one way to organize the stages of a strategic management process that we have successfully used in the past. In the figure, boxes with solid lines represent activities that occur at the same time or the same meeting. Boxes with dashed lines indicate information collected by survey. The boxes at the top of the figure identify the discrete number of meetings or steps that were taken to complete one cycle of the process.

To show how this process unfolds, one cycle of the process is described in Figure 8.1. The time to complete the first cycle of the process can vary considerably by lengthening or shortening meetings. The example shown in Figure 8.1 has six sessions of approximately four hours in duration, every two weeks. These meetings and activities can be configured in many other ways, as we demonstrate in the cases located in Part Five. Other workable combinations would include twelve two-hour sessions and nine three-hour sessions.

Waiting longer than two weeks between these sessions leads to lost momentum. Holding sessions more frequently than every other day can be logistically difficult, both for participants and facilitators, who must do summaries and tabulations between meetings. Waiting more than two weeks between sessions results in memory loss and the need to remotivate participants. Whatever the choice, each SMG member must be prepared to invest at least twenty-four hours to initiate this type of strategic management process. The twelve activities required in regenerative strategic management are listed below:

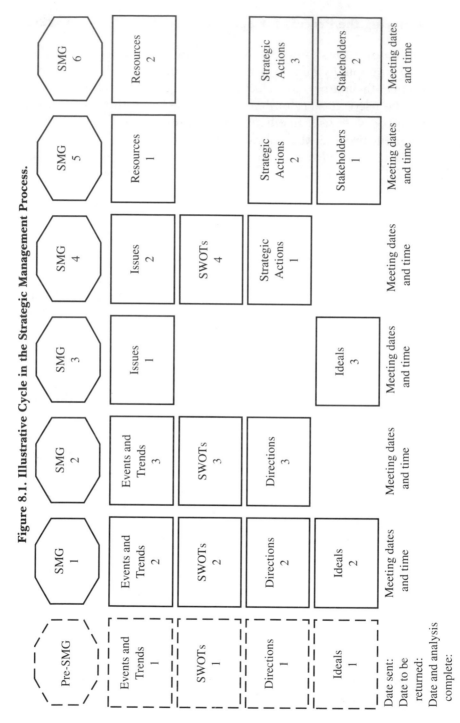

Figure 8.1. Illustrative Cycle in the Strategic Management Process.

1.   Document trend and events
2.   Identify strategic direction
3.   Determine ideals
4.   Carry out situational assessment (SWOTs)
5.   Set strategic issue agenda
6.   Identify issue-relevant SWOTs
7.   Generate strategic actions
8.   Synthesize strategic themes
9.   State strategic criteria
10. Select strategy for implementation
11. Analyze stakeholders and resources
12. Implement the selected strategy

Pre-SMG Activities

The first process activity calls for data gathering in which SMG members are polled to determine historical context. Situational assessments are collected in this same way. These steps provide substantial background information about events and trends, directions (organized according to the demands or needs, resources, program, and management practices), ideals, and SWOTs. This information is summarized to create lists that sum up the results of the surveys. Typically, a long list of items in each topic area is obtained. The summary mixes suggestions from each respondent, interposing ideas to ensure a complete review by the SMG members.

Formats useful in collecting this information are provided in Resource A. We find that a modified Delphi survey (Chapter Nine) can be used to poll SMG members prior to the first meeting (pre-SMG in Figure 8.1). Form A.1 in Resource A provides a letter useful for orienting SMG members, describing the recommended steps to fill out Forms A.2, A.3, A.4, and A.5 that we use to collect directions, events and trends, ideals, and SWOTs. In some instances, a second round Delphi is used to rank the items collected by each survey. Illustrations of the information obtained from these surveys can be found in the cases described in Part Five.

Session One

In session one, the members of the SMG are given a brief orientation to strategic management in which the purposes of the process, the role of the facilitator, and expected results are explained.

The first meeting (SMG 1 in Figure 8.1) is called to review, discuss, and rank items on these lists drawn up in the pre-SMG session. In this meeting, the SMG members become acquainted with concerns that have a historical origin and begin to confront the current situation facing the organization. Typically, a review of the items on each list is made, one at a time, beginning with events and trends. Discussion turns to directions, then ideals, and finally SWOTs. This ordering is essential for the group to come to grips with significant contextual concerns that the organization must respond to. Discussion terminates with ranking (procedures for ranking are discussed in Chapter Eleven).

The SMG reviews priority events and trends to position the organization in the milieu that describes its environment. This review is followed by a discussion of organizational directions. During the discussion of directions, the SMG members become aware of where the organization is going, and they highlight directions thought to have crucial importance. In each case, discussion is followed by a ranking to specify importance.

Ideals are discussed to establish where the organization should be going, in contrast to where it is going, given its direction. Discussion is directed toward selecting elements in the suggestions for ideals that can be amalgamated into a coherent statement in subsequent meetings. The elements suggested by the SMG for ideals are ranked at the end of this discussion.

The SWOTs lists are discussed and ranked as the last step in this meeting. Discussion is directed toward appraising the importance of the strengths, weaknesses, opportunities, and threats that were suggested by the SMG during the premeeting survey.

Session Two

The tabulated rankings provide the focus of discussion in session two (see Figure 8.1). This discussion centers on which items in the lists of trends and events, directions, and SWOTs will be emphasized and which will be treated as less urgent or important. Session two continues to center on historical context and situational assessment, bringing out what is crucial about each. This procedure gets the SMG members to gradually build their knowledge by engaging in periodic reappraisals of past actions to create a joint understanding of context and situation. Group process techniques that can be used to manage these sessions are discussed in Chapter Nine, and guides to select an appropriate group process are discussed in Chapter Twelve.

Session Three

The SMG briefly reviews the priority events and trends, directions, and SWOTs from the previous session. Attention then shifts to a review of ideals, which is followed by issue identification. Form A.6 can be used for issue identification (see Resource A), using an appropriate group process (Chapter Twelve).

Ideals are formed by an analysis of the priorities assigned to elements that make up ideals in the vision of each SMG member. This summary is presented for review and comment. Often this review produces suggestions to fine tune the statement. Suggestions are incorporated in the ideals statement that will guide subsequent actions.

Issues are identified using one of several group processes that can produce discovery and encourage disclosure (Chapters Nine and Twelve). Issues are identified, discussed, combined, and then ranked. This combination, or integration, is managed using synthesis techniques to cut the issues to a manageable set of four to seven critical issues expressed in the tension format. Sorting is carried out to identify relationships among the issue tensions, such as precedence and producer-product, using techniques described in Chapter Ten.

Session Four

The SMG continues its review of prior actions, both to evolve its commitments and its understanding. Review in session four considers all of the concerns addressed thus far but concentrates on issues. The structure among key issue tensions is reviewed using the precedence and causality relationships. Figures 7.2 and 7.3 in the previous chapter provide examples of precedence and causality relationships. The issue tension selected for management usually precedes the others and tends to be produced instead of being a product of the others. Forms to collect this information can be found in Resource B.

This review sets the stage for the generation of strategic actions. Form A.7 can be used with an appropriate group process (see Chapter Nine) to generate strategic actions. As with issue tensions, discovery is emphasized but in identification of strategies, creativity and innovation are also sought. The ideals, the issue tensions and the SWOTs are used as cues to generate action. The list of actions is subjected to synthesis to identify five to ten strategic themes, or core strategies, and is sorted to identify important relationships, such as precedence and producer-product using techniques discussed in Chapter Ten.

Session Five

A review of strategic themes and their relationships is carried out to orient the group to implementation concerns. The key strategy emerges from the precedence and producer-product (causality) analysis. As with the core issue, the priority strategy precedes and tends to produce the other strategies. This core strategy is used to focus a discussion about stakeholders and resource controllers that is essential to implement the strategy. Forms A.8 and A.11 are used to collect this information. Resources and stakeholders are identified, using a group process, and ranked to create the assessments shown in Figures 7.4 and 7.6 in the previous chapter, using Forms A.9, A.10, A.12, and A.13.

Session Six

In this session, key stakeholders and resources for the priority strategy are identified. Tactics are selected to deal with stakeholders and resource controllers using the approach described in the implementation stage.

The final area of discussion in this session deals with ways to continue the process. It can be treated as a one-time event, used to select a way to reposture the organization. However, it is more desirable to "recycle" on issue tensions or strategies and work through the list by devoting some time to strategy making in subsequent meetings of the organization's management. Strategy making is a crucial activity that merits considerable time and attention by organizational leaders on a continuing basis.

Process Recycles

The strategic management process recycles in several ways, as shown in Figure 8.2. This figure captures the four types of management required in fashioning strategy, the information carried forward, and the points where feedback can occur between these blocks of activity.

The most basic recycle is found in the innermost box of Figure 8.2, called *action management.* In action management, the SMG cycles between Stages Four, Five, and Six to fine tune strategy and set in motion ways to implement strategy. Action management is a variant of the focused-action strategic management process, in which issues are taken as given and implementation is added. Feedback shown at the bottom of Figure 8.2 provides information that indicates degrees of success and failure, suggesting the need for new ideas and ways to fine tune old ones. Both innovation and acceptance are key concerns in action management.

Including issue tensions in the recycling process creates *issue management.* The recycle moves back to pick up another issue tension and generates strategy to deal with the new issue

Figure 8.2. Recycling of the Strategic Management Process.

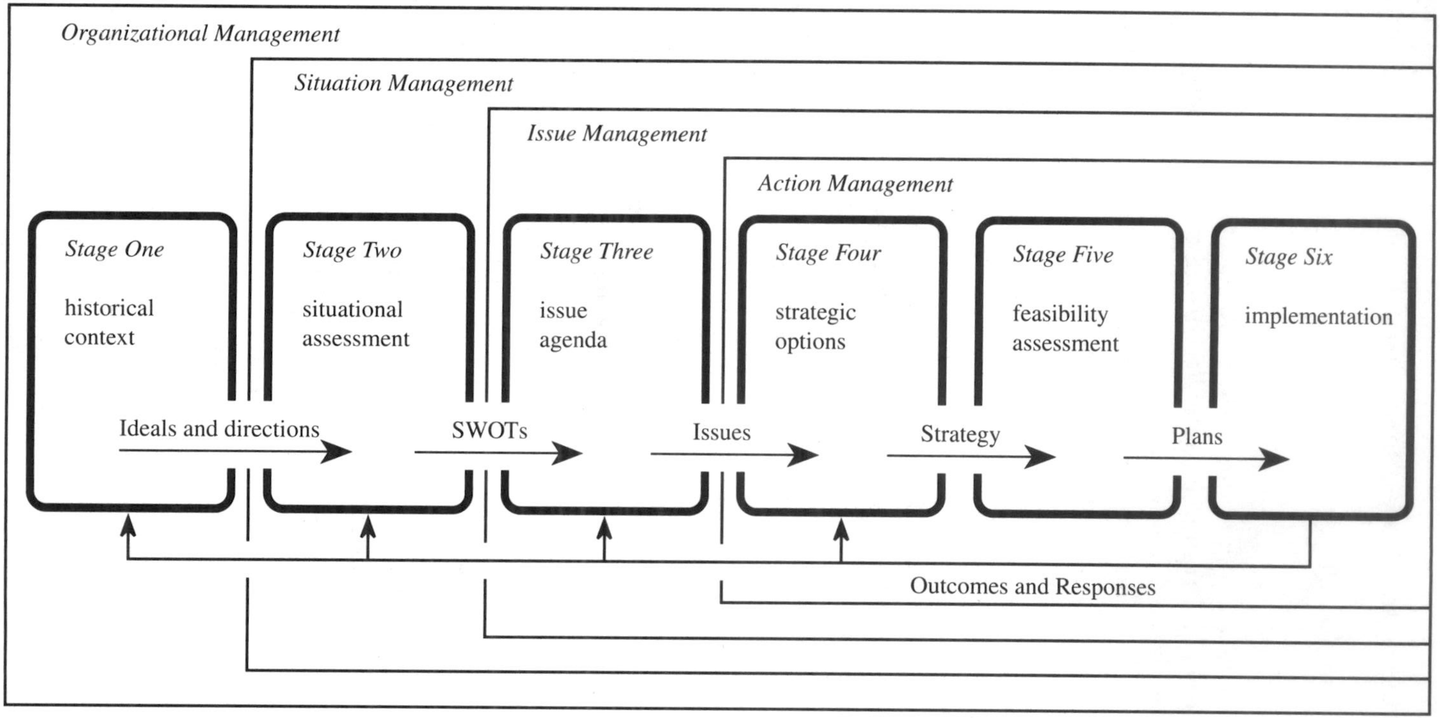

Organizational Management

Situation Management

Issue Management

Action Management

Stage One	Stage Two	Stage Three	Stage Four	Stage Five	Stage Six
historical context	situational assessment	issue agenda	strategic options	feasibility assessment	implementation

Ideals and directions → SWOTs → Issues → Strategy → Plans

Outcomes and Responses

tension. The issue agenda is reviewed and modified with each recycle (Figure 8.2). The key concerns are of agenda building disclosure and discovery.

Including a SWOTs review in the recycle produces *situation management*. As with the list of issues, the SWOTs list is revised and updated. The key concerns of situation management are recognition and disclosure.

Finally, *organizational management* occurs as the SMG revises its ideals vis-à-vis trends, events, and directions. This inquiry is carried out to determine if strategic action has changed directions enough so that the organization can reach its ideals. This analysis also picks up new events and trends that are significant enough to challenge the process anew. The key concern of organizational management is discovery and finding values that require preservation.

These recycles occur at various time periods throughout an organization's life. Emphasis shifts from understanding to action taking as salient needs emerge and the organization begins to understand what works by taking action. The notion of continual strategic management should be clear from this discussion. A single cycle through the process can help make regenerative change, but continually attending to the requirements of strategic management is needed to forge the ideas and relationships required to enable an organization to grow and evolve in meaningful ways.

Strategic Management for Continuous Change

Process recycles lay out the steps to follow in carrying out strategic management to produce continuous change. Ideally, a strategic management process is carried out in a continuous manner in which the process is flexibly applied to guide the deliberations of an organization, shaping and evolving it in beneficial ways.

Action Management

Action management should be viewed as a continuous activity in any organization that is seriously committed to managing strategically. The SMG leader is the key figure in such a process, although SMGs and SMG leadership may be needed at several levels of a reasonably complex organization. Strategic leadership calls for the SMG leader to devote some time to a strategic action agenda on a regular basis. Some action plans may create assignments as delegations to staff or line managers or to task forces. Other actions, particularly actions that are politically sensitive, would remain under the control of a top manager or chief executive officer. The body empowered to act as an SMG is expected to periodically review and appraise progress as it continually develops strategy that addresses issues on the issue agenda.

Issue Management

Periodically, the strategic manager updates and appraises the issue agenda. Updating is done by following the procedures described in this chapter and the last. Appraisal draws on the ideas discussed in Chapter Five.

As a prelude to revising the issue agenda, the strategic manager tests the current issue agenda by classifying issues with the six types of issue tensions described in Chapters Five and Six. This classification reveals some of the dominant values of the organization (Quinn, 1988; Nutt and Backoff, 1992). It also reveals unattended concerns. For example, if productivity developments are linked only to equity and preservation, the organization may be ignoring the need for transition. If any of the six tensions tend to be overlooked in the initial issue agenda, considering the implications of the missing tension is a top priority and should precede further issue identification or dealing with new developments that are clamoring for attention.

As a prelude to a search for missing tensions, the framework discussed in Chapters Five and Six is used to define terms and set out the reasons to consider the types of issues that can confront an organization. The revision of an issue agenda is carried out by searching for issues in each of the six categories. This can be done in one of two ways. A directed search can be carried out for each of the six types of tensions, one at a time. Alternatively, another search for issues can be carried out using procedures discussed in Chapter Seven. The results of this search can be classified by the SMG to identify gaps. A second search is then carried out to fill the categories that seem underrepresented or have been ignored.

A search directed toward each of the six types of issue tensions is more apt to uncover hidden concerns that the organization has failed to face in the past. Disclosure of hidden concerns can be difficult during the first attempt at strategic management. Therefore, we also incorporate these steps as an aid to revise the issue agenda. In other instances, it is desirable to develop the issue agenda with the tension framework before strategic action is sought. In both cases, the search for missing values helps to alert the SMG to important concerns that may be confronting the organization and may have eluded recognition because of value preferences and orientations of key organizational actors. If the organization is aware of these concerns, each can be attended to before it reaches crisis proportions.

There can be considerable variation in the time periods between the revision of an issue agenda. Organizations in volatile environments need a more frequent view of issues than do organizations in stable environments (see Chapters Three and Four). A reasonable guideline calls for annual revision of the issue agenda. However, the time period for revision can range from as little as three months to as much as two years, depending upon environmental volatility.

Situation and Organizational Management

Factors characterizing the situational and contextual features of an organization are less apt to shift abruptly in the short term. New developments are recognized when they take shape as an event or a trend or create a new SWOT entry. More pervasive changes tend to occur over longer time periods due to the subtle interaction of many developments that take emerge in many ways. Together, these changes can deflect organiza-

tional directions away from its ideals. Ideals may also change
with new circumstances, such as the insights that are brought
by new leaders.

Situational changes are more apt to occur than changes
in historical context. The situation merits review in a somewhat
longer time period than issues. Bryson (1988) suggests five years.
This may be too long for some organizations. A two- to four-
year cycle corresponds to elections, creating a sensible review
period for federal, state, and many local agencies. Again, environmental volatility stipulates the frequency of revision. Annual funding drives, like those of a United Way agency, create
the need to review the organization's situation yearly. In other
instances, a situation can be stable for long periods. A five-year
cycle for situational reappraisal is a reasonable upper limit.

Historical context can be expected to change less frequently than the situational context. A guideline for revision is
twice the time period allowed for situational reappraisal. This
produces a two- to ten-year review period, depending on the
volatility of the organization's environment.

Management of Change

The strategic manager can meet the strategy-making requirements of his or her job by following the guidelines in Figure
8.2. These guidelines call for four cycles of activity. Organizational management is carried out every two to ten years to appreciate historical context by denoting key events and trends
that establish directions away from ideals. Situational assessment searches for strengths, weaknesses, opportunities, and
threats in one- to five-year intervals. Situation management takes
the SWOTs and attempts to draw on desirable features of the
situation facing the organizations while deflecting the undesirable. Issue tension management is done in three-month to one-
year intervals to revise the issue agenda. This revision is carried out to search for hidden issue tensions and bring them
out for early management. Action management goes on continually, building responses to deal with priority issues drawn
from the issue agenda. The search for strategy is directed by

current SWOTs and ideals. Implementation follows from each strategy, which is tested for feasibility and carried out by managing the needed resources and stakeholders.

Key Points

1. A strategic management process can be carried out in various ways. Drawing on the stages and steps called for in strategic management, a process can be assembled for one-day retreats, in-depth explorations, and ongoing organizational change. Focused action can apply some aspects of strategic management in a one-day time frame. A process called regeneration provides an organization with in-depth exposure to strategic management ideas as key people work on the priority issue tensions confronting the organization. Continuous change management calls on organizational leaders to incorporate strategic management principles into their agenda of concerns, giving them equal standing with the other activities carried out by a leader.
2. The process of action management is continuous and it involves periodically updating the issue, situation, and organizational management agendas to recognize recent developments that have important implications.
3. The phasing of activities in strategic management calls for a recursive review of key activities to gradually build a joint understanding in an SMG of both organizational context and situation. These reappraisals create a basis and urgency to take strategic action that energize the process of change.

PART FOUR

■   ■

Useful
Support
Techniques

■   ■

Our approach to strategic management has two types of processes. One calls for a movement through six stages that are essential for strategic management, as discussed in Part Three. In the other, the strategic management group moves through three steps that are repeated for each of the six stages. *Search, synthesis,* and *selection* steps are carried out to describe the historical context, conduct situational assessment, form an issue agenda, generate strategy, assess feasibility, and implement strategy.

Information and ideas are sought during search, patterns are uncovered in synthesis, and priority actions are identified in selection. For instance, the SMG searches for issues, forms issues as tensions, identifies relationships (order or importance) among the issue tensions, and selects an issue tension for immediate management. Techniques that can be used to

223

aid the SMG in conducting search, carrying out synthesis, and setting priorities are described in Part Four.

It should be noted that some of these techniques apply to all of the steps. For example, in the nominal group technique (discussed in Chapter Nine), participants search for ideas but also create some synthesis when they combine ideas after listing and create a basis for selection when they set priorities. Other techniques, specifically developed to aid synthesis or selection, can be combined with the nominal group technique to improve the patterning of information and to make the setting of priorities more reliable. Most search techniques can be improved in this manner (Nutt, 1982a, 1984a; Nutt and Backoff, 1987). Combining techniques creates *hybrids* that improve results and add variety to the process. We have grouped techniques under search, synthesis, or selection headings in order to highlight their primary use or value.

Also in Part Four, guidelines are provided to select among the techniques. Performance requirements imposed on a strategy are derived from the strategic manager's expectations. In Chapter Twelve, several techniques are identified that can meet these requirements and offer technique options for the SMG leader or SMG facilitator to draw on. Using a repertoire of techniques that meet performance requirements is more effective than applying one technique over and over again. Without such a repertoire, there is a tendency to rely on past practices, which leads to overusing favored techniques.

Chapter Nine

Search Techniques for Uncovering Information and New Ideas

In the search step, the strategic management group or SMG seeks information that is required for each stage of the strategic management process—identifying historical context; making system assessments; specifying SWOT's, issues, action sets, resources, stakeholders; and so on, as described in Part Three. A number of techniques are particularly useful in the search for such information. These techniques can aid the SMG in uncovering ideas, making judgments, and exchanging views. Each of the techniques shown in Table 9.1 is described in this chapter to show how it works and how it can be used to support the strategic management process.

The categories in Table 9.1 identify classes of techniques with somewhat different benefits. Within each category, the techniques provide opportunities to vary one's approach and produce comparable benefits. Each technique can deal with

Table 9.1. Techniques Useful in Search.

Silent Reflective Techniques
> Nominal group technique (NGT)
> Brainwriting and its variations
> Nominal-interacting technique (NI)
> Kiva technique
> Delphi survey

Interacting Techniques
> Traditional face-to-face groups
> Focus groups
> Dialectic groups

Special Purpose Techniques
> Synectics
> Scenarios

specific types of problems that often arise during strategic management. These virtues are highlighted along with illustrations that show how the technique can be used for various activities called for by the strategic management process.

Silent Reflective Techniques

The process of silent reflection has been developed to overcome the barriers to full group participation and to encourage the development of innovative ideas. During the silent reflection phase, the SMG members feel a certain tension that promotes a form of competition for good solutions. This helps the group avoid superficial arguments, tired diagnoses, and pet ideas that stifle innovation. There are several group processes that use silent reflection, including the nominal group technique (or NGT), brainwriting, the nominal-interacting technique (or NI), kiva, and Delphi.

Silent reflective techniques have three distinct benefits.

First, they have been found to stimulate creativity and innovation in groups (Nutt, 1976a, 1977). New ideas are essential for several activities called for in the strategic management process. Second, silent reflective techniques promote disclosure (Van de Ven and Delbecq, 1974). Disclosure is particularly important in learning about roadblocks, such as weaknesses and threats, that must be confronted and overcome if change is to occur. Third, these techniques encourage acceptance (Nutt, 1976b). The SMG must develop a shared vision of needs and ways to meet them and in doing so agree on actions that should be taken. Silent reflective techniques have a good track record for promoting ownership, enticing the members of a group to support the consensus for action that emerges (Van de Ven and Delbecq, 1974).

Silent reflective techniques require each member of the strategic management group to identify SWOTs, issues, and the like before group discussion begins. There are several difficulties that stem from using an open discussion for such a search. Open discussion entices group members to make premature commitments and hasty evaluations, which keep people from offering potentially valuable ideas and thus shut off useful lines of inquiry (Bouchard and Hare, 1970). Giving group members a chance to reflect before discussion helps to overcome these barriers to candor, stimulates creativity, and increases acceptance of the results.

Silent reflective techniques produce these benefits by following two key principles. Deferring judgment and many ideas breeds quality (Osborn, 1963). These rules are essential for any situation in which innovation and disclosure are valued outcomes.

The value of deferment stems from the distinctions between the judicial and the creative mind. The judicial mind carries out analyses and comparisons that are required to make a choice. The creative mind constructs free associations to visualize new ideas. These mental processes are incompatible. The judicial mind and judgment making tend to dominate in group processes, making the free association needed to be creative impossible. As a result, all forms of judgment are deferred in these processes. Silent reflection creates an environment that allows members of the SMG to visualize ideas without any concern for their acceptability or importance.

Many ideas are needed to innovate. A person's thoughts tend to have a hierarchical structure. The dominant thoughts in the hierarchy are conventional. To get beyond these conventional notions considerable effort is needed to create new associations. The dictum that quantity breeds quality forces the SMG members to exhaust or purge their conventional ideas to get at the creative ones. The silent listing step encourages many ideas, enhancing the prospect of getting at the innovative ideas.

Nominal Group Technique

Nominal groups work silently to encourage reflection (Delbecq and Van de Ven, 1971; Delbecq, Van de Ven, and Gustafson, 1986). The nominal group technique can be applied throughout the strategic management process to identify events, trends, ideas, SWOTs, issues, strategies, stakeholders, and resources.

The nominal group technique (NGT) was derived from the behavioral science literature, tempered by experience. Most groups have an ideation phase and an evaluative phase. Ideation provides a search for ideas, and evaluation screens and merges ideas into a coherent picture. Different steps are best for each phase: silent reflection for ideation and interaction for evaluation. NGT can also control leaders who try to dominate a group through rhetoric, lowering both innovation and member satisfaction. The steps used in NGT control this behavior by ensuring equal participation.

The NGT group should be small, composed of seven to ten members who are seated so they can view each other. An introduction is required to pose the question to be resolved by the group and to give the leader legitimacy in regulating the group's efforts. This introduction should define the issue and introduce the SMG leader or facilitator. The leader outlines all steps in the process. It is quite important that each group member understands the steps and agrees to follow them. When the leader is unknown to the group members, an outside source of authority is often essential to get the group to accept the process.

The nominal group technique has the SMG initially work without discussion to encourage reflection. This reflective phase is followed by a systematic consideration of ideas. The leader begins by stating the purpose of each step in the NGT (identifying trends, ideas, and so on). In step one, each member is asked to write his or her ideas on a pad of paper, without discussion. Those who wish to talk during this phase should be discouraged in a friendly but firm manner. The silent listing phase continues until all SMG members have stopped writing or until a given time period elapses, preferably the former. The SMG leader or facilitator resists all but process questions and works silently to create a role model for the group.

In step two, the SMG leader or facilitator solicits and records ideas from each member. This phase is useful in depersonalizing the ideas and allowing each member equal time to present his or her views. It also provides a written record. Each individual is asked to give one idea from his or her list, which the leader records on a flipchart, taping sheets to a wall when filled. The leader should be sure the member agrees with the written version of the problem before proceeding. The leader rotates among the members, getting their ideas one at a time and recording each on the flipchart so all can see, until members confirm their ideas are exhausted. At this point, several sheets should be taped to the wall in full view of the members. NGT groups typically produce between twenty and forty ideas.

In step three, each idea is discussed. The SMG leader or facilitator asks first for clarification and then the merits and demerits of each item that has been listed. Considerable discussion may result, and the leader should make notes on the flipchart indicating significant elaborations. The leader should avoid focusing on one idea and should point out the logic in each idea by asking for clarification and recording differences of opinion. Consolidation attempts follow, in which the leader merges similar ideas, asking for the consent of the members. The leader must avoid arguments and must leave both options when a consensus to merge them does not develop.

In step four, the group is asked to create a consensus by selecting the most important problems. Several voting techniques that can be used for this purpose are explained in Chapter Eleven. In summary, the four steps in NGT are: (1) silent recording of ideas, (2) listing ideas, giving each member a turn, until the ideas are exhausted, (3) discussing the ideas to consolidate the list and sharing information about the merits of each idea, (4) voting to select a priority list.

Brainwriting

Brainwriting (Gueschka, Shaude, and Schlicksupp, 1975) is another group technique that uses silent reflection. In *cued brainwriting* (Nutt, 1984a), the SMG leader or facilitator initiates the session by placing sheets of paper that contain several written cues (that is, ideas that focus the group's attention) in the center of the table. The SMG participants are asked to take a sheet, read it, and silently add their ideas. When members run out of ideas or want the stimulation of another's ideas, they exchange their current list with one in the center of the table. After reviewing the new list, ideas are added. This process continues until ideas are exhausted.

A variation called *structural brainwriting* induces more synthesis (Nutt, 1984a). Members are asked to list their ideas in particular categories. Cues are provided for particular themes, such as strengths, weaknesses, opportunities, or threats, or for directions, via demand and needs, programs, resources, and administrative systems. After two ideas have been added in each category, the worksheet is exchanged for another member's worksheet in the center of the table. This process continues without discussion, with members exchanging their worksheets until ideas are exhausted or time is called. The structured brainwriting approach creates synthesis around the themes initially selected and allows members to sort within theme options, creating a second form of synthesis. These steps improve the quality of ideas but limit innovation because constraints implied by the cues are considered.

The round-robin recording step of NGT is used to list ideas. (In the structured form, several listing steps are carried out at the same time.) Each member is asked to describe one item on his or her current worksheet. The leader records the ideas one at a time, moving from one member to the next. This listing continues until all members pass. A discussion phase follows, permitting members to comment and elaborate on their ideas or the ideas of others. Prioritizing is the final step.

Nominal-Interacting Technique

An adaptation of the nominal-interacting technique (Souder, 1980) is particularly useful in providing a forum for "anteroom lobbying" during a group process (Nutt, 1984a). Group meetings are held, following NGT or brainwriting steps. The procedure is truncated at several points to allow for lobbying. A special room is provided with refreshments, ostensibly for a break. Between thirty and forty-five minutes are allocated for SMG members to share views and lobby each other. These steps are particularly valuable when considerable accommodation among members is needed because of conflict. The process, adapted from Souder, is shown below:

Round One

Step one: Silent reflective listing (NGT or brainwriting)
Step two: Round-robin recording
Step three: Anteroom lobbying
Step four: Group discussion
Step five: Anteroom lobbying
Step six: Initial prioritization
Step seven: Anteroom discussion
Step eight: Final prioritization

Round Two

Repeat steps three through eight on another day

The NI procedure introduces informal lobbying into the idea generation and ranking procedures. These breaks allow the natural urges that people have to share views and lobby each other to emerge. The SMG leader or facilitator can be more direct, asking SMG members to share opinions, exchange facts, challenge views, and bargain during the break. Members can ask for one another's priorities and their justification. These informal exchanges create mutual understanding and help the group avoid premature closure. Three lobbying sessions typically are needed before final vote on priorities can represent the level of consensus possible in a particular group. Typically, the first session identifies the diversity of opinions. In the second, members begin to adopt or reject ideas. After the third, judgments can emerge based on new understandings.

Kiva Technique

The kiva technique was devised by the Hopi Indians to make important tribal decisions (Nutt, 1989a). The name kiva is drawn from the structure used by the Hopi in their deliberations.

A kiva begins with the key decision body, such as the tribal elders, conducting an open discussion that leads to making preliminary judgments. This group is surrounded by several rings of tribal members, who listen to the discussion. The ring adjacent to the tribal elders is made up of individuals who have status just below that of the inner ring. The rings terminate with adolescents. After discussion, the tribal council moves to the outer ring, and then all groups move one ring toward the center. The group members now in the center discuss what they think they heard, with all others listening. This process repeats until the tribal council is again in the center ring. The council members then reconsider their decision in light of their reflections on what they proposed, aided by reflections on the reflections of others. This type of process is useful for strategic management carried out in decentralized organizations because it can involve many groups or levels in the organization's structure.

A kiva arrangement allows representatives of various groups or levels to reflect on what an SMG proposes and permits an SMG to gather an in-depth appreciation of reactions, and reactions to reactions, before making final decisions. NGT, brainwriting, or NI can be carried out in each circle or an interactive discussion can be used to uncover the views of each circle.

Delphi Survey

A Delphi survey (Dalky, 1967; Delbecq, Van de Ven, and Gustafson, 1986) systematically solicits and collates judgments to form a synthetic group. A series of questionnaires is used. The first questionnaire solicits ideas, information, opinions, or viewpoints and may ask the members to state the rationale behind their ideas. Forms A.1, A.2, A.3, A.4, and A.5 (in Resource A) provide examples of a Delphi format that is often used to gather information prior to the first SMG meeting. Should meetings of the SMG be difficult, due to logistical problems, subsequent questionnaires can be used to consolidate and feed back the ideas and associated rationales to the SMG.

The initial Delphi questionnaire asks broad questions, and subsequent questionnaires are built on responses to the preceding questionnaire. Each SMG member can review the logic behind the arguments of others, which stimulates consensus. The process continues until consensus is reached or sufficient information has been obtained, or it can be terminated with a vote to prioritize the information that has been collected (Nutt, 1984a).

Delphi was devised to do technological forecasting. The Department of Defense applied it to provide up-to-date technological information not readily available in a literature search. It has value when used prior to a meeting because it allows members of a group to efficiently clarify and share views.

Time, skill, and motivation are essential ingredients for a Delphi survey. Delphi participants must have time, writing skills, and the motivation to carefully set out their views. Between ten and fifteen members is a manageable group size using Delphi. The survey can be time consuming. About forty-five days are usually required for three rounds of the survey. This time can be cut to two to three weeks if an initial round of Delphi is used to gather information, such as information on historical context and situational assessment. Steps in the Delphi survey include development of question, development of survey instrument, analysis and feedback, and prioritization.

The Delphi question specifies the query that the panel will consider. Examples include: listing events, trends, directions, ideals, and SWOTs as shown in Forms A.2, A.3, A.4, and A.5. to initiate a process. Delphi can also be used to identify and prioritize issues, strategies, stakeholders, and resources later in the process, as shown in Forms A.6, A.7, A.8, A.10, A.11, and A.12. The first Delphi survey concentrates on getting ideas. The second and subsequent surveys concentrate on elaborating and adding to the ideas. The final surveys can evaluate the feasibility of ideas and establish priorities.

The survey instrument is developed and pretested to eliminate possible biases. The Delphi question is usually posed succinctly, with plenty of space for detailed responses. Sample forms for historical content and situational assessment are provided in Resource A. The participants should be given a deadline within which to respond (usually a week) and told when the next questionnaire will arrive. A week may be required to finish the first analysis. In this analysis, the ideas are summarized and returned to the participants. This list comprises the next questionnaire. A minimum of three days to summarize the results and return them is usually required.

In the second round, members are asked to critique each response, adding still other ideas should they come up. The process is repeated until both the critiques and new ideas stop or for a predesignated number of rounds. The facilitator or SMG leader, with the help of staffers, consolidates the information to find areas of agreement and disagreement and items needing verification. Subsequent questionnaires may take the form of lists of SWOTs, strategies, or so on, with a consolidated commentary of the panel under each. Examples can be found in the cases in Part Five.

Prioritization can be done by voting. Voting usually accompanies the third, and all, subsequent surveys. Each participant is asked to prioritize the list of ideas. Average scores are fed back to the participants for reconsideration in the final round of the survey. The final votes are taken to represent the views of the Delphi panel. In other cases, no final vote is needed. The process is stopped when no new information is obtained or when views seem to have been adequately explored.

Delphi surveys can be used in various ways in the strategic management process. A single survey of SMG members before a meeting can be a time saver, as discussed in Chapters Seven and Eight. Permitting each participant to reflect on the issue raised by the survey over a period of time helps to create consensus. Occasionally, meetings of an SMG can be delayed because of vacations and other member obligations. When this kind of situation arises, Delphi surveys can be used to collect information without a meeting. Delphi surveys can also be used to explore aspects of strategic management with a panel of outside experts, asking for their views of directions or trends If a complete Delphi survey is used, three rounds are minimal: one to list, a second to react and add to the listings, and a final to prioritize. Five or six rounds can be required to get at complex questions.

A Delphi survey is an excellent information dredge. It is also useful when confidentiality is essential, when meetings are costly, and when travel distances are long. Confidentiality can be needed to get suggestions about historical context and situational assessments from various work groups or centers of power in the organization. Ensuring anonymity encourages frank and candid responses for the SMG to contemplate as a prelude to a brainwriting session or discussion. Efficiency is produced by having participants fill out the surveys at their convenience.

Multiple rounds of a Delphi survey can be cumbersome, time consuming, and arbitrary. The individuals who summarize the information must have (or acquire) considerable knowledge to know how to reduce the information obtained

from the survey to manageable proportions. During information reduction, unconscious views held by the summarizer and
preconceived notions can creep in to bias or manipulate the
results. Considerable study is often needed to appreciate the
concerns being expressed by a Delphi panel before the nature
of disagreements and other insights become apparent.

Interacting Group Techniques

Traditional Face-to-Face Group

Interacting groups have no discussion format. Free-flowing and
open-ended discussion is encouraged, and little in the way of
process is provided. The group facilitator uses an agenda to
focus discussion. An SMG with complex interpersonal relationships may require an open discussion environment (Guetzkow
and Simon, 1950; Guetzkow and Dill, 1957; Guetzkow, 1960).
However, an individual in an interacting group will be pro-
foundly influenced by other group members. As a result, group
members will divide their time between the task and the social
environment. When suggesting their ideas, group members must
attend to personal considerations that arise, promoting both
needed information exchanges and acceptance of the decision
that is reached. This step promotes consensus, a feature that
makes interacting groups a superior means of making judgments on key questions, such as which issue tensions or strategies to initially address.

The performance of an interacting group can be improved by dealing with the interpersonal obstacles that occur
in a group. Collins and Guetzkow (1964) provide several guides
based on their review of the literature.

1.   Members of a group will withhold information they know
      to be relevant. To some extent, social rewards like praise
      and solicitous requests for contributions will overcome the
      inhibition to share information.
2.   Group members who lack competence have a depressing

effect on the quality of a group's judgment. A group *can* come to grips with a difficult choice, where some members of the group will lose something, when all members view each other as competent. Demonstrations of competence (such as a group leader citing the past accomplishments of each member) are useful when group members are not acquainted.

3. Group members experience participation penalties when their views are not readily accepted or are rejected outright. A leadership style that stresses good interpersonal relations reduces these penalties, which suggests that leaders with considerable skills are needed to lead judging groups.

4. Groups become inhibited by large status differences among members. Those members who perceive themselves as "high-power" will talk with "low-power" members until they make their status clear; then they will restrict their communication to other high-power members. This behavior creates tension and conflict in the group.

5. The behavior of some members can be inhibiting to the group. Nonparticipants have a chilling effect, as do isolates (people without a clear role). A socioemotional style of leadership is useful to draw out nonparticipants and seek ways for the isolate to participate.

6. Group members who seek gratification from severing and members who seek issue power (changing the course of events) are incompatible and should not serve on the same group.

7. Group members who support their views with logical arguments and show how their views are consistent with the past experiences of other group members have the most influence.

There are important variations to interacting groups that provide diversity and offer specific benefits. Focus groups and dialectic groups are variations that have particular value in strategic management.

Focus Groups

In the focus group technique, outside experts describe opportunities to the SMG. The experts can be brought in one at a time or as a panel, with the intent of provoking a dispute over their differing positions. Focus groups can be useful in informing the SMG and helping it focus on the most pertinent questions before it.

Dialectic Groups

The systematic examination of an idea from several points of view produces a dialectic (Mason and Mitroff, 1981; Emshoff, 1980). For instance, subgroups of the SMG can be asked to develop ideas based on different assumptions about the environment, constituencies, SWOTs, or the like. One subgroup presents its ideas, and the SMG debates the merits of those ideas. The purpose of the debate is to spell out the implication of each strategy, strategic theme, or SWOT and to challenge it by exposing weaknesses in its underlying assumptions. Discussion of two competing alternatives is not a dialectic. A dialectic involves discussion of ideas that are based on different assumptions. For example, a strategic theme can be discussed under assumptions that call for budget increases and budget shortfalls.

Dialectic groups have several benefits. First, the debate forces the group to consider a wide range of information. Pet opinions can be subjected to careful and systematic scrutiny, in which group members note how internal and external stakeholders would view the situation. This leads SMG members to develop fuller appreciation of each other's rationales, which may lead to synthesis and innovation. Dialectic groups may not work, however, when an issue is well structured or when there is preexisting conflict between certain group members.

Synectics

The synectics technique was devised to promote creativity for situations in which new ideas are essential (Gordon, 1961). The facilitator uses the technique to get the SMG to visualize a new perspective and purge preconceived notions. The SMG studies analogies or metaphors to come up with innovative ideas. In the final step, ideas are modified to make them feasible. For example, Velcro fasteners were identified using this procedure. Their widespread use in apparel stems from a proposed, but impractical, application for space suits.

In synectics, creativity stems from the use of analogies and metaphors in a systematic framework to deal with both strange and familiar problems. To enhance comprehension, a metaphor or an analogy is used to make the unfamiliar familiar. Obvious responses cause people to quickly embrace the conventional and not seek the innovative. In such instances, the metaphor or analogy is used to move the problem the distance needed for the group to visualize innovative ideas, making the familiar unfamiliar.

In strategic management, synectics can be applied to discover issues and strategies. Stakeholders and resources can also be examined by looking at them in new ways. Metaphors and analogies create excursions or creative trips to bring home new and hopefully different perspectives about issues, strategies, stakeholders, or resources. The use of analogies and carrying out these excursions are at the heart of the synectics technique.

The process of innovation is both emotional and intellectual. The synectics process seeks to engage a person's preconscious and unconscious to draw out emotional or nonrational linkages through the use of metaphors.

An analogy or a metaphor has been the key to many important discoveries. For example, Einstein used an image of himself riding on a ray of light to develop the theory of relativity. Composers such as Mozart and Tchaikovsky were found to have drawn on some form of image before composing their best works. Handel claimed to have had visions of God before he wrote the *Messiah*. Mental rehearsal has become a key aid in improving athletic performance (Garfield, 1985). Olympic diving coaches have their divers repeatedly think through each motion that they will use, concentrating on producing a perfect score for each dive. Other uses of visualization include the relief of chronic pain and fear management. Images have been used to help cancer patients decrease pain intensity and to reduce fears in patients with phobias.

Innovative organizations have sprung up from imagining a new way to do things. For example, Banana Republic found new ways to sell clothing using a catalogue. Analogies (the popularity of movies such as *Out of Africa*) were used to identify what the company's leaders thought would sell (safari clothing). They found out what sold at flea markets and used clothing stores and reproduced these items for sale by catalogue. Analogies were also used to find new ways to present their wares. Catalogues were thought to all look alike: glossy photos of glossy people in glossy clothes. The founders of Banana Republic looked for something that would speak to a buyer. They merged writing and art, using analogies to their disciplines of journalism and illustration: the ability to get things done fast and to get to the bottom of things. The operation has grown from a cottage industry to the most-demanded store in malls today.

A demonstration of the power of using images can be made by asking a group of executives to identify their problems. The group that is just asked to list problems will find fewer new ideas to pursue than another group that is asked to do a *mental excursion* (Wheatley, Anthony, and Maddox, 1987). Mental excursions are carried out by asking participants to imagine that there is no roof or walls in their place of business. Participants are told to close their eyes and float over their operation without any barriers: they can go anywhere and see everything. In just five to ten minutes, executives who follow this procedure identify many more problems that they have not thought of previously than when they just list problems.

To be successful, synectics teams should have expertise, motivation, and willingness to seek new ideas. A key criterion is expertise—including only people able, both psychologically and intellectually, to deal with the demands of visualizing issues, strategies, and so on. Stein (1975) adds several other qualifications. Group members should have a high energy level and flexibility. Those with demonstrated ability to generalize, seeking the broader picture in a problem, make good group members. In addition, appropriate education and job training are essential. Some potential members are excluded because they have vested interests or a low tolerance for ambiguity and others because they lack up-to-date knowledge.

Either the SMG, a subcommittee made up of SMG members, a mixed group made up of SMG members and others, or members outside the SMG can be used. The synectics participant should be acquainted with all steps in the process. The typical session lasts up to four hours.

The synectics facilitator should have four characteristics: optimism, a grasp of the environment, a capacity to maintain control over personal involvement so others can participate, and a clear understanding of the synectics technique. The last requirement is key, often demanding some training (Stein, 1975).

Synectics, like brainstorming, involves the generation of ideas under conditions of suspended criticism. Attempts are made to get participants to take a trip (mental excursion) to see where their thoughts will lead. The synectics procedure directs members of the team to focus their thoughts using several approaches that can create analogies and metaphors. The excursion is charted by guideposts, which aid members to visualize responses in new ways.

The facilitator begins by first carefully explaining what is wanted, such as strategic ideas or themes that combine strategic ideas. The synectics process is then carried out to make the *strange familiar* or to make the *familiar strange*.

The mind tends to draw on a person's experiences and to force these experiences, even when strange, into recognizable patterns. Often one becomes distracted by the detail, in part because the detail can be rationalized more easily than a new experience. In this case, the synectics team is forced to generalize to bring the original (strange) image back. To make the familiar strange, distortion, inversion, and transposition are attempted. The familiar has been made strange when a workable analogy is found. Four mechanisms are used to create analogies: personal analogy, direct analogy, symbolic analogy, and fantasy analogy.

Personal Analogy

In a personal analogy, members attempt to identify with elements in a problem statement. Each member tries to become the thing on which the group is working. The identification metaphor stems from the group attempting to "relate" to the problem.

The critical element in personal analogy is empathy, not role playing. For example, to understand how a debt collection system might work, the team members would be asked to imagine that they were various types of nonpayers, such as low-income people or bill shirkers, and imagine what would force payment from them. In mechanical systems, the team members put themselves in place of the system. For example, in the design of a system to increase the speed of a bank transaction, each team member would imagine that he or she was a financial transaction and would move through all steps in a process from activation to various points of data entry and, finally, to termination: data storage. The personal analogy is then tested to see if it can improve the efficiency and effectiveness of operations.

Four degrees of involvement can be attempted for personal analogies.

1. *First-person factual description*—The identification rests on a mere listing of facts. For instance, imagine that your Visa card minimum had not been paid and you were contacted about the nonpayment by your bank. The bank uses a "sweet young voice" to verify that you, the nonpayer, are on the phone and then plays a recording that presents veiled threats about bank action if payment is not received. Group

members are told, "Play this situation through your mind and imagine your reaction. Does it sound like a good tactic? Why or why not?"

2. *First-person emotional description*—The lowest order of personal identification stems from some form of emotion. The team members could imagine their reaction to the contact by the Visa office under various conditions, such as being unable to pay or just forgetting to pay.

3. *Empathetic identification*—The true personal analogy is based on kinship and attachment. The team members think about how they feel about the Visa office that had contacted them and the fact that they could pay but had not.

4. *Empathetic object identification*—The identification is shifted to the object. The synectics team member visualizes the place of residence in which the call was received and that the person also received it without any way to make contact.

The personal analogy exercise helps the group become more cohesive. Good personal analogies make the other steps easier.

Direct Analogy

The basic mechanism used in synectics is the direct analogy. To construct a direct analogy, facts are placed side by side and compared. The comparison seeks to extract the similarity or likeness of one thing with another. Facts, knowledge, or technology from one field are translated to another. Things that have closely corresponding purposes or tendencies make excellent analogies. For example, knowing how certain activities or purposes are achieved in biological organisms has provided a basis for extrapolation. Bell used knowledge of the human ear to design the telephone. The Wright brothers designed a stabilizing system for the Kitty Hawk after watching a buzzard fly. Darwin drew his natural selection theory from animal husbandry, realizing that selection could be random as well as planned. Laplace used the human body's self-healing processes to visualize the equilibrium found in celestial mechanics. Biological systems are a good source of direct analogies. Most operating systems must work in equilibrium so homeostatic analogies can be useful.

Gordon (1971) distinguishes between the cognitive strain introduced by the analogy's distance and the analogy's inventive elegance. For example, a new form of radar may be designed using the analogy of pigeons' sensitivity to the earth's magnetic field or a blind African freshwater fish's ability to create an electrical field that can distinguish between predators and prey and can communicate to others of its species. This degree of elegance is often hard to achieve. When using synectics for the first time, analogies that have a small psychological distance from the problem are best. For difficult problems, a greater distance is desirable. As the distance increases, the chance for an innovative leap also increases.

Symbolic Analogy

A symbolic analogy is created when the generalized image from the first step is used. A symbol is anything that stands for something else, such as an organization's logo. Firms recognize the importance of a logo and strive to make logos daring, original, and modern. Imagine the logos used by Sun Oil, CBS, Olivetti, Westinghouse, and IBM and note how they conjure up images of heraldry in our modern age. Labeling creates another type of symbol. For example, calling management information system options, "people-people," "superscore," and "microscope" creates distinct images about the data to be collected by each option. The idea is to create a new inference that opens up new thought patterns.

To use a symbolic analogy, a person seeks analogy that is esthetically appealing, if not an accurate representation. The analogy compresses the problem, disregarding some, or even many, of its elements. A paradoxical or even a controversial analogy is often sought.

Fantasy Analogy

Fantasies can be used to create images that offer solutions. Gordon (1971) sees them as a link between problem and solution because a new mechanism is required. The fantasy can be any unreal image or illusion, including any strange notion or whimsical suggestion. For example, Goddard's fantasies about travel to Mars, stimulated by attending the lectures of Percival Lowell at the turn of the century, led to modern rocketry. Goddard formulated the basic components that are used today while sitting in a large cherry tree, staring at the moon, and imaging each step in such a trip. Einstein thought up paradoxes concerning the behavior of light and created "thought experiments" that he solved while walking in rural Italy where he worked as a patent clerk. Runners who think about winning can run faster. A fantastic analogy often comes up while the group is attempting to draw on other analogies. It may create a deadend but can lead to productive new directions of inquiry.

The synectics leader moves through one or several of these analogy-producing approaches and lists the ideas that flow from the group. The synectics procedure has seven steps: (1) Problem as given, (2) Analysis, (3) Purge, (4) Problem as understood, (5) Excursion, (6) Force fit, and (7) Viewpoint.

Step One: Problem as Given

The first step begins with a description of the problem (such as, identify issues, strategic actions, strategic themes, and so on). The description should conjure up obstacles so an "opportunity to solve" posture is created.

Step Two: Analysis

The analysis step begins with a review of the information generated in previous stages of the strategic management process. In presenting the information, the leader asks the group to discuss what is central or essential. For example, when the intent is to reduce the costs of patient billing, the group could discuss the meaning of the term *bill*, attempting to make the familiar strange. When the objective has uncertainty, the leader initially attempts to make the strange familiar. For example, if the group was attempting to design a management information system, the group could begin by discussing information thought to be key to decision making. In each case, the group tries to come to grips with the problem and reveal some of its elements.

Step Three: Purge

Immediate suggestions often stem from step two. While seldom useful, they should be verbalized. This purges the group of off-the-shelf responses and allows it to consider other possibilities. Experts in the group are called on to point out the limitation of ideas that persist, which serves as a basis to purge them. A by-product is a further clarification of the group's mission.

Step Four: Problem as Understood

The new group aim becomes "the problem as understood." Each person is called on to describe the problem as he or she sees it and to offer a wishful solution. These problems and idealized solutions are recorded by the leader on a flipchart. After discussion, a direction is selected, often an amalgam of those in the list. The leader then asks the group to dismiss the problem and begin a mental excursion.

Step Five: Excursion

Excursion marks the beginning of the creative process. Various analogies are used to make the familiar strange. The facilitator questions each member and tries to get a response. The participants are asked to make analogies further and further from the problem. The excursion process usually takes the following course:

1. First direct analogy—asking for a similar analogy in a comparable field
2. Personal analogy—each member personally identifying with the direct analogy
3. Symbolic analogy—forming an abstract or seemingly contradictory idea from the personal analogy
4. Second direct analogy
5. Repeat steps

After the analogies are listed, some can be selected for further examination. Selection can be based on inherent interest, analogies very detached from the problem or seemingly irrelevant, or analogies for which the group may have information with which to elaborate the analogy. This is a critical step and demands both facilitator skill and insight into the problem.

Step Six: Force Fit

A force-fit phase, where the results of the final estrangement step (making the familiar strange) are connected to the problem, ends the inquiry for a particular analogy chain. Several such chains are used.

The analogy and the problems are connected. Members are given considerable latitude in responding, so any connection, no matter how seemingly farfetched, is permitted. The forcing stems from the link between the analogy and the problem. A fantasy force fit is followed with a practical force fit. In this step, the group substitutes a practical force fit with fantasy. For instance, assume participants are working with a Trojan horse analogy to design a superior mousetrap. The fantasy force fit to this analogy is to leave something that mice will covet so they will put it into their nests (Stein, 1975). For the practical force fit, the group must identify materials that the mice can use to build a nest that can be treated to be lethal to mice but not house pets or children.

Step Seven: Viewpoint

The terminal step in the technique is the discovery of an interesting issue, strategic action, or strategic theme. To have a useful viewpoint, one must begin to see how to create issue understanding or a viable strategy. The viewpoint associated with this discovery is the basis to suggest a strategy or to return to step five for another excursion, in hopes of elucidating the now somewhat better-understood problem.

Scenario

Search is the most important step called for to carry out activities in a strategic management process. If ideas are poor or trivial, attempts to organize them or decide which is the more important can follow all the best prescriptions and produce little of value.

A search can become very complex when the future conditions facing the organization are unclear or ambiguous. Scenarios are used to deal with the complexity by providing a window for the search process around various contingencies. Each window in the scenario provides a focus in which to search, focusing and simplifying the hunt for responses. Scenarios provide a way to frame the search for concerns that occur in stages three through six. Issues, strategies, stakeholders, and resources in these stages can be identified using various windows to guide a search.

Scenarios are constructed as a contingency framework that specifies how various possibilities combine to produce a variety of political, technological, or external event situations in which the strategy may have to function (Vanston and others, 1977). Different issues, strategies, stakeholders, and resources emerge when each of these scenarios is used as a context for strategic management.

The simplest form of scenario contrasts high and low

levels of two crucial factors. For example, several types of organizations, such as mental health centers and publicly funded hospitals like those in the state of Mississippi, face contingencies that can be defined in terms of prospects of new clients and the amount of support from local levies. Table 9.2 identifies four situations or cases, based on the interaction of these two factors.

The best-case scenario, successful marketing to new clients and the enactment of a levy, calls for a *general user* strategy. The focus of such a strategy is to identify new programs or services that fit within the ideals of the mental health center or hospital. Fee-for-service and publicly funded patients must coexist under any proposed strategy. Coexistence and new initiatives become the frame within which strategy is sought.

If neither marketing nor efforts to increase the levy size are successful, a worst-case situation results, calling for *cutback management*. The priorities are set on clients' needs, and low-need, nonpaying clients would be dropped, along with their providers. Reimbursement strategies are sought that maximize revenue from sources that provide publicly assessed care. Programs and services can be offered if they produce additional revenues or if reimbursement from third-party payers (such as medicaid) will be sufficient to cover the costs of the other services offered.

The other cells in Table 9.2 produce mixed outcomes in terms of desirability. A *public service* approach is adopted if the

Table 9.2. Defining Scenarios for Growth.

| | | Effects of Marketing on Demand | |
		Small	Large
Levy Size	Small	Cutback management	Lean and mean
	Large	Public service	General user

levy increases the level of support and marketing fails. The strategy would call for the expansion of free care. Attention would be directed toward high-need groups that lack means, such as people who are severely retarded and are educable. A second mixed case occurs when the levy increase fails but marketing suggests that new fee-for-service clients can be obtained. A *lean-and-mean* context results, in which strategy would stress cost-effective responses to new users. Industry-based programs are tested to ensure that these new services and programs, such as mental health education and drug testing services, will produce revenue at low cost. Such a strategy would dramatically change the makeup of the center, calling for retraining and a substantial number of new hires. The SMG tries to find the common threads in these strategies and treats the remaining strategies as options that could be used if the contingencies shown in Table 9.2 emerge.

By altering the definition of the factors slightly, new interpretations emerge. For example, consider the scenario shown in Table 9.3. In this example, the levy prospects can be treated as pass/fail. This situation applies to many public organizations that face the loss of public funds and seek to maintain their mission, such as libraries or publicly funded children's services. The levy could fail or pass and demand could grow or remain constant. The current situation creates a *business-as-usual* context, or BAU, in which to search. Levy failure coupled with current demand and levy failure coupled with

Table 9.3. Defining Scenarios for Decline.

| | | Demand | |
		Current	Increased
New Levy Prospect	Pass	Business as usual	Growth
	Fail	Austerity	Allocation

Table 9.4. Scenarios Relevant to Various Industries.

		Environment	
		Business as Usual	Change
Demand Prospects	Increase	Capacity enhancement	Austerity plans
	Decrease	New program initiatives	Adjustive and allocative

Segment	BAU	Change
Government	Flat budget	Decreased budget
Utilities	Old arrangements	Projected profit shortfalls
Banks	Stable discount rates	Increases in cost of money
Hospitals	Reimbursement on charges	Reimbursement on costs with deductibles

increased demand create *austerity* and *allocative* contexts. Only the passage of a levy and increases in demand would permit a *growth* context in which to devise strategy.

A scenario applicable to utilities is shown in Table 9.4. The categories also apply to nonprofit hospitals, many banks, and other organizations in which the economic situation is expressed in terms of regulatory control of markup, limits on profit allowed, or caps to charges or budgets. These organizations are facing key environmental contingencies, given by the prospect of changes in markup and by changes in the demand for their services.

In a utility, the economic situation is determined by a public utility commission that sets rates and other policies, such as shutoffs, that influence the level of recoverable costs. These rulings produce an economic situation in which strategic plans must be made. A second crucial factor is expected demand.

When a business-as-usual attitude prevails and increases in the demand for power are forecasted, a best-case scenario results that allows the utility to engage in *capacity enhancement*. In no other situation is capacity enhancement relevant as a strategy. The worst case is observed when the acts of regulators result in reduced markups and increases in demands for power occur. Austerity plans may be needed to deal with this contingency. New programs or initiatives are needed when normal markup is maintained in the face of conservation that leads to reduction in use. Advertising showing the benefits of using a particular form of power is one kind of response. *Adjustive* and *allocative* strategies are called for when profits are squeezed. Who gets what becomes a key issue, calling for an allocative strategic response.

Ways to define the BAU and the change situation for several industry types are also shown in Table 9.4. For instance, governmental hospitals, such as the Veterans Administration hospitals, face fixed or falling budgets. Other examples include: utilities with profit shortfalls, banks facing increases in the cost of money, and nonprofit hospitals dealing with prospective reimbursement rates.

Three-by-three and more complex representations of future conditions that depict intermediate representations of crucial factors can be desirable. An example is shown in Table 9.5. In this example, a hospital is considering ways to deal with a renal disease service. Demand is treated as low, current or forecast, and high in this example. Delays in reimbursement can be low (less than 90 days), expected, or high (more than 270 days). Long reimbursement delays produce a cash-flow crisis because most dialysis patients rely on public funds to pay for services. The nine contingencies in Table 9.5 identify potentially important contexts to devise strategy for the renal department of a hospital.

The combinations of an extreme value for delays and low or high demand create crisis situations that merit exploration as contingencies. Lacking funds and facing a high demand, the hospital will create a situation in which delays occur

Table 9.5. Scenarios for a Renal Disease Program Strategy.

| | | Demand | | |
		Low	Current or Forecast	High
	Less than 90 Days	Cost reduction	Use of reimbursement	Use of windfall
Delays in Reimbursement	Expected	Marketing	Business as Usual	Use of small markup windfall
	More than 270 days	Program change or termination	Borrowing due to cash-flow shortfalls	Margin shortfall

and expectations cannot be met. Low demands coupled with cash-flow delays pose a situation in which program termination must be considered. Should delays in reimbursement vanish, a windfall of unexpected cash can result, and steps must be taken to develop a defensive posture should this windfall be noticed. A group such as the Gray Panthers could call attention to "profiteering" by an organization not permitted to make profits.

Hybrid Techniques for Search

Combining techniques to conduct search can produce useful hybrids. The hybrid is created to produce or enhance particular benefits. For example, NGT and cued brainwriting can be combined to incorporate constraints by subtly suggesting directions in a search process. To merge these techniques, the silent reflective step of cued brainwriting is substituted for the NGT silent listing procedures. Combining NGT with synectics emphasizes creating and testing new ideas. To merge these techniques, NGT would be used for the synectics discussion in

Table 9.6. Hybrid Techniques for Search.

Hybrids	Why Used
Level One Interacting and focus group Interacting group	Create token discussion
Level Two NGT and Dialectic group	Create tension for change
Level Three NGT and Kiva NGT and NI	Produce insight and compromise in situations with potential conflict
Level Four Cued Brainwriting, Synectics, and NI Cued Brainwriting and NI	Introduce core values to be maintained as constraints before a search for new ideas is mounted
Level Five NGT and Synectics NI and Synectics	Produce needed creativity and innovation
Level Six Scenario, NGT, and Synectics Scenarios, NGT, and Synectics Scenarios, Kiva, and Synectics	Search in contexts to find ways to deal with important contingencies

Note: Techniques listed at each level have comparable benefits.

steps five, six, and seven of the synectics procedure. NGT and NI can be combined to introduce new ideas for a situation in which views are volatile and comprise essential.

Cued brainwriting merged with NI allows constraints to be subtly introduced into a tension-filled situation that must produce compromise. Scenarios can be combined with NGT and cued brainwriting (with or without synectics) to create multiple perspectives in which to search (Linstone, 1984). This hybrid is useful when the strategic management process must be carried out vis-à-vis ambiguous and shifting future conditions that suggest several important contingencies that must be managed. Hybrid techniques that are particularly useful for search along with their benefits are summarized in Table 9.6.

The levels in the table indicate increasingly more complex combinations.

Key Points

1. Group process techniques help to efficiently and effectively manage the search activities of an SMG. Silent reflective techniques are best to uncover new ideas and interaction to produce compromises and make judgments.
2. Hybrids that combine search techniques can be constructed for specialized uses. The SMG leader or facilitator, knowledgeable of the range of search techniques that are available, can combine them to create a repertoire of techniques that meets the special circumstances posed by doing strategic management in a given organizational situation.

■   ■

Chapter Ten

Making Sense
of Information:
Synthesis
Techniques

■   ■

In the synthesis step, the strategic management group seeks generalizations, patterns, or themes in the information (for example, SWOTs, issues, strategic themes, and stakeholders) produced by the search step. Techniques that can help a group identify patterns, themes, and generalizations in an unorganized mass of information produced by the search step are described in this chapter. Snowball, morphology, relevance tree, and interpretive structural modeling techniques are presented.

As in the search step, a repertoire of techniques is presented to provide a facilitator or group leader with a variety of techniques and to give techniques that have unique benefits. Habitually applying a particular technique can be avoided. The SMG facilitator or leader can become stale using the same approach over and over again. Also, each technique has particular benefits that can be exploited by applying techniques in situations that draw out these benefits. Merging techniques into hybrids, as discussed in Chapter Nine, further tailors techniques to a situation and enhances their benefits.

Techniques That Produce Synthesis

Snowball, morphology, and relevance tree techniques find patterns or themes in a mass of information. The snowball technique can be used by a group, such as an SMG. Morphology and relevance tree techniques can be applied to elaborate the results of a snowball or can be applied to raw information. Although not as useful in a group setting, the morphology and relevance tree techniques can be used to refine the relationships among items, such as strategic actions in stage four, to produce strategic themes that have more coherence than the results obtained from a snowball technique. The morphology and relevance tree techniques are typically carried out by the facilitator between meetings to lay out action relationships in a strategy. First we discuss each technique and then offer an example, showing how each technique can be applied.

Snowball

The snowball technique (Greenblat and Duke, 1981) is similar to the "storyboarding" approach applied by the FBI in kidnapping cases. The FBI has its agents bring all information regarding a kidnapping to a room and organize it according to categories (such as motives, MO's, and so on). These categories and the information each contains are periodically updated by agents as they gather new information about the case. The room becomes a repository of information that is organized into categories that gradually reveal characteristics (themes) of importance in solving the case. Storyboarding is also used by firms to sum up competitor intelligence and market information.

The snowball technique is like the storyboard approach and is specifically devised for use by groups. A group process used to generate ideas often creates long lists of partially integrated and overlapping ideas. The snowball technique can be used to find labels that identify themes or generalizations that sum up bundles of ideas, such as creating public awareness, redefining clientele, modifying services, expanding services, and the like.

To delineate such categories, the SMG sorts cards (or large sheets of paper) that list the individual ideas that resulted from a search step. Each card describes one of the items identified in the search step. The SMG members are asked to tape the cards to a wall, grouping similar ideas, and then to label the resulting categories. No ownership of ideas or categories is allowed; anyone can change any label or exchange cards among categories. The SMG members study the labels or categories and reorganize them without discussion. Stable patterns often emerge after three or four attempts at labeling and content modification. These classifications provide a more general set of categories than the initial pool of ideas, thus identifying important themes or generalizations in the ideas.

Morphology

Zwicky (1968) devised the morphology technique to create many diverse options for the strategist to ponder. In morphology, a strategic option is defined by all possible combinations of elements for key components. For example, key components in a mental health plan could be the type of care and its urgency. All combinations of the acute, chronic, rehabilitative, and custodial care elements for the "care" component and the convenient, urgent, or emergent elements for the "urgency" component create nine strategic themes or options, such as "chronic-convenience" care.

Relevance Tree

A relevance tree has a hierarchy and subdivisions within hierarchical levels (Warfield, 1976). The tree relates an overall objective to intermediate actions. Connections between levels show the relevance of these relationships. The highest level identifies the problems to be solved or objective to be met. Intermediate levels consider concerns, such as environment, and enumerate key elements, such as regulatory changes in reimbursement policy. The tree terminates with a list of specific actions. The relational properties in a relevance tree can be explored by using network techniques, such as interpretive structural modeling, described in the next section of this chapter.

Example of Using the Techniques

Consider the actions suggested by an SMG formed to do strategic management for a family medicine department. Strategic actions for the issue tension of "increased growth versus lack of funding to support growth" were grouped using the snowball technique into categories of:

1. Increase funds
2. Alter financial allocations
3. Improve management
4. Increase patient volume
5. Increase services
6. Cope with promotion and tenure
7. Increase research money

The top-ranked theme of increase funds was identified by the snowball from the following individual action suggestions:

1. Seek endowments.
2. Redefine the budget process.
3. Increase teaching tied to budget subsidies.
4. Decrease teaching not tied to budget subsidies (such as physical exams).
5. Increase grant funding.
6. Tie budget subsidy of university hospital to admissions from department's satellites.
7. Increase subsidy from state legislature.
8. Reduce all faculty to part time to reduce costs of liability insurance.

9. Allow faculty moonlighting for a salary reduction proportional to time off.
10. Increase residents' time at satellite hospitals (where it is compensated) and reduce it at university hospital.
11. Get college of medicine to take over debt in the practice plan.
12. Give faculty a personal discretion budget linked to money raised in grants.
13. Seek money from special programs offered by the university regents.
14. Get college of medicine to pick up more of faculty salary support in order to reduce pressure to provide patient care to pay employee salaries.

These action ideas could use additional sorting to relate the overall objective to intermediate steps. First, divisions can be made to separate revenue enhancements from cost cutting. Revenues can be internal or external, and costs can be cut through changes in allocation and outright reductions. Figure 10.1 shows a relevance tree that sorts the individual ideas from an NGT, after they have been grouped by the snowball technique. The relevance tree clarifies the actions to be taken and opens the door to search for more useful ideas. Using the tree, the SMG can be asked to search for more solutions, such as identifying for more ways to find revenue inside the university or outside.

The morphology technique takes items from categories and combines them into a series of possible solutions. Some combinations will be nonsensical, others insightful.

A morphology is shown in Table 10.1. Unlike the tree, which elaborates solution ideas, a morphology indicates combinations of items in each column that can be further combined to identify new solution ideas. In all there are $3 \times 3 \times 3 \times 4$ or 108 solution ideas that can be studied which combine inside and outside revenue enhancements with allocative and cost reduction actions. For example, one such program would tie admissions to a university subsidy, giving faculty discretionary money based on grant money raised. The time to pursue grant

Figure 10.1. Relevance Tree for Increasing Funds.

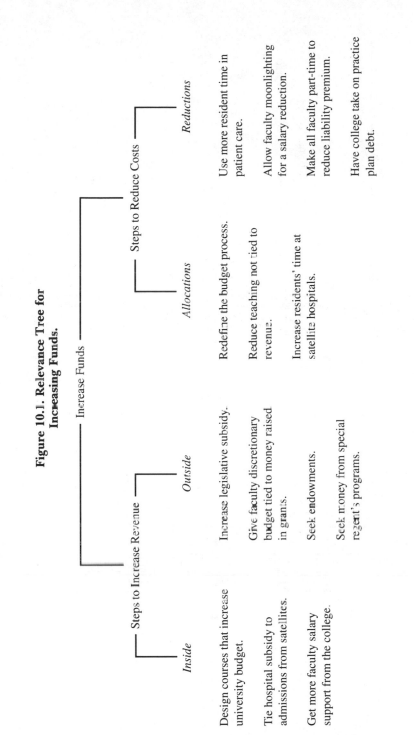

Increase Funds

Steps to Increase Revenue

Steps to Reduce Costs

Inside

Design courses that increase university budget.

Tie hospital subsidy to admissions from satellites.

Get more faculty salary support from the college.

Outside

Increase legislative subsidy.

Give faculty discretionary budget tied to money raised in grants.

Seek endowments.

Seek money from special regent's programs.

Allocations

Redefine the budget process.

Reduce teaching not tied to revenue.

Increase residents' time at satellite hospitals.

Reductions

Use more resident time in patient care.

Allow faculty moonlighting for a salary reduction.

Make all faculty part-time to reduce liability premium.

Have college take on practice plan debt.

261

Table 10.1. Morphology for Increasing Funds.

Inside Revenue Enhancements	Outside Revenue Enhancements	Allocative Cost Reduction	Outright Reduction
Design courses that bring in university subsidies.	Give faculty discretionary budgets tied to money raised in grants.	Redefine budgets.	Use more resident time in patient care.
Tie admissions from satellites to university hospital subsidy.	Seek endowments.	Reduce teaching not tied to budget allocations.	Allow faculty to moonlight.
Get more faculty salary support from the college.	Seek money from regent's programs.	Increase resident's time at satellite hospitals.	Make faculty part time.
			Have college take on practice plan debt.

writing stems from increasing resident involvement in patient care at the satellite hospitals to treat patients. The linkage of substituting residents for faculty to provide time for research is moderated by financial incentives in the arrangements made with the university hospital and the satellites. Negotiations with the various hospitals are implied to see if a more appropriate package of subsidies and payments can be arranged to free up faculty to pursue research. Each of the 108 programs can be examined one at a time to uncover interrelationships that offer insights into the fundraising strategy and ways to make it work.

Technique That Describes Structural Relationships

Interpretive structural modeling, or ISM (Warfield, 1976; Nutt and Backoff, 1987), is a technique that can be used to describe relational properties, such as causality, severity, importance or priority, and precedence (order) to make an implicit structure explicit. The technique can be applied to issues, strategies, problems, objectives, and other items that have relationships to develop a consensus about how they are related. Interpretive structural modeling is particularly useful in sorting out relationships among themes from ideas produced by a group process.

The SMG can use ISM to determine the order in which issues or strategies should be addressed and to identify producer-product relationships among issues or strategies. To capture this ordering, the SMG uses a paired comparisons ranking technique (Chapter Eleven). To make paired comparisons, each SMG member compares each item (for example, strategy or issue) with all other items, specifying the relationship in question (for example, order or causality). Counts of how many members judged an item to be more severe, of higher priority, or a first consideration are made. The count provides an index of severity, priority, or precedence for each item. Alternatively, a consensus about the relative priority of items can be determined. After an initial ranking, discussion is allowed, encouraging the more informed SMG members to comment on linkages they know best. The discussion allows the SMG to learn about the structure of issues or strategies. The paired comparison technique is repeated after discussion so that the final ranking reflects these matured views.

To illustrate the procedure assume that an SMG has produced four strategies, listed below:

> Strategy one: expand clientele
> Strategy two: develop alternative methods of service delivery
> Strategy three: contain costs of services provision
> Strategy four: stabilize funding for subsidized care

In this example two relationships are sought: precedence and producer-product. Each member of the SMG is given lists of all combinations of the four strategies.

Precedence Relationships

The order relationship is determined by asking each SMG member to compare each pair of strategies and indicate which precedes the other. To help make the comparisons, all combinations are listed, as shown below:

Pairs of Strategies	*Order*
Clientele and methods	P
Clientele and costs	P
Clientele and funding	S
Methods and costs	P
Methods and funding	P
Costs and funding	P

The SMG members work through each pair in this way, designating which strategy precedes by the letter *P* and which follows by *F,* with *S* (for same) being used for pairs of strategy that seem the same in terms of order.

A scoring format is shown in Table 10.2. To illustrate how to use the format, consider the method-clientele compar-

**Table 10.2. Precedence Relationships
from One SMG Member.**

	Clientele	Methods	Costs	Funding
Clientele	—	P	P	S
Methods	F	—	P	P
Costs	F	F	—	P
Funding	S	P	F	—

Note: The cells marked with a dash are not used in order relationships but may be used in other relationships, such as capturing information flows among strategies.

ison. Methods were thought to follow clientele, so an *F* is put in the cell located by the row next to methods and the column under clientele and a *P* is placed in the cell located by the clientele row and the method column in Table 10.2. Scoring is done by following these steps for each pair of items. Form B.1 (see Resource B) can be used to collect this information in a strategic management session.

Table 10.2 lists hypothetical data collected from one SMG member. The lower half of the matrix in the table provides a check of the logic that was applied. To check the logic of the ordering provided by an individual SMG member, the designations in the lower half of the matrix must be reversed from those in the upper half. For example, if clientele precedes methods there should be a *P* under the method, in the clientele row, and an *F* under clientele in the method row.

Assume that the data in Table 10.3 has been collected from a ten-person SMG. The consensus of an SMG about order is determined by counting the number of times there is a *P* in each cell. The ordering between any pair of items is determined by comparing the appropriate row cells. For instance, in the ordering of methods and clientele, the score in the methods row is 2 and the score in the clientele row is 8, indicating that this SMG believed that clientele precedes methods. A diagram is created by connecting the strategies with arrows to show the ordering of actions between all combinations of strategies, as shown in Figure 10.2. The direction of the arrow is determined by reading across each row in Table 10.3.

A strong relationship is given by votes of eight or more

**Table 10.3. Precedence Relationships
from an SMG.**

	Clientele	Methods	Costs	Funding
Clientele	—	8[a]	8	1[b]
Methods	2	—	8	9
Costs	2	2	—	1
Funding	8	1	9	—

[a]This number of people in a ten-person SMG that believe methods precede clientele.
[b]A sum of less than ten would result if one member thought funding and clientele could occur simultaneously.

in the ten-member group. In the example, there is a strong relationship running from clientele to funding. For methods, there is a strong relationship running from methods to cost and to funding. Cost follows clients, methods, and funding, so an arrow runs from each of these strategies to cost in Figure 10.2. Funding precedes clients and costs, so the arrow runs from funding to these two strategies.

As shown in Figure 10.2, each strategy has three arrows, which depict its relationship to the other three strategies. The direction of these arrows indicates which strategy should be primary in terms of its order. One strategy (contain costs) has arrows flowing toward it, suggesting that it is a resultant, or a

Figure 10.2. Precedence Among Hypothetical Strategies.

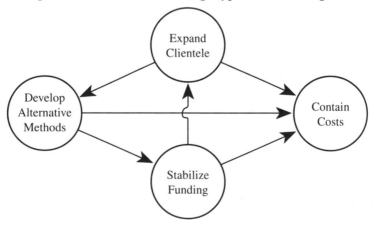

downstream, action. The other three have a reciprocal relationship, each with two arrows flowing out and one flowing in. A reciprocal relationship suggests that methods, clientele, and funding are linked and must be managed simultaneously during implementation.

For more complex strategic situations, closer votes and ties may occur. A tie or a close vote suggests the absence of an order relationship. To capture the absence of order between two issues or strategies, these issues or strategies would not be connected by an arrow, suggesting indifference to an ordering relationship.

Producer-Product Relationships

To capture the producer-product relationships among the items being considered, the SMG determines which of two items is the producer, also using the paired-comparison technique. In this case, the arrows in the diagram show the relative strength of an item (such as a strategy or issue) as both a producer (cause) and a product (an effect). (A producer-product relationship is similar to a cause-and-effect relationship, but is broader, which allows for reciprocal and other types of complex linkages among factors.) These relationships indicate how action in one arena enhances or retards action in another. The SMG then explores the relationships among strategies to consider these effects as implementation plans are developed. (The producer-product relationships among issues guide the search for strategy, which is discussed in the next section of this chapter.)

To establish producer-product relationships, each pair of strategies is compared to see which is the producer. In addition, each pair is rated on a -5 to $+5$ scale to depict the extent to which a strategy is a producer or a product. In this type of rating, the lower half of the matrix may not be the reciprocal of the upper half. The producer-product relationships between two strategies need not be symmetrical. For example, some clients can increase funding prospects and funds can increase who can be served. Both are positive relationships.

To construct the diagram, each pair of strategies is rated by comparing the extent that one strategy affects the other in a positive or a negative manner. For instance, if clientele affects methods very negatively, such as a mental health center dealing with the severely retarded individuals by legislative mandate, a −5 would be entered. The other combination can be rated differently. For instance, methods may affect clientele somewhat positively (a change in procedure may benefit some clients and not others) yielding a +2 rating.

The relationships between each pair of strategies are considered one at a time by the SMG members. To help make the comparisons, all combinations are listed, as shown below:

Producer	Product	Relationship Rating
Methods	Clientele	+2
Clientele	Methods	−5
Costs	Clientele	−3
Clientele	Costs	+2
Funding	Clientele	+5
Clientele	Funding	+5
Costs	Methods	−4
Methods	Costs	+5
Funding	Methods	+5
Methods	Funding	0
Funding	Costs	−3
Costs	Funding	+2

The SMG members work through all twelve combinations in this way, indicating the strength of the relationship.

Table 10.4 shows how the data collected from the hypothetical SMG member is summarized. Consider the relationship between methods and clients. Because methods were thought to have a moderately positive influence on clients, a +2 was entered in the cell identified by the methods row and clientele column. The influence of clients on methods was thought to be strongly negative, that is clients change methods, so a −5 was entered in the cell under the methods column and the clientele row. To list the data, one works through all the combinations in this way. Form B.2 (Resource B) can be used to collect this information from an SMG.

Table 10.4. Producer-Product Relationships from One SMG Member.

	Clientele	Methods	Costs	Funding
Clientele	—	–5	+2	+5
Methods	+2	—	+5	0
Costs	–3	–4	—	+2
Funding	+5	+5	–3	—

The SMG member rankings are averaged to create a consensus view for each of the twelve producer-product relationships. Assume that the ratings in Table 10.4 represent the average of the ratings assigned by an SMG. A diagram is created from the average ratings to show the strength of the producer-product relationships. Figure 7.3 (see Chapter Seven) captures the relationships in Table 10.4. Because strategies influence and are influenced by each other, each pair of strategies has two connecting arrows in the figure. Dark lines indicate strong relationships (say, average scores of 4 to 5). Light ones indicate weaker relationships. Solid lines indicate positive relationships and dotted lines, negative relationships. For instance, the arrow connecting clientele to methods is a dark dotted line, indicating that clientele produce a strong negative effect on methods. The arrow from methods to clientele is a light solid line, indicating a moderately positive relationship. The remaining arrows are specified using Table 10.4 in the same matter. A missing arrow denotes the absence of a causal relationship.

The figure shows that stabilizing funding and expanding clientele have a strong positive reciprocal relationship, suggesting that stakeholders for these strategies require careful consideration during implementation. Alternative methods and cost containment also have a strong producer-product relationship. Alternative methods have a strong positive effect on costs and costs have a strong negative effect on methods. This relationship suggests that attention to stakeholders for the methods strategy can have a desirable influence on the costs picture. But, dealing with the stakeholders to influence costs can change methods in ways that may be undesirable. This suggests that an implementation of strategy focusing on methods should precede one for costs. The influence of funding on methods also merits attention because changes in funding may force changes in methods.

In this example, funding was found to be crucial. By dealing with stakeholders to stabilize funding, noting both method and clientele changes that must be anticipated, an implementation plan begins to emerge. These changes should precede the formation of a plan to manage stakeholders calling for cost containment, such as regulations. This producer-product chain gives clear direction about where to begin strategic change in this hypothetical organization.

Interpretation of an ISM Using Issues

The interpretation of issues follows the same logic as applied to strategy. Diagrams order issues and spell out their producer-product relationships. The first issue to be attacked precedes most, if not all other issues, and tends to be a producer instead of a product. Issues that fall lower on the issue agenda would be preceded by all other issues and be products of other issues, making them the result of other considerations. These issues can be safely deferred for later considerations. When more issues are considered, issues in the center of a diagram will have significant interactive or feedback effects, which depict their influence on other issues and how the other issues influence these issues. Issues in the center of the diagram cannot be ignored during the identification of a strategy to deal with the priority issues.

The search for strategy is guided by these relationships. High priority is given to issues that are producers and that tend to occur first in a chain of events. These issues, and issues with important relationships with them, provide the focus of the search for strategic actions. They lay out an arena in which to search and identify important auxiliary concerns as the search unfolds. The cases described in Part Five give several concrete examples of ISM used to identify the relationships among issues and strategic themes.

Hybrid Techniques for Synthesis

Combinations of synthesis techniques can be used to identify important relationships and patterns in the pool of information produced by a search. As with the search step, combining techniques for synthesis creates a variety of benefits, each of which can be important in particular applications.

Several combinations of techniques are recommended for synthesis (Table 10.5). The snowball technique can be combined with ISM, morphology, and relevance trees. To use snowball with ISM, the SMG derives categories that capture key themes in a pool of issues or strategies. These themes are then subjected to analysis by the group to establish relationships, such as precedence and producer product, using ISM. This hybrid is useful in capturing a group's views and should be high in acceptance.

Snowball can also be merged with morphology and relevance trees. This hybrid takes the categories produced by the SMG using snowball and applies morphology and relevance trees to further uncover and explore relational patterns. This hybrid lacks acceptance or buy-in because it may not capture important beliefs about ordering. It does offer opportunity to study

Table 10.5. Hybrid Techniques for Synthesis.

Hybrid	Why Used
Snowball and ISM	Uncover themes and determine beliefs about theme relationships, such as order and producer product
Snowball and morphology and relevance trees	Explore relational structure, divided by components and elements, showing a detailed ordering of activities
Synectics and ISM	Derive innovative themes and capture relationships among these themes
Synectics and morphology and relevance trees	Derive innovative themes and explore structures in the theme relationships
Synectics and ISM	Derive innovative themes and capture relationships among these themes

relationships and introduce a competing relational pattern for SMG review and discussion. The detail in each snowball category can be organized in a hierarchical manner, showing the ordering and relationships within categories.

Other combinations apply synectics (discussed in the previous chapter) in place of snowball. The hybrid of synectics plus ISM and synectics plus morphology trees place a premium on innovation and creativity. The ISM procedure is used to promote acceptance, and morphology or relevance trees are used to study patterns carefully, improving the precision of the relationships.

Key Points

1. Synthesis techniques provide a way to identify patterns and generalizations in the mass of information gleaned from the search step.
2. Techniques that can be used to create synthesis (snowball, morphology, and relevance tree) find labels and categories that sum up a bundle of ideas and organize its contents to suggest themes.
3. Interpretive structural modeling is used to describe the relational properties among themes, such as order and producer product.
4. Hybrids that combine synthesis techniques can be constructed and have specific benefits. The SMG facilitator who is able to use each of these techniques and is aware of its benefits can create hybrids tailored to specific needs that emerge during a strategic management process.

Chapter Eleven

■   ■

Techniques for Setting Strategic Priorities

■   ■

In the selection step, the strategic management group orders the ideas produced in each process stage. The purpose of this step is to set priorities among the generalizations, patterns, or themes that emerge from the synthesis step. The priorities set at the end of a process stage provide a focus for action as the SMG moves to the next stage of the process.

Priorities can be set in one of two ways. Either a global assessment can be made or an index of merit, which combines the rankings made by applying several criteria, can be constructed. Useful techniques for setting priorities include anchored rating scales, paired comparisons, rank-weight techniques, distribute points techniques, and Q sort. This chapter shows how these techniques can by used by an SMG to set priorities as it considers events, trends, ideals, SWOTs, issues, and strategies and makes stakeholder assessments. The chapter

273

also discusses how priorities can be reconsidered in a group and how hybrids that combine techniques in useful ways can be created.

Anchored Rating Scales

Anchored rating scales, or ARS, can be used to elicit the ranking of strategies, issues, trends, events, and SWOTs from members of an SMG or others the SMG wishes to poll. The technique is easily understood and can be applied quickly, making it useful in a survey and when fairly precise discriminations among items are needed. A continuous scale with descriptors at several points along the scale is constructed to help to define the scale's increments and the endpoints (Nutt, 1980a). The annotations help the SMG member (or survey respondent) to visualize the meaning of scale intervals and scale endpoints. A variety of scale sizes can be used including 0 to 100 (or equivalently, 0 to 1.0), minus to plus infinity, and 0 to infinity. A scale anchored with a zero is used for items that have natural zero points, such as cost. A negative endpoint can be used for items in which negative values are possible, such as profit. Positive or negative infinity endpoints convey the notion of no theoretical limits to item values. To use a scale with positive or negative infinity as an endpoint, log increments are required. To simplify the scale, linear increments with -100 to $+100$ endpoints are recommended for applications in which values can be very large or very small. In most cases a 0 to 100 linear scale can be used.

To illustrate how ARS scales can be used, assume that an SMG wishes to set priorities for strategies such as clientele, methods, costs, funding, and public awareness. These strategies could be presented to members of an SMG using the format shown in Figure 11.1. Strategy can be listed alphabetically or randomly to avoid placement biases. Each SMG member draws an arrow from each of the strategies to a point on the scale that indicates his or her view of its importance. These scale values are normalized to convert them to percentages. For example, if a line was drawn from the cost strategy to .80

Figure 11.1. ARS Technique Used for Establishing Priorities.

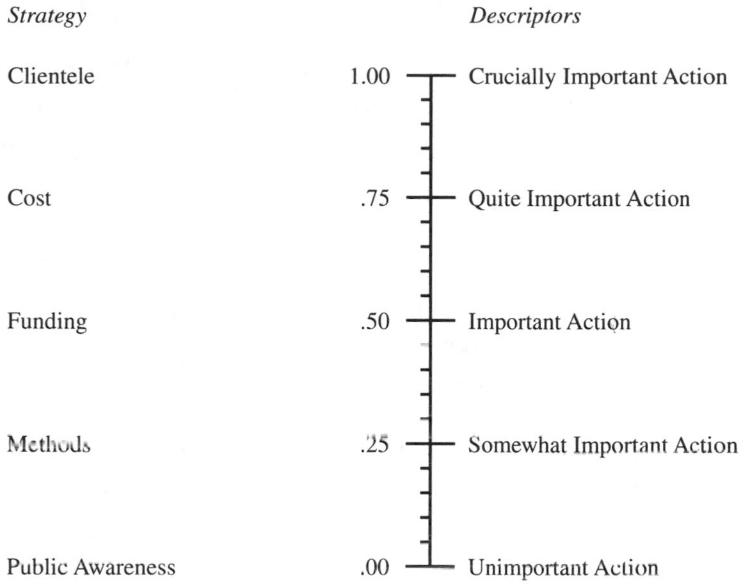

Strategy		*Descriptors*
Clientele	1.00	Crucially Important Action
Cost	.75	Quite Important Action
Funding	.50	Important Action
Methods	.25	Somewhat Important Action
Public Awareness	.00	Unimportant Action

and from the public awareness strategy to .60, cost would be weighted as:

$$.80 \div (.80 + .60) = .57$$

Public awareness could be weighted as:

$$.60 \div (.80 + .60) = .43$$

This computational tactic provides a way to find the weight of one item in relation to all others. (If more than two items are considered, one divides by the sum of the weights assigned to all items.) This approach provides a rank or priority that establishes the relative importance of all items being compared. An average value, indicating the consensual views of an SMG (or group being polled) is determined by averaging the percentage scores for each SMG member.

The technique can be applied when priorities for a number of criteria (for example, impact, implementation prospects, and so on) are required by creating a rating scale, like that shown in Figure 11.1, for each criteria. Each SMG member rates the strategy using each criterion. These values can be combined into a consensual rating by averaging across SMG members and the criteria.

Paired Comparisons

The paired comparison technique helps members of a strategic management group make comparisons that yield a very precise picture of priorities. Considering items, such as issues or strategic themes, in pairs permits the SMG member to concentrate on the differences between any two items, reducing the information-processing demands. Consider the previous example in which members of an SMG were asked to prioritize five strategic themes. To apply paired comparisons, a facilitator lists all combinations of the five themes, two at a time. SMG members are asked to compare the two themes (more generally, items) in each pair of strategic themes and indicate which is more important. Assume that the following choices were made by an SMG member:

Pairs	*Choice*
Methods versus costs	Methods
Methods versus funding	Funding
Methods versus clientele	Methods
Methods versus public awareness	Methods
Costs versus funding	Funding
Costs versus clientele	Clientele
Costs versus public awareness	Costs
Funding versus clientele	Clientele
Funding versus public awareness	Funding
Clientele versus public awareness	Clientele

Table 11.1. Strategy Priorities Determined Using Paired Comparisons.

	Methods	Costs	Funding	Clientele	Public Awareness
Methods	—	0	1	0	0
Costs	1	—	1	1	0
Funding	0	0	—	1	0
Clientele	1	0	1	—	0
Public Awareness	1	1	1	1	—
Raw Score	3	1	4	3	0
Normalized[a] Score	3/11	1/11	4/11	3/11	0/11
Percent	27	9	36	27	0

[a]Either row or column tabulations can be made. This example uses column tabulations, so columns are scored with a 1 to indicate the choice of strategy shown in the column.

277

The chart shown in Table 11.1 is used to tabulate a weight for each strategy from these choices. (Note that this discussion considers how column items affect row items, so a column tally is carried out in Table 11.1. It should be understood that the logic is the same and the same results will be produced using row or column tallying.) First, the first column and first row in the table are used. Alternative methods were rated as more important than cost, clientele, and public awareness so 1 is entered next to cost, clientele, and public awarenenss in column one, under methods. Method is less important than funding so a 1 is entered in the first row under the funding column. Zeros are entered in the remaining cells of the first row and first column. Now the first column and first row can be eliminated from further consideration.

The remaining cells in the second row and second column are considered, scoring each cell in the same manner. The process is repeated for the remaining columns and rows. The totals in each column are normalized to define a ranking for each strategic theme as shown at the bottom of Table 11.1. In most cases, an average value, indicating the consensus of the SMG, is determined by averaging the weights for each SMG member.

When multiple criteria are used, a paired comparison is made with each criterion. The results can be averaged or combined according to the importance accorded each criterion, which produces a weighted index. In some cases, the ratings for each criterion are kept separate so that the SMG can appreciate differences that can arise as strategy, issues, and the like are prioritized from different perspectives, such as importance or feasibility.

Rank-Weight Technique

This technique has SMG members first rank each item (such as SWOTs, directions, issues, and so on) and then specify its importance. Ordering the items in terms of their importance and then weighting them eases the information-processing demands of the task. Each item is placed on an index card. The SMG member first orders the items and then weights the items.

One of several approaches can be used to carry out the weighting. In the *odds procedure,* the SMG member compares the items to the top-ranked item one at a time, recording items that are more important (Nutt, 1984a). The most important item is given a value of one. If the first item was found to be twice as important as the second, a value of one-half is assigned to the second item. The odd ratios are normalized to convert them to percentages. Priorities can also be assigned using linear scales of − 100 or 0 to 100, log scales, or index numbers. The consensus view of the SMG is determined by averaging the values obtained from each SMG member, as described previously. The procedure can be repeated for criteria such as feasibility and importance to create ratings according to each of these notions of priority.

Distribute Points Technique

The distribute points technique is useful in prioritizing large numbers of items. The procedure can be carried out with or without anchors. Using the technique with anchors calls for three steps—selecting labels, recording item names on cards, and classifying the items according to the labels. Labels and values can be assigned as shown below.

Label	*Value*
Most desirable	10
Highly desirable	8
Desirable	6
Somewhat desirable	4
Marginally desirable	2
Undesirable	0

As the number of intervals increases, precision increases but the ease of designation declines, leading to blurred discriminations. Five to ten intervals are typically selected. Item names are then recorded on index cards. Each SMG member sorts the cards into piles associated with each label. The sorts are repeated several times. This step helps to ensure that the items have been reliably placed into categories.

To speed up priority setting, like that called for in a formal meeting, the direct assignment of ranks can be used. In this case, the integers can be associated with descriptors, such as 10 equals most important and 1 equals least important, and assigned to each item to describe its importance. Scales, such as -5 (least) to $+5$ (most) or -10 to $+10$, can also be used. These scales should be anchored by endpoint descriptors (such as most and least) whenever possible to increase ranking precision. Form B.3 (in Resource B) offers a format that can be used to distribute points among items, such as issues, by applying several criteria.

Q Sort

A group process, survey, or public hearing often produces many candidate items. The members of an SMG are often called on to set priorities for more than sixty strengths, weaknesses, threats, opportunities, trends, events, directions, stakeholders, and resources. Priority setting considering this number of items often becomes unreliable. Because of their sheer number, these items are difficult to prioritize. The situation is complicated by the value-laden, complex, and partially overlapping nature of SWOTs, directions, and so on that are obtained from several different sources. The Q sort technique (Kerlinger, 1967) provides a way to reduce the information-processing demands and improve reliability.

The Q sort improves reliability by having an SMG member first look for the most important items in a pool of items and then the least important ones, switching back and forth until all have been categorized. The number of items considered on each pass is equal. The items considered in all of the sorts have the approximate shape of a normal distribution.

Three steps are required to rank large numbers of items.

First, using the Q sort procedure, items are prioritized. The second step repeats the first to ensure that the ranking is reproducible, creating reliability. In the final step, items are ordered applying one of the ranking procedures discussed previously.

The Q sort can be used for item pools ranging from 30 to 130. Below 30 and above 130, reliability declines (Kerlinger, 1967). When fewer than 30 items are screened, the direct assignment technique can be used because the information-processing demands are manageable. Above 130, the task becomes tedious and items tend to be overlooked in the sorting process.

The first step in a Q sort calls for items (such as SWOT elements) to be written on index cards, along with a brief definition. To begin a sort, the members of a group read through the items to be ranked. The simplest sort is to put the items into three categories of importance such as important, unimportant, and the residual. The residual category is always made up of items that have an intermediate level of importance.

To illustrate the procedure, consider an example with fifty-five items to be ranked (Brown and Coke, 1981). The rater selects the three most important items from the fifty-five and enters a code number for each item under the $+5$ column. (Form B.4 in Resource B provides a scoring sheet useful in capturing these ratings for an SMG.) Next, the rater selects the three least important items and enters them under the -5 column. The rater then selects the four most important items from those that remain. These items are listed under the $+4$ column. Four unimportant items are selected next and put under the -4 column. The rater continues, adding items with each pass until seven remain. These items are located under the 0 column. The sorting process is repeated until the same sets of items begin to appear in each category. This type of ranking takes from one-half to three-fourths of an hour the first time that the procedure is used and considerably less time thereafter (Brown, 1980).

Different scoring schemes are needed for different-sized item pools. These distributions should be normal or as close to a normal distribution as possible to impose desirable statistical properties on the sort. Several such distributions (Kerlinger, 1967) are shown below.

$N = 80$

Scoring	−5	−4	−3	−2	−1	0	+1	+2	+3	+4	+5
Number Selected	2	4	6	9	12	14	12	9	6	4	2

Scoring	−4	−3	−2	−1	0	+1	+2	+3	+4
Number Selected	4	6	9	13	16	13	9	6	4
	4	6	10	12	16	12	10	6	4

$N = 70$

Scoring	−5	−4	−3	−2	−1	0	+1	+2	+3	+4	+5
Number Selected	2	3	5	8	11	12	11	8	5	3	2
	2	3	4	8	11	14	11	8	4	3	2

Scoring	−5	−4	−3	−2	−1	0	+1	+2	+3	+4	+5
Number Selected	2	3	4	7	9	10	9	7	4	3	2

Scoring schemes use a ± 5 scale and ± 4 scale. For eighty items, with ± 5 scale, two items are initially selected. With the ± 4 scale, four items are selected in the first sort. Any other scoring scheme with frequencies similar to the classic bell-shaped curve of a normal distribution can be used. To set up a scoring system, a set of index numbers is created that specifies each category's value, providing a scale. An example using a five-item scale follows.

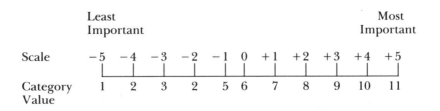

	Least Important									Most Important
Scale	−5	−4	−3	−2	−1	0	+1	+2	+3	+4	+5
Category Value	1	2	3	2		5	6	7	8	9	10	11

An example using a four-item scale follows.

	Least Important						Most Important		
Scale	-4	-3	-2	-1	0	$+1$	$+2$	$+3$	$+4$
Category Value	1	2	3	4	5	6	7	8	9

A *Q* sort permits SMG participants to carefully determine their attitude toward a large number of items. The technique is ideally suited to ranking tasks with more than thirty items and can be quickly administered and scored. Divisions of opinions about priorities among key stakeholders or SMG members can yield important insights. Factions can be isolated by comparing sorts to identify disagreements among the raters. The items supported by each faction suggest potential disagreements that should be addressed before consensus is sought.

Reconsideration of Priorities in Groups

To set priorities in a group, both reconsideration and reflection should be encouraged. Initial views of SMG members can be influenced by uncertainty in both their position and the position of others. To overcome these problems, a group would first set priorities without discussion, using any of the techniques previously described. Next, average values, representing the initial consensus, are computed and displayed to stimulate discussion. Discussion is directed toward defending or critiquing the initial priorities. The SMG considers these views as they emerge during discussion. After discussion, the SMG prioritizes the items again. The average weights that result represent an informed SMG consensus that shows more agreement than the initial weights. This procedure, called estimate-discuss-estimate, or EDE (Nutt, 1984a), can be summarized as:

1. Solicit individual priorities.
2. Pool individual priorities into a mean score, to specify the initial group consensus.

3. Discuss initial group consensus.
4. Reconsider initial priorities by ranking the items a second time.

      EDE is a useful way to organize the setting of priorities. A strategic management group often wants time to reflect and regards all choices as preliminary, pending more information. Reconsideration helps to reduce uncertainty about each member's position. The EDE technique brackets discussion with ranking. Discussion allows for information lobbying that encourages disclosure and mutual adjustment among the SMG members. An initial priority will always shift after group members share information.

      The EDE procedure was developed to obtain parameter estimates from groups for tasks in which a precise estimate was required. EDE was found to be a very accurate way to make these estimates (Gustafson and others, 1973). The procedure works for several reasons. First, it allows the current group consensus, not an individual, to be criticized. Second, EDE simulates what a group typically does when faced with setting priorities (Nutt, 1976a). In most situations, a decision body wants time to reflect. Groups typically treat their initial choices as preliminary, subject to change pending more information on how members feel and the facts they offer. Third, public vot-

Table 11.2. Comparison of Priority-Setting Techniques.

Technique	Speed	Precision	Adherence to Assumptions
Anchored Rating Scales	Moderate	Moderate	Moderate
Paired Comparisons	Moderate (for more than ten items)	High	Moderate/high
Rank Weight	Moderate	Moderate	Moderate
Distribute Points	High	Low	Low
Q Sort	Low	High	Moderate

ing by the show of hands or through open discussion subjects a member of a group to social pressure by other members. Members of a group that feel less knowledgeable are reluctant to take a position until they see how others are voting. Public voting will entice some members of a group to vote in ways that differ from how they would vote without knowledge of these sentiments. The initial ranking step gets each member to think through his or her preferences, which avoids the pressures to conform. After the initial ranking, changes are more apt to stem from the persuasiveness of the other members' arguments than from their status or personality (Huber and Delbecq, 1972).

Hybrid Techniques

Each priority-setting technique has strengths and weaknesses that stem from its speed, precision, and adherence to assumptions (see Table 11.2). Hybrids can be formed that overcome some of these limitations for specific applications. The most fundamental combination adds the EDE procedure to any one of the techniques (Table 11.3). EDE combined with any of the priority-setting techniques will improve its precision. This hybrid can be used to rank lists of SWOTs, events, directions, trends, and so on. Separate meetings can be needed to carry out an EDE.

Table 11.3. Hybrids for Selection.

Hybrids	Why Used
EDE and ARS	Speed not essential, moderate number of items
EDE and rank weight	Speed not essential, moderate number of items
EDE and distribute points	Speed essential
EDE and paired comparison	Small number of items are being considered and precision is important
EDE and Q sort	Large numbers of ambiguous items that must be prioritized are being considered and precision is important

The combination of EDE and the distribute points technique has the advantage of speed and precision. The combination of EDE and *Q* sort is useful for large item pools when there is time, during or between SMG meetings, to carefully sort items such as SWOT elements. EDE used with ARS and the rank-weight technique increases the precision of ranking and has time requirements between that of *Q* sort and the distribute points technique. EDE plus paired comparison is a very precise way to prioritize a small number of items. It can be used for strategies and issue themes but is less useful in other applications.

Key Points

1. Selection techniques help the SMG facilitator prioritize items (such as trends, SWOTs, or issues) that are identified during a strategic management process. Priority setting is required to help the SMG make the decisions that are required in each of the process stages. ARS, rank weight, distribute points, paired comparison, and *Q* sort can be used to help the SMG set priorities.
2. Hybrids combine selection techniques to bring out specific benefits for particular uses. SMG facilitators who build an awareness of these techniques and their benefits can create hybrids for particular uses.

Chapter Twelve

■   ■

Combining
Techniques
to Match Types
of Strategy

■   ■

It is particularly important to carefully consider the nature of strategy being devised in public and third sector organizations because of their complex environments. These environments are laced with politics and have many internal and external stakeholders that must be managed. Techniques to carry out a strategic management process should be selected with the needs of these organizations in mind. This chapter identifies combinations of the hybrid techniques, presented in the last three chapters, that meet the needs of strategic management carried out in public and third sector organizations.

Needs are defined by the requirements or expectations of the strategic manager for the strategy to be created. Four types of requirements, or performance expectations, are used to differentiate types of strategy: quality, acceptance, innovation, and preservation (Nutt, 1977; Quinn and McGrath, 1982;

Table 12.1. Types of Strategy.

Performance Expectations	Type
Quality, acceptance, and innovation	Comprehensive
Quality, acceptance, innovation, and preservation	Qualified comprehensive
Quality and acceptance	Traditional
Quality, acceptance, and preservation	Constrained traditional
Quality and innovation	Ideal prototype
Quality, innovation, and preservation	Constrained prototype
Quality	Utility
Quality and preservation	Quality utility
Acceptance and innovation	Awareness
Acceptance, innovation, and preservation	Constrained awareness
Acceptance	Seductive
Acceptance and preservation	Constrained seductive
Innovation	Idea
Innovation and preservation	Constrained idea
None	Gesture
Preservation	Ratification

Backoff and Nutt, 1988). Sixteen types of strategy can be identified by combining these performance requirements, as shown in Table 12.1. Matching these strategic types to hybrid techniques for search, synthesis, and selection brings out the benefits of the techniques in the most economical manner, minimizing the time and effort of the SMG members.

The strategic management approach described in Parts Three and Four has three key features: process, techniques that support the process, and guidelines for technique selection. The movement through six process stages tailored to meet the needs of third sector and public organizations has been described in Chapters Six, Seven, and Eight. This process recognizes some of the paradoxes and unique problems involved in doing strategic management in public and third sector settings and points a way to avoid such difficulties.

Three steps are repeated as the strategic management process moves through each of its six stages. The steps of search, synthesis, and selection are carried out to describe the historical context, conduct situational assessment, form an issue agenda, generate strategy, assess feasibility, and implement strategy. Techniques useful in carrying out the search, synthesis, and selection activities required in each stage have been described in Chapters Nine, Ten, and Eleven.

In this chapter, we offer guidelines for the selection of techniques based on performance requirements imposed on the strategy, derived from the strategic manager's expectations. These guidelines should not be used to make decisions for managers. They encourage managers to think carefully about their needs and point out how these needs influence the conduct of a strategic management process.

Criteria to Judge Needs

Expectations for strategy development are described by the terms *quality, acceptance, innovation,* and *preservation. Quality strategies* call for services that have desirable performance features, such as cost benefit or cost effectiveness. *Acceptance strategies* deal with the subjective views of people who can block or subvert both the strategic management process and its product. A strategy with high acceptance has the support of boards of directors and other key groups.

Innovative strategies are derived from ideas not previously recognized or attempted, in the hopes that some of these ideas will offer a decisive advantage. For example, an innovative strategy has an organization deal with unfamiliar interest groups, new clientele, or new services. *Preservation strategies* recognize that requirements to maintain current arrangements and to work within them are often imposed on strategy development. Examples of these requirements include sacrosanct procedures, policies, programs, or relationships as depicted by an organizational chart that the organization does not want to challenge or change. The organization seeks to retain this order in the face of the chaos that strategic change may bring. These commitments become real values that the organization commits to, not merely constraints, and thus they become performance expectations in their own right. These commitments set out an arena in which people can assume that there will be order and continuity or can act to preserve certain values.

Types of Strategy

The strategic management process is shaped by these performance requirements. The stages of the process, discussed in Part Three, were devised to meet the needs of public and third sector organizations. The hybrid techniques, in contrast, are selected according to their ability to produce specific types of results. Specific performance expectations for a strategy can be matched to the merits of results that stem from using each technique. Hybrid techniques were assembled in Chapters Eight, Nine, and Ten according to their ability to produce specific types of results for the process steps of search, synthesis, and selection. Specific performance expectations for the strategy can be matched to the expected merits of the hybrid techniques (Nutt, 1982b). The hybrid techniques recommended for strategic management are summarized in Table 12.2.

The notion of selecting techniques according to process

Table 12.2. Hybrid Techniques That Support the Strategic Management Process.

Techniques for Search	Techniques for Synthesis	Techniques for Selection
Interacting	Snowball and ISM	EDE and ARS
Interacting and focus group	Snowball, morphology, and relevance trees	EDE and paired comparisons
NGT and dialectics	Synectics and ISM	EDE and rank weight
NGT and Kiva	Synectics and NI	EDE and distribute points
NGT and NI	Synectics, morphology, and relevance trees	EDE and Q sort
Cued brainwriting		
NGT and synectics		
NI and synectics		
Cued brainwriting and NI		
Scenarios and NGT		
Scenarios and cued brainwriting		
Scenarios, NGT, and synectics		
Scenarios, cued brainwriting, and synectics		

Table 12.3. Hybrid Techniques Best Suited for Each Type of Strategy.

Strategy Type	Requirements	Search Step	Synthesis Step	Selection Step
1. Comprehensive	Quality, acceptance, innovation	Structured brainwriting with dialectics and synectics	Snowball, ISM, and scenarios	Q sort, EDE and paired comparisons
2. Qualified comprehensive	Quality, acceptance, and innovation, with important constraints	Cued brainwriting	Morphology	EDE and rank weight
3. Traditional	Quality and acceptance	NGT	Snowball and scenarios	Q sort and EDE and rank weight
4. Constrained traditional	Quality and acceptance, with important constraints	Cued brainwriting	ISM	EDE and rank weight
5. Ideal prototype	Quality and innovation, with important constraints	Delphi with synectics	Snowball and scenarios	Q sort
6. Constrained prototype	Quality and innovation, with important constraints	Focus group and structured brainwriting	Morphology	Q sort
7. Utility	Quality	Brainwriting	Relevance tree	ARS
8. Qualified utility	Quality, with important constraints	Cued brainwriting	Relevance tree	
9. Awareness	Acceptance and innovation	NGT	Snowball, ISM, and scenarios	EDE and paired comparisons
10. Constrained awareness	Acceptance and innovation, with important constraints	Cued brainwriting	ISM	EDE and rank weight
11. Seductive	Acceptance	NI	Morphology with NGT	Any

Strategy Type	Requirements	Search Step	Synthesis Step	Selection Step
12. Constrained seductive	Acceptance, with important constraints	Cued brainwriting and NI	Morphology with NGT	Any
13. Idea	Innovation	NGT and synectics	Snowball and ISM	EDE and paired comparison
14. Constrained idea	Innovation, with constraints	Cued brainwriting and synectics	ISM	EDE and paired comparisons
15. Gesture	None	Interactive group	None	Pooled rank
16. Ratification	Recognizing important constraints	Synthetic group (for example, survey stakeholders)	None	Any

requirements has an added benefit. The techniques identified in the last three chapters can be merged into hybrids that have particular benefits. For example, using Q sort combined with the nominal group technique can make selection more effective. The snowball or the interpretive structural modeling technique can be used with nominal groups to make synthesis easier. Using brainwriting in place of the nominal group technique increases variety and incorporates constraints into the search process. Some other hybrids include: synectics merged with brainwriting and paired comparisons, the nominal group technique merged with morphology and EDE, and brainwriting merged with snowball and paired comparisons.

All possible combinations of the ways to search, to synthesize, and to select create several hundred hybrid techniques that a facilitator or leader can use when working with a strategic management group. The strategic manager identifies the situation he or she believes that the organization is confronting by laying out performance expectations. Hybrid techniques are selected that meet these performance expectations, as shown in Table 12.3.

Comprehensive

Comprehensive strategies require quality, acceptance, and innovation but pose minimal constraints. The strategist has a wide latitude of action, but the strategy that is sought poses extensive expectations. This type of strategic management process would be initiated when an organization makes a commitment to consider significant changes in its services and clientele. The group processes used for search should engage the SMG in far-reaching considerations. As a result, structured brainwriting with a dialectical group process and synectics is recommended. Snowball, ISM, and scenarios are recommended to aid in the synthesis of ideas. Q sort and EDE are recommended to prune the idea list and paired comparison to set priorities among items in the winnowed list.

The imposition of constraints calls for a *qualified comprehensive strategy*. A broad search is undertaken, but the strategic manager announces core values that the organization will attempt to preserve. When constraints are present, cued brainwriting can be used to subtly introduce these requirements into the process without lowering acceptance and innovation. Morphology and EDE with rank weight are recommended for synthesis and selection, again to ensure that constraints are recognized.

Traditional

Traditional strategies do not stress innovation but require quality and acceptance. Such a strategic management process could be mounted in response to external agents, such as regulators, that can impose certain sanctions unless the organization changes its policies, services, and practices. For example, medicare reimbursement policy forced hospitals to consider expanding outpatient services. Regulators of power generating utilities call for the use of locally available gas and oil by the utility regardless of its storage and transportation costs. The strategy used by respected competitors faced with the same external pressures is often mimicked. NGT is suggested because it promotes both quality and acceptance. Snowball, scenario, Q sort, and EDE with rank weight are recommended for synthesis and selection tasks.

When constraints are added, the process is called a *constrained traditional strategy*. For example, a power-generating utility may attempt to purchase locally available gas but continue to transport gas from other states to avoid lawsuits and to ensure adequate gas supplies for worst-case scenarios stemming from extremes in weather. Cued brainwriting, ISM, and EDE with rank weight are recommended for the reasons previously cited.

Ideal Prototypes

The ideal prototype strategy calls for quality and innovation. The prototype creates a benchmark to gauge future efforts. Such a strategic management process could be undertaken by consulting firms to specify the range of strategic alignments that make sense for their current or projected clients. Because acceptance is not an issue, Delphi surveys are recommended. The surveys are designed to tap people with state-of-the-art information by involving individuals inside and outside the organization. The Delphi survey is used to dredge up ideas for SMG consideration prior to using synectics. Snowball and scenarios are used for syntheses. A *Q* sort winnows ideas.

In a *constrained prototype strategy,* a focus group is used to ensure that ideas the organization wants considered get introduced to the SMG and that the group is oriented toward core values the organization wants to preserve. Structured brainwriting is applied to introduce quality. Morphology imposes a structure and a *Q* sort creates a winnowed list of possible options for future consideration. In both the ideal and constrained prototype strategies, formal selection awaits selling a strategy to a client.

Utility

Strategies devised to seek only quality are called utility. This type of strategy is preferred when organizational leaders are both powerful and relatively independent of their board and regulatory agents. Nonprofit organizations with fee-for-service revenue generation could adopt such a posture. Examples include consulting firms, such as RAND, and some state organizations, such as departments of natural resources, that can charge for licenses and inspections mandated by law. Such an environment permits a proactively inclined leader to operate in a highly autonomous manner. When such a leader is less interested in what is new than in what works, a utility strategy seeking process can be called for. The brainwriting technique is suggested. A relevance tree structure can be used to capture the actions being called for the chief executive officer. ARS offers a quick way to set priorities. A *qualified utility process strategy* (quality and constraints) could be managed by cued brainwriting, synthesized by a tree structure, and selected by ARS.

Awareness

Awareness strategies are carried out to inform an SMG about possibilities and to seek acceptance to act on possibilities that seem particularly relevant. Organizations that seek to coax key stakeholders into exploring possibilities would use this type of strategy. An NGT is proposed for search; snowball, ISM, and scenarios for syntheses; and EDE with paired comparison for selection for awareness strategy development. A *constrained awareness strategy* also seeks the acceptance of possibilities but imposes constraints on the search. For instance, a utility could use such a process to get top management to see new vistas for the organization, while recognizing pet ideas that pose constraints. For these strategies, cued brainwriting is suggested for search, ISM for synthesis, and EDE with rank weight for selection.

Seductive

For the seductive strategy, only acceptance is important. Such strategy can arise when leaders are confronted by board members who insist that the organization devises a strategic plan. For example, business representatives on a school board may contend that schools without a formal strategy are run by the "seat of the pants." The school superintendent may have a strategy, but prefers to keep it hidden, for example, because of impending desegregation litigation or because he or she does not see the merit in a strategic management process. In either case, only acceptance would be sought. Search techniques are preferred that make the member feel that something was accomplished but that do not limit the leader's ability to maneuver (Mintzburg and Waters, 1982). The NI process is recommended. Morphology with NGT can be used to explore emergent factors and to seek a synthesis of ideas acceptable to all. Any quick voting technique (such as ARS) can be used.

A *constrained seductive strategy* (acceptance with constraints) calls for cued brainwriting to introduce constraints and

NI with plants (people who lobby for ideas thought to be crucial) to promote acceptance. Synthesis and selection use the same
techniques recommended for seductive strategy.

Idea

Idea strategies develop possibilities for contemplation, not action. Hospitals that explore ways to replace revenue losses due
to reimbursement caps may develop such a strategy to inform
themselves about possibilities without the friction of acceptance
or the need to make assessments of quality. A creative process
is needed for search, which calls for synectics with each step of
the synectics process managed by NGT. Synthesis calls for
snowball and ISM to capture the relationship. Selection is done
using EDE and paired comparison.

A *constrained idea strategy* identifies areas to be preserved
before the organization sorts through possibilities. Cued brainwriting and synectics can be used for search, ISM for synthesis,
and EDE with paired comparisons for selection to identify approximate ordering among a constrained list of ideas.

Gesture and Ratification

A gesture strategy is created when the process to derive strategy is mounted merely to impress third parties. Such a process
may be rational when regulatory or legislative bodies give special consideration to organizations that carry out strategic management or appear to have produced a new strategy. For example, health regulators require evidence of a strategic plan
before capacity expansion plans of a hospital will be considered. An interacting group, made up of people that the leader
can control, is asked to elicit ideas and act as the SMG for a
gesture strategy. The ideas can be recorded and voted on using a pooled rank voting technique.

For a *ratification strategy,* synthectic groups (for example,
surveys) are used because constraints are important. Analysis
of the survey can ensure that these constraints are identified.
For instance, newspapers use this type of strategy when they

conduct surveys of readers' preferences and then ignore preferences that conflict with editorial policies of the paper. Any format that makes voting easy can be used. The synthesis step can be ignored for gesture and ratification strategies.

Key Points

1. Strategic management requires knowledge of process; techniques that support the search, synthesis, and selection demands of a process; and the combination of techniques into hybrids to meet the special needs of strategic management in a given situation.

2. Hybrid techniques are created by combining or merging the techniques for search, synthesis, and selection in creative ways. Some of these combinations were described in Chapters Nine, Ten, and Eleven, but still others are possible. The process facilitator who becomes familiar with these techniques can fashion still more hybrids tailored to his or her specific needs.

3. Types of strategy are defined by whether or not quality, acceptance, innovation, and preservation are required for the strategy to be devised. Each strategy is matched to hybrid techniques that can be used to deal with the search, synthesis, and selection requirements of each process stage.

PART FIVE

■   ■

Strategy
in Practice:
Three Cases

■   ■

In Part Five, three cases are presented that describe how strategic management can be carried out by following our process prescriptions. The cases are selected to indicate some of the unique needs that arise in nonprofit organizations, local governments, and state agencies. The cases differ in the involvement of staff and boards of directors, numbers of sessions and intensity of effort, the role of oversight bodies in the strategic management process, continuous versus single-cycle attempts at strategic management, and types of strategy pursued.

Each case details the organization's history; the triggering events that prompted change; and the aftermath, in which the issue agenda is reshaped. We illustrate how to collect needed information, use techniques, classify issues, and identify and interpret environmental factors using all of the tools and concepts discussed in the book.

■   ■

Chapter Thirteen

Strategic Challenges
to a Nonprofit
Social Services
Agency

■   ■

This chapter describes strategic management activities for a mental health center. The triggering development was the loss of federal funding. This cutback was to eliminate, over a three-year period, 34 percent of the revenues used to operate the center. The center was groping for ways to replace these lost revenues without curtailing services to needy groups who had become dependent on the center.

The triggering development had a production value. The strategic management process uncovered a tension between the values of productivity and equity that had gone unrecognized by the center's management. The most obvious way to replace revenue lost from federal block grants was to charge for services. However, the traditions of treatment professionals in the center made this difficult. The therapists encouraged the use of mental health services by divorcing payment from the service. Even questions about private fees and the ability of a service user to pay through insurance had been ignored, making service fees that could have been collected go undetected. The sliding-fee scale used by the center was not acceptable to welfare agencies, which made collection from medicaid and other public assistance programs impossible. The therapist's negotiation with a client set treatment goals as well as payment levels. The sliding scale for payments was strongly rooted in the organization's traditions. As a result, the productivity-equity tension was moderated by preservation.

This chapter outlines the process that was used to shape the agency's strategy and develop an implementation plan for its installation. First, we give some background that describes the history and nature of the center. This discussion is followed by a description of how we phased activity in the strategic management process and formed the SMG. The information gleaned for each stage of the process and techniques applied are then presented. The section called "Aftermath" gives a summary of how the agency used these ideas and integrated strategic management into its organization. The executive director sought a comprehensive strategy that had quality, acceptance, and innovation. We selected techniques that matched these requirements (see Chapter Twelve).

Agency Background

The organization was founded when a steering committee was formed to open a mental health center in the early sixties. Within two years, five counties were involved in the center through membership on the steering committee. The center opened two years later to provide mental health service for a five-county catchment area. Funding from the state created expanded mental health and retardation services in 1969. The center's growth and its continuous service to clients was recognized by a mental health levy that was passed in 1975. In the center's locality, and throughout the nation, the awareness of the need for mental health service was growing. In 1978, the center received a grant from the National Institute of Mental Health (NIMH) to design a comprehensive service package.

The rapid growth led to a decentralization of services to local communities. This step helped to assure that local communities would become involved in the center, with a central management structure providing oversight for financing and development. NIMH funding led to designation as a "comprehensive center." Staff grew to 130 professional and support personnel, who provided services to 1,500 clients by 1980. In 1981, two new clinic buildings were opened in two of the counties. Another was added in 1982 and two more in 1984. Also, a fifteen-bed inpatient unit was completed during this time period.

The center tailored services to the needs of each of its five counties and involved the community in each local center. This approach helped to provide services that were responsive to local needs, rather than programs that must meet needs preferred by center practitioners and federal policy makers.

The center's existence depended on volunteers who gave it the initial impetus and provided support for the subsequent growth of its services. In addition, strength was drawn from 200 crisis volunteers. These volunteers were thought to demonstrate the center's commitment to its community and partnership with the community in service development and delivery.

The commitment to offer services of the highest quality to anyone who needed them resulted in huge growth, doubling the center's number of cases over the past six years. In addition, 18,000 contacts were served through a crisis line.

Current Situation

The center operates on a $4 million budget and has one hundred twenty professional staff members, including psychiatrists, psychologists, social workers, counselors, and technicians. Through five clinics, about 2,700 clients were being served. The center offers a range of services including aftercare, adult outpatient care, day treatment, children's residential care, consultation and education, emergency services, and substance abuse treatment.

The center described its mission as providing leadership and services on a community basis to foster positive mental health. The center was committed to finding ways of preventing, reducing, and minimizing the residual effects of mental health problems. The center believes that services should be made available to everyone in its catchment area without regard to factors that distinguish people, including ability to pay. A strict confidence between client and the agency is maintained in all service delivery.

The center provides services for people with mental disabilities, substance abusers, and people with stress-related ailments. Programs have been fashioned to serve suicide attempters, people having difficulty coping with marital and economic problems, and victims of domestic violence and of rape or abuse. Substance abuse programs are focused on drugs and alcohol. A variety of special programs have been mounted to deal with displaced homemakers, children services backup, unemployed care givers, survivors and survivor families, correctional institutions, the hungry and needy, the deaf, stress victims, Alzheimer's disease support groups, teen parents, single parents, persons in life crisis, the elderly, farmers in economic strife, and the unemployed.

Funds to operate the center are received from several sources. State and local funding through state appropriations and local levies made up about 33 percent of the revenues, Title XX and XIX made up 12 percent, self-pay and insurance made up 6 percent, and children's residential and LEAA made up 4 percent. Income from services sold to local industry made up 10 percent of the revenues. The source of revenue had to grow if the 33 percent of the budget currently provided by federal block grants was phased out.

The center was under the general direction and oversight of a multicounty volunteer board. A politically appointed "648" board contracts with the center for the delivery of the mental health services. The 648 board distributes state mental health funds to multicounty areas by contracting with mental health centers to offer services in those areas.

Motivation

The center's interest in using a strategic management process was triggered by productivity developments: the termination of federal funding for mental health centers, increased competition from hospitals and other providers, and shifts in sources of revenues. The center's leadership wanted to establish a more dynamic, anticipatory approach to planning. They sought to supplement their annual planning activities with a long-range, action-centered process.

In the following sections we describe our approach to strategically managing the center, identifying the principal participants, and describing the results obtained. The purpose of this discussion is to illuminate both the how and the what of the process by describing how it is carried out and the results obtained.

Strategic Management Process

The strategic management process was carried out by a strategic management group (SMG), composed of organizational insiders. The fifteen SMG participants were all senior agency staff members. They included the agency executive director (chief executive), controller, assistant director, director of administration services, director of research and evaluation, consultation coordinator, four satellite directors, director of rehabilitation services, emergency services coordinator, substance abuse coordinator, and inpatient unit coordinator. Outside stakeholders were involved in legitimizing the process at the beginning and became involved again during implementation.

Facilitators carried out the process by holding four-hour meetings each month for seven months with the SMG. The phasing of activities used in this case is shown in Figure 13.1. Note how key activities are repeated to review and update the

Figure 13.1. Phasing of Activities for Mental Health Center.

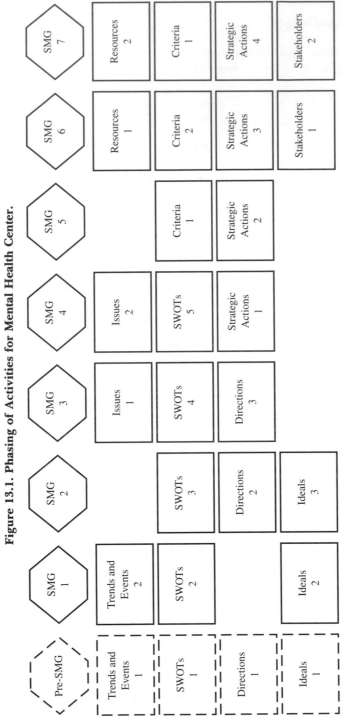

SMG's mutual understanding throughout the process (see Chapter Eight).

The SMG engaged in a series of activities to launch the strategic management process and develop the SMG as a strategic management team. The SMG was given a listing of events in the form of an agenda to be specific about the time commitments. A listing of events for the mental health center, drawn from Figure 13.1, follows.

Session 1: Orientation to Strategic Management and Context Appreciation
Discuss intent of process
Define strategic management
Discuss steps to be taken in the seven sessions
Review and rate situational assessment (survey feedback)
Review and rate trends and events (survey feedback)
Review and rate ideals (survey feedback)

Session 2: Situational Assessment
Review and rate strengths, weaknesses, opportunities, and threats (SWOTs)
Review directions
Review ideals

Session 3: Strategic Direction
Discuss relationships among issues
Compare issues with SWOTs
Review situational assessment
Establish directions
Identify issues

Session 4: Strategies
Review SWOTs
Discuss strategic principles
Develop strategic actions

Session 5: Strategic Action I
Develop strategic actions
Analyze strategic actions
Identify strategic criteria

Session 6: Strategic Action II
  Synthesize strategic actions
  Apply criteria to select priority actions
  Identify resources
  Identify stakeholders
    (stakeholder interviews between sessions)
Session 7: Planning for Action and Implementation
  Test strategies
  Plan action
  Analyze stakeholders
  Review situational assessment
  Establish directions
  Identify issues
  Analyze resources
  Manage the strategic implications

An agenda, identifying specific activities for individual sessions, was prepared for each meeting.

Stage One: Historical Context

In the first stage, the strategic management group identified trends, critical events, and directions that characterize the historical context of the mental health center and its ideals. The SMG reconstructed history by examining past trends, events, and directions of emphasis, noting how they have changed in the past and may change in the future for the center.

Collecting the Information

A modified Delphi survey (Chapter Nine) was used to collect data describing trends, events, and directions prior to the first meeting (pre-SMG in Figure 13.1). Two weeks were needed to complete the first round of the survey and two more to summarize the results.

The SMG was sent Form A.1 and asked to fill out Form A.2 (see Resource A). Staff members summarized these results by taking one item from each SMG member's list until all items were recorded. This mixed the responses from an individual member with the others in the SMG. In the initial meetings, the SMG rated each trend, event, and direction by applying the direct assignment technique using a 1 (least important) to 10 (most important) rating scale (see Chapter 11). The rating process was repeated to allow for reflection and sharing of information among SMG members. To give a sense of dispersion, individual ratings were listed along with the average depicting current consensus.

External Trends and Events

The SMG was asked to list specific external trends and events that will influence how the center will function for the next three to seven years and that must be confronted. Each member was asked to think broadly and include economic, client, managerial, technical, social, political, and demographic factors that should be considered for their strategic impact. Fifty-nine trends and events were identified, rated, and sorted into economic, user-related, and political categories. The lists that follow note the five top-ranked trends and events identified by the SMG in each category. (A complete listing can be obtained by writing the authors.)

Average Rating:	Economic Events and Trends
9	1. Loss of federal funding and levy renewal
9	2. Limits on health care costs by insurance regulations as well as caps on third-party reimbursement growth
8	3. Use of fewer services when people are made to pay
8	4. Increased encroachment and competition
7	5. Pressure by 648 board to do more with less

Average Rating:	*User Related Events and Trends*
9	1. Demand for improved services
9	2. Specialized programs and services that cater to business and industry
8	3. Increasing numbers of homeless and awareness of need for mental health services in this group
7	4. Continuation of high unemployment and underemployment in center's catchment area, leading to more consumers without funds
7	5. Assistance for formation of community support groups (such as groups for parents of troubled teens, and so on), cancer victims, parents of gays

Average Rating:	*Political Events and Trends*
9	1. Recruitment of business leaders as board members
8	2. State department of mental health expectations regarding services for severely mentally retarded
8	3. Demands by state for non-duplication, leading to more interagency cooperation and coordination
7	4. Continued conflict over substance abuse funding

6   5. Community reaction against
                                        group homes

Directions

The SMG was asked to identify the current strategic direction
of the center by characterizing its movement in the past and
projecting this movement into the future. Each SMG member
was asked to look back over the past three to seven years and
ahead over a similar time period to identify major changes that
had been or will be experienced. Directions were classified by
the four components of a system: needs and demands, programs, resources, and administrative or managerial capacities.
The raw responses were placed into these categories for subsequent review. The SMG members listed twenty-two directions for *needs and demands*. The top five follow:

Moving Away From	*Moving Toward*
1. Free services and services to poor	1. More business or finan- cially related activities
2. Staff independence	2. More regulation, structure
3. Responding to basic needs with one approach (psychi- atric evaluation, medica- tion, and counseling)	3. Responding to needs, pre- sented by target groups (such as hospital dis- charges, battered women and men, groups of em- ployees needing service)
4. Responding primarily to needs as perceived by mental health system em- ployees	4. Comprehensive approach to diversity of needs
5. Therapy as the major treatment modality	5. Case management as ma- jor program activity

The SMG listed twenty-one directions for *programs*. The
top five follow:

Moving Away From	*Moving Toward*
1. Referrals from public welfare and state institutions	1. Middle income, insured, and employed patients
2. Programs lacking in directions or targets based on whim of staff	2. Increased emphasis on specific targets
3. Funding for services based on broad definitions	3. Funding for services based on specific services and clients
4. Comparative isolation of mental health services from other agencies	4. Working collaboratively with others
5. Working mostly with lower-income and lower-functioning clients	5. Working with higher-functioning and higher-income clients.

The SMG listed fifteen directions for *resources*. The top five follow:

Moving Away From	*Moving Toward*
1. Poor physical facilities	1. Good physical facilities
2. Productivity as the number one priority	2. Increased evaluation of efficacy of service delivery
3. Giving away services	3. Improved collection of fees and more sources of funding
4. Staff with avant-garde image	4. Staff with professional, conservative image
5. Stable environment with abundant resources	5. Uncertain environment with limited resources

The SMG listed twenty directions in *management*. The top five follow:

Moving Away From	*Moving Toward*
1. Autonomy	1. Increased accountability
2. Diffuse image	2. Clearer image

3. Clear roles and tasks for board in governance and committee work

3. No clear tasks for board in governance and more relinquishing of authority to administrator

4. Decentralized model, with autonomy at the lower level

4. Decentralized but specialized model, with dual levels of accountability

5. A variety of public images created by different staff approaches to media

5. Unified image of the center consciously shaped by the board, executive director, and media specialist

Ideals

A third and final activity in stage one had the SMG members create idealized images of the mental health center five or more years into the future, while the analyses of trends and events and of shifting directions were still fresh in their mind. The SMG participants were asked to describe attributes that would make up an ideal vision of their organization.

The SMG filled out Form A.4, following the procedure used for trends, events, and directions in SMG 1 (Figure 13.1). Looking ahead into the future, the SMG identified fourteen attributes to characterize the best of all possible worlds for the center. After synthesis, the following ideas emerged: *"Balance between decentralization which insures client sensitivity about needs and centralization to maintain high standards of services for all, fiscal balance between income source (third party, self pay, levy, state funds, and industry contracts); balance of resources allocated to hospital and residential treatment, day treatment, aftercare, EMC house, outpatient counseling, crisis and educational programs; balance between clinical skill development to sustain and increase quality of treatment, and use of outside programs."*

The SMG identified fourteen attributes to characterize the worst of all possible worlds for the center. The following ideas emerged: "Loss of balance, leaving the agency with: centralized decision making, a shift to narrow range of services for a narrow range of consumers, more paper work leading to less time for service provision, and movement away from treatment for excellence to financial incentives."

Interpreting the Information

The SMG noted external trends and events such as decreases in federal funding, increasing need for health care cost containment, and pressures from its board to increase productivity. Changes in directions were keyed to needs and demands, resources, programs and services, and general management practices. Specifically, the SMG envisaged a change in service demands from a historical pattern of free services to a rationing of services. The center's SMG viewed the center's past use of resources as typified by the building of facilities, whereas it saw the future as emphasizing full use of those facilities with no new construction. A movement from nonspecialized services for the poor to specialized services for business and industry was envisaged. The SMG saw the center as moving from a reactive to an anticipatory orientation in planning and from management by the staff's clinical preference to management for organizational survival.

The mental health center's SMG saw its ideals as a balance between individual client's needs and high standards of services for all, a balance between income sources, a balance of resources allocated to various programs, and a balance between clinical skills development and use of outside programs. The idealized vision of the organization captured the tensions in opposing forces that will take shape as issues. Ideals also provide a target, offering a way to assess movement toward desired ends.

The SMG members examined their initial mindsets by using directions and trends to reconstruct the organization's history. Ideals were used to push the organization's planning horizon forward. Surveys were used to collect this information from each member. The survey results were aggregated and fed back to the SMG to promote discussion and refinement during meetings. Discussion allowed the SMG to develop a shared interpretation of the organization's history and its idealized future.

Stage Two: Situational Assessment

Exploring historical context brought the strategic management group to an understanding of the center's past and its idealized future. In the next stage, the immediate situation of the organization was considered. To carry out this stage, the SMG identified and ranked the organization's current strengths and weaknesses as well as its future opportunities and threats.

Collecting the Information

The modified Delphi survey used to collect information in stage one included a section for SWOTs. Form A.5 (Resource A) was used and included in the pre SMG survey activities (see Figure 13.1). Rating and summary followed the steps taken for stage one.

The rating of SWOTs was repeated in several SMG meetings (see Figure 13.1). Discussions and rerating allowed for the sharing of information among SMG members and encouraged a movement toward a consensus. Individual votes are listed in the rankings below to give a notion of the dispersion of values among SMG members.

SWOTs are rated and rerated several times in most of our SMG meetings. In the case of the mental health center, SWOTs were considered five times before a consensus emerged. Finding consensus on SWOTs can take less time in some settings but seldom more time than that observed in this case.

Strengths were collected by asking the SMG members to identify skills, distinctive competencies, capabilities, competitive advantages, or resources that could be affected by internal actions or policies and must be drawn on to carry out new strategy. The SMG identified seventy-four strengths and rated them with a scale on which 10 equals most and 1 equals least. Note how the priorities shifted following discussion. The five top-rated strengths are listed below.

Mean Score	Priority New	Old	Strengths
9	1	20	Varied programming and comprehensive services
9	2	13	Present financial position
8	3	4	Quality of therapists and clinical staff and their commitment to excellence
7	4	18	Active and supportive board and strong board relationship
8	5	54	Support of key community leaders, particularly legislators and public officials

Weaknesses were collected by asking the SMG members to list skills, distinctive competencies, capabilities, competitive advantages, or resources that are missing and must be overcome to make strategic change. The SMG listed sixty-four weaknesses. The five top-rated weaknesses are listed below:

Mean Score	Priority New	Old	Weaknesses
8	1	8	Inadequate, complicated, and confused billing system that lacks timeliness and capacity
7	2	12	Impending loss of public dollars and low third-party reimbursement
6	3	6	No psychiatric leadership
6	4	26	Staff members who do not understand how to operate in climate of resource scarcity
5	5	35	Poor relationships with physicians

Opportunities were collected by asking the SMG to describe situations in which benefits are fairly clear and likely to be realized if a correct set of actions is taken. The SMG identified forty-seven opportunities. The five top-rated opportunities are listed below:

Mean Score	Priority New	Old	Opportunities
9	1	3	Growth of third- and first-party revenue
9	2	7	Passing of levy
9	3	18	Increased use of services by employed (paying) persons
9	4	2	Industry programming
8	5	5	Becoming a fixture in the community, increasing acceptance, improving reputation, and improving credibility with state

Threats were described as situations giving rise to potentially harmful consequences to the center's future if action is not taken. The SMG identified forty-three threats. The five top-rated threats are listed below:

Mean Score	Priority New	Priority Old	Threats
9	1	1	Bizarre behavior by 648 board
9	2	2	Scheduled decline of federal block grant over the next two to three years
9	3	12	Loss of local levy support (fighting by five county commissioners over levy percentage)
7	4	16	Erosion of support of care for seriously ill
7	5	27	Tendency of people who can pay for services to disregard local agencies

Interpreting the Information

The SMG perceived the mental health center's strengths to include service variety, current financial position, and quality of therapists, staff, leadership, and management. Their perceived weaknesses included an inadequate billing system, dependence on uncertain public dollars, low levels of revenues from third-party payers, and weak leadership in psychiatry resulting from a long-standing vacancy in its medical director position. In terms of future opportunities the members of the SMG believed they might increase third-party revenues, get a levy approved, increase industry contracts for services, and actively market their services to new clients. They perceived threats as the phaseout of federal block grant monies, limits on the amount of levy support that they could get county boards to put on a ballot for voter approval, the capriciously shifting priorities of the "648" board, and the increasing control of mental health dollars by health maintenance organizations.

The situational assessment made by the SMG candidly confronted crosscurrents in the pressures that the center faced. Reviewing history in stage one and conducting a situational assessment in stage two made it possible for the SMG to own up to the center's weaknesses and threats without attributing blame to others. Clarifying strengths allowed the SMG to see capabilities that the organization possessed and reinforced their sense of competence in managing their weaknesses and threats. The idealization process stimulates a more active search for opportunities in the direction of the ideals. The first two stages built great pressure to get at the core issues that must be managed, which ushered in the next stage.

Stage Three: The Issue Agenda

We define an issue as a difficulty that has a significant influence on an organization's ability to achieve a desired future and for which there is no mutually agreed-on response. Issues can be internal or external to an organization or both.

Public and third sector SMGs typically uncover four to seven high-priority issues for active management, thus creating an issue agenda. The dynamic nature of both the organization and its environment ensure that, over a year or two, the strategic issue agenda will shift as new items enter and old items disappear. For that reason, an SMG should review and update its issue agenda periodically, as discussed in Chapter Eight.

Collecting the Information

Issues represent a departure from previous activities in both content and procedure. In stages one and two, the emphasis has been historical—finding and building on a consensus about the forces acting on the organization. A shift to the present is made in stage three by dealing with these concerns. We used an NGT (Chapter Nine) to uncover issues and the ideas about tensions discussed in Chapters Five and Six to frame issues, and direct assignment to rank them (Chapter Eleven). During the NGT session, Form A.6 (Resource A) was used.

Thirty issues emerged from the NGT session. The six top-ranked issues are listed below:

Rank	Mean Score	Issues
1	8	Increasing the number of paying consumers while meeting the needs of those whose ability to pay is low

2	7	Remaining financially stable
3	6	Developing a billing system that incorporates business concepts and professional values (sliding-fee scale)
4	6	Developing new ventures independent of 648 board control
5	6	Allocating a limited number of staff to increasing demands for productivity
6	6	Attracting and maintaining quality staff

These issues were then put in terms of opposing forces pulling or pushing the center various directions and away from idealized images of its future. These forces identify the underlying tensions at work on the organization. This format for expressing issues illustrates polar opposites, or contradictions, within the organization or between it and external actors. Issues were examined to find the implied tension. Six issue tensions emerged after discussion:

1. Billing system philosophy that incorporates both business and humanitarian values (for example, fee for service or sliding-fee scales)
2. Maintenance of financial stability while searching for new sources of revenue
3. Maintenance of quality staff while meeting system demands for new services
4. Productivity demands and the values held by professional staff about quality care
5. New ventures that threatened the center's old stakeholders
6. Need for revenues and dealing with users who cannot pay for service

The issues were then compared two at a time to determine precedence and producer-product relationships among the issues, following procedures described in Chapter Ten. The resulting diagrams are shown in Figures 13.2 and 7.3.

Interpreting the Information

The humanitarian values of service for all, without regard to a client's ability to pay, and the need for a businesslike approach

Figure 13.2. Issue Precedence for Mental Health Center.

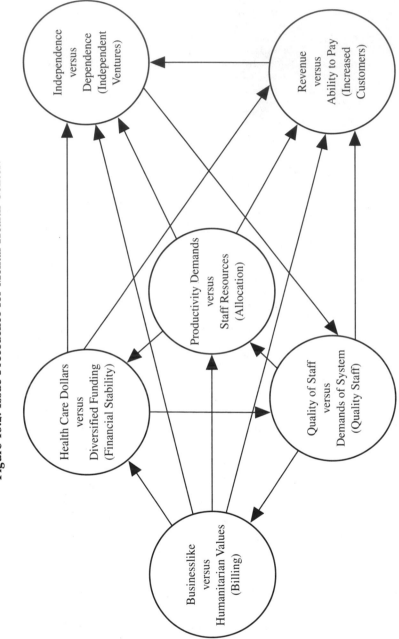

in the collection of fees for service created the fundamental tension. By framing issues as opposites and confronting the historical context and situational assessment, the SMG members felt a strong need to reconcile these contradictory pressures. A second issue, related to the center's financial stability, involved the twin pressures of declining health care subsidies and the need for diversified funding in the face of cutbacks. Again, the issue called for a solution that reconciled dual pressures. A third issue concerned the maintenance of high-quality treatment and the simultaneous demand for more productivity in processing of clients. The center's dependence on the 648 board for its funding, the expected decrease in funds available to that board (resulting from cutbacks in federal subsidies that the board administers), and the potential for independent funding through new ventures by the center caused a tension between independence and dependence, creating still another issue. Figure 7.3 shows how these issues have a mutually causal relationship, making them the key concerns in the search for strategic action.

The strategic management group uncovered issues, discussed them, and ranked them in one meeting. At the next meeting, the top issue was selected for management by the SMG. The issue selected was to reconcile humanitarian and business values, and its selection is confirmed by the precedence relationship in Figure 13.2, because this issue precedes the others in importance. The billing issue had to be managed before marketing and funding issues could be considered.

The issue agenda typically is set by the third or fourth meeting and marks a turning point in the process. The remaining sessions focus less on the context and more on identifying substantive actions to manage the key issues. Note that specific goals are not needed to orient strategic thinking. Instead, participants reconstructed history and formed ideals as targets to create an anticipatory mindset. By shifting to the current operating tensions, the SMG was able to develop an agenda of issues to be managed now rather than goals to be achieved at some distant future. A network of relations (Figures 13.2 and 7.3) is the underlying focus of action, not a linear movement toward an abstract goal.

Stage Four: Strategic Options

The strategic management group identified possible strategies for dealing with each issue on the agenda, beginning with the most important issue to be managed. The list of strengths, weaknesses, opportunities, and threats, identified in stage four, was reviewed for each issue to see which SWOTs were most relevant and to uncover ones that had been overlooked. Different issues brought out different configurations of SWOTs and different rankings of the items in each. The shifting SWOT priorities allowed the strategic management group to see the complex dynamics at work in the center. Using the SWOTs as guidelines to generate ideas for action helped the center come to grips with its complex dynamics.

Collecting the Information

A synthesis of the forces underlying the issue was sought. The issue of billing system philosophy called for a reconciliation of humanitarian values with business realities. Strengths, weaknesses, opportunities, and threats suggested concerns that led to the new billing philosophy issue.

To identify strategic actions, SMG members were given worksheets with the issue and its relevant strengths, weaknesses, opportunities, and threats listed next to it (see Form A.7 in Resource A) and were given the following instructions: considering the ideals we have identified for our future, suggest concrete actions we could undertake to manage the issue described below so as to build on strengths, overcome weaknesses, exploit opportunities, and blunt threats. The SMG was asked to find or invent actions that addressed all four aspects.

The worksheet given the group members for the issue of billing system philosophy is shown in Figure 13.3. It was used in conjunction with the brainwriting approach described in Chapter Seven. Two groups were used. SMG participants in

Figure 13.3. Strategy Worksheet for Issue of Billing System.

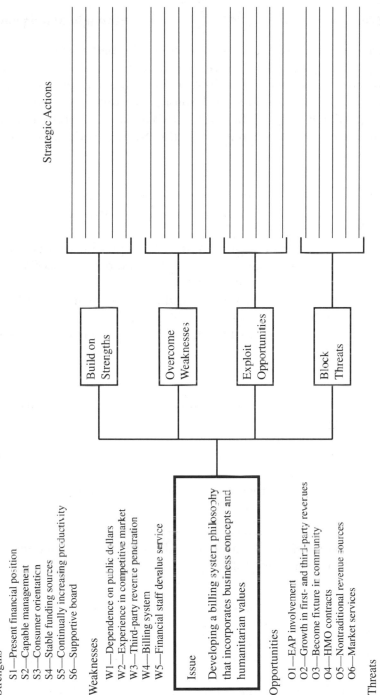

Strengths

S1—Present financial position
S2—Capable management
S3—Consumer orientation
S4—Stable funding sources
S5—Continually increasing productivity
S6—Supportive board

Weaknesses

W1—Dependence on public dollars
W2—Experience in competitive market
W3—Third-party revenue penetration
W4—Billing system
W5—Financial staff devalue service

Issue

Developing a billing system philosophy
that incorporates business concepts and
humanitarian values

Opportunities

O1—EAP involvement
O2—Growth in first- and third-party revenues
O3—Become fixture in community
O4—HMO contracts
O5—Nontraditional revenue sources
O6—Market services

Threats

T1—Reimbursement and billing
T2—Withdrawal of 648 board purchases
T3—Loss of local levy support
T4—HMO control of mental health dollars
T5—Federal block grant phaseout

each group listed actions and then swapped their sheets and added new ideas. This process continued until all members were passing the sheets and no longer recording actions. The results were listed in a round-robin fashion, discussed, and then ranked. A partial listing of the twenty-two ideas for strategic action produced by group one, with the SWOT code and priority noted, follows:

1. Get all staff to invest in the need to collect fees. (W4)
2. Support the 648 board's campaign strategy to get levy support. (T3)
3. Use a service representative concept with clients and insurance company to market the value of services and encourage sales. (O2)
4. Elicit the support and assistance of consumers and their families to educate the public. (T3)
5. Hire a professional fundraiser with salary based on amount raised. (T5)
6. Support efforts to lobby for third-party insurance coverage. (T1)
7. Identify and prioritize third-party markets in all areas for pilot action. (W3)
8. Recruit good billing staff. (S2)
9. Develop impact statement of what it would be like if service were cut. (T3)
10. Identify competitors and seek collaboration before becoming competitive. (W2)

Some of the twenty-seven ideas for strategic actions produced by group two follow:

1. Get each therapist to set dollar value on his or her services (W1) then focus on question, "What would help you be worth full agency charge?" (W2)
2. Give year-end bonus or award based on fees collected. (S1)
3. Use lost revenue figures to spotlight need for therapists

to get fees and answer questions for clients regarding fee collection. (O1)

4. Set aside reserve for those unable to pay to replace write-off system. (T1)
5. Develop reports to inform clinicians how much money they have generated. (W3)
6. Employ financial counselor to help clients deal with budgeting and finances. (S2)
7. Have consumers pay after each visit with billing and fees more differentiated by service. (T2)
8. Hire a consultant from a successful doctor's office or an administrator from a health maintenance organization for fee collection. (T3)
9. Use fees as tool in clinicians' work with clients (T4)
10. Set up "profit centers" responsible for generation of percentage of revenue for total budget. (T5)

A strategy is made up of action ideas that have a common theme. The SMG was asked to identify labels for separate bundles of actions to suggest themes. Themes may emerge from actions that launch a new program, identify resultant consequences and outcomes, or describe a process. The snowball technique was used to capture themes. The following themes emerged.

1. *Scholarship:* Use lump sum in lieu of payments agreed to at outset of therapy, with release forms to seek reimbursement for any additional therapy needed.
2. *Sales and Marketing:* Use multiyear contracts that offer services to industry. Market to insurance companies and create publicity that produces consumer support by demonstrating the value of services. Use media creatively to make these points.
3. *Contracting Procedures:* Involve clinicians in contract negotiation.
4. *Ownership:* Get consumer support and collaborative grants. Use service cut scenario to dramatize needs. Stress the need for mutuality.

5. *Pilot Collections:* Identify and prioritize third-party markets.

Interpreting the Information

The strategy selected by the mental health center stemmed from a need to change its past practice in charging for services. Historically, the mental health center had based its fees on the client's ability to pay; fees were negotiated by each therapist for each client. This negotiation allowed therapists to treat low-income clients who could be significantly helped by their services, but it also led to variations in charges for clients with similar resources and problems. Welfare agencies and insurance carriers interpreted this practice as a sliding-fee scale, which had two consequences for the center. First, third-party reimbursements were lost. Most welfare agencies and insurance carriers refuse to reimburse unless the provider organization has a fixed fee for services. Second, sliding fees led many clients to view the services of the mental health center as free: fully covered by public funds. With the anticipated cutbacks in federal subsidies, the center's cost recovery from these funds would fall from 80 percent to 50 percent, putting the center in an untenable financial position.

The SMG selected a strategy it called *scholarships*. The scholarship represented that portion of the cost of a client's care that would be borne by the center, that is, paid for by public funds. Clients would be asked during admission to help the center determine how they would pay for the remainder of their care using a variety of sources, such as self-pay, insurance, medicaid, and so on, and to authorize the center to pursue reimbursement from those payers. This strategy resulted in fixed fees, which allowed the mental health center to pursue aggressive fee collection from welfare and insurance sources and did not call for payments from low-income clients. It allowed the center to simultaneously increase its revenues and maintain the humanitarian nature of its services. Having selected a strategy for implementation, the SMG did a pre-implementation feasibility assessment and entered a new stage.

Stage Five: Feasibility Assessment

The operating environment of the regional mental health center was quite complex. Introducing a new strategy ushered in considerations that went beyond forecasting what services consumers would purchase. Besides the standard concerns for clients' or customers' and employees' views of change, political, financial, and legal implications had to be considered. To deal with this broader set of considerations, two steps were taken. First, extended discussions of who will be affected by the new strategy and how other parties could affect successful implementation were carried out using stakeholder analysis. Specific parties who could affect or were affected by the scholarship strategy were identified to determine the people and organizations with political, financial, managerial, professional, or other interests or stakes in the strategy and to anticipate how they might respond as the scholarship strategy was communicated and implemented. Second, resources required to implement the strategy were determined. The analysis went beyond finances to consider political, legal, managerial, professional, and other resources and who could supply them.

Stakeholder and resource analysis clarified the range of joint commitments that must exist or be built between the center and its stakeholders and resource suppliers if implementation of the strategy was to be successful. Top management was responsible for building these commitments. The operational, technical design, and installation activities were delegated to others.

Collecting the Information

The mental health center's scholarship strategy called for a movement from a policy of free care to a more aggressive posture toward fee collection. The scholarship would underwrite a portion of the costs of care but would commit clients to help find ways to pay the rest.

The limitations of time and resources called for the targeting of high-priority stakeholders. First, the SMG identified stakeholders for the scholarship strategy. To aid in this listing, the SMG considered users of services, key providers of support, cooperating units, providers of services, and the like. The SMG used Form A.8 (see Resource A) to list the required information. Information collection was carried out during SMG 6 (see Figure 13.1) and managed using NGT, described in Chapter Nine. The SMG listed both stakeholders and their stakes or interests in the strategy in this step.

After the list was completed, each stakeholder was ranked in terms of importance using Form A.8. When assigning ranks, the SMG noted the nature of the stakeholder's interest or stake and whether the stakeholder came from inside or outside the organization. (The ranking procedures were described in Chapter Seven.) A direct assignment approach was used in the stakeholder segment (see Chapter Eleven).

To score the stakeholder list in terms of position, SMG members were asked to find stakeholders *most* likely to be supportive of the scholarship strategy and rate them +5, and then find stakeholders most likely to oppose the strategy and rate them −5. Neutral stakeholders were rated 0, and the other stakeholders were scaled using these anchors (see Form A.9).

Position on the Issue
(−5 = Negative +5 = Positive).

Internal Stakeholders	*Priority*	*Average rating*
MHC board	#4	1.50
MHC management	#1	4.00
Supervisors, first level	#3	2.58
Clinical staff	#5	.83
Support staff	#6	.75
Billing staff	#2	3.42

External and Internal Stakeholders		
Clients		−.75
External Stakeholders		
648 board	#9	−1.83
648 staff	#8	−1.67

State department of mental health	#7	− .67
Local government		
State officials	#5	− .5
Referring agents	#3	0
Community at large (taxpayers)	#4	− .33
C&E contractors	#6	− .58
Insurance companies	#1	1.17
Anti–mental health power groups	#10	− 2.17

To score the stakeholder list in terms of importance, SMG members were asked to find the most important stakeholders and rate them 10 and then find the least important stakeholders and rate them 1, rating the remainder using these anchors. A rating of 5 or less identified stakeholders who required no formal contact (see Form A.10).

Importance
(1 = Least 10 = Most).

Internal Stakeholders	Priority	Average rating
MHC board	#2	8.75
MHC management	#1	9.08
MHC Supervisors	#3	8.00
Clinical Staff	#5	7.58
Support Staff	#6	5.83
Billing Staff	#4	7.83

External and Internal Stakeholders

Clients		5.92

External Stakeholders

648 board	#2	7.17
648 staff	#3	6.67
State department of mental health	#5	4.50
Local government		
State officials	#8	3.67
Referring agents	#7	3.83
Community at large (taxpayers)	#9	3.67
C&E contractors	#10	3.50
Insurance companies	#1	7.25
Anti–mental health power groups	#6	4.33

Resources were ranked in the same way as stakeholders (Forms A.11 and A.12).

Interpreting the Information

Ranking clarified how much and what kind of power the stakeholder had, suggesting the extent to which each stakeholder could influence the actions required by the strategy. Each stakeholder's importance and posture (support, neutrality, or opposition) was identified to classify stakeholders (see Figure 7.7 in Chapter Seven). The ranking put stakeholders in categories called *low priority, antagonistic, problematic,* and *advocates* for the next stage of the process.

Stage Six: Implementation

Our approach to implementation dealt with the broad-scale concerns raised by a change to the scholarship strategy, not with steps to install new billing procedures. Programs were devised to monitor and evaluate stakeholders' predicted actions.

The SMG evaluated each of the stakeholder categories. First, the numbers and proportions of stakeholders in each category were determined. Additional analyses were carried out to suggest the extent of support or opposition; determine the homogeneity of the stakeholders in each category; determine the prospects for a coalition; and identify neutral stakeholders who could be targeted for lobbying.

Plans

The chief executive officer (CEO) of the mental health center took over the process at this point. Figure 7.7 was used by the CEO to identify stakeholders for the mental health center and its scholarship strategy. The importance of the stakeholders in the antagonistic category suggested a need for considerable caution. Stakeholders who were closest to a neutral position (clients) were approached initially. The CEO attempted to win these individuals over. The center held public meetings to involve clients in careful discussions of the issues, asking for their suggestions of ways to replace lost sources of revenue.

Many of the external stakeholders were problematic stakeholders, and initial implementation avoided prematurely drawing attention to the scholarship strategy. The CEO also assessed these stakeholders to determine whether coalitions among them were possible and the probable implications of such coalitions for the scholarship strategy. For example, a coalition was possible between the state department of mental health and local governments, so the CEO took steps to allay local government officials' fears, assuring them that the mental health center did not anticipate asking for funding from local governments. Then the community at large was targeted for education attempts using the mass media. From that point on, the implementation moved to industry contractors. The center made presentations attempting to convert these stakeholders to at least a neutral, if not a supportive, position. Then the center was ready to deal with the members of the 648 board and its staff. The 648 board was empowered to contract for mental health services using state funds. These potentially antagonistic stakeholders presented a crucial barrier to implementation.

The center anticipated objections to dropping the sliding-fee scale and developed counterarguments. The center also developed a downside scenario: it described various actions, such as cutbacks in services and the like, that the center would have to take if a larger proportion of its service costs could not be reimbursed (see Chapter Ten). The analysis included the proportion of its costs that it currently captured and showed different targets, associating various downside possibilities with each target. For example, after federal cutbacks, revenues would be at 50 percent of costs; therefore, the center articulated scenarios at that level, at 65 percent, and at 95 percent, representing the current untenable situation, a problematic situation, and a good situation, respectively. The mental health center's scholarship strategy was presented as a way to preserve the humanitarian nature of its mental health services while assuring the center's survival.

Actions

The SMG uncovered a tension between billing for services and humanitarian service provision and selected it as the most important issue to be managed. This tension identified the need to deal with both equity in providing services and fee collection in any strategy to be developed. The center came up with a scholarship strategy, which created a win-win approach to managing the tension between billing versus humanitarian service provision. Patients were offered a scholarship, with the amount dependent on their financial circumstance and their prognosis for improvement. Patients were asked as a condition for receiving the scholarship to indicate whether they had insurance and to authorize the center to seek reimbursement from other sources, such as welfare agencies. This step made previously lost revenues recoverable. By having set fees and deferring payment for a period of time, the sliding-scale notion was preserved while reimbursement from federal and state sources was made possible. The tradition of delegating the fee decision to professional staff members was preserved by these arrangements.

The outcome of the process created a vital new face for the mental health center. This new face was used to hire key executive staff members, challenge and redirect a board of directors, and communicate with and bring cohesion to a diversity of staff members in a time of intense activity in the mental health industry. At an external level, understandings that emerged have helped conceptualize a new relationship with the 648 mental health board. The center confronted the threat of "bizarre 648 board behavior" and by doing so has helped a more mature relationship with the 648 board to emerge. The constant shifting of priorities has been recognized and steps have been taken by the 648 board to phase in new concerns and priorities.

The center has seen considerable success for their graphics marketing project and will open an intensive adult treatment center to help patients make the transition from state hospitals back to the communities. They have begun to market center products by establishing a sales position in the organization.

Reshaping the Issue Agenda

After this cycle of the process, the issue agenda for the mental health center had five issues yet to be considered. We helped the strategic leader test the issues that were uncovered by the SMG, using the framework in Chapters Five and Six to determine the issue agenda's comprehensiveness.

The issues were classified as shown below.

> *Productivity-Equity*
> Businesslike versus Humanitarian billing
> Demands for increased productivity versus staff demands for quality services
> Revenues versus ability of users to pay
> *Transition-Productivity*
> New business versus funding stability
> *Transition Equity*
> New services versus maintaining quality staff
> *Transition-Tradition*
> New ventures versus center independence

Review of this list suggests a preoccupation with the productivity-equity tension and a recognition of the impact that the expected transitions will have, without being specific about these transitions. The triggering development of productivity (loss of federal funds) was linked to equity in the first cycle of strategy making. Many of the issues that remained also concerned equity, including the ability of users to pay and therapists who control the conditions under which services were given (to the most indigent and those who could benefit most).

The budget shortfall (productivity) triggered concerns about the future. The SMG, made up largely of therapists, translated productivity into an equity tension. Dealing with equity suggested the need to move to actions that can replace lost revenue. The SMG was reluctant to confront the need to deal with transitions without linking it to tradition and equity. All other issues dealing with transition were linked with productivity.

The issue tension framework suggested the need to examine the issue tensions neglected in the first attempt at uncovering issues to find hidden concerns that may merit attention. For example, the equity-tradition tension suggests the need to explore whether therapists' demands for control over the conditions of service may influence the number of people that can be served, which may affect equity from the user's perspective. The tradition-productivity tension was also ignored in the first issue agenda. This tension suggests that the mental health center may be wedded to certain ways of doing things and will find it difficult to initiate new ventures that will reach out to businesses and offer mental health services. This new source of clients may restrain the therapists' freedom in deciding the conditions and provisions of service.

In forming a new issue agenda, the strategic leader was advised to search for issues that specified transitions and the issues that each transition may provoke. The search could then be directed toward finding issues buried in the equity-tradition and tradition-productivity tensions. After this search, a new issue agenda was to be formed and analyzed to find relationships before prioritizing issues for the next round of strategy development.

This approach recognizes that the initial issue agenda reflects the blind spot of an organization, but these initial attempts at action must deal with values perceived to be critical. The scholarship strategy allowed the mental health center to deal with the equity concerns posed by productivity threats. The agency then had the capacity to deal with transitions. Going to transitions initially would have been resisted. With these objections neutralized, a new issue agenda could be fashioned to continue strategy development.

Aftermath

The mental health center was emerging from a period in which it had considerable external control and moderate internal capacity. Historically, the external control stemmed from exclusive prerogatives to receive payments for the treatment of several types of mental illness. The center's attempts to maintain these arrangements had created a moderately *political* type of organization (see Figure 4.3). The strategic emphasis was to maintain relationships in the center's authority network, which ensured block grants from state and federal sources that underwrote the center's budget. The impending elimination of federal funds was shifting the center from a political to a *buffeted* organization.

External control was lost as the center groped for ways to deal with the loss of one-third of its revenues. The center's leader recognized the need to become more proactive and was searching for ways to increase internal competence and replace the lost control to reach this aim.

The center had been operating in a placid environment in which its clients had been stipulated by federal mandates. Local levies had been approved to expand treatment and subsidize the indigent. The center had become adept at managing its oversight bodies. These bodies had become center advocates, giving the center an exclusive franchise to deal with people needing mental health services in a five-county area and assisting in the passage of local levies that underwrote care for the indigent and others. A *bureaucratic* strategy emerged in which the center's strategic responsiveness was directed toward meeting federal and state edicts that governed the expenditure of state and federal funding (see Figure 4.1). The conditions of service provision were delegated to treatment professionals to carry out. The decision-making power of the professionals extended to deciding how much of the normal fee would be waived for each client.

The impending cuts in federal funding moved the center from a *placid* to a *turbulent* environment (Figure 4.1). The center's management sensed that its bureaucratic strategy must be changed. There was a need to produce new revenues, make major budget cuts, or do both budget slashing and look for new revenues. Expanding revenues called for new clients and a more proactive posture toward new ventures. Budget cuts called for tough choices among client groups that could damage future levy prospects. An *accommodator* strategy (Figure 4.1) emerged because of the center's need to become responsive to the demands posed by these new initiatives.

The center sought a way to manage two important clusters in its environment—relationships that maintained state and local funding and the new ventures. Each had special interests and demands that were not always complementary. The center believed that new ventures might draw in low-need services that catered to local employer perceptions of mental health issues and needs in their companies (such as stress management). These new initiatives could drive out services that were high need and poorly funded (such as services for the educable mentally retarded). Dealing with issues such as services for the educable mentally retarded posed issues that could be termed *sitting ducks* (Figure 4.2). The educable mentally retarded and other key clients served by the center posed problems for which there can be substantial progress and high public support, as indicated by local levy success. The more avant-garde services (such as counseling of rape and abuse victims and AIDS support groups) stemmed from issues that can become *angry tigers*. The clients of these services were becoming vocal about their needs and the quality of services they received. Allegiances to a particular source of care were not seen by members of these groups as either appropriate or needed. The center's carefully orchestrated image could be damaged by vocal clients who have a history of being highly critical of health care treatment professionals.

The priority issues tensions identified for management by the SMG, classified as a portfolio, are shown below. Their initial priority is given in parentheses.

Dark Horses
   Billing versus free care tension (1)
Angry Tigers
   Financial stability versus new revenue tension (2)
   Quality staff versus increased productivity tension (3)
   Productivity versus care quality tension (4)

Sitting Ducks
New ventures versus center independence tension (5)
Revenue versus ability to pay tension (6)

The mental health center selected a dark horse, the billing issue, for issue management, ignoring a sitting duck and a number of issues that could become angry tigers. To build capacity, it may have been essential for the center to pursue new ventures before confronting the angry tigers. However, success in dealing with new ventures would have defused the financial stability issue and reduced pressure to deal with the quality of staff and ability to pay issue.

Chapter Fourteen

Innovation in Local Government

This chapter describes the strategic management of a county library. The triggering development stemmed from a "preservation" value. A new tax law had been passed that threatened the library with a severe budget reduction. The library, widely accepted as one of the more progressive in the country, sought to preserve its programs and initiatives from being dismantled.

The strategic management process uncovered a tension between the value of preservation and both transition and productivity that had been overlooked. Current programs and capabilities were found to be in tension with allocation among categories of users in the inner city and suburbs (productivity) and a new state law that collected tax revenues and called for libraries to work out funding allocation (transition). The old law allocated tax revenues according to a population-served formula. The county library had the largest target group, so it received the biggest appropriation. Several wealthy suburbs had proposed to change the formula from population served to circulation. This would substantially increase the suburbs' share of the allocation and leave the county library's programs that serve low-income and minority children, who are historically relatively infrequent users of books, without support. The county was attempting to make the library a haven for these children between school hours to encourage educational values. This initiative would be more difficult to maintain if budget allocations were based on circulation, which was defined as books taken out of the library.

At the same time, this library, like libraries across the country, was undergoing a transformation. Its transaction system was being strained by a steady increase in demand, causing slow response time and down time, which created bottlenecks at circulation desks. Extra terminals and a system update were needed. The microfilm readers were obsolete and over 100 new ones were needed. The physical plants at several sites were in a critical state, and new branches were being demanded. All of this was occurring as the library was experiencing success in attracting unprecedented use by both minority groups and its traditional users.

The library had initiated "help line" and "morning memo" information systems, considered some of the best in the country before electronic mail had become a novelty. The morning memo reminded employees of tasks (such as meetings, programs, and job openings) and sent new items to the staff. The help line provided trained staff to help branches track down and repair terminals. The help line was essential to keep branches running with their obsolete equipment. The budget cuts that would result if a new allocation formula was enacted threatened these systems.

This chapter describes the process that was used to shape the program and funding strategies developed by the library. Background is provided describing the history of the library. This discussion is followed by a description of the SMG and the strategic management phases. The information obtained from each process phase is described. The "Aftermath" section provides a summary of how the library used these ideas and made strategic management a part of its ongoing management. The library director selected a qualified comprehensive strategy that sought quality, innovation, acceptance, and preservation. We selected techniques to identify and synthesize information that matched these requirements (see Chapter Twelve).

Organizational Background

The county library system had a large main library with twenty branches and a total collection of 25,000 items. It served a county with a population of 870,000. The branches had a combined circulation of 3.5 million, user visits of 2.6 million, and 2,800 registered patrons in the last year. The branches were augmented by bookmobile, hospital, home, and jail services that brought library services to areas without branches or with special needs for outreach programs. The branches with the largest per capita user visits and circulation were located in the suburbs, and those with the smallest were located in low-income areas found in the inner city. The branches varied considerably in size and newness of facility, and they attempted to keep services in line with turnover (the ratio of circulation to collection, a measure of utilization) and user visits. The branch libraries were designated "large" if their circulation was above 120,000, user visits above 100,000, and registered borrowers above 8,000. All branches sought this designation because large branches were staffed at fifty-seven hours a week, compared to forty hours for small branches.

Historical Development

The library began service in 1873 with magazines and newspapers, providing service in the old city hall. A new main library was opened in 1907, providing public meeting rooms. A music collection was donated in 1908, courtesy of a local women's music club. The first audiovisual programs began in 1908, which led to the establishment of an audiovisual division in 1950.

The library began a braille collection in 1937, donating it to the city board of education in 1968. A microfilm collection began in 1948, and a photo collection and books-by-mail service were added in 1974, with a video-studio service added a year later. The first videotapes were purchased in 1978, which also marked the creation of a newspapers and magazines division. A circulating visuals collection was initiated in 1981.

To support its diversified and growing collection, the library developed a number of notable administrative and program initiatives. Branches date from 1928, when an expansion to two central city and two fringe village sites was completed. A library station to help public schools was begun in 1937 and, in 1950, was absorbed into school libraries when they were capable of handling the service load. Services for hospital patients and homebound readers were started in 1949, and the first bookmobile was put into service in 1951. A drive-in window opened in 1975. The "classrooms without schools" program was begun in 1977 to provide services to low-income children. Writer-in-residence programs and the secondhand prose bookstore also date from 1977. Genealogy classes were first offered two years later. A home and garden line began in 1984.

A number of notable administrative services were added to support these program initiatives throughout the years. Computer payroll programs were added in 1963, and the IBM information system became operational in 1975, pioneering computerized communication to branches. The library grew beyond the city to become a countywide library in 1975. This change brought with it a new support group called Friends of the Library, which linked the new users with the new service areas. This change led to voter registration and other community services being offered by the library. Automated gaylord circulation systems were installed in 1978 to deal with the sharp increase in usage that was expected because of service area growth.

To promote these programs, a number of actions were taken. Alex Haley, the author of *Roots*, keynoted the dedication of an expanded central city branch. Noted children's authors who had special recognition in low-income areas were brought in to promote books for young people. Speakers were brought in to promote adult literacy. Individuals such as the first black Miss America, Suzette Charles, made appearances at library branches. A number of well-known authors, cartoonists, and writers of children's books made appearances seeking to bring people into library branches in order to introduce them to the library and encourage them to use its services. The wives of state and national political leaders also made appearances for the same purposes. Sales of books removed from the library's collection were initiated to support the impending levy campaign and to mount a summer reading club, which attracted 12,000 youngsters.

The board had just carried out a major organizational restructuring to promote improved operations. The changes split information systems into three divisions dealing with library automation, administration (wages and salaries), and operations and repair and also added several new positions.

A seven-member library board of trustees provides oversight and hires the executive director and controller. Four board members are appointed by the county commissioners (an elective body) and three by the county judge of common pleas for terms of seven years. The board has been very active in library affairs and management. Current members represent unions, local companies, and the city's public school system. The executive director and controller serve as ex officio board members. The executive director was acting as director and hoped to be appointed as director. Other administrative staff members included an assistant director, three coordinators, seven department directors, and the main and branch library directors and staff members.

Current Concerns

The 1990s opened with high expectations for the library and limited funds to meet them. Branches were not strategically located, causing the library to neglect some parts of the service area. Bookmobile services could not supplant the needed branch services. Collections were somewhat out of date. All branches needed a continuously staffed information desk with video-tapes, compact discs, and records; an extensive collection of newspapers and magazines as well as other periodicals; and a current collection of books. The computer system was out-dated, and suburbs had been calling for branches to be con-structed in their service area. Some of the more wealthy sub-urbs had built a competitive library, eroding the service area and posing questions about competition among public organi-zations.

Funding for the library came from several sources, in-cluding levies, allocations from state tax collections, and dona-tions. Both sources of public support were being changed. New legislation allowed libraries to extend the maximum levy pe-riod, previously limited to five years, to twenty years and even indefinitely, the way public schools do. The governor had just signed a law that earmarked 6.3 percent of the state income tax revenues for public libraries. Previously, a portion of prop-erty tax revenues had been earmarked for library use accord-ing to population served. The basis to allocate the new tax was not specified. Libraries were to work it out among themselves. The library board and staff were concerned that a new for-mula would be pushed by the new suburban libraries that had greater per capita circulation, which would put minority groups that the county library was trying to reach at a disadvantage.

Also, a state income tax, unlike a property tax, is volatile. The board and staff were concerned that tax revenue short-falls and calls by taxpayers for sharp reductions in state tax could severely cut long-established levels of funding for the library. The current library levy was up for renewal. Asking for a large levy increase might offend county voters who had been library supporters. The library also had to continue to cultivate grants and donations. The state had just awarded $73,000 in a grant to start a media center and to improve the library's collection of high-tech and cultural arts books. Inter-nal and cash contributions of $82,000 had been collected in the past year and were earmarked for various purposes. Facing these dilemmas, the library director and board decided to start a major strategic management initiative. Previous planning efforts had done little more than create a list of fiscal year objectives.

The Strategic Management Process

Strategic management in this case was carried out by two strategic management groups. This arrangement was deemed necessary to involve the board of trustees (denoted SMGB) and key staff members (denoted SMGS). The SMGB was made up of the seven board members, the executive director, and the controller. The SMBS had sixteen members, including the executive director and controller along with all department directors (building operations, communications, finance, information services, personnel, technical services, and extension services) and coordinators for volunteer, adult, and children's services. Outside stakeholders were involved during implementation.

Facilitators carried out the first process cycle by holding fourteen four-hour meetings over a fifteen-month period. The phasing of activities for this case is shown in Figure 14.1. The phasing departs from the other cases in two ways. First, the phasing was different because two SMGs were used. The board initiated activity in SMGB 1 and verified proposed actions at the end of the process in SMGB 2 and 3. The SMGs made an independent organizational and situational assessment and proposed strategy with implementation plans in SMGS 1 to SMGS 11 (see Figure 14.1). Second, two pre-SMG surveys were carried out, one for the board group and one for the key staff members. These surveys covered the topics shown in the pre-SMG activities noted in Figure 14.1.

The sessions were organized as follows:

Session SMGB: Orientation to Strategic Management and Context Appreciation (with Board)
  Define strategic management and how it is done
  Review trends and events (board survey feedback)
  Review SWOTs (board survey feedback)
  Review directions (board survey feedback)
  Review ideals (board survey feedback)

Session SMGS1: Orientation to Strategic Management and Context Appreciation (with the Key Staff)
Define strategic management and how it is done
Review trends and events (staff survey feedback)
Review SWOTs (staff survey feedback)
Review directions (staff survey feedback)
Session SMG2: Situational Assessment
Revise SWOTs
Revise directions
Review ideals (staff survey feedback)
Session SMG3: Strategic Direction
Finalize SWOTs
Identify directions
Select ideals
Session SMG4: Issue Assessment
Identify issues
Identify issue relationships
Session SMG5: Strategic Issues and Actions
Identify issue priorities
Identify strategic actions
Session SMG6: Strategy Development I
Assess strategic action
Identify criteria
Identify stakeholders
Identify resources
Session SMG7: Strategy Development II
Synthesize strategic actions
Assess stakeholders
Assess resources
Session SMGS8: Feasibility Assessment
Review strategic action
Review stakeholders
Review resources
Review implementation concerns
Session SMGS9: Implementation I
Review strategic actions
Select criteria
Discuss implementation plans

Figure 14.1. Phasing of Activities for Library.

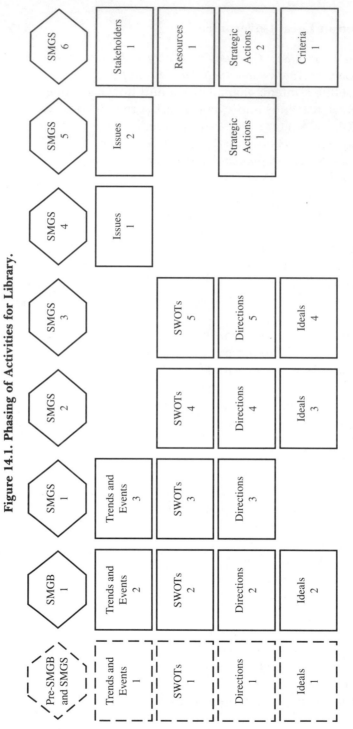

SMGB = strategic management group with board

SMGS = strategic management group with staff

348

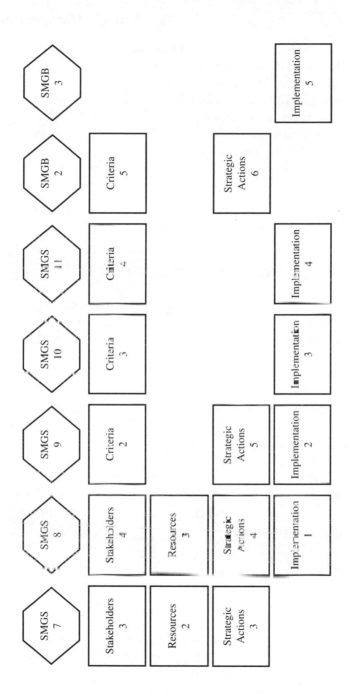

   Sessions SMGS10 and 11: Implementation II and III
        Discuss criteria application
        Discuss implementation plan decisions
   Session SMGB2: Review by SMGB
        Review strategic actions
        Review criteria
   Session SMGB3: Decisions
        Discuss implementation plans

An agenda was prepared for each meeting that detailed the
actions called for by each of these activities.

Stage One: Historical Context

In the first stage, each SMG identified trends, critical events,
and directions that described the historical context of the library and selected ideals. A comparison of the reconstructed
history by the board and key staff members shows how perceptions differed and the implication of these differences. Using
two SMGs and comparing their perceptions is recommended
whenever boards have been actively involved in the organization and have formulated policy and when key staff members
have considerable tenure. Both groups have important insights
that must be shared to create a basis for action.

   A modified Delphi survey was used to collect data describing events, trends, and directions prior to the formal
meetings. This procedure and the rating steps follow those described in Chapter Thirteen.

Trends and Events

The SMGs were asked to list trends and events that will influence the library for the next several years. Members were asked
to think broadly to include economic, client, managerial, technical, social, political, and demographic terms. What follows is
a summary of the top five priorities.

Economic
1. Increase in the public library's importance and visibility in the community as a resource center because of community responsibility
2. Change in the economic base for library funding and a possible interpretation by public as having lots of money
3. Increased competition from cultural groups for funds (such as right to read programs) because of funding cutbacks
4. High cost of property, building, and maintenance.
5. Difficulty in replacing or adding to the library's .60 mill general property tax operating levy, which expires in two years. An addition or replacement levy will not be easy to sell to the public.

User Related
1. Change in public's attitude toward library services: was recreational neighborhood institution, now a resource for informational needs
2. Increased technological competence of users and higher demand on library for technological services for businesses and students
3. Conflict between higher level of user competence and the more basic needs of the inner-city population
4. Continued growth of city as a diverse economy, requiring additional areas of special interest within library
5. New user groups wanting different services and collections because of upswing in economy

Managerial
1. Movement to full automation, which has an impact on style of technical and public services and level of staff needed to work in automated environment
2. High cost of personnel
3. Constant upgrading of management and administrative skills in order for library to remain viable organization in the community
4. Growing need for security in library

5. Library schools producing fewer candidates for librarian and manager positions

Technical

1. Development of library resources as a strong support system for increasing technology in business community
2. Desire for quick access to growing information base by public
3. Development of laser disc and video, significantly changing the media available to libraries
4. Information explosion, causing people to change the ways in which they obtain needed information in the future

Political

1. Local emphasis on county and downtown expansion and development, requiring more leadership from library
2. Attempts by various legislators from time to time to reduce the 6.3 percent of state tax revenues earmarked for libraries, especially when harder economic times return
3. Public officials who may not like the library tax issue to be on the ballot with their issues
4. The use of library administration as lobbyists and the need to pursue funds for existence
5. Distribution of the 6.3 percent of state income tax revenue
6. Shift in political climate that views library service as a luxury
7. Change in length of library levies

Social/Cultural

1. Homeless and deinstitutionalized people using the libraries as a shelter and a source of social contact
2. Single parent homes and homes with two working parents
3. Growing problem of illiteracy and three-year national literacy program beginning
4. Expansion of city's cultural arts opportunities
5. New flurry of at-home entertainment technologies and services

Demographic

1. Rapid growth of population and development in northwestern city and county

2. Shift in population age: more babies, fewer children in high school and college, more senior citizens
3. Use of library's services by children of the 1984–1985 baby boom (expectations about services by well-educated, economically comfortable parents)
4. Suburban residential sites still popular

After reviewing these trends and events the following priorities were set, listed by their importance:

1. Change in funding and the public view that library has a lot of money
2. Expiration of operating levy in the next year
3. Movement to full automation
4. Distribution of the 6.3 percent of state income tax revenues
5. Attempts by various legislators to reduce distribution percentage
6. Population trends
7. High cost of personnel
8. Library administration as lobbyists
9. Constant upgrading of skills to meet external requirements

Directions

The SMGS was asked to identify the current strategic direction by characterizing the library's movement in the past and projecting it into the future. A period of about five years was suggested. Responses were classified as programs and services, resources, patron needs and demands, and general management and organizational style. The top five are listed.

Programs and Services

Moving Away From	Moving Toward
1. Superficial attention to patron needs/patron self-help	1. More in-depth concern for individual patron needs/user assistance

2. Programming limited to library materials and services

2. Programming by whim of programmer, duplicating programs conducted by other community agencies

3. Decades of slow growth and development

3. Rapid expansion of facilities and services as well as usage

4. Service hours convenient for staff

4. Service hours that meet patron needs

5. Slight emphasis on reference service

5. Quality reference service with librarians and trained LTA's

6. Waiting for patrons to come to library

6. Actively campaigning in business communities to promote service possibilities

7. Low circulation of collections

7. Collections with high turnover rates

Resources
   Moving Away From

Moving Toward

1. Going after big grant money

1. Using the administrative staff for their collective knowledge and experience

2. Materials budget based on size of facility

2. Budgets based on percentage of circulation contributed to system

3. Costly resources and minimal service

3. Cost-effective service

4. Shotgun acquisitions

4. Centralized purchasing

Technologies
   Moving Away From

Moving Toward

1. A pioneer in video production and cable television programming

1. No video production and no cable television programming

2. Seemingly glamorous technology and systems

2. Viable computer systems, realistically purchased with endurance and production in mind

3. Unsophisticated, inadequate circulation system

3. More sophistication about acceptable circulation systems and public catalogues

4. Clerical tasks requiring filing and use of typewriters

4. Use of word processors and microcomputers for basic routines

Patron Demands and Needs
  Moving Away From

Moving Toward

1. Perceived as a stodgy warehouse for books

1. A public image of a responsive and lively learning agency

2. Passive participation
3. Grateful patron
4. Busy season versus slow season
5. Provincial image

2. Active participation
3. Demanding patron
4. Constantly busy through whole year
5. Cosmopolitan image, leading people to expect more sophisticated services

6. The "free rider" concept

6. Accountability

General Management and
Organizational Style
  Moving Away From

Moving Toward

1. Risk taking

1. Better cooperative planning

2. Political agency

2. Developing intergovernmental relations

3. Authoritarian leadership
4. Management by crisis

3. Increase in participation
4. Management style requiring vision and leadership, bringing diversity to bear on common purpose

5. Internal territorial concepts
6. System feeling politically autonomous

5. System management integration
6. Integration with city and county governments as support unit

After review, the following directions were seen as priorities. The listing is in order of importance. (Items 2, 3, and 5 emerged during discussion.)

Moving Away From	*Moving Toward*
1. Management by crisis	1. Management style requiring vision and leadership, bringing diversity to bear on common purpose
2. Jumping on the bandwagon in response to new technologies	2. More careful planning and analysis before decisions are made related to new technologies
3. Thinking of each facility as a separate library	3. Thinking systemwide toward unity and some degree of uniformity
4. Previous executive director's priority of time away from PLCFC	4. Current executive director's attention to this library and working through problems rather than serving as consultant to others
5. Materials selection based on interests of branch or division staff	5. Materials selection based on interests of the community
6. Slight emphasis on reference service	6. Quality reference service with librarians and trained LTA's
7. Service hours convenient for staff	7. Service hours that meet patron needs
8. Unsophisticated, inadequate circulation system	8. More sophistication about acceptable circulation systems and public catalogues

Ideals

A third activity had SMG members create idealized images of the library five or more years into the future with the trends and events and shifting directions in mind. The SMG members described attributes that would make up an ideal vision of the library: "A user oriented organization with dynamic leadership providing the best possible service to the public, including the handicapped, minorities, and the disadvantaged. Stabilized budget to support needed services insuring adequate staffing and larger, better equipped main and branches. Board and director roles defined and followed, creating a strong commitment to staff development and making the library an integral part of the community."

Stage Two: Situational Assessment

The exploration of history by the board and staff SMGs enhanced each group's understanding of the library's past and an idealilzed future. In the next stage, the immediate situation facing the library was explored. To carry out situational assessment, each SMG assessed the library's strengths, weaknesses, opportunities, and threats. This information was collected by a modified Delphi survey in the pre-SMG (see Figure 14.1), and rankings were obtained as noted in the last chapter. Note that SWOTs were discussed and rated in four separate meetings. This helped to create a consensus. The following SWOTs were identified as priority considerations. The board and staff groups agreed on each SWOT unless noted.

Strengths
1. Aggressive director, strong management style
2. Competent and concerned staff on all levels dedicated to serve the public
3. Strong public support
4. A creative and innovative library system
5. Strong commitment from library board
6. Professional public relations staff and products

7. High visibility: twenty-one facilities
8. Children's services (board only)

Weaknesses

1. Inadequate funding
2. Problems with technology
3. Need for direction (strategic planning and leadership)
4. Staffing levels at some facilities (understaffed)
5. Age and condition of main library (staff only)
6. Staff morale and burnout (staff only)
7. Space limitations (staff only)
8. Service hours
9. Plan for collection

Opportunities

1. Increased funding—sound finances including capital improvements bond issue
2. New leadership style and directional philosophy (board only)
3. Circulation system development
4. Securing of appropriate funding levels (board only)
5. Expansion or renovation of new main library (board only)
6. Continuing and solid relationships with governmental officials (board only)
7. Quality reference service
8. Business support for main library project (financial and other)
9. Being at forefront of computer technology
10. Plan for orderly growth (board only)

Threats

1. Perception of decreased need because of state funding
2. Volatile nature of tax revenues and problems due to new funding scheme
3. Current computer system, VTLS shortcomings, and circulation system
4. Continuation of "lean machine" concept and inadequate staffing level

5. Inability to meet internal and external demands, including space problems
6. Lack of long-range plan showing administration's belief in the future
7. Service inequities perceived in some suburbs (board only)

Stage Three: The Issue Agenda

Issues mark a departure from previous stages in both content and procedure. In the previous two stages, a consensus about key concerns facing the library was created. In stage three, an action agenda is identified. Recall that a strategic issue is an actual or anticipated condition or tension, internal or external to the library, that, if it continues, will have significant effects on the library's functioning and ability to achieve its desired future. We used the brainwriting procedure to uncover issues, the tension ideas in Chapters Five and Six to articulate the issues, and direct assignment to rank them.

Thirty-five issues were identified by SMGS during the brainwriting session. The issues listed below stemmed from using a snowball technique to merge the issues into ten themes.

1. Planning for long-range capital improvement of the main library and library service outlets.
2. Creating an integrated internal computer system (hardware and software). Present cataloguing records are inadequate, data base is "dirty," and the material acquisition system needs to be integrated with library general ledger system.
3. Assessing new external technologies and their impact on system.
4. Providing adequate staffing levels (quality, training, quantity) to support and provide library service programs. Also, providing appropriate levels of communication to keep staff informed of where library is heading.
5. Stabilizing levels and sources of funding. Issue centers on securing and maintaining funding, stabilizing the county

distribution, and changing the public's perception of the library as being financially well off.

6. Promoting a systemwide concept that has a management team with a common focus and is consistent in the decision-making process.
7. Enhancing public support of the library through image, involvement, and visibility.
8. Identifying market and prioritizing services. Determining how to meet market criteria and priorities.
9. Providing security for both staff and patrons.
10. Keeping staff members informed and their morale high.

These issues were then articulated as opposing forces that are pulling or pushing the library in various directions and away from its ideals. These forces identify the underlying tensions at work on the library. This format for expressing issues illustrates conditions within the organization and between it and external stakeholders. These issue tensions are given in order of priority in the following list.

1. Identification of market and prioritizing of services (tension between old services and new services)
2. Adequate and stable funding (tension between maintaining current funding versus getting new funding)
3. Adequate staffing levels (tension between staff productivity and participation in key decisions)
4. Long-range capital improvement planning (tension between improving the physical plant and needed new funding)
5. Integrated internal computer system (tension between past computer innovations and new technological developments)
6. Systemwide focus (tension between needs of branches and needs of system)
7. Enhancement of public support (tension between serving everyone and meeting special needs)
8. Staff morale and communication (tension between stress

from working conditions and funds required to improve
these conditions)
9. New technologies and their impact (tension between being
current and funding innovations)
10. Security for staff and patrons (tension between staff and
patron safety and access)

The issue precedence relationship was determined using
ISM and is shown in Figure 14.2.
The SMGS saw services and funding as the key issues
that called for management and chose to attack both issues in
their first attempt at creating strategy. The tensions between
old and new services suggest that steps must be taken to find

Figure 14.2. Issue Precedence for Library.

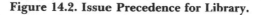
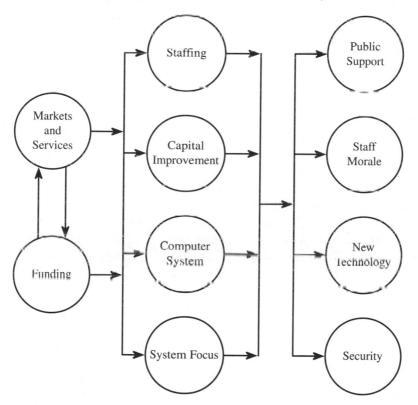

unserved market areas and determine needs as well as to identify current services that capture the core values of the library and must be retained. To provide these old and new services and take care of the clients and markets they serve, new funds must be secured and old funds protected. There is a tension between the priority attached to creating new sources of revenue and protecting old ones. These issues were used as the focus to search for strategic actions in the next stage of the process.

The other issues either called for downstream considerations or followed from the service and funding issues. The second set of issues considers staffing, capital improvement, computer support, and system focus. In staffing, the tension between participation in development and productivity was identified. More participation stresses an already stressed system, but unilateral action would damage implementation. Capital improvement creates a tension between the needs for new buildings and equipment and other uses of available funds, including staffing and training. The computer support issue captures the tension between past innovations that the library wants to preserve and new developments that do the same thing better and at less cost.

The third set of issues deals with public support, staff morale, new technologies, and safety. The issues seem resolvable when the preceding issues have been managed. For instance, the tension between serving everyone and serving patrons with special needs (such as the economically disadvantaged) can be managed after services and funding have created staffing, capital improvements, computer support, and a system focus. A similar relationship can be noted in the remaining issues.

Stage Four: Strategic Options

The SMGS identified possible actions for dealing with the two key issue tensions. The list of strengths, weaknesses, opportunities, and threats was reviewed for each issue to ensure that each SWOT was relevant. Using the SWOTs as guidelines, the

SMGS sought a way to reconcile the tensions between new and old sources of funding and old and new services. First, the SMGS attacked the service issue and then moved to the funding issue.

To identify strategic actions, SMGS members were given worksheets listing the issue and its relevant SWOTs. They were asked to consider their ideals and suggest concrete actions to manage the issue tension that built on strengths, overcame weaknesses, exploited opportunities, and blunted threats.

The worksheet is shown in Figure 14.3. (Note that this

Figure 14.3. Worksheet for Current and Future Markets for Library.

Users

		Current	Potential
Services	**Current**	*Service:* videotape library *Users:* young white males	*Service:* videotape library *Users:* families, social clubs, fraternities, and sororities
	Potential	*Service:* use of personal computers *Users:* business professionals *Service:* software library *Users:* business professionals *Service:* coupon exchange *Users:* consumer enthusiasts	*Service:* use of personal computers *Users:* school children and parents *Service:* software library *Users:* school children and parents

approach differs from the one used in the other cases, which indicates useful ways to extend the analysis when there are many stakeholders.) The group used a structured brainwriting variation in which SMGS members identified current services (clients and markets) that must be preserved and passed the sheet to another member, who identified new services. This sensitized members to one another's preservation values. Old and new services and users were recorded separately. Two subgroups of the SMGS were set up to generate strategic actions following this approach. One of these groups developed sixty-five ideas, the other forty-six. The ideas were then merged, creating lists of the current and future users, services, and service modes. Illustrations of items in each category are provided.

Users (current and future) include *individuals* (such as categories that include school-age preteen, preschool, toddlers, upper-middle, business people, aged, retired, English as a second language, homebound patrons, institutionalized); *groups* (such as friends of the library, special-interest groups, retailers, neighborhood business associations, book club members, organized "golden agers," and services areas with new branches); and *institutions* (such as other libraries, government officials, contract service users, schools, corporate users, and credit and collection agencies). *Current services* had several categories that include material circulation services (such as book circulation, pamphlets, magazine circulation, videocassette circulation, film circulation, audiocassette, games and toys circulation, audiovisual equipment loans, and puppet shows); *reference and information retrieval services* (such as public catalogue of library holdings, noncirculating material, government documents, and maps), tapeline for home and garden/health/law line services, reference questions, and research; *other recreational, educational, and information services* [such as educational/informational programs, personal computer services, coin-operated machine services (photocopier, typewriter, and microform reader/printer machine services), meeting rooms, talking books, Golden Buckeye registration, voter registration, and polling], and *future services* (such as by mail, laser discs, language lab, automated community bulletin board, electronic keyboards, satellite accessibility, circulating microcomputers, and automated trip tickets). Finally, categories for delivery include *current modes* [such as phone, mail, buildings (main and branches), and outreach], and *future modes* (such as local area networks, portable kiosk, on-line references in branches, telephone access to public catalogue, electronically supported conference room, videotape vending, fax machines, and microwave up-link).

Morphology was used to merge these ideas into strategies. The strategies were constructed according to services and

Figure 14.4. Markets Matched to Service Delivery Modes for Library.

Service Delivery Modes

	Current	Potential
Current	*Market:* data base access *Delivery Mode:* access at library site	*Market:* data base access *Delivery Mode:* access at home or office from telephone modem hookup
Potential	*Market:* software library *Delivery Mode:* checkout from library site	*Market:* software library *Delivery Mode:* van delivery to technical parks or businesses

Markets

Figure 14.5. Resource Requirements Matched to Service Delivery Modes for Library.

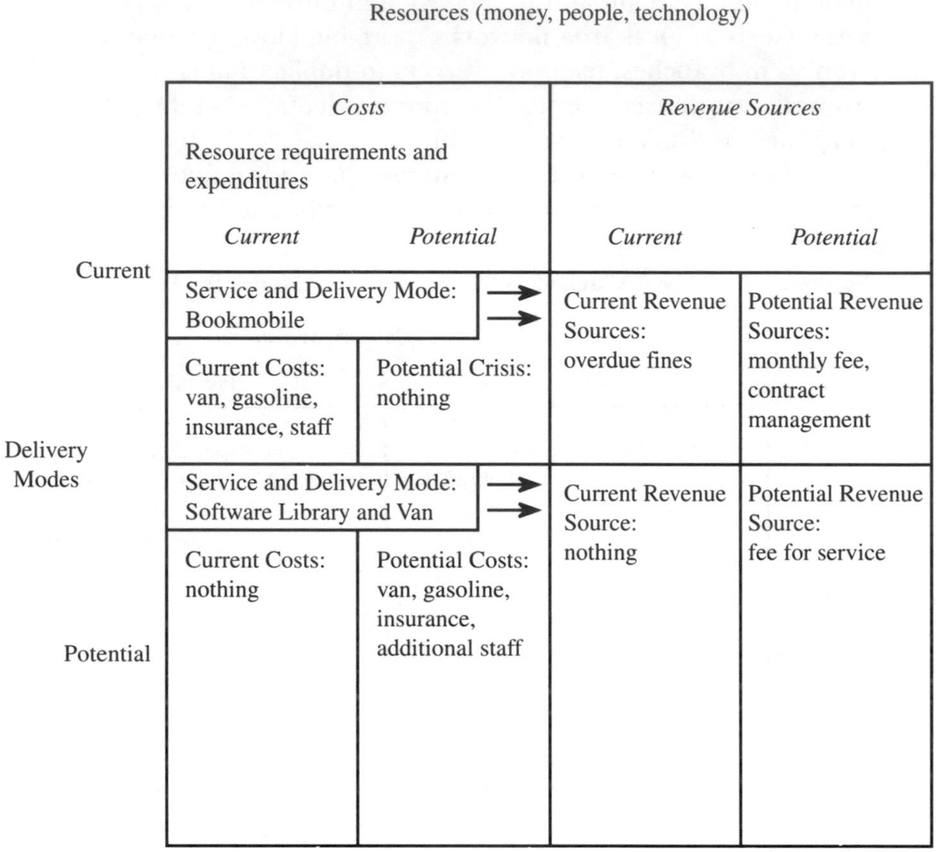

Resources (money, people, technology)

	Costs		Revenue Sources	
	Resource requirements and expenditures			
	Current	*Potential*	*Current*	*Potential*
Current Delivery Modes	Service and Delivery Mode: Bookmobile → →		Current Revenue Sources: overdue fines	Potential Revenue Sources: monthly fee, contract management
	Current Costs: van, gasoline, insurance, staff	Potential Crisis: nothing		
	Service and Delivery Mode: Software Library and Van → →		Current Revenue Source: nothing	Potential Revenue Source: fee for service
Potential	Current Costs: nothing	Potential Costs: van, gasoline, insurance, additional staff		

Figure 14.6. Strategies for Library.

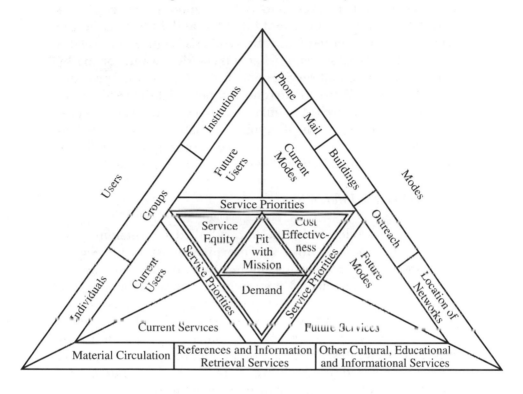

Service Priorities for Next Decade

users, identifying current ones to be preserved and new ones to be developed, markets and delivery modes, and resources and delivery modes. Figures 14.3, 14.4, and 14.5 describe the strategies that emerged from the synthesis. Figure 14.3 relates users and services, showing what stakeholders want, sorting by current and potential services and users. Figure 14.4 provides the relationship between current and potential delivery modes and markets. Figure 14.5 links resources to delivery modes, providing another form of resources analysis. Finally, in Figure 14.6, all these relationships are captured in one figure showing users (stakeholders), services, and resources.

Interpreting the Information

The strategies selected by the library called for retaining and enhancing services. A three-way morphology, shown in Figure 14.6, shows the relationship among users, modes, and service priorities. Having selected a strategy for implementation, the SMGS entered a new stage by considering implementation feasibility. The future driving forces to be considered were determined to be leisure time competition, increased number of functional illiterates, an aging population, religious groups, the deinstitutionalized, inner-city residents (need versus demand), and the type of economic growth attracted to the county.

Stages Five and Six: Feasibility Assessment and Implementation

The library has a board of trustees that helps it connect to sources of support. The board had a long-standing relationship with the library and had developed strong ties. These ties had two implications. First, the board had been a powerful advocate for the library and its programs. Second, the board had been involved in all past strategic initiatives and expected to be involved in the future. To use a board, it must be carefully managed. As a result, the strategic management process was fashioned to involve the board as an initiating and an approving body, as shown in Figure 14.1. The board was asked to frame what was done and to approve any proposed action.

The board was brought up to date by carrying out a comparison of its trends and events, directions, ideals, and SWOTs with those of the staff group. This comparison revealed a large degree of agreement. The six top-priority external events were listed by both staff and board. The bulk of the priority SWOTs appeared on both lists. The top two issue tensions were identified by both groups. This gave the results produced by the SMGS special credibility.

The SMGB reviewed proposal actions and approved them. The next step was to secure the needed funds. This occurred in the next round of strategic management, carried out by the library without the participation of the facilitators. This case marks a success in moving from regenerative to continuous-change strategic management, as noted in Chapter Eight.

In part because of the strategic plan, the acting director was appointed by the board as its permanent director. The board decided to adopt the politically risky tactic of seeking a new operating levy while maintaining the current level of state allocations to support its plans. The board authorized and then supported a countywide library levy that took advantage of the loosening of library levy rules in the state. The new levy would replace a .6 mill levy, scheduled to expire in a year. The county commissioners were approached and asked to put a 2.2 mill permanent (nonexpiring) levy on the ballot to support the library's strategy. The levy would raise $9.4 million a year and would support a $51.6 million capital improvement program. The improvements were to include the purchase of a new site and the construction of a new main library in the center city as well as new buildings for ten branches, major construction at two others, and two new branches.

This tactic assumed that voters were the key stakeholders and that they would be advocates. Community groups were also assumed to be no worse than neutral and possibly willing to support the levy. This proved to be overly optimistic. The chamber of commerce voted not to endorse the campaign or contribute to its costs. The library director saw the downtown power figures as typically nonsupportive of library interests and was confident that patrons and voters could be counted on for their support. The reception in the neighborhoods was quite positive, suggesting that the levy would pass, but the downtown business support worsened. Businesspeople began to resent the levy, fearing it would erode support for their pet projects (such as a convention center, and a sports arena). The city's only newspaper began to run articles claiming that the levy would increase the library's budget to be the largest in the state. The county commissioners voted to put the levy on the ballot, but did not endorse it. The media called the levy "excessive" and rallied against it with periodic "news" pieces in the paper, including the publishing of claims of campaign finance law violations. As opposition mounted, the board scaled down the levy, limiting the time period to fifteen years. Amid predictions of failure, the levy was overwhelmingly supported by voters.

Negotiations with other libraries proved to be difficult. The director tried to argue that the library serves 78 percent of the county's 870,000 residents and called for a formula that would give the library 70 percent of the state funds for the region. The six suburban and county library directors met to work out a distribution formula to allocate state funds. The session degenerated into a shouting match between the county director and some of the suburban library directors. After several unsuccessful attempts to allocate the funds, the county's budget commission intervened and imposed a formula based on population, circulation, and size of service area. Budget increases are now made through the county board's coordinating committee.

The library's construction projects have been completed. Its visitors and people with library cards have increased by more than 10 percent a year. The number of circulation and reference questions also shows sharp increases systemwide.

Reshaping the Issue Agenda

After the initial cycle of the process, the issue agenda had eight issues yet to be managed. The facilitators helped the library director reshape the agenda by testing the issues for comprehensiveness, using the tension framework in Chapter Five.

The issues were classified as shown below. (The numbers indicate priority on the initial issue agenda.)

Preservation-Transition
   Market and services (old services versus new services) (1)
   Adequate and stable funding (old versus new funding sources) (2)
   Integrated computer system (past innovation versus new developments) (5)
Productivity-Transition
   Capital improvement planning (new plant versus new funding) (4)
   New technologies (being current versus funding innovations) (9)
Equity-Productivity
   Adequate staffing (staff productivity versus participation) (3)
   Systemwide focus (needs of branches versus needs of system) (6)
   Public support (serving all versus special needs) (7)
   Staff morale (working conditions versus funding) (8)
   Staff and patron security (safety versus access) (10)

The issue agenda raises two points. First, note that every issue is implicated in every other issue. Resolving the pivotal issues (market and services, adequate and stable funding) also helped to relax the tensions concerning capital improvement, staffing, public support, staff morale, and systemwide focus. Also, questions regarding new technologies and integrated computer systems were resolved in part. Second, the list of issues shows a preoccupation with preservation and transition. Note that three types of tensions did not emerge: productivity-preservation, equity-preservation, and equity-transition. The library had a culture that had been tied to productivity and preservation. Transition (innovation) was foreign to the library and occurred only when a threat to its funding emerged on the horizon. This led the library to see tensions of change in both productivity and preservation.

We counseled the library's leaders that issues in the three overlooked tensions should be considered in reshaping the issue agenda, as well as the three tensions considered in the last round of strategy formation. This step will help the library to confront questions that caused problems with branches in the past. In particular, equity concerns seem to have been overlooked in dealing with the suburbs and their perceptions of fairness. If these concerns are examined, a new way to manage the competing interests with a win-win strategy to serve the county may emerge.

Aftermath

The county library was a *professional* type of organization that sought to become more proactive in its strategic development but had no idea how to develop a strategy. Its internal capacity was high and control was moderate. The key players wanted to increase capacity further but were ill-prepared for the control expectations. The strategic management effort attempted to get key players to create a vision of what the library could become. The leadership never quite realized that by giving up control (such as to county commissions) they could create new options and thereby increase the organization's internal capacity.

Historically, the library had relied on a *director* strategy. However, the library was operated in an environment that had become increasingly turbulent, which called for increased responsiveness and considerable need for action. The library correctly identified these features, as noted in its trends and events and directions, and chose to become proactive in dealing with them. The library chose a *compromiser* strategy, attempting to win by garnering all available funds and underwriting expansions into its market area. The library chose moderate cooperation and high need for action in following this strategy.

To move toward a *mutualist* strategy, the library must become more collaborative. Collaboration is needed in several ways. First, the competitive posture with the six suburban libraries could again become destructive. By seeking ways to work together and sharing resources and programs, the far reaches of the county that are not well served by the library can be helped. Second, patrons do not see boundaries that bureaucrats recognize, as noted by many patrons that have library cards for several libraries. Competing for patrons' attention runs considerable risks of alienating them and losing the support that has been crucial to levy success. It remains to be seen if the library director can devise a mutualist strategy and implement it.

The priority issue tensions identified for management by the library classified as an issue portfolio are given below. The numbers in parentheses indicate priority.

Sitting Ducks
   Markets and services (1)
   Staffing (3)
   Systemwide focus (6)
   Public support (7)
   Staff morale (8)
Angry Tigers
   Adequate and stable funding (2)
   Capital improvements (4)
   Integrated computer system (5)
   New technologies (9)
   Patron and staff security (10)

Note that the library selected sitting ducks for issue management but had several issues calling for funds that could become angry tigers. The library misjudged the numbers and intensity of efforts to block their new strategic initiatives. In the future, it would be wise for the library to devote more time to stakeholder and resource management and to confront issues that are apt to become angry tigers.

This case had a tilt toward innovation at the expense of implementation. As noted in Chapter Six, both formulation and implementation are essential in strategic management. The library was fortunate to have built a solid relationship with voters that could deflect criticism by the downtown standers and shakers and special interests. The next time funds are needed, it may be more difficult to get voter support in the face of such opposition. Also, the suburban libraries could form alliances and block future attempts at innovation.

Chapter Fifteen

■   ■

Forging a New
Mission
for a State
Health Agency

■   ■

This chapter outlines the strategic management of a crippled children's services bureau, located in a state department of health. The triggering development was production. The bureau of crippled children's services (BCCS) saw a number of threats to its budget from both inside and outside the organization. A new governor had taken office with a "prevention plank" in his platform. The emphasis on prevention could take funds away from BCCS because it was set up to provide services and had no role in prevention.

Problems in operations were also of concern. Only 37 percent of the services authorized by BCCS were actually used, raising questions about the procedures used to determine eligibility. Changes in eligibility were being considered that could reduce the funds from both state and federal sources. The bureau was vulnerable to large and hard-to-predict claims. Although unlikely, one legitimate claim from a severely handi-capped child could take a significant portion of a year's budget. Several such claims could exhaust the budget in the first few months of a fiscal year. The bureau's management wanted to anticipate and deal with these concerns before a crisis emerged. Strategic management was initiated to act before things got out of control and to plan for the future.

The strategic management process uncovered a tension between the production value and both transition and preser-vation that had been overlooked. The anticipated budget shortfalls (production) were in tension with needed changes in claims processing (transition) and the need to maintain current commitments (preservation). The current authorization and claims processing systems were labor intensive operations that could be computerized. The manual system could not be changed without adhering to rules and procedures set up in state and federal enabling legislation.

This chapter describes the process that was used to shape and implement the service strategies devised by BCCS. Changes led to a name change to describe the bureau's new mission. The bureau dropped the term *crippled* from its name and re-placed it with *handicapped*. The name change indicates the bu-reau's strategy. First, we provide background, indicating the historical role of BCCS. This discussion is followed by a de-scription of the SMG and phasing of strategic management ac-tivities for this case. The information obtained from each pro-cess stage is outlined. The "Aftermath" section shows how BCCS applied the ideas discussed in the book and engaged in a pro-cess of continuous change strategic management to manage its affairs. This process is still in place, providing guidance. The bureau's management wanted a comprehensive strategy that stressed quality, acceptance, and innovation. The techniques that we used to identify and synthesize information were se-lected to meet these requirements (see Chapter Twelve).

Agency Background

Services for crippled children began in 1935 through federal legislation that provided the first public source of support for the care of low-income children. More children became eligible for services in the 1960s when medicaid and a variety of categorical programs were begun. The original legislation provided federal grants that states were to match. Agencies in state government were set up to administer and distribute these funds. The agency was to locate, diagnose, and offer services to children with crippling conditions.

In 1981, Congress set up maternal and child health block grants that included the functions of most crippled childrens' service (CCS) agencies. Many states continued their CCS agencies because state legislation had previously set standards for cases, income limits, and range of services. In these states, CCS agencies still play a major role in the care of crippled children. Annually, $300 million are spent by these agencies, of which 31 percent comes from federal funding sources.

The State Program

BCCS is a state-administered program that establishes the eligibility for services of children (from birth to twenty-one years of age) with either crippling or potentially crippling health problems. This BCCS began operation in 1919. The bureau moved to a state department of health in 1980, where it became an operating unit of the maternal and child health division. BCCS serves 35,000 children in the state annually and has a budget of $4 million. It identifies children with crippling conditions, refers them to appropriate health providers, and authorizes payment for services. Its key functions are: service authorization, case processing, and invoice payment. Service authorization is made up of medical and financial case management. The medical case management involves assessment, eligibility for diagnostic and treatment services, and plans of care.

Service authorization activities identify clients and their conditions. In this state, acceptance of a client is dependent on disease condition, severity of the condition, client's age, and family income. BCCS applies guidelines based on these criteria and determines eligibility for service. The plans of care identify units of service that are authorized for payment. The patient is then referred to a physician for treatment. The case is monitored by a member of the nursing staff to ensure that the plan is followed.

In the previous year, BCCS had authorized over 650,000 units of service in seventy service categories. The most frequent service categories included: physician visits, physician consultations, radiology, laboratory, public health nurse visits, and hospital outpatient and inpatient visits, which accounted for 75 percent of the referrals. BCCS authorizes services for its own funding as well as for medicaid and private insurance payers. Thirty-eight percent of the services in this state were supported by BCCS funds, and 62 percent were authorized for medicare and insurance payers. The bulk of the caseload stemmed from diseases of the musculoskeletal system; musculoskeletal deformities; infantile cerebral palsy; diseases of the ear; cleft lip and palate; endocrine and metabolic diseases (cystic fibrosis); spina bifida; and prenatal conditions.

The bureau pays for services that involve treatment, education, and training. These services also provide special prostheses, diets, physical therapy, counseling, medicines, recreational activities, and transportation. The total cost of such services can devastate a family's income. For instance, the Cystic Fibrosis Foundation found that respondents to a survey reported out-of-pocket costs of more than 30 percent of the family income. Families with children who had spina bifida report a figure of 12 percent. These figures double when income loss and nonmedical expenses (such as transportation) are included. The services of BCCS improve a child's quality of life through improved joint function, enhanced employment prospects, and an improved outlook.

The bureau is organized around its care plan and reimbursement activities. A staff of nurses handles care management, and data processing specialists handle the payment decision system. Each inquiry received by BCCS is processed and classified according to needs for plans of care or financial support for new or old cases and invoices. Plans of care and financial support deal with service authorization. First, eligibility is determined and then the individual's family is notified by mail that treatment is authorized and is also given the location of the city and county health department in that jurisdiction. If eligibility is denied, the letter states the medical or financial grounds for the denial. The information is entered into the data-processing system, along with updates. The administrative activities call for establishing case files, determining medical and financial eligibility, terminating care support, tracking cases, handling inquiries, updating data bases, and coding and storing relevant information. BCCS has 210,000 care plans stored in its data-processing system.

Of the 21,000 cases considered in the last year, about half were new cases and the rest continuing ones. Ninety-three percent were approved and 7 percent were denied. Twenty-seven thousand eligibility determinations were made and verifications were sent and 61,000 terminations were made. Over 160,000 notifications were mailed to providers, patients, and field staff.

Bills are paid to certified providers on the behalf of patients with approved plans of care. Invoice processing involves several steps that screen unpayable invoices from the rest. Payable invoices are checked for missing information and errors. If incomplete, the invoice is returned to the provider (who typically initiates claims). The accepted invoices are checked against the case data base to verify acceptability by checking provider names, diagnostic codes, and the like. If codes are valid, plans of care are updated to show services rendered. An invoice can be rejected at this point for several reasons. For example, an invoice may be rejected if a patient has insurance coverage. The remaining invoices go to accounting so that a voucher may be prepared. The voucher is sent to the state auditor's office so that a warrant can be written. The time required from invoice receipt to warrant writing is eight to ten weeks.

BCCS strives for a 100 percent match between invoices and plans of care. To ensure that comparisons can be made, there is a two-month delay between the plans of care being completed and the payment of an invoice. In the previous year,

BCCS had authorized 225,000 units of care and had paid for 76,000, or 32 percent. The highest rate of payment (that is, services actually rendered) is near 100 percent for surgery and inpatient hospital days. Physician visits run at 41 percent, with laboratory services at 11 percent. Cystic fibrosis is the medical problem with the highest percentage of authorizations paid (87 percent), and musculoskeletal deformities had the lowest (57 percent).

   If all of the units of service were consumed, BCCS would not have the funds to operate. The bureau depends on the low rate of conversion of its authorizations to survive. According to data we collected, cost increases of 140 percent for physician visits, 169 percent for consultants, 816 percent for radiology, 439 percent for laboratory services, and 257 percent for out-patient fees could occur. A 49 percent increase in budget would be needed if the authorized services were actually consumed.

Problems and Prospects

BCCS believed the failure to use authorized services stemmed from several sources, including families with inadequate funds to travel to sources of care, lack of motivation, and little understanding of the need for care. Also, BCCS's bureaucratic payment system may have discouraged providers. And providers may have requested more services than needed to increase prospects that a claim would be considered. Whatever the case, BCCS believed there was ample evidence that the payment systems needed to be streamlined. Also, families may need incentives to use the services. The role of BCCS in determining eligibility from medicaid and others was also being questioned.

   A new governor had taken office and had a liberal agenda that called for an emphasis on prevention. BCCS saw this as a threat to its existence. The bureau was firmly rooted in a treatment program that had no linkage to preventive programs and served a set of conditions for which prevention is still not possible. BCCS believed that new funding would become remote and that cuts might be made to draw funds away from it and toward maternal and child health programs, such as screening, early detection, and prenatal care, which were in vogue. Such a step would correspond to the governor's priorities and initiatives. BCCS believed that the notably low use of their authorized services could be used to call for cutbacks. Various suggestions for cost cutting were under consideration, but none had been implemented. Simulations revealed that proposed changes could cut internal processing time from 12 percent to 57 percent without affecting patient care, although the cost of services may increase.

National studies have suggested that crippling conditions are unrelated to the services provided by CCS agencies. Medical programs in the bureau's state had little relationship to the needs of the state's crippled children. Eligibility was being questioned. The free care dictates of Title V, which provided for care without cost to low-income families, were being questioned. Proposals for co-payments were in the works. The definition of low-income was being questioned. The U.S. Office of Management and Budget poverty line, determined annually, had been used as a cutoff for aid. Changes in the cutoff could drastically reduce federal funds. State funding was apt to follow this lead. These flames were fanned by claims that some children were eligible for several free care programs for the same condition.

The Strategic Management Process

Strategic management was carried out by an SMG made up of bureau insiders and key members of its parent body, the state's division of maternal and child health. The division's personnel director and controller participated along with the bureau's acting director and representatives drawn from the nursing staff and from the fiscal and data-processing staffs, giving the SMG twelve members. The bureau sought to develop the SMG into a viable planning unit capable of guiding its management into the future. Outside stakeholders were involved during implementation. The views of field staff members were also obtained at that point in time.

Facilitators carried out the first process cycle by holding

seven meetings over a period of six months. The phasing of activities is shown in Figure 15.1. Surveys were used to gather information to initiate activity, shown as pre-SMG in the figure.

The sessions were then organized as follows:

Session 1: Orientation to Strategic Management and Context Appreciation
  Define strategic management and how it is done
  Review trends (survey feedback)
  Review SWOTs (survey feedback)
  Review ideals (survey feedback)
Session 2: Situational Assessment
  Rank SWOTs
  Review and rank direction (survey feedback)
Session 3: Strategic Direction
  Review directions
  Identify and rank issues
Session 4: Issue Assessment
  Identify issue relationships
  Review SWOTs
  Identify strategic actions
Session 5: Strategic Action
  Identify strategic criteria
  Identify strategic action relationships
Session 6: Feasibility Assessment
  Review strategic criteria
  Review strategic action
  Identify resources
  Identify Stakeholders
Session 7: Implementation
  Synthesize strategic action
  Analyze resources
  Analyze stakeholders
  Implement plans

An agenda was prepared for each meeting, detailing the actions required, following this outline.

Figure 15.1. Phasing of Activities for BCCS.

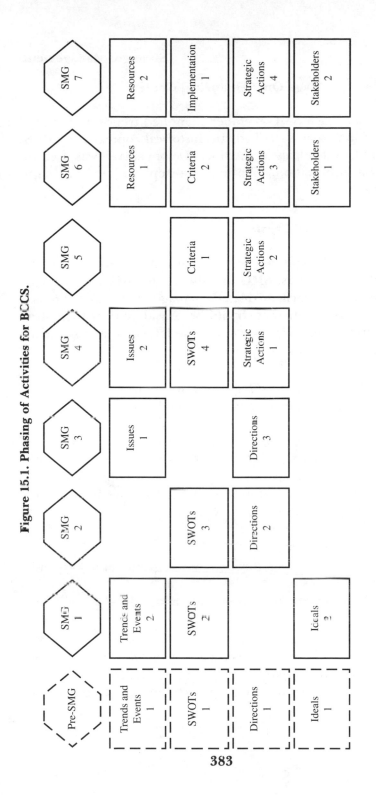

Stage One: Historical Context

In stage one, each SMG member identified trends and events and directions that described the historical context for BCCS and identified its ideals. A modified Delphi survey was used to collect this information, following the steps outlined in Chapter Thirteen.

External Trends and Events

The SMG listed trends and events that will influence BCCS for the next several years. SMG members were asked to think in terms of economic, client-related, managerial, technical, political, and social factors that should be considered for their strategic impact. After setting priorities, the following list emerged:

Administrative Technology
1. Computerization of service authorizations
2. Office automation—mainframes, and microcomputers

Cost Containment/Diagnostically Related Groups
1. Continuing cost containment pressures from the legislature, administration, and Department of Public Welfare
2. Diagnostically related groups (DRGs)—as set forth by the state Department of Public Welfare

Funding Mechanisms
1. Change in funding through block grants and local millages
2. Possible budget cuts at both state and federal levels

Increased Demand for Service
1. Increased numbers of people eligible due to economic conditions (unemployment, loss of insurance)
2. Continued pressure from parents and providers to expand services

Medical Technology
1. Advances in health care methodologies, resulting in increased services at an increased cost
2. Rapidly changing medical technology, resulting in change in the kind of clients needing services (that is, high technology may result in more severely handicapped children surviving and needing long-term care)

Directions

The SMG identified BCCS's current directions by characterizing the bureau's movement in the past and projecting directions into the future for five to ten years. Responses were classified as need and demands, resources, services and clients, and managerial and organizational. Some of each category are listed in priority order below.

Demands and Needs

Moving Away From	Moving Toward
1. Disregard for political and special-interest groups	1. Strategies to respond to special-interest groups
2. Fragmented treatment plans	2. Comprehensive, standardized plans
3. Emphasis on intensive medical service at a few centers	3. Illusion of support services provided locally
4. Fragmented care, not coordinated	4. Coordination of care, such as medical centers and children's hospitals

Resources

Moving Away From	Moving Toward
1. Well funded	1. Cost containment and justification of program via accountability/performance measures

2. More dependence on state dollars

2. More dependence on other than state dollars

3. Lack of proper data base

3. Development of reliable data base

4. Isolated view of BCCS

4. BCCS as part of health care delivery system

Services and Clients
   Moving Away From   *Moving Toward*

1. Hospital stays

1. Increased outpatient services

2. Limited services to patients with all handicapping conditions

2. Broader services to patients with a limited number of handicapping conditions

3. Low-income clientele

3. Low- to middle-income clientele

4. Efforts to prevent handicapping conditions

4. Increased services for patients with the more complex conditions

Managerial and Organizational
   Moving Away From   *Moving Toward*

1. Focus on short term

1. Focus on long term

2. Manual operations

2. Computer record keeping and planning

3. Conflicts between medical and financial administration

3. Planned and integrated organization

4. Crisis management, reactionary

4. Responsive organizational system, management through planning

Ideals

SMG members created an idealized image of BCCS five to ten years into the future, with the priority trends and directions in mind. After consolidation and priority setting, the SMG identified the following features for an ideal bureau: "The BCCS would have the authority to see that *all* children in the program that need care at a comprehensive care center. Funding would be sufficient to increase conditions covered and income eligibility. BCCS would become a leader in the balance of containing costs while assuring high quality of care to handicapped children." To establish a floor for planning, the SMG identified the following attributes of a worst-case scenario: "A lessening of services with an increase in need. Being slow in providing services, delaying treatment, not providing all the necessary services to rehabilitate the client totally."

Stage Two: Situational Assessment

This stage explored the immediate situation facing BCCS. To carry out this stage, the SMG assessed the bureau's strengths, weaknesses, opportunities, and threats. This information was collected by a modified Delphi survey in the pre-SMG and rankings were obtained as noted in Chapter Thirteen. Note that SWOTs were discussed and rated in three separate meetings. This helps to create a consensus. The following SWOTs were identified as important considerations and are listed in priority order.

Strengths
1. Diversification of funds and fiscal resources
2. Federal commitment to maternal and child health
3. Genuine concern for the disabled population
4. Widespread public support
5. Beginnings of a good computer system
6. Cooperation (internal, providers, and so on)

Weaknesses
1. Rate of growth and control over funds decreased relative to service demands
2. Program not perceived as fitting current policy emphasis on prevention

3. Lack of needs assessment to plan
4. Perception of delays and inefficient operation
5. Dependency on manual operation

Opportunities
1. Legislation
2. Current climate emphasizing innovation and change in governmental programs
3. Grass-roots support for BCCS
4. Use of technology to increase efficiency and effectiveness
5. Emphasis on health care costs

Threats
1. Funding problems
2. Poor understanding of BCCS
3. Diagnostically related groups
4. Close identification with welfare

Stage Three: The Issue Agenda

Issues mark a departure from previous stages in both content and procedure. In the previous two stages, a consensus about key concerns facing BCCS was created. In stage three, an action agenda is identified. Recall that a strategic issue is an actual or anticipated condition or tension, internal or external to BCCS, that, if it continues, will have significant effects on the bureau's functioning and ability to achieve its desired future. We used NGT to uncover issues, the tension ideas in Chapters Five and Six to articulate the issues, and direct assignment to rank them.

Twenty-five issues were identified by the SMG during the NGT session. The issues listed below stemmed from a snowball technique that pooled these issues into four themes. The issues are listed by the rank assigned for each theme. The numbers in parentheses indicate the initial rating of the individual issues.

1. *Political Environment*
   Program and service integration with maternal and child health division (2)

Cost-containment policy—DRGs, prospective payment systems (3)

Understanding of program by external stakeholders (4)

Reaction to changes in other resources and programs (10)

Determination of uniqueness of program (17)

2. *Financial Concerns/Competing for Dollars*

Reasonable share of maternal and child health budget (6)

County and local concerns—refinancing and accountability for local funds given to state (7)

Assessment of financial impact of any action (16)

Demonstration of cost effectiveness of program (17)

3. *Comprehensive Services to Limited Population or Less Service to More People*

Determination of the bureau's role—direct service, referral, education, and so on (9)

Emphasis on community-based ambulatory services rather than on provision of tertiary care (13)

Decentralization of services to build grass-roots support (20)

Concern for quality of care versus paying bills (25)

4. *Complexities of Program Management*

Align ducks in a row to identify and address external concerns (5)

Paperwork (11)

Referral process in need of improvement (19)

Evaluation of reimbursement mechanism to ensure cost-effective quality of care and adequate services (22)

Feedback system to let bureau know how its programs are affecting the community (24)

The SMG broke into two subgroups and discussed each issue. This discussion altered the priorities, and the third theme was selected as the priority consideration. The reformulation of this theme offered by the subgroups was: to define the bureau's role with respect to handicapped children and their families.

The issues on the issue agenda were then articulated as opposing forces that are pulling or pushing BCCS in various directions away from its ideals. These forces identify the underlying tensions at work on the bureau. This format for expressing these issues illustrates conditions in the bureau and between it and external stakeholders. Issues articulated in this way are listed in order of priority.

1. Bureau's role with respect to handicapped children (tension between the broader role for the bureau and the governor's emphasis on prevention)
2. Political environment (tension between limiting the bureau's role and growing needs)
3. Financial concerns/competing for dollars (tension between historical commitments and emerging realities of cost cutting)
4. Complexities in program management (tension between needs for efficiency and rules and regulations that must be followed)

The priority issue tension illustrates how resources and change are linked. The expansion of the bureau's mission to dealing with handicapping (versus crippling) conditions implied new funds when the political environment seemed to call for a cutback. The tension shows that steps must be taken to confront both concerns if the bureau is to be successful.

The political environment issue brings out pressures to cut the bureau's budget and limit its role, which are in tension with the growing needs. The financial concerns issue identifies the agency's historical commitment to crippled children and the possibility of budget cuts. Finally, the program management issue illustrates how rules and regulations that govern how decisions must be made are in tension with initiatives to streamline systems and to improve efficiency. In each case, the issue tension brings out considerations that must be dealt with as the issue is managed.

Stage Four: Strategic Options

The SMG identified possible actions for dealing with the key issue tensions. The list of strengths, weaknesses, opportunities, and threats was reviewed for each issue to ensure that each was relevant. Using the SWOTs as guidelines, the SMG sought a way to reconcile the tensions between a broader role for BCCS and the governor's emphasis on prevention.

To identify strategic actions, SMG members were given sheets of paper with the issue and its relevant SWOTs written on them, shown in Table 15.1. They were asked to consider their ideals and to suggest concrete actions to manage the issue tension that built on strengths, overcame weaknesses, exploited opportunities, and blunted threats.

The SMG used a structured NGT variation to identify strategic actions. First, actions were identified for each SWOT. These ideas were then listed according to the SWOT. Mergers took place by applying a snowball technique to a list of actions. Themes were identified, as listed below.

1. Redefine the bureau's clientele and services (its role).
2. Establish alternative methods of service provision or delivery.
3. Enhance political support for the bureau and its programs and services.
4. Build coordination and cooperation with other programs.
5. Increase public awareness.
6. Assure stability of funding.
7. Find ways to contain service costs.

The SMG ranked these strategic themes using criteria of fiscal impact, salability, and quality of care emphasis. The strategy of role redefinition had the highest ranking.

The SMG explored the relationships among these strategies by applying the ISM procedure (see Chapter Ten). Figure 15.2 summarizes the relationships identified for precedence. These relationships tend to confirm the ranking of role redefinition as the key strategic action. Note, however, that four of the strategies must play an important role. In each case, arrows flow both in and out, indicating that each of these strategies by applying the ISM procedure (see Chapter Ten). Figure 15.2 summarizes the relationships identified for precedence. These relationships tend to confirm the ranking of

Table 15.1. Strategic Issues Worksheet.

ISSUE: To define the bureau's role with respect to handicapped children and their families

Building Upon Strengths
Market the program.

Make the public aware of the costs of care and the costs of not receiving care.

Draw upon outside expertise to sell the program to the counties, the staff, and the division.

Lobby the legislature using outside support groups and professional organizations and available data to show how BCCS contains costs.

Overcoming Weaknesses
Publicize positive aspects of BCCS (use good data).

Work on PHC rules and state law.

Use staff and consumer groups to influence the state department of health director, legislature, and governor.

Redefine program as preventive and expand prevention activities.

Coordinate preventive aspects with genetics, family planning, and child health departments.

Exploiting Opportunities
Educate and lobby the legislature.

Collaborate with other state department of health programs, other agencies, and the division to expand on health prevention programs for children.

Project the program's image as innovative, preventive, and cost saving.

Institute regional coordinators.

Raise income standards.

Blocking Threats
Market, sell, and lobby the bureau to the legislature and get other departments to help.

Emphasize quality of care, uniqueness, and differentness from welfare (for example, middle-class families are helped).

Do planning using DRG, prospective payment, long-term, and contingency plans if not enough funds.

Figure 15.2. Strategy Precedence for Bureau of Crippled Children's Services.

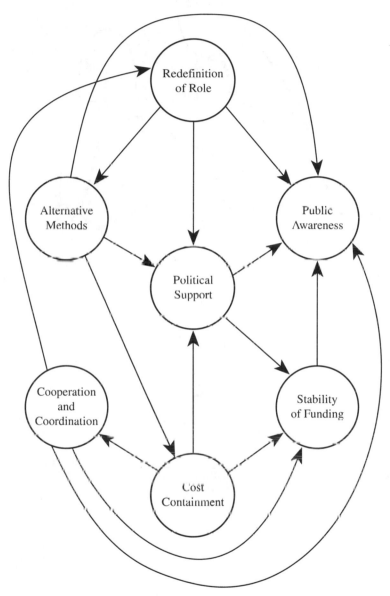

Figure 15.3. Producer-Product Relationships Among Strategies for Bureau of Crippled Children's Services.

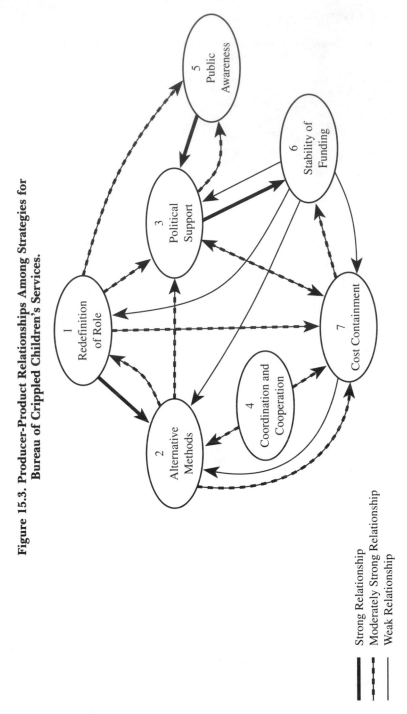

 Strong Relationship
Moderately Strong Relationship
Weak Relationship

Note: Arrowheads show direction of relationship.

these strategies in Figure 15.2. Both are essential but depend on the other strategies being in place before either can be realized. This demonstrates that a linear movement through the strategies, considering them one at a time, is undesirable.

Figure 15.3 summarizes the extent to which each strategy is a producer or a product and the strength of this relationship. This figure also brings to light important feedback effects that make it difficult to attack the strategies one at a time. These analyses helped the SMG see the need to deal with these seven strategies at the same time during implementation.

Stage Five: Feasibility Assessment

The SMG identified stakeholders and resources using an NGT for each of the seven strategies. The first analysis determined the resources needed by the seven strategies. After listing, prioritization, and the like, the final list was reorganized to link it to strategies and suppliers.

Listed below are the types of resources available to the bureau. Listed after each resource are the suppliers or controllers of that resource. Finally, whether the supplier is internal or external is indicated by an *I* or an *E*. These include *investment capital* [such as private corporations (E) and physicians (E)]; *professional support groups* (such as medical advisory committee (I), state nurses association (E), and academy of pediatrics (E); *computer and telecommunication technology* (such as state agency working in this area (E) and the corporate sector (E); *good image* (with groups that include field staff (I), local health departments (I), providers to BCCS clients (E), and BCCS medical advisory subcommittee (I); *legitimacy* (with groups such as office of budget and management (E), bureau chief as medical doctor (I), general assembly (E), and BCCS clients (E); *child advocacy groups* (such as Children's Defense Fund (E) and county children's services agencies (E); *federal mandates* (such as Department of Health and Human Services (E) and Congress (E); *expertise* (from groups such as state department of health and legal services (E), BCCS staff (I), COMPASS consulting group (I), state department of health cost containment (E), and state department of health, public information officer (E); *decision-making ability* [by bureau chief (I) and State department of health chain of command (E)]; *computer data for bill paying* (serving BCCS data staff (I), state department of human services (E), providers (E), and CCS programs in other states (E); *flexibility under current law; grant money; out-of-state programs; third-party resources; federal funds; department of health; diagnostic advocacy groups; research; state funds; manpower;* and *county funds.*

The resource list was used to stimulate the SMG's thinking about stakeholders, who were often key resource suppliers. Stakeholders were identified with an NGT and organized according to strategy and whether the stakeholder was internal or external. Then they were coded according to the stakes. The codes for the stakes are (1) professional relationship, (2) clientele, (3) services, (4) economics or profit motive, (5) consumers, (6) expertise or advice, (7) political success, (8) professionalism, (9) advocacy, and (10) public information and education. A partial listing of stakeholders follows:

Strategy One: Redefine the Bureau's Clientele and Services

Internal Stakeholders (examples below)	*Stake Code*
Physicians in the bureau	1, 2, 3, 6
Division	2, 3, 4
Department of health legal counsel	2, 3, 6
Chief of division	2, 3, 4, 6
State workers who have other roles	4, 5, 9

External Stakeholders (examples below)	*Stake Code*
Insurance companies/third-party payers	2, 3, 4, 6, 10

Disabled child and family	2, 3, 4, 5
BCCS provider physicians	2, 3
Rehabilitation services commission	2, 3, 6

*Strategy Two: Establish Alternative Methods of Service Provision/
Delivery*

Internal Stakeholders (some examples)	Stake Code
Physicians in bureau	1, 2, 3, 6
Preventive medicine	2, 3, 6
Unions	4, 9, 10

External Stakeholders (some examples)	Stake Code
Local health departments	1, 3, 4
Insurance companies and third-party payers	2, 3, 4, 6, 10
Disabled child and family	2, 3, 4, 5

*Strategy Three: Enhance Political Support for Bureau and Its
Programs/Services*

Internal Stakeholders (some examples)	Stake Code
Physicians in bureau	1, 2, 3, 6
Staff of BCCS	3, 4, 10
State workers who have other roles	4, 5, 9

External Stakeholders (some examples)	Stake Code
Legislators	2, 5, 7
Parent support groups	3, 5, 9
County commissioners	4, 7

Strategy Four: Build Coordination and Cooperation Among Child Health Service Providers

Internal Stakeholders (some examples)	Stake Code
Unit head and administrative staff	1, 6, 8
Medical services	2, 3, 6
Women, infant, children (WIC) food supplement program	2, 3

External Stakeholders (some examples)	Stake Code
Disease-specific interest groups	2, 3, 5
Rehabilitation services commission	2, 3, 6
Providers of services, therapy, and so on	3, 4, 6
Parent support groups	3, 5, 9

Strategy Five: Increase Public Awareness

Internal Stakeholders (some examples)	Stake Code
Physicians in bureau	1, 2, 3, 6
Unit heads and administrative staff	1, 6, 8
Preventive medicine	2, 3, 6

External Stakeholders (some examples)	Stake Code
Regional office of health and human services	1, 2, 3, 6

Director of health	1, 2, 3, 7
Primary care physicians	3, 4

Strategy Six: Assure Stability of Funding

Internal Stakeholders (some examples)	Stake Code
Physicians in bureau	1, 2, 3, 6
Division chief	2, 3, 4, 6

External Stakeholders (some examples)	Stake Code
Director of health	1, 2, 3, 7
Legislators	2, 5, 7

Strategy Seven: Find Ways to Contain Costs of Programs and Services

Internal Stakeholders (some examples)	Stake Code
Division chief	2, 3, 4, 6
Unions	4, 9, 10

External Stakeholders (some examples)	Stake Code
Insurance companies, third party payers	2, 3, 4, 6, 10
Legislators	

By examining the recurrent stakeholders in these lists, the SMG was able to pinpoint several groups that seemed to merit special management. These groups included the field staff, the medical advisory group for the BCCS, as well as local physicians and public health departments. An NGT was used to identify the desired outcome for each of these stakeholders and the actions to take regarding each stakeholder. Table 15.2

Table 15.2. Worksheet for Analyzing Stakeholders, Desired Outcomes, and Actions.

Directions: For each Stakeholder to the left identify the following under the appropriate headings (see Form A.11).

1. Enter the most important stakeholders, internal or external, who affect or are affected by strategy one: redefining the bureau's clientele and services.
2. Then, working with one stakeholder at a time, briefly state what desired *outcome* BCCS wishes to achieve relative to this strategy for the stakeholder. Enter in column two.
3. Next, given the stakeholder and the desired outcome(s), what *actions* should BCCS take to achieve that result? Enter in column three.

Continue on through the list of stakeholders in this fashion, completing the process for each one.

Stakeholders and Stakes	Desired Outcomes	Actions Toward Stakeholders (Direct and Indirect)
1. Staff of BCCS	1. Informed about CCS program direction.	1. Ask for their input and inform them of final plan.
	2. Each has a defined job contributing to desired plan direction.	2. Look at Japanese method of management and redesign management to incorporate what works well.
	3. Eliminate "deadwood."	3. Personnel to assist with this (document need for change).
	4. Eliminate conflicts between staff.	4. Committee of peers to hear and resolve problems can be established.
	5. Decision making at the lowest levels.	5. Increase accountability as related to program goals.

Table 15.2. Worksheet for Analyzing Stakeholders, Desired Outcomes, and Actions, Cont'd.

Stakeholders and Stakes	Desired Outcomes	Actions Toward Stakeholders (Direct and Indirect)
	6. Contribution of realistic input to policy.	6. Establish evaluation mechanisms using case data and personal activities to evaluate policy.
	7. Strategic management group continues as top priority.	7. Provide tools to staff to use business cards, telephone credit cards, toll-free lines, computer terminals, and so on.
	8. Utilize computer data, other tools to broaden role.	8. Hire consultant group on an ongoing basis to guide strategic management group.
	9. Acceptance of plan.	9. Participate in interagency groups and consult on local level.
	10. Gain bureauwide direction.	10. Involve whole staff in another level of participation and produce commitment.
	11. Increase productivity and motivation.	11. Direct participation to kinds of staff: (1) clerical, (2) management, (3) supervisory, and (4) data professional.

summarizes one of these assessments and the worksheet that was used. In the next stage, steps were taken to manage these interests.

Stage Six: Implementation

Implementation was carried out by repeating the pre-SMG surveys with key stakeholder groups and by conducting telephone surveys with others. The field staff and others repeated the surveys, which allowed them to identify trends, directions, and the like. There was a close agreement among the items and the priorities. Because of this agreement, it seemed safe to share proposed actions. Next, the strategies were shared with these groups, and they were asked for their endorsement, which was obtained.

Telephone surveys were carried out with various external stakeholders to share proposed strategies and ask for comments. These calls ended by asking the respondent for his or her endorsement. In each case, the information illustrated in Table 15.2 provided a guide to structure the interview and probe for the things needed to support the strategies.

These interviews were structured using the arguments posed by Figure 7.5 (Chapter Seven). First, the respondent was asked which clients should be served or not served. The question typically authorized BCCS to fold in more clients. Second, services to be included or excluded were identified, usually with the same result—increasing services. Then rules regarding eligibility were tested. The consensus of these responses allowed BCCS staff to compute the revenue and expenditure effects of the recommendations.

The BCCS has successfully implemented its strategic plan. The extent of its success can be seen in its name change. It is now known as the Bureau of Handicapped Children's Services. The name change was used to signal the new approach to be taken by the bureau.

The bureau initiated the continuous change approach to strategic management described in Chapter Eight. The SMG has continued to identify issues and to develop strategic responses, managing the agency's plans in this manner.

Reshaping the Issue Agenda

After the initial cycle of the strategic management process, the issue agenda had three issues yet to be managed. The facilitators helped the BCCS director reshape the agenda by testing comprehensiveness using the issue tension framework in Chapter Five.

The issues were classified as shown below (the numbers in parentheses indicate priority on the initial issue agenda).

> *Productivity-Equity*
>   Bureau's role with respect to handicapped children (1)
> *Productivity-Transition*
>   Political environment (2)
> *Productivity-Preservation*
>   Financial concerns/competing for dollars (3)
>   Complexities of program management (4)

The initial issue agenda raises several points. First, the bureau was primarily concerned with productivity. We were able to show how productivity was in tension with other values and raised the consciousness of the SMG about competing ideas and interests, which led to a successful implementation of the first cycle of the process.

Three of the issue tensions did not emerge in the first process cycle: preservation-equity, preservation-transition, and transition-equity. We counseled the SMG to consider issues in these categories as the issue agenda was reshaped for the next cycle of activity. This step helped the bureau to confront inequities that often arise as changes are being made, what should be retained in the face of change, and problems various individuals will have in making changes. None of these values were foreign to the bureau, but they were not being formally considered. These values were considered as the strategic management process began its second cycle in the bureau.

Aftermath

The bureau was a *professional* organization that wanted to become more proactive, anticipating rather than reacting to events that could be predicted. Initially, the bureau's internal capacity was fairly high and control was moderate. The bureau sought to increase its control over events to become more proactive. To become proactive, the bureau's leaders wanted key insiders to develop a vision of the future. The vision that emerged called for a broader role in dealing with handicapping conditions, which meant expanding the bureau's services and clients.

To gain acceptance of this broader role, the bureau's management allowed a large number of stakeholders to comment on the bureau's plans, potentially giving up control over some features of the strategy that would be carried out. By accepting more oversight (and thereby control), the agency was able to expand its purview and to reduce its threats simultaneously, becoming a more relevant agency. The bureau's management recognized the paradox of control; by giving up control, letting outsiders have a voice in deciding what would be carried out, control was increased. This approach to implementation enhanced the bureau's role, which increased its purview and made the bureau more proactive. Success in the first cycle of the strategic management process encouraged the bureau's leadership to continue with this approach, which thus created an even greater proactive posture.

The bureau had been operating in a placid environment with little need for action and a low level of responsiveness, using a *bureaucratic* strategy. The bureau saw signs of turbulence on the horizon and wanted to deal with directions that would pull it into this turbulence. Both an increased need for action and increased collaboration were incorporated into its plans, creating a *compromiser* strategy. The bureau attempted to increase its budgetary claims by expanding its role through agreements with other agencies.

The bureau has continued its strategic development, moving toward a *mutualist* strategy. By seeking services with a preventive potential in subsequent cycles of its strategic management process, the bureau anticipated needs that the governor's office had targeted as priorities. The bureau also sought to build more cooperative arrangements with outside groups to serve children with handicapping conditions. These actions moved the bureau from being a control agency, authorizing actions by others, to being a proactive agency that anticipated needs and led the movement to take corrective action.

The priority issue tensions identified for the management of the bureau, classified as a portfolio, were all found to be *dark horses*. Issues regarding the bureau's role, political environment, financial concerns, and program management were potentially tractable but had little stakeholder support. The bureau recognized that by acting to deal with issues that were dark horses, it could build the needed support to capitalize on issues that could be presented as tractable. Without action, several of the issues could become *angry tigers*. This shift seemed particularly likely for the "role" issue. Had the bureau not acted, the political appeal of children's services could bring other players into the arena, who might claim that the bureau had shirked its obligations. Competition would drive out cooperation, making mutualist strategies very difficult to initiate and hard to maintain. By broadening its base of support to act in a defensible arena (services for handicapped children) through collaborative initiatives, the prospect that the total needs of handicapped children would be addressed was increased.

Conclusion:
Strategic Principles for Organizational Transformation

This conclusion is both summative and integrative, offering principles that suggest how to manage an organization strategically. We summarize the theory and process of strategic management and offer our view of its future. Strategic principles are derived from the unique needs posed by the public and third sector, from the way change is made in and for this type of organization, and from the demands for transformation that will redirect and channel the energies of strategic leaders in the future.

Creating Strategy

To create strategy, an organizational leader must address aims, identify key players, recognize the setting in which development is to take place, specify timing, and carry out a process

(Figure C.1). The key players are stakeholders, who must play a role in the formation and implementation of strategy. Some stakeholders will become members of the strategic management group (SMG) that will undertake strategic development and implementation. Some SMG members can enter and exit as the strategy unfolds and other will be recognized for their influence during feasibility assessments. The process, or the *how* of strategic management, is used by the SMG to create content, or *what* makes up strategy. Strategy is devised to meet aims (the *why*) and is carried out in particular settings (*where*) and with certain timing (*when*). These elements of strategic management have the relationship shown in Figure C.1.

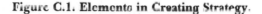

Figure C.1. Elements in Creating Strategy.

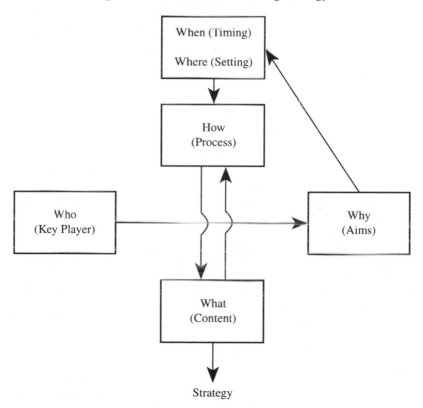

The dominant force in fashioning a strategy is an organizational leader who takes action by articulating an aim. Recall
the cases presented in Part Five. The leader of the county library wanted it to grow and modernize. The director of the
mental health agency sought new directions and funding continuity. Leaders get things going by recognizing the need for
change, which provides impetus and purpose. As shown in Figure C.1, questions about timing and setting follow. The leader
determines when results are expected and who is to be involved. In the case of the mental health and children's services
agencies, the SMGs were made up of key insiders.

In other instances, outsiders make up the SMG and a
consortium arrangement is used (see Chapter Five). In a consortium, members represent the interests or point of view of
agencies and organizations that must act together to fashion a
strategy. Consortia are becoming more important as demands
for integration in service delivery increase. For instance, the
state of Illinois has mandated "councils" and the state of Ohio
has initiated "cluster groups" made up of all state agencies that
deal with aspects of a particular topic, such as economic development, to coordinate strategic action. Such a group is needed
to deal with the equitable delivery of services and to appreciate
important values such as seeing that needs are met, eliminating
duplication, and ensuring continuity. The strategic leader who
elects to use a consortium recognizes the need for this type of
group, a recognition that begins to shape the process that will
be used.

The choice of timing also shapes the process. As noted
in Chapter Eight, scaled down one-day experiences will differ
from those that call for a one-process cycle. A one-time cycle
differs from the commitments and resources required to do
continuous change strategic management.

The process (how) used to form a strategy is partially
determined by timing and setting. Another important determinant of process is expectations. As described in Chapter
Twelve, aims (why) determine the type of information that is
required by the process. The strategic leader determines the
needs for quality, innovation, acceptance, and preservation (for

example, identifying centers of excellence that will not be changed). These choices help to identify the best way to collect and organize information needed by the process to increase the prospect that the desired type of strategy can be created. For instance, the mental health center in Chapter Thirteen sought a comprehensive strategy, which called for quality, acceptance, and innovation.

The arrows between the how (process) and the what (content) in Figure C.1 attempt to capture the interplay between process and content. One merges into the other as strategy is fashioned. This "dance of the what and how" is central to our approach of doing strategic management. The strategic leader energizes a process with ideas and uses process to fashion ideas. Learning occurs during energizing and development efforts. Strategic leaders who use the process wisely can position their organization so that change is both possible and desirable.

Strategic principles flow from the guidelines we provide to cope with the who, why, when, where, how, and what elements of strategic development as noted in Figure C.1. These principles, which are summarized in Table C.1, deal with understanding the special needs of context given by public and third sector organizations and how their features create constraints and possibilities. Principles also concern how such organizations should go about strategic management for change and transformation. Change occurs when an organization repositions in light of opportunities and threats. Transformation occurs when the organization commits to manage its fundamental tensions and continuously seeks innovative win-win responses to all types of issue tensions as they arise or are anticipated.

Special Needs of Public and Third Sector Organizations

Organizations with significant public features have unique needs. As noted in Chapters Two and Seven, publicness calls for new ways of thinking about the nature of strategy and its development.

Table C.1. Strategic Principles.

Elements of Strategic Action	What Is Done
Who (strategic leader makes a commitment)	Recognize change in organizational capacity and responsiveness needed to become a *proactive* organization.
Why (articulate aims and purposes)	Determine *ideals* to manage a vision, create a vision, or deal with demands.
Where (determine context to be managed)	Select *context* from which SMG membership is to be drawn (agency, mixed board and agency, or consortium).
When (make choices about duration)	Infer *type of process* to be established (trial experiment, one cycle, or continuous change).
What (select content of strategy)	Note special needs of *public* and *third sector* organizations. (How is organization apt to change and produce new constraints and possibilities?)

Match environments to *types of strategy*.
1. Bureaucratic strategy fits placid environments.
2. Accommodator strategy fits placid clusters.
3. Director strategy fits disturbed environments.
4. Mutualist strategy is required in turbulent environments.
5. Use strategies to focus effort by providing plans, ploys, patterns, positions, and perspectives.

Table C.1. Strategic Principles, Cont'd.

Elements of Strategic Action	What Is Done
How (make decisions about process)	Make *strategic changes.*

1. Recognize the importance of *issues* by applying tests that create issue tensions, and then classify them according to values. The tractability and public support in dealing with these issues suggest ways to package the issues to win agency support.
2. Manage the dance of the what and how. *Engage* the dance by
   a. Determining and evaluating directions, establishing ideals, assessing SWOTs, forming an agenda of issue tensions, searching for strategy, assessing needs, and making implementation plans.
   b. Recycle as needed to create action management, issue management, situation management, and organizational management.

   Organize the dance by
   a. Forming the SMG.
   b. Leader choosing among roles of process manager, process participant, or observer.
   c. Deciding on process timing.
3. Promote ownership by having SMG interpret needs and create responses based on shared meanings.
4. Select information-generating techniques to support the process according to expected results.
5. Coax leaders to accept and carry out responsibility to become a process facilitator, teacher, technician, manager, and politician.

Make *transformational* changes. Follow the principles for strategic change, emphasizing
1. Continuous change strategic management.
2. Innovation and creativity.
3. All types of issue tensions.
4. Mutualist strategy and consortiums.

Publicness stems from markets, constraints, goals, authority, authorization to act, accountability, and performance expectations that differ from those faced by firms, which create strategy to produce profit. The market in a public or third sector organization is made up of rule-making bodies, such as boards of trustees or legislatures. Publicness also arises when constraints limit flexibility and autonomy, goals are vague and in dispute, the leader's authority is limited, political interference and scrutiny by outsiders can be expected as strategy is formed, broad accountability is required, and performance expectations continually shift.

When just one of these features is present, strategic leaders should avoid using private sector approaches to strategic management. For example, the mental health agency in Chapter Thirteen had customers dictated by its controlling board. The board stipulated the scope of services to be offered and philosophy for charges and called for free care for indigent clients. State and federal structures governed what the agency had to do to get block grants that made up a significant part of the mental health agency's budget. Goals were articulated in terms of the scope of service and clients. The board was calling for increased collections while maintaining free care as well as increased productivity while maintaining professional control of services. It failed to see the conflicts that these demands produced. Any one of these features creates a "public environment" in which strategic management must take place. The process that is used to fashion strategy must be able to deal with each of these considerations.

The Changing Character of Public and Third Sector Organizations

Savvy leaders in public and third sector organizations have an acute appreciation of the constraints and possibilities that characterize these organizations. However, these organizations are facing turbulent times in which new developments can alter the nature of public and third sector organizations overnight. A new administrator enters or board members unexpectedly leave and old commitments are "out the window." These developments can alter markets, goals, accountability, performance expectations, and the other features in unexpected ways. The proactive leader must study how his or her organization can change and the impact of these changes, as noted in Chapter Two. These developments also bring with them the need to rethink historical strategy and consider the value of change.

Difficulties in Creating Strategy

Organizations with public features face three types of difficulties in fashioning a strategy. We find that strategic management is carried out to manage the visions of leaders, shape emerging demands, and create strategy in response to environmental signals.

To manage a vision, the leaders need to put their ideas into practice. Some way to give detail to the vision and get the commitments of key stakeholders is essential. As noted in Chapter One, the director of a board of regents that sets state policy for higher education sought to create a strategy to get people ready for school and ready for jobs. The director challenged his staff and the board to rethink the commitment to education in these terms. The process (how) is used to refine the strategy (what) and build commitments.

A vision emerges when a leader recognizes the desirability for expansion or growth, the need to stabilize funding, or new roles bring thrust on the organization or when someone in authority mandates the integration and coordination of services. These new aims initiate a process that seeks change in strategy that recognizes and incorporates these new ways of doing business and seeks coherence. The process (how) shapes a strategy (what) according to the emergent ideas that are thrust on the organization, as noted in the case of the library in Chapter Fourteen.

When a vision is not present at the outset or suggested in part by new demands being placed on the organization, strategy must be created by a process. The need for board education, leadership changes, or legal mandates for planning;

being caught in a rut; or facing practical threats suggests that strategic change is needed. These signals must be interpreted and expanded to form an issue agenda for which a strategy is sought. The process (how) is used to create a strategy (what) as commitments are being built, as noted in the case of the children's service bureau in Chapter Fifteen.

Strategic Change

The leaders of public and third sector organizations, seeking a way to manage, shape, or create a vision that will become the new strategy for their organization, seek change. We have offered several principles that guide the how of strategic change in the chapters describing process and theory. The principles that govern strategic change in organizations with public features are summarized below.

Identify Organizations Susceptible to Change

Organizations with high control that lack capacity (political organizations) or have high capacity without accountability (professional organizations) do not have any motivation to change. When capacity erodes or accountability increases, these organizations become buffeted and will seek to become proactive by increasing their capacity or accountability. This condition motivates leaders to seek ways to improve this state of affairs and creates the opportunity to do strategic management.

Match Environment to Types of Strategy

The intensity of the demands for action and expected responsiveness describe the environment in which change must take place. For the best results, strategic types are matched to environments best suited to them.

When demands are at a low ebb, a placid environment results. In such an environment, a bureaucratic strategy is carried out by programmed action and standardized procedure, as in the mental health center discussed in Chapter Thirteen, before federal funding cuts. The organization takes a defensive posture to protect these routines through budget maximization and the creation of slack for the inevitable budget cutback. The equivalent of protectionism in firms is sought. The strategist becomes a custodian and uses sagas, in which heroic exploits are used to reaffirm values and protect important competencies. For example, sagas were used by professionals in the mental health center to fashion war stories to protect their fee-setting prerogatives.

Organizations that have high responsiveness and low demands for action create clustered placid environments. In this environment, an accommodator strategy is applied to deal with each cluster by recognizing and dealing with its unique needs. Priorities must be set to allocate available funds among clusters, based on the compelling nature of the needs in each cluster. Such a strategy was adopted by the mental health agency to deal with funding cuts. Allocation is carried out by parlays, in which a move is made to create an opportunity to make a subsequent move. This tactic is used in budget hearings, media reports, and the like to gradually reveal allocations and read reactions.

Disturbed environments arise when responsiveness has been low and the need for action becomes high. This environment calls for a director strategy, in which new demands are dealt with by taking unilateral action. The county library in Chapter Fourteen had used such a strategy to provide countywide services until its service area began to erode. New ways to meet needs are tried out as ventures, in which speculations about emergent issues and ways to respond are considered.

Turbulent environments arise when responsiveness and the need for action both dramatically increase. A compromiser strategy is typically used. An agency plays one constituency off against another, meeting the needs of important constituents, needy constituents, or both when resources permit. Such a strategy was adopted by the county library. A mutualist strategy is usually a better approach because it attempts to create collaborative arrangements to meet all important needs that arise with umbrella organizations, such as the National Kidney

Foundation and the highway safety consortia. This strategy takes shape as a quest, which mounts new initiatives that create a grand vision. Leaders that create the sense of adventure and tests of courage of a quest create such a vision. A mutualist strategy gets stakeholders to search for new ways to meet emergent needs and entices key people to collaborate in meeting needs that prove to be crucial.

Strategy is used by an organization to focus effort in reaching for its goals by providing plans, ploys, patterns, positions, and perspectives. As a plan, a strategy offers a way to take action, such as finding new clients and services. Ploys are strategies invented to deceive an opponent. Note how ploys are not useful in a mutualist strategy but are essential to a compromiser strategy. As a pattern, strategy captures the stream of actions that puts together emergent opportunities with planned action. Strategy as position seeks services that seem needed by reading environmental signals. Positioning, such as protecting budgets or becoming territorial by staking out a service area, often accompanies director and accommodator strategies. As a perspective, strategy captures an organization's traditions and commitments, becoming a touchstone for future action.

Recognize the Importance of Issues

Issues are crucial to strategic management because they direct the search for strategy, like problems do in problem solving. Trends or events produce developments that capture attention. To ensure that these developments are not symptomatic or misleading, two steps are applied. First, the triggering development is paired with other developments to create what we call an issue tension. The tensions show how organizations are being pulled and pushed in several ways at the same time by all important issues. Second, issue tensions are classified using generic tensions of productivity-equity, productivity-transition, productivity-preservation, equity-transition, equity-preservation, and transition-preservation to ensure comprehensiveness. Organizations frequently recognize issues that stress some of these values but not others. The overlooked tensions offer new insights into useful strategy. Strategy is sought that attempts to balance opposing forces in each type of tension, being cognizant of both values. Managing tensions in this way increases the prospect of fashioning win-win responses.

Issues can be classified according to stakeholder support and tractability. When both are high, issues that are sitting ducks emerge. When both are low, issues called sleeping dogs arise. Issues become dark horses when resolution is possible but stakeholder support is lacking and angry tigers when stakeholder support is present but resolution is difficult. The portfolio of issues classified in this way suggests how people will react to strategic efforts and the manageability of the issue agenda.

Manage the Dance of the What and the How

Practitioners and the literature describe strategy as both content and process, making it both a noun and a verb. We believe this idea calls for a periodic shift in emphasis from what to how and back again, which creates a "dance of the what and how." To engage this dance, we call for the following steps:

1. Determine and evaluate directions and how directions have been influenced by key trends and events. This information establishes historical context and points out where the organization is going.
2. Establish ideals that indicate who should be served, what the organization should be doing, how the organization wants to be regarded by key stakeholders, and what persona the organization wants to have in the future.
3. Assess the current situation facing the organization in terms of key strengths, weaknesses, opportunities, and threats (SWOTs).
4. Establish an agenda of issue tensions to be managed that considers the values of transition, preservation, equity, and productivity.
5. Search for strategy that responds to priority issue tensions

by building on strengths, overcoming weaknesses, seizing opportunities, and blunting threats.

6. Assess strategy to determine needed resources and the extent of stakeholder support.

7. Devise implementation plans that garner the required resources and build stakeholder support to take action.

8. Recycle as needed. First, to pick up additional issue tensions from the issue agenda, repeat steps five, six, and seven. This is called action management. Second, periodically revise the issue agenda, repeating step four. This is called issue management. Third, reassess the situation repeating step three. This is called situation management. Finally, repeat steps one and two to look at directions and ideals for shifts and revisions. This is called organizational management. Together, these recycles provide a way to carry out the continuous strategic management of an organization.

To organize the dance, leaders must:

1. Specify SMG membership, determining whether or not a consortium will be used.

2. Select a role, choosing among roles of process manager, process participant, or process observer.

3. Decide on timing, determining if the process will be shortened, be carried out on a one-time basis, or be carried out continuously, as noted above.

Promote Ownership

The SMG is made up of people who represent key power centers inside and outside the organization. The participation of key players in the SMG helps both in formulation and implementation of strategy.

The social world of the SMG arises out of the interaction of its members as they explore and interpret their views. What counts are the constructions of reality that the SMG makes. This social construction of reality guides what is seen or believed. Process is crucial in helping the SMG make constructions that square with reality. Process also creates an opportunity to create shared meanings that can be sustained to provide a basis for action. The dance of the what and how is designed to build the knowledge and insight in an SMG that is needed to formulate and implement strategic change. Participation helps the SMG members appreciate what can be done and their role in carrying out strategic change. When the SMG develops ideas jointly, an appreciation of needs and stakeholder interests emerges which creates the basis to act.

Select Information-Generating Techniques According to Expectations

Strategic managers should develop a broad knowledge of techniques that can support the strategic management process. Such a repertoire allows the strategic leader to fashion hybrid techniques that combine useful features of several techniques according to the expectations of strategy development. These expectations stem from the need to produce quality, acceptance, innovation, or preservation in a strategy. Techniques that support the strategic management process are selected according to these needs. Strategic leaders with these insights become very good technician supervisors.

Get Leaders to Accept Multiple Responsibilities

Organizational leaders who wish to strategically manage their organization must move from observer or participant to process manager, facilitating the work of an SMG and changing its members as required. The leader of the future must adopt several roles in addition to process manager, including facilitator, teacher, technician (or technical supervisor), and politician.

Recognize the Intent of Strategic Management

Strategic management is carried out to realize organizational ideals. Trends, events, directions, and SWOTs that pose issue tensions; actions taken in response to issue tensions; and political and social forces that facilitate or constrain action must be considered as the organization reaches for its ideals.

The organization of the future must create a process of continuous change in which leaders take an active role, encouraging creativity and innovation and applying a mutualist strategy. This seldom occurs today but will be essential to meet the turbulent times ahead.

Transformational Change

In the future, the leaders of public and third sector organizations must find a way to create and manage transformations. Transformation is required to continuously alter both internal structure and external commitments in response to dynamically changing needs that will characterize the future of most organizations with public features. Turbulent environments have high need for action and call for collaborative responses, in which organizations form alliances and garner and allocate resources in response to emergent needs. This process calls for continuous strategic management that is carried out by the organizational leader, careful attention to tensions in issue agendas, creative responses, and the use of a mutualist strategy. Tomorrow's strategic leader must follow the principles of strategic change and emphasize principles noted in Table C.1 that are essential to produce transformational strategy. These principles follow.

Initiate Continuous Change Strategic Management

In our case examples and in our experiences, organizations treat strategy development as a one-day affair or as one concerted effort facilitated by outsiders. In the future, this must change. This prescription for continuous change strategic management, in which cycles of action, issue, situation, and organizational management are carried out repeatedly, will mark the successful organization in the twenty-first century. If organizational transformations are to occur, strategy development must become an ongoing activity within the organization that involves a significant amount of the leader's time. Leaders who fail to follow such an approach will be replaced by individuals who can follow this approach.

Promote Innovation and Creativity

One of the biggest problems that we encounter is the resistance to creativity and creative techniques. (It should be noted that this resistance is a problem in the private sector as well.) Many organizations with public features have been able to ignore the demands for new ideas in the past, relying on legislative edicts and the innovations of others. In the turbulent environments that we anticipate, organizations with public features will no longer have this luxury. The demands for action will come and go before leaders can see what others are doing and mimic it. Creative strategy will become increasingly important and organizational leaders who fail to innovate will be replaced. Creativity and innovation are essential ingredients of organizational transformation.

Recognize and Deal with Issue Tensions

Creative strategy can be inferred, in part, from the cues provided by issue tensions. Issue tensions broaden the arena of search for strategy to beyond the developments that initially capture attention.

The notion of an issue tension is similar to paradoxical or Janusian thinking, in which contradictions between two defensible interpretations are confronted. The arguments posed by each are plausible, but together they seem contradictory. The contradictions are explored to find ways to understand these opposing interpretations. Seen in this way, issues identify forces based on core values that are pulling and pushing an organization in many directions at the same time. Thus, strategic management seeks to manage opposing forces, such as budget cuts and emergent service needs. Values that undergird tensions stem from productivity, equity, transition, and preservation. Strong claims and counterclaims based on these values are being made, for which a response is required. Strategic leaders who deal with but one of these opposing forces create a dangerous situation, in which barriers to action or possibilities are overlooked.

Treating issues as tensions makes the identification of a win-win strategy more likely. The "and" relationship in the tension makes it essential to consider both developments that make up the opposite poles of the tension. For example, by looking for equity concerns in productivity and productivity concerns in equity, the need to deal with each type of concern becomes apparent. This coaxes the organization to search for remedies to both equity and productivity, increasing the chance of locating a win-win strategy. Extending the search to deal with each of the six types of tensions helps organizations find issues that have been overlooked in the past and expands strategy into these new areas. Implementation prospects are enhanced by uncovering interest groups that have been overlooked and must be managed. The prospect for innovative strategy increases because the emergent issues call for new ways of doing business.

Contending with both poles of an issue tension increases the chances of finding innovative strategy. Each opposing force is accepted as equally valid and accurate. The seeming incompatibilities of developments, such as the need to change (transition) and the need to maintain a culture (tradition), produce creative insights. For example, managers who think about cost and quality to form strategy produce more innovative results. Excellent organizations learn how to recognize and manage issue tensions. The successful organizations of the future must have such a creative edge. Creativity at all levels will be essential to meet this aim.

Use Mutualist Strategies

Mutualist strategies distinguish between growth and development. Growth calls for more, an increase in size, whereas development seeks an increase in net worth. Developmental strategy increases the net benefits to all relevant stakeholders. To meet this aim, mutualist strategy deals with turbulent environments in which compelling needs explosively emerge with little warning by substituting collaboration for competition. The best outcome from a competitive posture would have competing agencies serving people thought to fall under their jurisdictions. Such an approach leaves important needs unmet or underserved and encourages duplication. A collaborative posture calls for negotiation with taxing and budgeting authorities to parcel out service areas so that all service responsibilities can be met. The mutualist strategy calls for consortia and other kinds of umbrella organizations to be created to serve emergent needs. Although relevant examples such as the Highway Safety Program and the National Kidney Foundation can be identified, they have occurred far too infrequently in the past and will become more essential in the future.

A collaborative approach will be needed to ensure that emergent needs in a dynamically changing environment will be met. The mutualist strategy will be managed by resources and programs drawn from many sources. The self-interests of these sources are subordinated to the greater interest of serving people's needs. The mutualist strategy recognizes the need to develop novel structural arrangements and to create new ways to meet emergent needs.

To initiate a mutualist strategy, tomorrow's strategic leader must have vision, commitment, and leadership qualities. Vision is needed to recognize when compelling issues arise and to formulate creative responses or to anticipate needs with an innovative strategy. Commitment is required to set an example for others. One must sacrifice personal aims and parochial interests to set the tone called for by a mutualist strategy. Leadership skill is needed to strike a posture that avoids being pretentious but takes a moral position, which calls for collective action. Many are apt to interpret such a posture as a clever way to promote the leader's interests.

Successful and unsuccessful leaders engage in many of the same behaviors. Success depends on putting things into a frame in which mutualist values are believable, so others will adopt and emulate these values. Successful leaders of the future must be able to marshal the resources and commitments needed to realize their vision.

Key Points

1. The unique needs of organizations with public features and ways to make strategic change in these organizations suggest strategic principles.
2. The principles of strategic change include identifying organizations susceptible to strategic management, matching strategy to environments, recognizing issues as tensions, managing the dance of the what and the how, promoting ownership that encourages implementation, selecting leaders who accept each of the strategic management roles, selecting information generators according to desired type of strategy, and meeting the expectations called for by strategic management.
3. The principles of transformational strategy requires continuous change strategic management, innovation and creativity, recognizing and dealing with all six issue tensions, and using mutualist strategies. Transformational strategy will be essential for organizations with public features to be successful in the twenty-first century.

Resource A

Forms, Worksheets, and Handouts to Support Process Stages

Form A.1. Delphi Instructions.

On _____, you and your fellow members of the strategic management group will meet to launch a strategic management process. I am looking forward to working with you and to an opportunity to assist you in identifying your strategic management position.

    In order to make the best of the limited time we will have together and, perhaps more important, to give you time to think about some things that are central to effective strategic management, we are asking you to complete the enclosed forms. Effective strategic management is premised upon sound analysis of the organization, its characteristics, and the environment in which it operates. The questions we are asking are designed to gather your perceptions about where the organization is in its world and where you see it heading.

    Please note that the forms call for answers of short phrases or paragraphs. Your responses should focus on capturing the essence of what you are raising. You will note, too, that some questions seem to build on others. For this reason, it will be best if you find a block of time sufficient to permit you to work through all the forms at one sitting.

    We will be providing feedback based on the overall group response. Anonymity will be protected, but you may place an identifying notation on your responses if you think you might want them back after the work session. Please return the completed forms to me by _____, at the address below. Please contact us if you have any questions.

Thank you.

Form A.2. Strategic Direction Worksheet.

Briefly describe the current strategic direction of the organization. What basic movement does the organization have? It is helpful to look back over the past three to seven years and ahead over a similar period to identify major changes the organization has experienced or will experience. Describe below the organization's movement in the areas (dimensions) listed.

Dimension

Demands/Needs (things we must or should respond to in order to serve the needs and wants of clients or to give recognition to groups important to the agency)

In my opinion, we are moving away from   *In my opinion, we are moving toward*

Dimension

Resources (means at our disposal to carry out our program—our fiscal, human, and physical facility resources, including data)

In my opinion, we are moving away from	*In my opinion, we are moving toward*

Dimension

Programs (the mix of programs and services we offer and the clientele we target)

In my opinion, we are moving away from	*In my opinion, we are moving toward*

Dimension

General Managerial and Organizational Practices (the competencies and strategies around which our administrative mechanisms are organized)

In my opinion, we are moving away from	*In my opinion, we are moving toward*

Form A.3. External Events and Trends Worksheet.

List below the specific external events and trends that you feel
will impact upon the functioning of the agency over the next
three to seven years. Think broadly in terms of the economic,
client-related, managerial, technical, political, and social factors
that ought to be considered because of their strategic impact.
This is your chance to explicitly identify the external events
and trends that you think the organization will be confronted
with in the future.

1.

2.

3.

4.

5.

6.

7.

8.

9.

10.

11.

12.

Form A.4. Ideal Agency Attributes Worksheet.

Looking into the future, what attributes do you think would describe the organization in the best of all possible worlds? What attributes would characterize the organization in the worst of all possible worlds?

Best-case attributes

Worst-case attributes

Form A.5. Situational Assessment Worksheet.

Strengths are defined as one or more skills, distinctive competencies, capabilities, competitive advantages, or resources that the organization can draw on in selecting a strategy. List the strengths that the organization can use in any future strategy.

1. _____   6. _____

2. _____   7. _____

3. _____   8. _____

4. _____   9. _____

5. _____   10. _____

Weaknesses are defined as the lack of one or more skills, distinctive competencies, capabilities, competitive advantages, or resources. List the weaknesses that any future strategy for the organization must take into account.

1. _____   6. _____

2. _____   7. _____

3. _____   8. _____

4. _____   9. _____

5. _____   10. _____

Opportunities are situations in which benefits are fairly clear and likely to be realized if certain actions are taken. List the opportunities that are open to the organization.

1. _____ 6. _____

2. _____ 7. _____

3. _____ 8. _____

4. _____ 9. _____

5. _____ 10. _____

Threats are situations that give rise to potentially harmful events and outcomes if action is not taken in the immediate future; they must be actively confronted to prevent trouble. List the threats that currently confront the organization.

1. _____ 6. _____

2. _____ 7. _____

3. _____ 8. _____

4. _____ 9. _____

5. _____ 10. _____

Form A.6. Strategic Issue Agenda Worksheet.

Strategic issues are anticipated or actual conditions or tensions, internal or external to the organization, that, if they continue, will have a significant effect on the functioning of the organization or its ability to achieve its desired future.

List below strategic issues that the organization must manage to be successful in the future. To state an issue as a tension, follow two steps. First, identify the issue using the definition above. Second, find the most significant factor pulling in the opposite direction and pair the issue with this factor. For example, the issue of cutbacks in a medical school department of family medicine due to loss of state funds can be paired with increased service demands by low-income patients.

1.

2.

3.

4.

5.

6.

7.

8.

9.

10.

11.

To explore issues, it is often useful to expand the issue's significance by identifying its important features and why it merits the organization's attention. For example, if you were to make a presentation to someone not as closely involved with the organization as you, what would you say are the significant aspects of this issue? Why is it worthy of attention?

Issue #1 _____

    1.

    2.

    3.

    4.

    5.

Issue #2 _____

    1.

    2.

    3.

    4.

    5.

Issue #3 _____

    1.

    2.

    3.

    4.

    5.

Issue #4 _____

   1.

   2.

   3.

   4.

   5.

Issue #5 _____

   1.

   2.

   3.

   4.

   5.

Issue #6 _____

   1.

   2.

   3.

   4.

   5.

Form A.7. Strategy Worksheet.

1. On the attached worksheet, list as many strategic actions as you can that relate to the priority issue. Use the issue relevant SWOTs to assist you in this task.
2. In applying the SWOTs principles, feel free to suggest both conventional and novel action ideas. We have found that if you consider possible action that could build on strengths, overcome weaknesses, exploit opportunities, and blunt or block threats, a comprehensive yet creative set of ideas can be produced for further discussion and refinement. Enter your action ideas at the right of the worksheet.
3. When you enter the action ideas on the right-hand lines under "Strategic Actions," be sure to list the number of the SWOTs the action targets (for example, S1, S2, and O1). An action may target only one SWOT factor or several. Strategic actions that simultaneously affect strengths, weaknesses, opportunities, and threats are important to discover. If you run out of space, use the back side of the page.
4. There is no need to sign the sheets. Do write legibly so that others can read your writing.
5. When you have exhausted your ideas, let the facilitator know.

Definition and Guiding Principles of Strategic Management: Strategic management is movement toward our mission, built upon an understanding of our current situation and an identification of our desired future, which permits us to

Build on our strengths
Overcome our weaknesses
Exploit our opportunities
Block or *blunt* our threats

Form A.7. Strategy Worksheet.

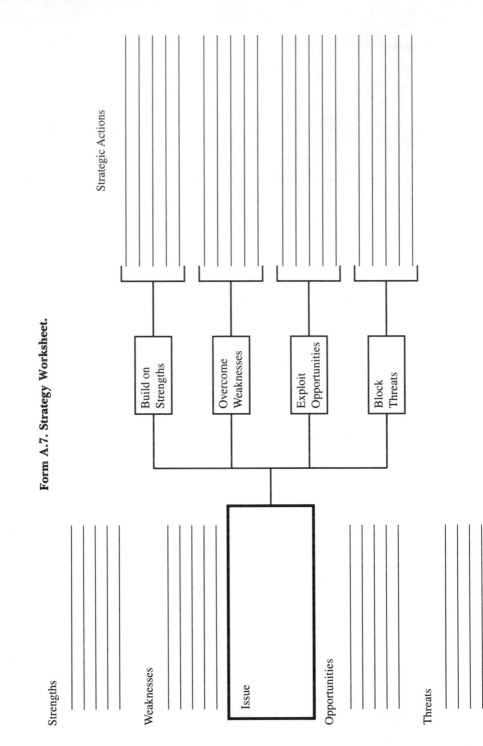

Strengths

Weaknesses

Issue

Opportunities

Threats

Build on Strengths

Overcome Weaknesses

Exploit Opportunities

Block Threats

Strategic Actions

438

Form A.8. Stakeholder Identification Worksheet.

Both within and outside the organization, there are individuals, groups, and organizations who share an interest or have a stake in the strategies that we are considering. Stakeholders include all parties who will be affected by or will affect the priority strategy.

List below to the left the stakeholders for the strategy. List to the right the interest or stake involved (user of services, suppliers of clients, cooperation in service delivery, costs of access, and so on). In our discussion, we will not ask whether the stakeholder is internal or external; you can make an *I* or *E* next to each party to communicate this. Work slightly. Shift back and forth between strategies if you reach a dead end in your thinking.

Strategy: _____

Stakeholder   Interest/Stake

_____   _____

_____   _____

_____   _____

_____   _____

_____   _____

_____   _____

Form A.9. Stakeholder Issue Position Worksheet.

Score the stakeholder list by finding the stakeholders *most* likely to be supportive of our priority strategy and rating them +5. Find the stakeholders most likely to oppose the strategy and rate them −5. Rate neutral stakeholders 0. Rate the remainder of the stakeholders using these anchors.

Position on the Issue

(+5 = Positive, −5 = Negative)

Stakeholder or Code   Rating

_____   _____

_____   _____

_____   _____

_____   _____

_____   _____

_____   _____

_____   _____

_____   _____

_____   _____

_____   _____

Form A.10. Stakeholder Importance Worksheet.

Score the stakeholder list by finding the most important stakeholders and rating them 10. Find the least important stakeholders and rate them 1. Rate the remainder of the stakeholders using these anchors. A rating of 5 or less indicates that
stakeholders do not require formal contact during implementation.

Importance

(1 = Least, 10 = Most)

Stakeholder or Code   Rating

_____   _____

_____   _____

_____   _____

_____   _____

_____   _____

_____   _____

_____   _____

_____   _____

_____   _____

_____   _____

_____   _____

Form A.11. Resources Identification Worksheet.

For each strategy listed below, identify the type of resource
that might be required for successful achievement of the strategy, together with who might be a supplier or controller of
that resource. In thinking about resources as they relate to the
strategies, look for both external and internal resources. Look
for both fiscal (money) and nonfiscal resources (such as labor,
legitimacy, status, acceptance, knowledge, expertise, power, time,
and an existing program) that could be used as a resource by
us to achieve a strategy objective or other form of assistance
that could be tapped by us.

Strategic Theme	Resource Types	Suppliers	How to Acquire
_____	_____	_____	_____
_____	_____	_____	_____
_____	_____	_____	_____
_____	_____	_____	_____
_____	_____	_____	_____
_____	_____	_____	_____
_____	_____	_____	_____
_____	_____	_____	_____
_____	_____	_____	_____
_____	_____	_____	_____

Form A.12. Resource Criticality Worksheet.

Rate the criticality or importance of each resource and its controller by first finding the most critical resources or controllers and rating them 10. Find the least important resources or controllers and rate them 0. Rate the remainder using these anchors. A rating of 5 or less implies that the resource is not essential to carry out the strategy.

Criticality

(1 = Least, 10 = Most)

Resource, Controller,   Rating
      or Code

_____   _____

_____   _____

_____   _____

_____   _____

_____   _____

_____   _____

_____   _____

_____   _____

_____   _____

_____   _____

Form A.13. Resource Potential Availability Worksheet.

Rate the potential availability (ease of funding or mobilization) of each resource by identifying easily acquired resources and rating them +5. Rate unavailable resources −5 and resources with uncertain availability 0. Rate the remaining resources using these anchors.

Potential Availability

(−5 = Not Available, +5 = Easily Available)

Resource or Code   Rating

_____   _____

_____   _____

_____   _____

_____   _____

_____   _____

_____   _____

_____   _____

_____   _____

_____   _____

_____   _____

_____   _____

_____   _____

Resource B

■   ■

Forms and Worksheets for Support Techniques

■   ■

Form B.1. Precedence Relationships Worksheet.

For each item in a row, enter in the column to its right whether the item precedes (P) or follows (F) the item listed above in the column in order of causal preference and consequence. If both items operate simultaneously, enter (S).

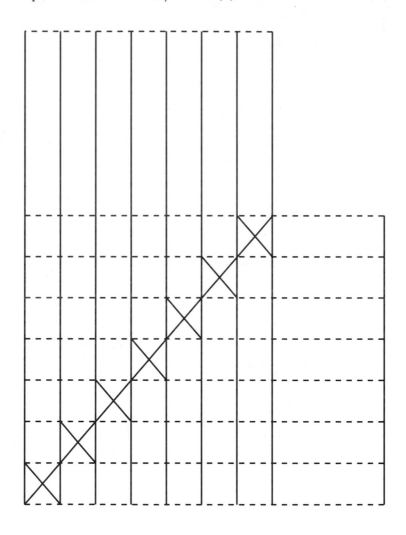

Form B.2. Producer-Product Relationships Worksheet.

Enter the extent to which the item in each row affects positively (+1 to +5) or negatively (−1 to −5) the item in each column. If it has no significant effect, enter a zero (0).

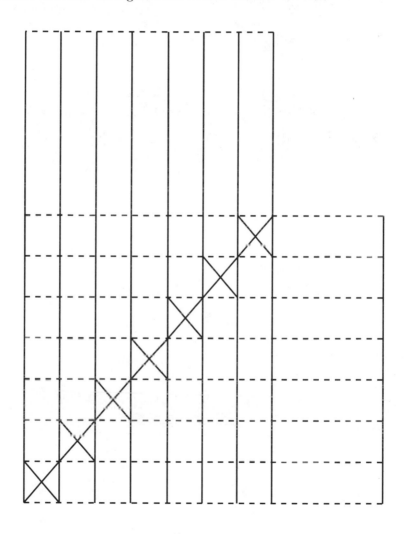

Form B.3. Ranking Worksheet for Criteria.

Any of the criteria that follow can be used to select strategy.

1. Impact
2. Importance
3. Timeliness
4. Control
5. Issue precedence*
6. Causality*

   If criteria 1 through 4 are used, the rating sheet on the facing page is used for each criterion.

*Implied by charts

Form B-3. Ranking Worksheet for Criteria, Cont'd.

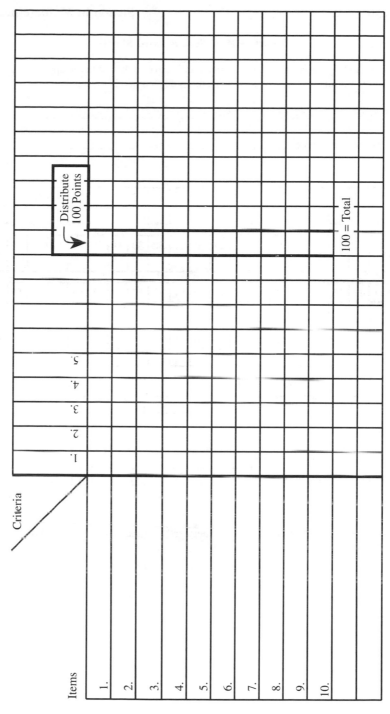

Form B.4. *Q* Sort Record Sheet.

After sorting, insert the category value number for each card in the appropriate box below. Be sure each category contains the specified number of cards.

Subject: _____ Sorter: _____

Information Source: _____ Date: _____

1	2	3	4	5	6	7	8	9	10	11	12	13	14	15	16	17	18	19	20

21	22	23	24	25	26	27	28	29	30	31	32	33	34	35	36	37	38	39	40

41	42	43	44	45	46	47	48	49	50	51	52	53	54	55	56	57	58	59	60

61	62	63	64	65	66	67	68	69	70	71	72	73	74	75	76	77	78	79	80

81	82	83	84	85	86	87	88	89	90	91	92	93	94	95	96	97	98	99	100	101

Category Value	1	2	3	4	5	6	7	8	9
Number of items in category	5	8	12	16	19	16	12	8	5

Note: A value of 9 indicates "most important." A value of 1 indicates "least important."

Source: Adapted from Nutt, 1984a.

References

Acar, W. "Organizational Processes and Strategic Postures: Cross-Classification or Continuum." *Proceedings of the General Systems Society,* 1987, J-70–J-81.

Ackerman, R. W., and Bauer, R. A. *Corporate Social Responsiveness: The Modern Dilemma.* Reston, Va.: Reston, 1976.

Ackoff, R. *Creating the Corporate Future,* New York: Wiley, 1981.

Allison, G. T., Jr. "Public-Private Management: Are They Fundamentally Alike in All Unimportant Aspects?" In B. Bozeman and J. Straussman (eds.), *New Directions in Public Administration.* Pacific Grove, Calif.: Brooks/Cole, 1984.

Andrews, K. R. *The Concept of Corporate Strategy.* Homewood, Ill.: Irwin, 1980.

Ansoff, H. I. "Managing Strategic Surprise to Weak Signals." *California Management Review,* 1976, *18,* 21–23.

Ansoff, H. I. "The Changing Shape of the Strategic Problem." In D. Schendel and C. Hofer (eds.), *Strategic Management.* Boston: Little, Brown, 1979.

Ansoff, H. I. "Strategic Issue Management." *Strategic Management Journal*, 1980, *1* (2), 131–148.

Ansoff, H. I. *Implanting Strategic Management.* Englewood Cliffs, N.J.: Prentice Hall, 1984.

Ansoff, H. I., Declerk, R. P., and Hayes, R. L. *From Strategic Planning to Strategic Management.* New York: Wiley, 1976.

Appleby, P. H. *Big Democracy.* New York: Knopf, 1945.

Arcelus, F. J., and Schaefer, N. V. "Social Demands as Strategic Issues: Some Conceptual Problems." *Strategic Management Journal*, 1982, *3* (4), 347–358.

Archebalt, D., and Backoff, R. W. "An Innovation Adoption Perspective for Marketing in the Government." In M. Mokwa and S. Permut (eds.), *Government Marketing.* New York: Praeger, 1981.

Argyris, C., and Schon, D. *Organizational Learning: A Theory of Action Perspective.* Reading, Mass.: Addison-Wesley, 1978.

Axelrod, R. *Structure of a Decision: The Cognitive Maps of Political Elites.* Princeton, N.J.: Princeton University Press, 1976.

Backoff, R. W., and Nutt, P. C. "A Process for Strategic Management with Specific Application for the Nonprofit Organization." In J. Bryson and R. Einsweiler (eds.), *Strategic Planning.* Chicago: American Planning Association, 1988.

Baker, R. "Organizational Theory in the Public Sector." *Journal of Management Studies*, Feb. 1969, pp. 15–32.

Bales, R. F. *Interaction Process Analysis.* Reading, Mass.: Addison-Wesley, 1951.

Banfield, E. C. "Corruption as a Feature of Governmental Organizations." *Journal of Law and Economics*, 1977, *20*, 587–605.

Bardach, E. *The Implementation Game.* Cambridge, Mass.: MIT Press, 1977.

Bass, B. M. "When Planning for Others." *Journal of Applied Behavioral Science*, 1970, *6*, 151–171.

Benn, S. I., and Gaus, G. F. *Public and Private in Social Life.* New York: St. Martin's Press, 1983.

Bennis, W., and Nanus, B. *Leaders.* New York: HarperCollins, 1985.

Berger, P., and Luckman, T. *The Social Construction of Reality.* New York: Doubleday, 1966.

Blaylock, B. K., and Rees, L. P. "Cognitive Style and the Usefulness of Information." *Management Science,* 1984, *15,* 74– 91.

Blumenthal, J. M. "Candid Reflections of a Businessman in Washington." In J. L. Perry and K. L. Kraemer (eds.), *Public Management: Public and Private Perspectives.* Mountain View, Calif.: Mayfield, 1983.

Blumenthal, M., and Michael, D. "Candid Reflections of a Businessman In Washington." *Fortune,* Jan. 29, 1979.

Boland, R. J., Jr. *Organizational Sense Making and Alternative Accounting Systems: A Case Analysis.* Faculty Working Papers, no. 695. Urbana, College of Commerce and Business Administration, University of Illinois, 1980.

Bouchard, T. J. Jr., and Hare, M. "Size, Performance, and Potential in Brainstorming Groups." *Journal of Applied Psychology,* 1970, *51* (1), 51–55.

Boulding, K. *The Image.* Ann Arbor: University of Michigan Press, 1956.

Bozeman, B. "Dimensions of Publicness: An Approach to Public Organization Theory." In B. Bozeman and J. Straussman (eds.), *New Directions in Public Administration.* Pacific Grove, Calif.: Brooks/Cole, 1984.

Bozeman, B. *All Organizations Are Public: Bridging Public and Private Organizational Theories.* San Francisco: Jossey-Bass, 1987.

Bristol, L. H., Jr. "The Application of Group Thinking to the Problems of Pharmaceutical Education." *American Journal of Pharmaceutical Education,* 1958, *22,* 146–156.

Brown, N. S. *Q-Sort Analysis.* New Haven, Conn.: Yale University Press, 1980.

Brown, S. R., and Coke, J. G. *Public Opinion on Land Use Regulation.* Urban and Regional Development Series, no. 1. Columbus, Ohio: Academy of Contemporary Problems, 1981.

Bryson, J. *The Role of Forums, Arenas and Courts in Organizational*

Design and Change. Discussion Paper, no. 6. Minneapolis: Strategic Management Research Center, University of Minnesota, 1984.

Bryson, J. M. *Strategic Planning for Public and Nonprofit Organizations: A Guide to Strengthening and Sustaining Organizational Achievement.* San Francisco: Jossey-Bass, 1988.

Bryson, J. M., Freeman, R. E., and Roering, W. D. "Strategic Planning in the Public Sector: Approaches and Directions." In B. Checkoway (ed.), *Strategic Perspectives on Planning Practice.* Lexington, Mass.: Lexington Books, 1986.

Buchholz, R. A. *Business Environment and Public Policy.* Englewood Cliffs, N.J.: Prentice Hall, 1982.

Burnberg, J. G., Pondy, L. P., and Davis, C. L. "Effect of Three Voting Rules on Resource Allocation Decisions." *Management Science,* 1970, *16,* pp. B356–B371.

Burns, T. "The Direction of Activity and Communication in a Departmental Executive Group." *Human Relations,* 1954, *7,* 73–87.

Burrell, G., and Morgan, G. *Sociological Paradigms and Organizational Analysis.* Exeter, N.H.: Heinemann, 1979.

Caiden, G. E. *The Dynamics of Public Administration.* Hinsdale, Ill.: Dryden Press, 1971.

Cameron, K. S. "Effectiveness Paradoxes: Consensus and Conflict in Perceptions of Organizational Performance." *Management Science,* 1986, *32* (5), 539–553.

Chaffee, E. E. "Successful Strategic Management in Small Private Colleges." *Journal of Higher Education,* 1984, *55,* 212–241.

Chaffee, E. E. "Three Modes of Strategy." *Academy of Management Review,* 1985, *10,* 89–98.

Chandler, A. D., Jr. *Strategy and Structure.* Cambridge, Mass.: MIT Press, 1962.

Child, J. "Organizational Structure, Environment and Performance." *Sociology,* 1972, *6,* 1–22.

Christenson, P. R., Guilford, J. P., and Wilson, R. C. "Relations of Creative Responses to Work Time Instructions." *Journal of Experimental Psychology,* 1957, *53,* 82–88.

Christenson, P. R., and others. *Business Policy: Text and Cases.* (5th ed.) Homewood, Ill.: Irwin, 1983.

Churchman, C. W. *On the Design of Inquiring Systems: Basic Concepts in Systems and Organization.* New York: Basic Books, 1971.

Churchman, C. W. *The Systems Approach and Its Enemies.* New York: Basic Books, 1979.

Cobb, R. W., and Elder, C. D. *Participants in American Politics: The Dynamics of Agenda Building.* Newton, Mass.: Allyn & Bacon, 1972.

Collaros, P. W., and Anderson, L. R. "Effect of Member Participation and Commitment on Influence Satisfaction and Decision Riskiness." *Journal of Applied Psychology,* 1974, *59,* 127–134.

Collins, B., and Guetzkow, H. *A Social Psychology of Processes for Decision Making.* New York: Wiley, 1964.

Cummings, L. L., Huber, G., and Arndt, S. "Effects of Size and Spatial Arrangements on Group Decision Making." *Academy of Management Journal,* 1974, *17,* 460–475.

Cyert, R. M., Dill, W. R., and March, J. G. "The Role of Expectations in Business Decision Making." *Administrative Science Quarterly,* 1958, *3,* 307–340.

Cyert, R. M., and March, J. G. *A Behavioral Theory of the Firm.* Englewood Cliffs, N.J.: Prentice Hall, 1963.

Daft, R. L., and Weick, K. "Toward a Model of Organizations as Interpretative Systems." *Academy of Management Review,* 1984, *9* (2), 284–295.

Dahl, R. A., and Lindblom, C. E. *Politics, Economics and Welfare.* New York: HarperCollins, 1953.

Dalky, N. *Delphi.* Santa Monica, Calif.: Rand, 1967.

Delbecq, A. L. "The Management of Decision Making in the Firm: Three Strategies for Three Types of Decision Making." *Academy of Management Journal,* 1967, *10* (4), 329–339.

Delbecq, A. L. "The World Within the Span of Control." *Business Horizons,* 1968, *11,* 47–56.

Delbecq, A. L., and Van de Ven, A. "A Group Process Model for Problem Identification and Program Planning." *Journal of Applied Behavioral Science,* 1971, *7* (4), 466–492.

Delbecq, A. L., Van de Ven, A., and Gustafson, D. H. *Group Techniques for Program Planning.* Middleton, Wis.: Greenbrier, 1986.

Deutsch, M. "The Effects of Cooperation and Competition upon Group Process." In D. Cartwright and A. Zander (eds.), *Group Dynamics.* New York: HarperCollins, 1962.

Dewey, J. *How We Think.* Lexington, Mass.: Heath, 1910.

Dewey, J. *Logic: The Structure of Inquiry.* New York: Putnam, 1938.

Dickson, G. W., Senn, J. A., and Chervany N. L. "Research in Management Information Systems: The Minnesota Experiments." *Management Science,* 1977, *23,* 913–923.

Downs, A. *Inside Bureaucracy.* Boston: Little, Brown, 1967.

Downs, A. "Up and Down with Ecology: The Issue Attention Cycle." *The Public Interest,* Summer 1972, pp. 38–50.

Drucker, K. "On Problem Solving." *Psychological Monographs,* 1945, *58* (5), entire issue.

Drucker, P. F. *The Practice of Management.* New York: HarperCollins, 1964.

Drucker, P. F. "Managing the Public Sector Institution." *The Public Interest,* 1973, *33,* 75–93.

Drucker, P. F. *Management: Tasks, Responsibilities and Practices.* New York: HarperCollins, 1974.

Dutton, J. E., Fahey, L., and Narayanan, V. K. "Towards Understanding Strategic Issue Diagnosis." *Strategic Management Journal,* 1983, *4,* 307–323.

Dutton, J. E., and Jackson, S. "Categorizing Strategic Issues: Links to Organizational Action." *Academy of Management Review,* 1987, *17,* 76–90.

Dutton, J. E., and Ottensmeyer, E. "Strategic Issue Management Systems: Forms, Functions, and Contexts." *Academy of Management Review,* 1982, *15* (4), 45–49.

Eadie, D. C., and Steinbacher, R. "Strategic Agenda Management: A Marriage of Organizational Development and Strategic Planning." *Public Administration Review,* May–June 1985, pp. 424–430.

El Sawy, O. A. *Exploring Temporal Perspectives as a Bias to Man-*

agerial Attention. Los Angeles: Center for Futures Research, Graduate School of Business Administration, University of Southern California, 1985.

Emery, F. E., and Trist, E. L. "Causal Texture of Organizational Environments." *Human Relations,* 1965, *18* (1), 21–32.

Emshoff, J. *Managerial Breakthroughs.* New York: American Management Association, 1980.

Engelbert, E. A. "The Professional Competencies of Public Managers." *ASPA News & Views,* 1974, *24* (7), 7–10.

Etzioni, A. *Modern Organizations.* Englewood Cliffs, N.J.: Prentice Hall, 1964.

Evered, R. "So What Is Strategy?" *Long-Range Planning,* 1983, *16* (3), 57–72.

Faust, W. L. "Group vs. Individual Problem Solving." *Journal of Abnormal Psychology,* 1959, *59*, 68–72.

Fiedler, F. "Engineering the Job to Fit the Manager." *Harvard Business Review,* 1965, *13*, 115–122.

Filley, A., and Grimes A. J. "The Basis for Power in Decision Processes." *Academy of Management Proceedings,* Dec. 1967.

Filley, A., House, R., and Kerr, S. *Managerial Process and Organizational Behavior.* (2nd ed.) Glenview, Ill.: Scott, Foresman, 1976.

Fleishman, A. "Leader Behavior Descriptions for Industry." In R. M. Stogdill and others (eds.), *Leader Behavior: A Description and Measurement.* Columbus: Bureau of Business Research, Ohio State University, 1975.

Fredrikson, J. W. "Strategic Process Research: Questions and Recommendations." *Academy of Management Review,* 1983, *8* (4), 565–575.

Freeman, R. E. *Strategic Management: A Stakeholder Approach.* Boston: Pittman Press, 1984.

French, J., Jr., and Raven, B. H. "The Bases of Social Power." In D. Cartwright, (ed.), *Studies in Social Power.* Ann Arbor, Mich.: Institute of Social Research, 1959.

Fryback, D. G., Gustafson, D. H., and Detmer, D. E. "Local Priorities for Allocation of Resources: Comparison with the IMU." *Inquiry,* 1978, *15*, 265–274.

Galbraith, C., and Schendel, D. "An Empirical Analysis of Strategy Types." *Strategic Management Journal*, 1983, *4*, 153–173.

Galbraith, J. R. "Matrix Organization Designs." *Business Horizons*, Feb. 1971, pp. 20–40.

Garfield, C. *Peak Performance*. New York: Warner Books, 1985.

Garnett, J. L., and Campbell, R. N. "Implementing Governmental Strategies: Models, Factors and Games." Paper presented at national conference of the American Society for Public Administration, Miami, Apr. 1989.

Gawthrop, L. C. *Administrative Politics and Social Change*. New York: St. Martin's Press, 1971.

Ghiselli, E. E. *Exploration in Managerial Talent*. Pacific Palisades, Calif.: Goodyear, 1971.

Gilmore, T. N. *Making a Leadership Change*, San Francisco: Jossey-Bass, 1988.

Gordon, W. J. J. *Synectics*. New York: HarperCollins, 1961.

Gordon, W. J. J. *The Metaphorical Way*. Cambridge, Mass.: Propoise, 1971.

Greenblat, K. S., and Duke, R. D. *Principles and Practices of Gaming Simulation*. Newbury Park, Calif.: Sage, 1981.

Grossman, R. M. "Voting Behavior of HSA Interest Groups: A Case Study." *American Journal of Public Health*, 1978, *68* (12), 1191–1193.

Gueschka, H., Shaude, G. R., and Schlicksupp, H. "Modern Techniques for Solving Problems." In *Portraits of Complexity*. Columbus, Ohio: Battelle Memorial Institute, 1975.

Guetzkow, H. "Differentiation of Roles in Task Oriented Groups." In D. Cartwright and A. Zander (eds.), *Group Dynamics: Research and Theory*. New York: HarperCollins, 1960.

Guetzkow, H., and Dill, W. R. "Factors in the Development of Task Oriented Groups." *Sociometry*, 1957, *20*, 175–204.

Guetzkow, H., and Simon, H. "The Impact of Certain Communication Nets upon Organization and Performance in Task Oriented Groups." *Management Science*, 1950, *21*, 233–250.

Gustafson, D. H. and others. "A Comparative Study in Subjective Likelihood Estimates Made by Individuals, Interacting

Groups, Delphi Groups and Nominal Groups." *Organizational Behavior and Human Performance*, 1973, *9*, 280–291.

Halpin, A. W. "The Leadership Behavior and Combat Performance of Airplane Commanders." *Journal of Abnormal and Social Psychology*, 1954, *49*, 19–22.

Hare, A. P. *Handbook of Small Group Research*. New York: Free Press, 1962.

Hare, A. P., Bogatala, E. F., and Bales, R. F. (eds.) *Small Groups: Studies in Social Interaction*. New York: Knopf, 1955.

Harrigan, K. R. "Strategies for Declining Industries." *Journal of Business Strategy*, 1980, *2*, 20–34.

Harrigan, K. R. "Barriers to Entry and Competitive Strategies." *Strategic Management Journal*, 1981, 2, 395–412.

Hatten, M. L. "Strategic Management in the Non-profit Organization." *Strategic Management Journal*, 1982, *3*, 89–104.

Hayes, R. H. "Qualitative Insights from Quantitative Methods." *Harvard Business Review*, July–Aug. 1969, pp. 108–117.

Hearn, G. "Leadership and the Spatial Factor in Groups." *Journal of Abnormal Psychology*, 1957, *54*, 269–272.

Henderson, B. *Henderson on Corporate Strategy*. Cambridge, Mass.: ABT Books 1979.

Herbert, T. T., and Yost, E. B. "A Comparison of Decision Quality Under Nominal and Interacting Consensus Group Formats: The Case of the Structured Problem." *Decision Sciences*, 1979, *10* (3), 358–370.

Hinton, B. L., and Reitz, H. J. *Groups and Organizations: Analysis of Social Behavior*. Belmont, Calif.: Wadsworth, 1971.

Hofer, C., and Schendel, D. *Strategy Formulation: Analytical Concepts*. St. Paul, Minn.: West, 1978.

Hogarth, R., *Judgment and Choice*. New York: Wiley, 1980.

Holloman, C. R., and Hendrich, H. W. "Adequacy of Group Decisions as a Function of the Decision Making Process." *Academy of Management Journal*, 1972, *15*, 175–184.

House, R. "Leader Initiating Structure, Performance, Satisfaction, and Motivation: A Review and Theoretical Interpretation." 1974. (Mimeographed.)

Howe, E., and Kaufman, J. "The Ethics of Contemporary

American Planning." *Journal of the American Planning Association,* 1979, *45* (3), 242–255.

Howell, I. T., and Becker, S. W. "Seating Arrangements and Leadership Emergence." *Journal of Abnormal and Social Psychology,* 1962, *64,* 148–150.

Huber, G. P., and Delbecq, A. L. "Guidelines for Combining the Judgments of Individual Members in Decision Conferences." *Academy of Management Journal,* 1972, *15,* 159–174.

Jackson, S. B., and Dutton, J. E. "Discerning Threats and Opportunities." *Administrative Science Quarterly,* 1988, *3* (3), 370–387.

Janis, I. L. *Crucial Decisions.* New York: Free Press, 1989.

Jantsch, E. *Design for Evolution: Self-Organization and Planning in the Life of Systems.* New York: Braziller, 1975.

Kaplan, A. *The Conduct of Inquiry: Methodology for Behavioral Science.* San Francisco: Chandler, 1964.

Keeley, M. "Organizational Analogy: A Comparison of Organizational and Social Contract Models." *Administrative Science Quarterly,* 1980, *25,* 337–362.

Kerlinger, F. N. *Foundation of Behavioral Research.* (2nd ed.) New York: Holt, Rinehart & Winston, 1967.

Kerr, S. and others. "Toward a Contingency Theory of Leadership Based on Consideration and Interaction Structure Literature." *Organizational Behavior and Human Performance,* 1974, *12,* 62–82.

King, W. R. "Using Strategic Issue Analysis." *Long-Range Planning,* 1982, *15* (4), 45–49.

King, W. R., and Cleland, C. *Strategic Action and Policy.* New York: Van Nostrand Reinhold, 1978.

Kingdom, J. W. *Agendas, Alternatives and Public Policies.* Boston: Little, Brown, 1984.

Kolb, D. A. "Problem Management: Learning from Experience." In S. Srivastva and Associates, *The Executive Mind: New Insights on Managerial Thought and Action.* San Francisco: Jossey-Bass, 1983.

Lawler, E. E. *Pay and Organizational Effectiveness: A Psychological View.* New York: Wiley, 1971.

Lawrence, P. R. and Dyer, D. M., *Renewing American Industry.* New York: Free Press, 1983.

Levine, C. H. "Organizational Decline and Cut Back Management." *Public Administration Review,* July–Aug. 1978, pp. 316–325.

Levine, C. H. and others. "Organizational Design: A Post Minnowbrook Perspective for the New Public Administration." *Public Administration Review,* July–Aug. 1975, pp. 425–435.

Lewin, K. "Group Decisions and Social Change." In J. E. Maccoby, T. W. Newcomb, and E. Hartley (eds.), *Readings in Social Psychology.* New York: Holt, Rinehart & Winston, 1958.

Lindblom, C. E. *The Intelligence of Democracy: Decision Process Through Adjustment.* New York: Free Press, 1965.

Linstone, H. *Multiple Perspectives for Decision Making.* New York: North Holland, 1984.

Lippitt, M. E., and Mackenzie, K. D. "Authority Task Problems." *Administrative Science Quarterly,* 1976, *21* (4), 643–660.

Locke, E. A. "Knowledge of Results: A Goal Setting Phenomenon." *Psychological Bulletin,* 1968, *70,* 474–485.

Lorange, P. *Corporate Planning: An Executive Viewpoint.* Englewood Cliffs, N.J.: Prentice Hall, 1980.

Lowi, T. *The End of Liberalism.* New York: Norton, 1969.

Lyles, M. "Formulative Strategic Problems: Empirical Analysis and Model Development." *Strategic Management Journal,* 1981, *2,* 61–73.

Lyles, M., and Mitroff, I. I. "Organizational Problem Formulation: An Empirical Study." *Administrative Science Quarterly,* 1980, *25,* 102–119.

Machiavelli, N. *The Prince.* L. Ricci, tr. Oxford, England: Oxford University Press, 1952. (Originally published 1903).

Maier, N.R.F. "Reasoning in Humans II: The Solution of a Problem and Its Appearances in Consciousness." *Journal of Comparative Psychology,* 1931, *12,* 181–194.

Maier, N.R.F. *Problem Solving and Creativity: In Individuals and Groups.* Pacific Grove, Calif.: Brooks/Cole, 1970.

Mainzer, L. C. *Political Bureaucracy.* Glenview, Ill.: Scott, Foresman, 1973.

March, J. G., and Olsen, J. P. *Ambiguity and Choices in Organizations.* Bergen, Norway: Universitets for Laget Press, 1976.

March, J., and Simon, H. *Organizations.* New York: McGraw-Hill, 1958.

Mason, R. "A Dialectic Approach to Strategic Planning." *Management Science,* 1969, 15 (8), B403–B414.

Mason, R. O., and Mitroff, I. I. *Challenging Strategic Planning Assumptions.* New York: Wiley-Interscience, 1981.

Meyer, A. D. "Adapting to Environmental Jolts." *Administrative Science Quarterly,* 1982, *27,* 515–537.

Miles, R. E. *Coffin Nails and Corporate Strategy.* Englewood Cliffs, N.J.: Prentice Hall, 1982.

Miles, R. E., and Snow, C. C. *Organizational Strategy, Structure and Process.* New York: McGraw-Hill, 1978.

Miles, R. E. and others. "Organizational Strategy, Structure, and Process." *Academy of Management Review,* 1978, *3* (3), 546–562.

Miller, D., and Frisen, P. H. "Archetypes of Strategy Formulation." *Management Science,* 1978, 24 (9), 921–933.

Millett, J. D. *Organization for the Public Service.* New York: Van Nostrand Reinhold, 1966.

Milliken, F. V. "Three Types of Perceived Uncertainty About the Environment: State, Effect and Response." *Academy of Management Review,* 1987, *12* (1), 133–143.

Mintzberg, H. *The Nature of Managerial Work.* New York: Harper-Collins, 1973.

Mintzberg, H. "Planning on the Left Side, Managing on the Right." *Harvard Business Review,* 1975, July-Aug.

Mintzberg, H. "Patterns in Strategy Formulation." *Management Science,* 1978, *24,* 934–948.

Mintzberg, H. "Crafting Strategy." *Harvard Business Review,* 1987a, July-Aug., 65–75.

Mintzberg, H. "The Strategy Concept I: The Five Ps for Strategy." *California Management Review,* 1987b, *30* (1).

Mintzberg, H. "The Strategy Concept II: Another Look at Why Organizations Need Strategy." In G. Carroll and D. Vogel (eds.), *Organizational Approaches to Strategy.* New York: Ballinger, 1987c.

Mintzberg, H., Raisingham, D., and Theoret, A. "The Structure of Unstructured Decision Processes." *Administrative Science Quarterly*, 1976, *21*, 246–275.

Mintzberg, H., and Waters, J. A. "Tracking Strategy in an Entrepreneurial Firm." *Academy of Management Journal.* 1982, *25* (3), 465–499.

Mitnick, B. *The Political Economy of Regulation.* New York: Columbia University Press, 1982.

Mitroff, I. I., and Emshoff, J. R. "On Strategic Assumption-Making: A Dialectical Approach to Policy and Planning." *Academy of Management Review*, 1979, *4* (1), 1–12.

Mitroff, I. I., and Kilmann, R. H. "The Stories Managers Tell: A New Tool for Organizational Problem Solving." *Management Review*, 1975, *64*, 18–28.

Mitroff, I., and Kilmann, R. H. *Methodological Approaches to Social Science: Integrating Divergent Concepts and Theories.* San Francisco: Jossey-Bass, 1978.

Mitroff, I. I., Nelson, J., and Mason, R. O. "On the Management of Myth Information Systems." *Management Science,* 1974, *21* (4), 371–382.

Mitroff, I. I., Shrivastra, P., and Udwadia, R. E. "Effective Crisis Management." *Academy of Management Executive*, 1987, *1* (3), 283–292.

Mohrman, S. "A New Look at Participation in Decision Making: The Concept of Political Access." *Academy of Management Proceedings,* Aug. 1979.

Mokwa, M., and Permet, S. *Government Marketing.* New York: Praeger, 1981.

Morgan, G. "Paradigms, Metaphors, and Puzzle Solving in Organizational Theory." *Administrative Science Quarterly*, 1980, *25*, 605–622.

Morgan, G. "Opportunities Arising from Paradigm Diversity." *Administration and Society*, 1984, *16* (3), 306–327.

Morgan, G. *The Image of Organizations.* Newbury Park, Calif.: Sage, 1986.

Murray, M. A. "Company Public and Private Management: An Exploratory Essay." In J. L. Perry and K. L. Kraemar (eds.),

Public Management: Public and Private Perspectives. Mountain View, Calif.: Mayfield, 1983.

Nadler, G. *Work Design: A Systems Concept.* Homewood, Ill.: Irwin, 1970.

Nadler, G. *The Planning and Design Approach.* New York: Wiley-Interscience, 1981.

Narayanan, V. K., and Fahey, L. "The Micro Policies of Strategy Formation." *Academy of Management Review,* 1982, 7 (1), 35–34.

Neustadt, R. E. "American Presidents and Corporate Executives." Paper presented at conference of National Academy of Public Administration, Oct. 1989.

Nisbett, R., and Ross, L. *Human Inference: Strategies and Shortcomings of Social Judgment.* Englewood Cliffs, N.J.: Prentice Hall, 1980.

Nutt, P. C. "A Field Experiment Which Compared the Effectiveness of Design Methods." *Decision Science.* 1976a, 7 (4), 739–758.

Nutt, P. C. "The Merits of Using Experts and Consumers as Members of Planning Groups." *Academy of Management Journal,* 1976b, *19* (3), 378–394.

Nutt, P. C. "An Experimental Comparison of the Effectiveness of Three Planning Methods." *Management Science,* 1977, *23* (4), 499–511.

Nutt, P. C. "On the Acceptance and Quality of Plans Drawn by Consortiums." *Journal of Applied Behavioral Sciences,* 1979, *15* (1).

Nutt, P. C. "Comparing Methods to Weight Decision Criteria." *Omega: The International Journal of Management Science,* 1980a, *8* (2), 163–172.

Nutt, P. C. "On Managed Evaluation Processes." *Technical Forecasting and Social Change,* 1980b, *4* (17), 313–328.

Nutt, P. C. *Evaluation Concepts and Methods.* New York: Spectrum, 1982a.

Nutt, P. C. "Hybrid Planning Methods." *Academy of Management Review,* 1982b, 7 (3), 442–454.

Nutt, P. C. "Implementation Approaches for Planning." *Academy of Management Review,* 1983, *8,* 600–611.

Nutt, P. C. *Planning Methods.* New York: Wiley, 1984a.

Nutt, P. C. "Types of Organizational Decision Processes." *Administrative Science Quarterly,* 1984b, *3,* 414–450.

Nutt, P. C. "The Tactics of Implementation." *Academy of Management Journal,* 1986, *29* (2), 230–261.

Nutt, P. C. "Identifying and Appraising How Managers Install Strategy." *Strategic Management Journal,* 1987, *8,* 1–14.

Nutt, P. C. *Making Tough Decisions: Tactics for Improving Managerial Decision Making.* San Francisco: Jossey-Bass, 1989a.

Nutt, P. C. "Selecting Tactics to Implement Strategic Plans." *Strategic Management Journal,* 1989b, *10,* 145–161.

Nutt, P. C., and Backoff, R. W. "Mutual Understanding and Its Impact on Formulation During Planning." *Technological Forecasting and Social Change,* 1986, *29,* 13–31.

Nutt, P. C., and Backoff, R. W. "The Strategic Management of Public and Third Sector Organizations." *American Journal of Planning,* 1987, *53,* 44–57.

Nutt, P. C., and Backoff, R. W. "Strategic Issues as Tensions." *International Journal of Behavioral Science,* 1992.

Nutt, P. C., and Hurley, R. "Factors Affecting Capital Expenditure Review Decisions." *Inquiry,* 1981, Summer, 151–164.

Osborn, A. F. *Applied Imagination.* (3rd ed.) New York: Scribner's, 1963.

Paine, F. T., and Anderson, C. R. "Contingencies Affecting Strategy Formation and Effectiveness." *Journal of Management Studies,* 1977, *14,* 147–158.

Parker, A. W. "The Consumer as a Policy Maker: Issues of Training." *American Journal of Public Health,* 1970, *60,* 2139–2153.

Parnes, S. J. "Effects of Extended Effort in Creative Problem Solving." *Journal of Educational Psychology,* 1961, *52,* 117–122.

Parnes, S. J., and Meadow, A. "The Effects of Brainstorming Instructions on Creative Problem Solving by Trained and Untrained Subjects." *Journal of Educational Psychology,* 1959, *50,* 171–176.

Perry, J. L., and Rainey, H. G. "The Public Private Distinction in Organization Theory: A Critique and Research Strategy." *Academy of Management Review,* 1988, *13* (2), 182–201.

Peters, T. J., and Waterman, R. H. *In Search of Excellence: Lessons from America's Best Run Companies.* New York: HarperCollins, 1982.

Pettigrew, A. M. "Strategy Formulation as a Political Process." *International Studies of Management and Organization,* 1977, *7,* 78–87.

Pfeffner, J. *Power in Organizations.* Marshfield, Mass.: Pitman, 1981.

Porter, M. E. *Competitive Strategy: Techniques for Analyzing Industries and Competitors.* New York: Free Press, 1980.

Porter, M. E. *Competitive Advantage.* New York: Free Press, 1985.

Posner, M. I. *Cognition: On Introduction.* Glenview, Ill.: Scott, Foresman, 1973.

Post, J. E., and Epstein, M. C. "Information Systems for Social Reporting." *Academy of Management Review,* 1977, *2* (1), 81–87.

Quinn, J. B., *Strategies for Change: Logical Incrementalism.* Homewood, Ill.: Irwin, 1980.

Quinn, R. E. "Applying the Competing Values Approach in Leadership: Toward an Integrating Framework." In M. J. Hunt, R. Stewart, C. Schecieshiem, and D. Hosking (eds.), *Managerial Work and Leadership: An International Perspective.* Elmsford, N.Y.: Pergamon Press, 1983.

Quinn. R. E. *Beyond Rational Management: Mastering the Paradoxes and Competing Demands of High Performance.* San Francisco: Jossey-Bass, 1988.

Quinn, R. E., and Cameron, J. "Organizational Life Cycles and Shifting Criteria of Effectiveness." *Management Science,* 1983, *29* (1), 33–51.

Quinn, R. E., and Cameron, J., *Paradox and Transformation.* New York: Ballinger, 1988.

Quinn, R. E., and McGrath, M. R. "Moving Beyond the Single Solution Perspective: The Competing Values Approach as a Diagnostic Tool." *Journal of Applied Behavioral Science,* 1982, *18* (4), 463–472.

Quinn, R. E., and Rohrbaugh, J. "A Spatial Model of Effectiveness Criteria: Towards a Competing Values Approach to

Organizational Analysis." *Management Science,* 1983, *29* (3), 363–377.

Raiffa, H. *Decision Analysis: Introductory Lectures on Choices Under Certainty.* Reading, Mass.: Addison-Wesley, 1970.

Rainey, H. G. "Public Management: Recent Research on the Political Context and the Managerial Roles, Structures, and Behaviors." *Journal of Management,* 1989, *15* (2), 229–250.

Rainey, H. G., Backoff, R. W., and Levine, C. H. "Comparing Public and Private Organizations." *Public Administration Review,* Mar.–Apr. 1976, pp. 233–244.

Ring, P. *Strategic Issues: What Are They and Where Do They Come From.* In J. Bryson and R. C. Einsweiler (eds.), *Strategic Planning.* Chicago: American Planning Association, 1988.

Ring, P., and Perry, J. "Strategic Management in Public and Private Organizations: Indications of Distinctive Contexts and Contraints." *Academy of Management Review,* 1984, *10* (2), 276–286.

Ritti, R. R., and Funkhouser, G. R. *The Ropes to Skip and the Ropes to Know: Studies in Organizational Behavior.* (3rd ed.) Columbus, Ohio: Grid Publishing, 1987.

Roessner, J. D. "Designing Public Organizations for Innovative Behavior." Paper presented at annual meeting of the Academy of Management, Seattle, Wash., Aug. 1974.

Roessner, J. D. "Incentives to Innovate in Public and Private Organizations: Implications for Public Policy." *Administration and Society,* 1977, *9,* 341–365.

Rothenberg, A. *The Emerging Goddess.* Chicago: University of Chicago Press, 1979.

Rowe, A. J., Mason, R. O., and Dickel, K. *Strategic Management and Business Policy: A Methodological Approach.* Reading, Mass.: Addison-Wesley, 1982.

Rubin, M. S. "Sagas, Ventures, Quests and Parlays: A Typology of Strategies in the Public Sector." In J. Bryson and R. Einsweiler (eds.), *Strategic Planning.* Chicago: American Planning Association, 1988.

Schendel, D. E., and Hofer, C. (eds.). *Strategic Management.* Boston: Little, Brown, 1979.

Schlisinger, L., Jackson, S. M., and Butman, J. "Leader-Member Interaction in Management Committees." *Journal of Abnormal and Social Psychology,* 1960, *61,* 350–354.

Schon, D. A. *The Reflective Practitioner: How Professionals Think in Action.* New York: Basic Books, 1983.

Schreisheim, C. J., Tolliver, J. M., and Behling, O. C. "Leadership: Some Organizational and Managerial Implications." In P. Hersey and J. Stinson (eds.), *Perspectives in Leader Effectiveness.* Athens, Ohio: Center for Leadership Studies, 1980.

Schultze, C. L. "The Role of Incentives, Penalties and Rewards in Altering Effective Policy." In R. Havenon and J. Margolis (eds.), *Public Expenditures and Policy Analysis.* Chicago: Markham, 1970.

Schumaker, E. F. *A Guide for the Perplexed.* New York: HarperCollins, 1977.

Scott, W. E., and Cummings, L. L. *Readings in Organizational Behavior.* (Rev. ed.) Homewood, Ill.: Irwin, 1973.

Selznick, P. *TVA and the Grass Roots.* Berkeley: University of California Press, 1949.

Simon, H. A. *Administrative Behavior.* New York: Macmillan, 1947.

Simon, H. A. *The New Science of Management Decision.* (Rev. ed.) Englewood Cliffs, N.J.: Prentice Hall, 1977.

Simon, H. A., and Newell, A. "Human Problem Solving: The State of the Art in 1970." *American Psychologist,* 1971, *26,* 145–159.

Simon, M. A. *Understanding Human Action.* Albany: State University of New York Press, 1982.

Skinner, B. F. *Contingencies of Reinforcement.* East Norwalk, Conn.: Appleton and Lange, 1969.

Smart, C., and Vertinsky, I. "Designs for Crisis Decision Units." *Administrative Science Quarterly,* 1977, *22,* 640–657.

Sommers, R. "Further Studies on Small Group Ecology." *Sociometry,* 1965, *28,* 337–340.

Sorensen, T. C. *Kennedy.* New York: HarperCollins, 1966.

Souder, W. E. *Management Decision Methods for Managers of Engineering and Research.* New York: Van Nostrand Reinhold, 1980.

Stahl, O. G. *Public Personnel Administration*. New York: Harper-Collins, 1971.

Staw, B. M. "Nationality and Justification in Organizational Life." In B. M. Staw and L. Cummings (eds.), *Research in Organizational Behavior: An Annual Series of Analytical Essays and Critical Reviews*. Vol. 2. Greenwich, Conn.: JAI Press, 1980.

Staw, B. M., Sandelands, L., and Dutton, J. E. "Threat-Rigidity Cycles in Organizational Behavior." *Administrative Science Quarterly*, 1981, *26* (4), 501–524.

Stein, M. I. *Stimulating Creativity*. Orlando, Fla.: Academic Press, 1975.

Steiner, G. *Top Management Planning*. (Rev. ed.) New York: Macmillan, 1979.

Steiner, G. A. *Strategic Planning*. New York: Free Press, 1979.

Stephenson, W. *The Study of Behavior*. Chicago: University of Chicago Press, 1953.

Stogdill, R. M. *Individual Behavior and Group Achievement*. New York: Oxford University Press, 1969.

Stogdill, R. M., and Coons, A. E. (eds.). *Leader Behavior: Its Description and Measurement*. Monograph, no. 88. Columbus: Bureau of Business Research, Ohio State University, 1975.

Strumpf, S. A., Zand, D. E., and Freeman, R. D. "Designing Groups for Judgmental Decisions." *Academy of Management Review*, 1979, *4* (4), 589–600.

Suchman, E. A. *Evaluation Research: Principles and Practice in Public Service Organizations*. Newbury Park, Calif.: Sage, 1967.

Sudman, S., and Bradburn, N. M. *Asking Questions: A Practical Guide to Questionnaire Design*. San Francisco: Jossey-Bass, 1982.

Sussman, L., and Herden, R. P. "Dialectic Problem Solving." *Business Horizons*, Fall 1985.

Thibaut, J. W., and Kelley, H. H. *The Social Psychology of Groups*. New York: Wiley, 1959.

Thompson, J. D. "Common and Uncommon Elements in Administration." *Social Welfare Reform*, Summer 1962, pp. 181–201.

Thompson, J. D. *Organizations in Action*. New York: McGraw-Hill, 1967.

Tichy, N. M. *Managing Strategic Change: Technical, Political and Cultural Dynamics.* New York: Wiley-Interscience, 1983.

Toulmin, S. *Knowing and Acting: An Invitation to Philosophy.* New York: Macmillan, 1979.

Tversky, A., and Kahneman, D. "The Framing of a Decision and the Psychology of Choice." *Science,* 1974, *211,* 453–458.

Tversky, A., and Kahneman, D. "Judgment Under Uncertainty: Heuristic and Beasis." 1985, *185,* 1124–1131.

U.S. Department of Health, Education, and Welfare. HCHSR, Dec. 1978.

Van de Ven, A. H., and Delbecq, A. L. "Nominal Versus Interacting Group Process Effectiveness for Committee Decision Making." *Academy of Management Journal,* 1974, *14* (2), 203–217.

Van de Ven, A. H., and Poole, M. S. "Paradoxical Requirements for a Theory of Organizational Change." In R. Quinn and K. Cameron (eds.), *Paradox and Transformation: Toward a Theory of Change in Organization and Management.* New York: Ballinger, 1987.

Vanston, J. H., Jr., Frisbie, W. P., Iopreato, S. C., and Poston, D. L., Jr. "Alternative Scenario Planning." *Technological Forecasting and Social Change,* 1977, *10,* 159–180.

Volkema, R. J. "Problem Formulation as a Purposive Activity." *Strategic Management Journal,* 1986, 7 (3), 267–279.

Wamsley, G., and Zald, M. N. *The Political Economy of Public Organizations.* Lexington, Mass.: D. C. Heath, 1973.

Warfield, J. N. *Societal Systems.* New York: Wiley, 1976.

Warwick. D. *A Theory of Public Bureaucracy.* Cambridge, Mass.: Harvard University Press, 1975.

Wechsler, B., and Backoff, R. W. "The Dynamics of Strategy in Public Organizations." In J. Bryson and R. C. Einsweiler (eds.),. *Strategic Planning.* Chicago: American Planning Association, 1986.

Wechsler, B., and Backoff, R. W. "Policy Making and Administration in State Agencies: Strategic Management Approaches." *Public Administration Review,* July–Aug. 1988, pp. 321–327.

Weick, K. *The Social Psychology of Organizing.* Reading, Mass.: Addison-Wesley, 1979.

Weinberg, M. W. "Managing the Public Portfolio: Strategic Perspectives from the Private Sector." *Association of Public Policy Management,* Sept. 1986, Austin, Tex.

Weiss, H. L. "Why Business and Government Exchange Executives." *Harvard Business Review,* July–Aug. 1974, pp. 129–140.

Wheatley, W. J., Anthony, W. P., and Maddox, E. N. *Enhancing Strategic Planning Through the Utilization of Guided Imagery.* Florida State University, Tallahassee, 1987 (mimeographed).

Wildavsky, A. "Rescuing Policy Analysis for PPBS." *Public Administration Review,* Mar.–Apr. 1969, pp. 189–202.

Wildavsky, A. *Speaking Truth to Power.* Boston: Little, Brown, 1979.

Woll, P. *American Bureaucracy.* New York: Norton, 1963.

Wortman, M. S., Jr. "Strategic Management in Not-for-Profit Organizations." In D. E. Schendel and C. Hofer (eds.), *Strategic Management.* Boston: Little, Brown, 1979.

Ziller, R. C. "Group Size: A Determinant of the Quality and Stability of Group Decisions." *Sociometry,* 1956, *20,* 165–173.

Zwicky, F. *Discovery, Invention, and Research Through the Morphological Approach.* New York: Macmillan, 1968.

Index